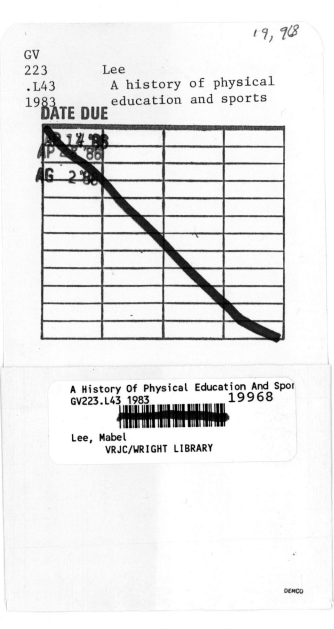

A History of
Physical Education and
Sports
in the U.S.A.

Publisher's note This book is an expansion and revision of Mabel Lee's work in Part III, "America," *A Brief History of Physical Education*, Fifth Edition, Rice, Hutchinson, and Lee, now out of print.

A History of Physical Education and Sports in the U.S.A.

Mabel Lee
Professor Emerita
University of Nebraska — Lincoln

John Wiley & Sons
New York   Chichester   Brisbane   Toronto   Singapore

To
Edward Mussey Hartwell
and
Fred Eugene Leonard
America's
First Historians
of
Physical Education

Library of Congress Cataloging in Publication Data

Lee, Mabel, 1886-
    A history of physical education and sports in the U.S.A.

    Bibliography: p.
    1. Physical education and training—United States—History.
2. School sports—United States—History. 3. Physical education
teachers—United States—Biography. 4. Physical education for
women—United States—History. I. Title.
GV223.L43   1983   613.7′0973   82-24746
ISBN 0-471-86315-7

Printed in the United States of America

10 9 8 7 6 5 4 3 2 1

PREFACE

Within the profession of physical education there is much interest today in researching and writing about the sociological, physiological, psychological, and philosophical aspects of the discipline. But there is little enthusiasm for the study of its history. True there is an awakening of interest in the history of sports, which are a subdivision of physical education. Also, sports themselves are split into numerous sub-subdivisions with, it seems, an enthusiastic following for each individual sport so that a great wealth of historical research and writing is being offered for the enrichment of the profession within that area. But few workers in the field have been concerned with the overall history of the profession in its relation to general education.

The historians of physical education have been for the span of the ninety years that their efforts have embraced but a very few compared with the total number of researchers and writers in the profession. I am happy therefore, even at a late date in my own career, to be at least one woman who has taken up this challenge. Much of this history, particularly in regard to physical education for girls and women, reflects my own experiences over seventy years of commitment to the profession.

This book has four purposes: first, to acquaint undergraduates with the profession of physical education as a part of general education—this is a basic textbook for students preparing for a career in physical education; second, to bring physical educators up to date in the overall history of physical education since their own student years—this is a refresher book; third, to all workers in any branch of physical education who need quick information on the historical development of various aspects of physical education, this is a reference book to have close at hand; and fourth, to persons of the lay world who are interested in the development of any one of the many facets of physical education, this is also a handy reference book.

The references at the end of the book are a valuable source of supplementary assignments for students. Also there is a wealth of history being published today that makes excellent supplementary material for a course in the history of physical education: these periodicals, small pamphlets, and booklets offer a collection of articles by a group of well-known authors on many of the subtopics discussed in this book. Much of such writing consists of biographies of leaders (many on file in college and university libraries as doctoral theses) and histories of a given sport, with the field generally well covered sport by sport.

The topic of sports presents a problem. In a book such as this, I have intended to include only amateur sport, but when it comes to the intercollegiate contests of the sports that are most popular with the lay world, amateur becomes deeply involved with what savors of professionalism. One must decide where to draw the line to keep the discussion objective and focused on the purposes and objectives of education. Therefore, I have tried to keep the line clear between professional and amateur sports by distinguishing between them on the basis of the sports that contribute toward the goals of education and those that do not. For example, in discussing the Olympics, I have played down a discussion of medals won in favor of accenting the coming together of athletes to build a brotherhood of Man. Hence, the accent on the Olympic Academy of today.

As to today's brand of sports called intercollegiate sports, especially of the big leagues for football, the brand supposed to be amateur is a far cry from actual amateurism. It seems that nothing short of doing away with scoreboards, getting rid of athletic scholarships and recruitment, giving the game back to the *bona fide* students of a college or university, sending the coaches to the bleachers during a game, will bring back true amateur sports worthy of an educational institution. At any rate, since sports are so large a part of physical education, and offered properly have a real place in education, it is impossible to ignore them in any discussion about physical education in general. I have tried to keep "quack" amateur sports in their correct place in relation to educational sports and have given educational sports a large coverage in keeping with their relative importance in the physical education program.

Today, authors are aware of the need to be watchful to avoid any form of discrimination in their writings. Especially since the Education Act of 1972 with its Title IX mandates, sex discrimination is readily suspect. But on the whole this is a small problem within the field of physical education itself. There is no denying the fact that there has through the years been much discrimination against girls and women in the physical education segment of education. But what has existed has come from male education administrators and male coaches, not from male physical educators. Generally, there has been little need to overcome prejudice from within the profession itself.

To give equal recognition to both sexes in the presentation of biographies of outstanding leaders, I decided to offer three photographs of each sex in each of the three eras—late nineteenth century and early and mid-twentieth century. It posed no problem for from the very beginnings in this profession in the United States, women have along with men led the way. In each period, women have been accepted as worthy partners of men. The problem was not to find as many capable women as men but to choose three of the several worthy ones. I made the selections to represent workers in a variety of interests in each era. I have devoted much space to biographies of the profession's talented leaders who have caused things to happen. There has always been a wealth of talented leaders in the United States in the field of physical education. The difficulty has been to limit recognition to so few.

If students are bothered about the seeming overabundance of dates throughout this history, they should be reminded that it is a date that ties a person, thing, or event to its proper niche in history and to its relative position in time in relation to other bits of history. Dates are not things to be memorized but to be recognized as reference material, quickly available in this form. A recital of history in any aspect requires dates to tie things together properly.

Several state and national offices of various organizations related to physical education have been most generous in their help. For such assistance I am particularly indebted to ACSM, AAHPERD, ICHPER, NCAA, NFHSAA, and to the National YMCA and the National YWCA.

I acknowledge the good help of Marie Cripe, who so painstakingly typed this manuscript for me and helped with other chores related to it, to James Crabbe, who until he left his position in the Department of Physical Education at the University of Nebraska—Lincoln was my chief library contact during the preparation of this manuscript, to Ruth Levinson, who took over in helping me after James Crabbe was gone and who ran countless errands for me to conserve my time to work at my desk, and to Ruth Schellberg, AAHPERD archivist, who procured for me much information on the international affairs of our profession and on related topics of organizations concerned with physical education.

For permission to use various photographs and for information from their archives I am grateful to Wellesley, Smith, Vassar, Oberlin, and Springfield colleges, and to the University of Iowa. For the courtesy of supplying me with copies of several photographs and for their generous sharing of records I am deeply grateful to AAHPERD.

Mabel Lee
Lincoln, Nebraska

CONTENTS

PART A

PHYSICAL
EDUCATION
HERITAGE

CHAPTER 1

Heritage From the Ancient and Medieval Worlds

THE ANCIENT WORLD

Records of ancient times available in museums throughout the world or in sculptured pieces and bas-reliefs in situ in ancient ruins assure us that ancient peoples participated in much physical activity common to all human life of all ages—activities fundamental to all physical education today—running, leaping, hurdling, chasing, throwing, hurling, catching, climbing, boxing, wrestling, swimming, boating, and rhythmical movements. Such records date back as far as 3200 B.C. and became known to today's world through archeological discoveries made during the last 150 years.

Mesopotamia: Sumer, Assyria, Babylonia

The earliest records of the Sumerians, Assyrians, and Babylonians have come from the ruins of their ancient cities, Warka, Nineveh, Ur, and Babylon, which are all located in today's Iraq (old Mesopotamia). These records dating back to mid-600 B.C. were discovered by the British Museum Archeological Expedition of 1849 in a collection of 25,000 cuneiform tablets in the King's Library in the ruins of the ancient city of Nineveh.[1] Also among the old Sumerian records were the tablets giving the great epic poem, *Tales of Gilsamesh*,[2] the man of great physical prowess, the Paul Bunyan, the Superman of the Ancient World—the first great public exponent of physical fitness! This great library had but a brief existence. The great city of Nineveh was destroyed in 612 B.C. Six years later the Medes laid what was left of it in desolate ruins, and the great library safely buried within the ruble of the palace waited for over 2400 years to be discovered by the British archeologists of the early nineteenth century. What a treasure they found!

Egypt

The bas-reliefs and other relics of ancient Egypt preserved today largely in museums throughout Europe and the United States as well as in Egypt give a clearer idea than do the relics of Mesopotamia of the great variety of physical activities engaged in by ancient people. Although there are Egyptian records dating back as far as 3400 B.C., those depicting participation in physical activities of a physical education nature are mostly of the fourteenth and fifteenth centuries B.C. Racing in two-wheeled chariots and boating are depicted along with wrestling, swimming, gymnastics, dancing and games with balls and sticks.[3]

Greece[4]

As the Sumarians arose out of the mists of prehistory to become the leaders of the world, flourished, and then declined to be succeeded by the Assyrians, Babylonians, and Egyptians, each of whom also flourished and then declined so in their turn, the Greeks arose to replace them in the ongoing flow of history. There are records in hieroglyphics of early Greece dating back to 2300 B.C. depicting women dancing and men engaging in acrobatics, boxing, and wrestling.

Development of Sports Contests and Establishment of the Olympic Games. As early as 1000 B.C. sports contests had developed. In 776 B.C. the Olympic Games were inaugurated, lasting 1170 years. They were open only to male athletes of Greek blood, with no criminal record. They consisted of foot races, a penthathlon, broad jumps, hop-step-jump, and javelin throw. Rewards were a crown of wild olive and palm branches. When the Greeks (10,000 against 60,000 Persians) defeated the army of the great King Darius at Marathon in 490 B.C., the Greek Pheidippides ran twenty-two miles to Athens and with his dying breath informed the Athenians of the victory. Almost 2400 years later, memory of this notable event is kept alive by the many marathon races run annually all over the world by many thousands of runners in behalf of both historical memories and physical fitness. No other event in the history of the world has received from youth such long-lasting, worldwide acclaim.

Not looking upon their games as contests for a few of great physical valor and excellence to put on entertainment for the public the Greeks invited all youth to enter into the activities for their own physical development. Success was not measured by winning a contest but by participating in good form, in control of temper, and with dignified manner. To excel in any one activity counted for little. The important thing was to excel in a variety of activities; hence, the stress the Greeks attached to being able to perform well in the pentathlon and decathlon. Awards for physical achievement were not monetary. The olive wreath was considered a great prize. Greek sport was amateur sport at its best.

A favorite sport event was the discus throw. No doubt one of Greece's most famous sculptured pieces is *The Discus Thrower* (Discobolus) by the sculptor Myron of the Golden Age. The discus throw is one of the oldest of field sports and the oldest known discus was found in archeological excavations, measuring 8 to 10 inches in diameter and weighing 4 to 5 pounds.

Birth of Physical Education As a Discipline. Within the next hundred years following the Battle of Marathon, Herodotus, the great Greek historian and traveler, and the three great teacher–philosophers were born. From the teachings and writings of these four came the birth of the idea of democracy and of the responsibility of the state to educate the youth. Clear ideas of the need of organized physical activities for all citizens arose with the birth of the idea of physical education as a discipline in itself, a concern and branch of education.

There is a great wealth of literature available in many languages that reveals the extent of knowledge the Greeks of this Golden Age had about physical education. Gymnastic exercises in themselves were considered the foundation of all physical education, the body conditioner upon which sports, games, and dance were built. Plato claimed that swimming and gymnastics engaged in, even on a compulsory basis, were of great value and that participation in them should be obligatory for all youth, girls as well as boys.[5]

From these Greek writers we learn that dancing reached a high form in the Greek Golden Age, their choric dance being considered the highest art form, and that preschoolers enjoyed swings, seesaws, stilts, hoops, kites, and games of hide and seek and, drop the handkerchief.

With the limited knowledge at that time of anatomy and physiology, the operation of the body in motion, or the physiology of exercise, it is astonishing how knowledgeable these learned Greeks were about the values of exercise and how varied a program of physical education they advocated. Common goals in the teaching for all youth were obedience to commands, respect for authority, and ability to act in unison with others.

Rome[6]

As early as 2000 B.C. people were migrating from Greece into territory that is today's Italy. By 760 B.C. there was great Greek colonization especially in the Bay of Naples area. By 507 B.C. the Roman Republic had been founded. By then Greece had experienced almost 300 years of Olympic Games, although things were different in Rome. Long periods of migrations of settlers from the north and northeastern lands had brought to northern Italy people quite different from the Greek settlers. Whereas the Greeks brought with them their idea of sports for all the citizens–sports engaged in not as ends in themselves but for the sake of life's enrichment, as a side issue to life's chief occupation, amateur sport in the true sense of the word—other races brought a love of watching other people engage in physical contests, leading to the development within their national life of what in today's parlance is called spectatoritis. They demanded highly skilled performers for their entertainment; out of this grew the great era of gladiatorial combat and chariot races. To acquire sufficient skill to please the enormous crowds that came to watch them, performers had to make a lifetime profession of the activity, creating professional sport as opposed to type of sport engaged in by the Greeks.

From the thirst of the populace for these professional contests grew a demand for a place large enough to handle the great crowds desiring to see the contests. This led in 329 B.C. to the first great Roman amphitheater, the Circus Maximus, which could seat 200,000 spectators. By 186 B.C. the Greeks of the Roman Republic put on their first demonstrations of their Greek form of physical education and sports. But the Romans of non-Greek ancestry were little interested in these demonstrations and were critical of the nakedness of their athletes. By 31 B.C. the Roman Republic had become the Roman Empire, and within the next few years a new religion was born to bring the world into the Christian Era. Following this came a period of great military conquests by Rome. In the first century Anno Domini (A.D.), the great Roman Coliseum was built with a seating capacity of 50,000 to 87,000.

By the fourth century A.D. the Olympic Games went into a decline. They had become corrupt, entangled in politics, and so subservient to degrading practices that the entire ideology of their purpose was lost. In A.D. 394 the Christian emperor Theodosius abolished the games as a debasing influence.

Throughout the later years of the Republic and the more than 200 years of the Empire, Romans, as well as Greeks on their own, engaged in several sports and physical activities. They played a game resembling hockey, and handball was so common that many private homes had handball courts.

The form of dance that Roman–Greek men and women engaged in, was considered by other Romans to be effeminate and the men refused to indulge in it. The dance forms they created were largely pantomimic and used almost entirely as a form of entertainment. It followed the pattern of Roman sports with but few specially trained professionals engaged in the activity and the great body of citizens partaking of it only as spectators.

Gradually in the fifth century a decline set in and by A.D. 476 the Roman Empire, not conquered by some enemy from outside but by inward advancing decay, came to the end of its glory.

THE MIDDLE AGES

From the fall of the Roman Empire until the discovery of the New World, a period of a little more than 1000 years, there were tremendous migrations throughout Europe of Teutonic tribes who finally settled down laying the foundations of the nations of the modern European world.

The Early Middle Ages

The earlier years of the Middle Ages were largely shrouded in mystery. It was a period when hordes of uncivilized and unlettered peoples left scant record of themselves. Thus it became known to many historians as the Dark Ages. Yet it is the period that gave the world yet another new religion, Islam, its great Christian cathedrals and great Moslem mosques, and also the beauties of illuminated manuscripts.

However some records have been preserved of the Eastern Roman Empire's Middle Ages when chariot racing was at its height of popularity in the hippodrome of Constantinople. But it was in the fifth century A.D. that this sport was at its height.[7]

Chariot racing had come to Constantinople from the Circus Maximum of Rome—the old racing and sports arena built around 600 B.C. But by the reign of Byzantine Emperor Justinian (A.D. 527 to 565) the sport was at its peak. At that time the Roman form of racing was used. It called for four chariots per race, four horses abreast per chariot, and seven laps around the hippodrome. In the sixth century a day's program called for twenty-five races per day, but 400 years later the number had dropped to eight races per day. These races were run off in three classes, according to the age of the charioteers: one of boys under 17 years of age, one of 17-to-20-year-olds, and one of over 20-year-olds.[8]

The Rise of Islam and the Preservation of Religious and Literary Works. In A.D. 612, Muhammed, a merchant of Mecca in Arabia and head of a successful caravan trade, inspired by secret revelations, began a career of preaching of One God. Ten years later, at Medina where he had more friendly reception than at Mecca, he founded the Islamic religion. This new religion spread widely throughout the Middle East and by A.D. 711 the Moslems (the followers of Islam) had conquered much of northern Africa and had even reached Spain where Cordova became the Islamic capital in Europe (A.D. 755). About this same time the city of Baghdad was built in Mesopotamia as the capital of all Islam. For a period of almost 500 years this city was the world center of learning of that period.[9]

To the University of Baghdad came the savants of the world. There the Arab scholars resurrected the lost Greek literary works, transliterating them into Arabic and sending them out throughout the worlds they were conquering, reaching into western Europe. There the Arabic writings were transliterated into various European languages and the ancient Greek writings were became known to the Medieval world.

From these translations the Western world learned of the riches of physical education born in early Greece of the great teacher–philosophers. Thus the views of Socrates, Plato, and Aristotle on physical education were available once more to the world of learning. Well that they were for the Dark Ages left no records of any advancements in ideas on physical education.

The Latter Middle Ages

As the Dark Ages gave way to the Age of Chivalry with its founding of great institutions of learning and the wondrous rediscovery that the world is indeed round, historical periods blended into each other, just as the Ancient World had blended into the Early Middle Ages, advancing toward a modern world. The Latter Middle Ages was a period of great advancement for humanity.

The Period of Knighthood. With the might of a strong Rome no longer available to protect the settled populace from the hordes of barbaric Teutons that had been roaming western Europe from the time of the fall of the Roman Empire in the fifth century, the feudal system gradually developed for mutual protection. Neither political nor governmental this was merely an informal clustering together for mutual benefit of groups of people into communities centered about the holdings of some nobleman who was a great landowner. Within this organization grew up three distinct classes of people, the serfs who worked the land, the vassals who offered counsel and military protection as needed and contributed to the common good in all manner of services above the work of the serfs, and the knights, military servants of high birth, who were subject to call into military service on horseback. In times of adversity and attacks by enemies, all classes were subject to call to the defense of their patron, to whom in exchange for his concern and protection they offered unquestioned allegiance and loyalty.

The feudal system lasted for about a thousand years, but knighthood found its greatest glory in the fourteenth and fifteenth centuries.

Each fief was largely dependent upon its knights for common protection against its most dangerous enemies. From this need there developed a class of young men of noble birth whose great aim in life called for superb physical fitness. Since heavy armor was worn for combat, even more than ordinary physical fitness was required, so that the education of these knights was predominantly a program of physical activity. The pursuit of this kind of well-being and the acquisition of the skills demanded by their calling took up almost the entire time alloted to their education.

From the legends of King Arthur and his Knights of the Round Table of the sixth century (preserved for posterity by twelfth to fifteenth century writers,)[10] there must have been carryover from the Greek ideals of a physical education handed down through Rome, reaching Britain through Caesar's conquests of 57 B.C. and the subsequent 500 years of Roman occupation. From the very beginnings of knighthood the youths trained as knights had to have great endurance, strength, and skill. Only men of virile physique could succeed in this career. They were trained in horsemanship, swimming, fencing, boxing, the handling of lances both on foot and on horseback, and scaling walls.

In later years there developed for entertainment of the nobles, jousts and tournaments which reached their height in the thirteenth, fourteenth, and fifteenth centuries when many of the tournaments became elaborate pageants. These jousts were held all over Christendom, being to the later Middle Ages what the Hellenic games were to ancient Greece and the chariot races and gladitorial contests were to ancient Rome.

It is doubtful that any other long period in history made such exclusive demands for physical fitness upon its privileged young men. If children, women, and men other than knights engaged in physical activities, as of course they must have, practically no records have come down the years to so inform us.

Old World Advances in Physical Education. Although there are only scant records of the physical activities available to the common people of the Middle Ages, there are interesting records of the activities of the persons attached to the courts of the various nobles as well as to those of the crowns. There was much hunting, horsemanship, horse racing, rowing, swimming, archery, dancing, and games similar to football, cricket, tennis, and golf.[11]

In 1560 the artist Vasari did a fresco of a football game engaged in on the Piazzo Santa Marie Novella of Florence, with spectators around the four sides of the great square on foot in the front rows, on horseback at the rear, with the center reserved for the players numbering about thirty, as best that can be counted, with an indefinite number huddled in a heap at the center. The twelve other players in the front half of the square in the fresco are well scattered about the field of play.[12]

It is reported that the British and French negotiators of truce terms for the Hundred Years War at Calais in 1439 took time out to play a friendly game of football. If true, the general run of the men of the governing class knew the game as participants.

In fact there are records that in 1303 an Oxford student was killed while playing football on High Street and that in 1409 because of football's ''grievous contention and contumely,'' the city of London stopped collecting money to buy new footballs. There are also records all through the 1300s and 1400s of royal decrees criticizing the game so that finally St. Andrews of Scotland forbade the playing of the game. As played in medieval times, football was a loosely organized game in which entire villages would put on contests with as many as a hundred or more on each side. This sort of football was played for centuries.[13]

As to dance of the Middle Ages, the choric dance of the classic Greek, generally considered the first dance of a purely artistic form, had long died out with the fall of Rome.

In the fifteenth century, dance as first preserved in the courts of the nobility of Italy and later catching on in France became a form of processions in celebration of events in the life of the court, including singing and dialogue and acrobatic feats. Devoid of religious motive or even of attempts to express emotions, it was purely for entertainment of the upper classes and became known as the ballet. The first such ballet was presented at Torona, Italy, in 1489. It was not until over a hundred years later, in France, that this form of dance included any attempt to express emotion, and it made little progress. However in folk dances of the French country people were adapted for court entertainment as a new dance feature.

In the mid-seventeenth century, a classic dance form emerged from the *Academie Royale* established by Louis XIV in 1661. The ballet master, Beauchamp, formulated a dance technique that gave the world the classical "five positions" of the ballet. More than 300 years later they are still accepted as the fundamentals of classic dance. Later two techniques developed—the "turning out" of the hip and the rising upon the points of the toes, which added markedly to the nature of the dance.[14]

Discovery of America.[15] In 1492 Columbus made his first voyage westward across the Atlantic, reaching land in three or four months, at today's Santo Domingo, and going on from there to Cuba. He was convinced that he and his men had reached China. On three succeeding journeys he discovered Porto Rico, Jamaica, and Trinidad, and made landings on South America. Finally on his last trip he went farther west than the West Indies to the coast of today's Honduras and on to Panama. He died in 1506 not knowing that he had discovered a new world. But savants back in Europe felt sure that places he had reached were not the eastern reaches of China.

During Columbus's third voyage, Amerigo Vespucci sailed from Spain to discover the mouth of the Amazon River. On a second voyage he sailed along the coast of Brazil and became convinced that this was a new world. His published account of this voyage led geographers of that time to agree that new lands had been discovered. In 1507, the year following the death of Columbus, they proposed that the new land be named America after the explorer who was convinced that this was not China. The proposal was accepted but only as applying to South America. Gradually the name was accepted for both the northern and southern lands.

Here was a new world apparently waiting to be settled. Sixty years later, Sir Walter Drake sent ships out to establish colonies in what is today's Virginia but they returned home with their would-be settlers. Twenty years later, Jamestown, Virginia, was founded. Thirteen years after that (1620) the Pilgrims arrived on Cape Cod. In another ten years, seventeen ships had arrived from England with 1000 emigrants for the Boston area, and in the next twelve years, 16,000 settlers had arrived from England alone, along with settlers from Holland and other countries. The American colonies were well underway.

2

Heritage from the Colonists of the New World

In the seventeenth and the first half of the eighteenth century there were but a few small colonies scattered along the Atlantic seaboard of America. By the opening of the Revolutionary War settlements had spread inland toward the mountains and a few even beyond into the Ohio Valley. By then the population of the thirteen colonies was reported to be around 3 million with Boston a metropolis of 30 thousand.

Throughout Colonial days the population was almost 95 percent rural. Settlements were far apart, and as travel was by foot, horse, or boat it was difficult for people to get together. The days were filled with the struggle for existence—the conquest of the soil and of the forests, protection from the Indians, building and repairing homes, obtaining food, and preparing meals. Everyone was busy most of the waking hours. However, since work at arts and crafts was a necessity everyone had some form of creative work to do, and therein lay much contentment for all.

EDUCATION IN GENERAL

The leaders among the colonists desired a common education for all children. Among their earliest undertakings was the establishment of schools of some sort. As early as 1647 the Massachusetts colonists decreed that for every town that had as many as fifty families, schools must be established, and all children, even those of the servant classes, girls as well as boys, were to be taught at least to read. By 1689, six schools were in existence in Virginia, one in Maryland, eleven in New York, and about twenty in Massachusetts.[1] The writings of the English philosopher John Locke were well known in America. His *Thoughts on Education,* published in 1693, exerted such influence on the colonists that his theory of formal discipline held sway in the schools. The elementary education of boys and girls was cared for through private tutors, district schools, and public schools for paupers. Reading, writing, ciphering, and spelling comprised the curriculum. The Bible was the main textbook, and all children were taught the catechism.

Benjamin Franklin, as early as 1743 in his *Proposals Relating to the Education of Youth*, recommended that academies be organized whose aim would be to prepare young people for life in the world of their day. He called for schools with a "healthful situation" with garden, orchard, meadow, and fields and with provision for students to engage in games, running, leaping, wrestling, and swimming. Franklin founded the first academy in Philadelphia in 1749. Samuel Moody followed in 1763 with the first boarding school.[2]

LEISURE ACTIVITIES[3]

Since the responsibilities of meeting the needs of everyday life were so time-consuming in Colonial days there was little free time for recreation. But the spontaneous urge for people to get together for companionship brought forth forms of recreational activities which, although born of their daily needs, resulted in much merrymaking for the great mass of the people. Also, some did manage to find time occasionally to engage in dance and sports. It is recorded that some boys played a form of football in the Colonies as early as 1609.

From the needs of the people to combine recreation with useful labor there arose quilting parties, cornhuskings, house- and barn-raisings. Even though the stern hand of the church was strongly felt in the land, the pious, who considered anything not connected with work or worship as a waste of time, could conscientiously join in this fun. The less pious and the young people engaged in the dances and the sports which some of the colonists had brought from the mother countries with them. Also, the need to market their products brought forth fairs, and amusements grew up around these such as wrestling matches and chasing greased pigs or climbing greased poles.

A leisure class developed around the large plantations of the South where there were slaves to do the work. Fox hunting, horse racing, and extravagant balls filled the leisure hours. In Philadelphia, as early as 1627, British soldiers quartered there brought to that community a form of old English pageantry, and other groups kept alive the traditional Maypole dances of England. Practically all the colonies except the strongly church controlled ones of Massachusetts, New Hampshire, and Connecticut soon developed some forms of festivals, fairs, and pageants.

Children of Colonial days played marbles, "fives," leapfrog, hop scotch, blindman's buff, and hop-skip-and-jump. They did a lot of kite flying and fishing, and in the spring they danced around the Maypole.

The children of the New England colonies, where the obdurate Puritans ruled both church and state, found it difficult to engage in these activities as much as they would have liked. The grown-ups, too, had their difficulties with stern authorities. On Christmas Day, 1621, when the Governor of Massachusetts ordered the men of Plymouth out to their daily work, the newcomers who had recently arrived on the ''Fortune'' excused themselves saying it was against their conscience to work on Christmas Day. So, as the Massachusetts archives tell the story:

> . . . he led away ye rest and left them: but when they came home at noone from their worke he found them in ye streete at play, openly: some pitching, ye barr & some at stoole-ball and such like sports. So he went to them and took away their implements and tould them it was against his conscience that they should play & others work. If they made ye keeping of it a mater of devotion let them kepe their houses, but ther should be no gameing or revelling in ye streets. Since which time nothing hath been attempted that way, at least openly.

Church rules or no church rules, the young people of Boston played football and squibs and in the winter threw snow balls so actively that ''His Majesties Justices'' passed a law in 1701 ''for preventing danger by Footballs, Squibs and Snowballs.'' Toward the latter part of the period the boys and young men of all the English settlements played football, cricket, fives, rounders, and many other games. The village commons, or greens as some called them, served as the first municipal playgrounds in America. The Dutch brought to New Amsterdam their great love of skating and ninepins. They used the Old-World Dutch skates and sleds, and, in their merrymaking, both old and young were a great contrast to the dour New Englanders.

In Virginia nearly all the British sports flourished. Fox hunting was the universal sport of a gentleman. Muster day, when all men were to report for military instruction, was an occasion for athletic competitions and games; foot races, jumping, boxing, wrestling, cockfights, and horse racing were the main attractions at these gatherings and at the fairs and picnics. The winners received prizes and considerable notoriety. According to records at William and Mary College, the Governor of Massachusetts in 1691 issued the following proclamation:

> To the Sheriff of Surry Co. I desire that you give public notice that I will give first and second prizes to be shot for, wrastled, play at backswords, and run for by horse and foot, all which prizes are to begin on the 22nd day of April next, St. George's Day, being Saturday, all which prizes are shott for, etc. by the better sort of Virginians only, who are Batchelors.

Such meets were crude but enjoyable and were engaged in without training.

In 1792 the Methodist Episcopal Church, fearing the trends of the day, issued the following statement on play for the students attending the schools under their management.

. . . we prohibit play in the strongest terms. . . . The students shall rise at five o'clock . . . summer and winter. . . . Their recreation shall be gardening, walking, riding, and bathing without doors, and the carpenter's, joiner's and cabinet-maker's business within doors. . . . The students shall be indulged with nothing which the world calls play. Let this rule be observed with the strictest nicety; for those who play when they are young, will play when they are old.[4]

Dance

The early settlers brought various forms of dance to the New World with them. The British gentry brought their stately and dignified dances, whereas the lower classes brought the jigs and reels and boisterous squares. The French brought their cotillions and quadrilles. After the Revolutionary War the few girls' schools then in existence were advertising dancing as one subject that would be taught to "the young ladies."

Sports

During the colonial years school hours were so long that there was little opportunity for boys to engage in sports. As for the colleges, the games of the students are as old as the colleges, but from the very start they met with opposition from the authorities, who were quick to rule against them as being harmful. As related in Princeton College archives, the boys at that school were playing some sort of ball game in 1761 as is evidenced by the outcry of the trustees of that year as follows:

The Trustees, having on their own view been sensible of the Damage done to the President's House by the Students playing at Ball against it, do hereby strictly forbid all and any of the Sd Students, the Officers and all other Persons belonging to the College, playing at Ball against Sd President's House, under the penalty of Five Shillings, for every offense, to be levied on each Person who shall offend in the Premises.

At all events, the Princeton trustees were not forbidding the playing, merely moving it to some other setting. Providing a playing field for the boys was as yet not considered necessary.

Bowling. A game called skittles, similar to modern bowling, was played in the South in particular, surviving today in the southeastern mountain regions, no doubt brought there by the early English settlers who, judging from the many references in various of Dickens' novels to his characters' enjoyment of "skittles and beer," were addicted to both the game and the liquid refreshment.

Cricket. From an advertisement carried in the March 1778, issue of *The Royal Pennsylvania Gazette*[5], it is evident that the game of cricket was being played at least by the British occupation forces around Philadelphia. The advertisement was as follows: "Any person acquainted with the making of *Cricket Bats* or *Balls* may have good encouragement. Enquire of the printer." However, the game was being played in Virginia as early as 1709.[6]

Football. A game called futballe was played in England as early as the eleventh century and the colonists brought it to the New World with them. However their game resembled soccer somewhat and was called long bullets. By the opening of the eighteenth century, a game then known as football was played so enthusiastically that the "freeholders and inhabitants" of Boston passed orders for "preventing danger by Foot Balls" and eighty-four years later still other orders to the effect that football was "not to be played at, or kicked through any part of the town."[7]

Golf. A game called goff was being played in the Carolinas in 1714, no doubt brought by the many Scots who settled there. Evidently the game was familiar in other colonies as well, since it is mentioned and recommended by the famous physician, educator, and politician of that time, Benjamin Rush (1745–1813).[8]

In the United States, the year 1795 is clearly the earliest recorded date for this game, in the form of an announcement in the Charleston, South Carolina *City Gazette* of a golf club meeting on the village green. There is a similar record from Savannah, Georgia, for 1796, and a third record from Riverton, New York, of April 21, 1779, announcing that golf balls and clubs could be purchased from the local printer. Other than these few scattered attempts, the game of golf seems to have died out until a revival in late nineteenth century.

Nine-Pins. In 1714 the British Coffee House maintained a bowling green in Boston which was open to "all gentlemen, merchants and others that have a mind to recreate themselves." In New Amsterdam a green was laid out in 1732 at the foot of Broadway for the use of the public, the land being leased from the city. Bowling Green of today's New York City marks the site of these activities. Originally nine pins were used, but, because of excessive betting, the game was outlawed, and later, to evade the law, a tenth pin was added.

Rounders. The Old English game of rounders came to America with the earliest colonists and flourished through the years, gradually evolving into today's baseball, which in its present form is essentially American. The earliest published recognition of the game of baseball is in *The Little Pretty Book*, published by Hugh Gaine in New York in 1762.[9]

Shinny. The boys at Princeton College played a game "in the back common of the college" with balls and sticks which caused so much annoyance to the faculty that in 1787, they voiced their objections declaring:

> The game is in itself low and unbecoming to gentlemen Students and in as much as it is an exercising attended with great danger to the health by sudden and alternate heats and colds and as it tends to accidents, almost unavoidable in that play, to disfiguring and

maiming those who are engaged in it . . . the faculty think it incumbent on them to prohibit both the Students and Grammar Scholars from using the play aforesaid.[10]

The diaries of the students of later years testify that the faculty prohibition was of no avail and that shinny was for many years the main college game.

Tennis. There is record that tennis, then known as court tennis, was being played in America as early as 1763. At that time the game was mentioned in the publication of *Temporary Acts and Laws of His Majesties Province*, Boston, New England.

FIRST THOUGHTS OF PHYSICAL EDUCATION

Although the colonists accepted English philosopher John Locke's ideas on formal discipline, they fell short of accepting his idea that vigor and discipline of the body were chief aims of education. Although the theories of French philosopher Rousseau and German education reformer Basedow on the need for physical as well as intellectual education also inspired America's leaders, it was difficult to put them into effect. Locke had specifically called for instruction in dancing, fencing, and horsemanship to be included in the school programs.[11] Jean Jacques Rousseau (1712-1770) called for instruction in swimming, leaping and jumping, and scaling cliffs. He proclaimed that children must be allowed to be children before they become adults. He felt that physical and intellectual education are so intimately bound together and interdependent that there should be no marked dividing line between them—they should proceed together. He believed in a sound body for a sound mind. Perhaps one of the best known sentences in his book *Emile* is the following: "If you would cultivate the intelligence of your pupil, . . .give his body continued exercise, make him robust and sound in order to make him wise and reasonable: let him work and move about and run and shout and be continually in motion."[12] He strongly recommended gymnastic exercises as well as games and outdoor activities for a physical education.

Johann Basedow (1723–1790), an ardent follower of Rousseau, opened a school in Dessau, Germany, in 1774, called the Philanthropinum, in which gymnastics were given a definite place in the school curriculum. This was the first time physical education was included as a part of a school program. However, the innovation in education did not receive a wholehearted reception and the venture lasted only a few years. But while it lasted the pupils spent one hour in the morning and two in the afternoon in gymnastics, sports, and manual labor. Physical activities engaged in were running, jumping, throwing, wrestling, fencing, riding, dancing, swimming, skating, walking on balance beams, and exercises on ladders.[13]

In the Colonies in America at this time, a few educational leaders, chief among whom was Benjamin Franklin, strongly urged recognition by the schools of the physical activity needs of children. But for the most part, physical education not only had no acknowledged place in education in Colonial days, but the educational spirit influenced by the prevailing Puritan attitudes, was hostile not only to play, believing it to be a sin but to all activities related to play, including sports and even physical exercises.[14] Although, particularly in New England, the boys from ten to sixteen were given military drill six days a year, only after the War of Independence did there arise an emphasis on the physical welfare of the students and the desirability, if not the necessity, of physical exercise as a part of the school program.

Thomas Jefferson (1743–1826) in his writings on education, expressed his belief in the necessity of physical exercise as a part of general education. In his plans for the University of Virginia, he included provision for a gymnasium, although he made no plans for the employment of a teacher to be in charge of it. The influence of these great leaders was gradually felt, and educators began to reevaluate their educational objectives.

EARLY PROFESSIONAL LITERATURE

Since no profession of physical education as yet existed in the early days of United States history, there was, of course, no local professional literature as such. However, there was developing a literature on physical activities which is of historic interest. From 1712 on, the first books mentioning physical activities came out in America, chief among them Hugh Gaines' *A Little Pretty Book* of 1762 which contains woodcuts of games and gives the first mention in the United States of cricket and baseball. Preceding this was Edward Blackwell's *A Compleat System of Fencing* of 1734 put out by William Parks of Williamsburg, Joseph Seacombe's *Business and Diversion Inoffensive to God* of 1739 dealing with fishing, and John Armstrong's *Art of Preserving Health*, first published in London in 1644 and reprinted for American readers in 1745 by Benjamin Franklin.

Following these were Benjamin Rush's *Sermons to Gentlemen Upon Temperance and Exercise* (published in 1772 by John Dunlap of Philadelphia), which mentions both golf and tennis, Bernard Roman's *A Concise Natural History of East and West Florida* of 1775 containing an account of lacrosse as a Choctaw Indian game, and Edmund Hoyle's *Hoyle's Games Improved* 1796, published by James Benfort of Philadelphia, containing material on tennis and quadrilles. Between 1796 and 1857 this last book ran to nineteen editions.[15]

EARLY LEADERS IN PHYSICAL EDUCATION

Benjamin Franklin (1706—90)[16]

America's first recorded promoter of physical education was Benjamin Franklin. He was the first voice raised in the Colonies in behalf of physical education. Not only did he as an educator interest himself and others in the kind of school and curriculum needed for the youth of the land but he also went far beyond that to offer detailed instructions and advice on setting up a physical-activity school program. He even gave instructions on the techniques of teaching some of the activities, notably swimming.

As a young boy Franklin became deeply interested in the skills of swimming. He experimented with a kite to draw himself across the water as he floated on his back with cork paddles for his hands and feet to propel himself more effectively through the water. He investigated the problem of muscle cramping and the physiological effects of sudden plunging into cold water. He became such an expert swimmer that as a young man he gave an exhibition of swimming in London and later gained an international reputation as an authority on the subject.

Samuel Moody (1727?-1795)

Before the Revolutionary War, Samuel Moody, first headmaster of the famous Dummer Grammar School of Byfield, Massachusetts (the first private boarding school in America, which opened in 1763) became the chief exponent of physical activities as an important part of education. After Franklin he was the foremost person of this period to promote this part of the program. He taught the activities to the pupils and participated in them. Among his pupils were several who were destined to become famous: two signers of the Constitution, twenty members of the Continental Congress, and two Chief Justices of the Massachusetts Supreme Court.[17]

B

PHYSICAL EDUCATION FOR A NEW NATION: LATE EIGHTEENTH AND EARLY NINETEENTH CENTURIES (1787-1865)

3

Physical Activities For a New Nation

The War of Independence setting the American colonies free of British deomination opened up vast territories, vast responsibilities, and vast opportunities for a free world. The territory of the new nation reached from the Atlantic Seaboard to the Mississippi River. By 1830 the population of the United States had increased from the three million of Revolutionary War days to 13 million. Throughout the mid-1800s immigrants from many lands continued to pour into America at every port. To Europe, America had become "the promised land"-the home of the free. In Germany, Metternich's Carlsbad Decrees of 1819 stifled political action and instituted strict censorship of the press and supervision of universities. Through the thirty years in which these decrees were in force, German students and professors by the hundreds fled to America bringing with them their deep interest in education and freedom. Many of them, also, brought their enthusiasm for physical education, materially enriching the educational system of that period.

At this same time the Irish and Scotch-Irish were being ruthlessly suppressed by the English. From 1816 on, immigrants from Ireland poured into America in astounding numbers, reaching by 1935 an annual number of 30,000. In the hundred years from 1820 to 1920, four and a quarter million immigrants came to the United States from Ireland alone.

Women were awakening in the early nineteenth century to their opportunities for advancement, both in politics and in education. In 1848 there was held in Seneca Falls, New York, the first women's rights convention ever assembled anywhere in the world. This beginning led to opened doors for women in the world of education, bringing thoughts of careers outside the home. A side issue of the women's rights movement was the campaign for dress reform championed by Amelia Bloomer (1818—1894), editor of a popular women's magazine, which led eventually through an unplanned side issue to acceptance of a type of garment that made it possible for women to dress in a manner fitting to the pursuit of a career in the teaching of physical education.

EDUCATION IN GENERAL

With the opening of the nineteenth century, elementary schools increased rapidly in number, the academies gained in popularity over the Latin grammar schools of Colonial days, and coeducation was becoming a recognized form of education. "Free public" high schools open to all children, however, were little known in the early part of this era. In fact, as late as 1850 there were only eleven public high schools in all of the United States, and college education for women became a reality for only a very few. Massachusetts in 1852 became the first state to pass a compulsory school attendance law. (It took sixty-four years for the last state— Mississippi—to fall into line.) This move created a need for changes in educational procedures and programs to take care of the special needs of children who had never before attended school, just as the civil rights movement in this century opened doors of heretofore segregated schools to many children whose special needs called for new adjustment and programming.

Treatises and books on education by European leaders were becoming readily available in the United States. Particularly did Froebel, the German founder of kindergartens and champion of education of women, begin to have marked influence on American educational philosophy, and the theories of Rousseau and Pestalozzi called for educational programs based on the interests and needs of pupils. Many national leaders took a deep interest in the schools, in particular Thomas Jefferson, who used his great influence for the establishment of universal free schools.[1]

In 1826 a public high school for girls was established in New York, and so many attended that it closed shortly because of lack of finanical support.

Although the number of schools financed by public taxation grew rapidly between 1800 and 1850, the private schools continued to carry the great burden of the responsibility for the education of the youth of the land.[2]

Lower Schools

In 1818 Boston added primary schools to its public school system, and followed shortly with the English High School, the first high school in America of the new free schools movement. From then on, the public high school began to replace both the Latin Grammar School of Colonial days and the Academy of the late eighteenth century. By 1825 New York City, and by 1829 Portland, Maine, had established high schools. The movement quickly spread to Philadelphia (1838), Baltimore (1839), Cleveland (1830), St. Louis (1853), and Detroit, Chicago, and San Francisco (1856), thus spanning the continent.

In 1837 Horace Mann (1796–1859), a famous reformer in the field of education and then Secretary of the Massachusetts State Board of Education, remodeled the entire state system of education, centralizing the supervision of local district schools, eliminating religious domination wherever it still existed, and introducing new methods based on the best to be found in Europe. He insisted that common schools were to be common to all and with lay control. To supply qualified teachers for the schools, he also established in 1839 the first public normal school in the country in Lexington, Massachusetts. His methods and theories were soon adopted throughout all common schools.

Heretofore secondary schools had not been considered necessary for the great mass of people, but now the idea of universal education—at least universal male education—was growing. By the end of the era, the idea included girls as well as boys, and enrollment of girls in public schools was beginning to make serious inroads upon the enrollment in girls' private schools; as early as 1820 a girls' high school was opened in Boston. By then the Moravian Academy for Girls in Bethlehem, Pennsylvania, had been functioning for forty years.

Higher Schools

In the late eighteenth century, the emphasis of education was shifted from the colleges to the lower schools. Now, in the new century, a renewed and greatly expanding trend for "higher education" began.

Following the Revolutionary War, fourteen states founded universities:

1801-South Carolina	1831-New York
1804-Ohio (Athens)	1836-Wisconsin
1807-Maryland	1839-Vermont
1817-Michigan	1839-Missouri
1819-Virginia	1844-Mississippi
1820-Indiana	1847-Iowa
1820-Alabama	1850-Utah

Many private colleges also were established in this period reaching from coast to coast, chief among them were:

1800-Middlebury (Vermont)	1831-Wesleyan (Connecticut)
1813-Colby (Maine)	1833-Oberlin (Ohio)

1841-Ohio Wesleyan (Delaware)   1846-Grinnell (Iowa)
1842-Willamette (Oregon)   1851-Coe College (Iowa)
1846-Beloit (Wisconsin)   1854-Iowa Wesleyan (Mt. Pleasant)

In this same period the first women's colleges were established:

Lindenwood (Missouri) starting in 1827 as a female seminary and achieving collegiate rating in 1863, to become then the second oldest women's college.

Mount Holyoke (Massachusetts) founded in 1837 as a female seminary but not achieving collegiate rating until 1893.

Rockford (Illinois) established in 1849 but not achieving collegiate rating until 1891.

Elmira (New York) started in 1851 and chartered as a college in 1853, to become the first women's college in the United States.

Vassar (New York) established in 1861 as a female college but not acquiring collegiate rating until 1867.

Also in this period, the first coeducational college (Oberlin, in 1833) from its beginnings admitted both blacks and women, the first college in America to admit either.

Most of the colleges established in this period were founded by religious groups, and in their beginnings many combined industrial training with intellectual education. The plan seemed well suited to the growing spirit of democracy in education, because students without financial means could defray a part of their educational expenses with the products of their labor. However, it was not until the theories of Pestalozzi and Fellenberg, two noted Swiss educators of the day, reached America that these ideas were put into practice. In 1831 the advocates of the movement for manual labor met in New York City and organized the Society for Promoting Manual Labor in Literary Institutions, and beginning in 1833 colleges founded on this idea sprang up throughout the Middle West in particular. In Indiana, the Presbyterians organized Wabash Manual Labor College in 1833 and Hanover in 1827; the Baptists founded the Indiana Baptist Manual Labor School in 1835; the Methodists, Asbury University in 1837; and the Friends, Earlham College in 1842. All these institutions long ago dispensed with the manual labor phase of their work and now exist as Wabash, Hanover, Franklin, Depauw, and Earlham.

LEISURE ACTIVITIES

As the western-moving settlers conquered the wilderness and settled down to establish homes and form communities, there grew up a division of labor made possible through group-living which produced some semblance of leisure time. With the coming of steamboats and railroads, recreation took on a new form. The *New York Herald* in 1838 advertised round-trip boat excursions to Coney and Staten islands and Hudson River trips with dancing and band concerts included. The quilting bees, corn-huskings, and square dancing of earlier days were still popular. Organized competitive sports had not yet come to the American scene, but there were informal games and contests to claim many participants.

By the late 1840s many Germans had come to America, bringing their Old-World ways of celebrating special occasions, setting the pattern for the Fourth of July celebrations particularly throughout the Middle West with parades, singing, bunting and flags, picnics, patriotic speeches, and reading of the Declaration of Independence. Games and contests filled the day and lasted far into the night. Freedom was indeed something very personal to these people who had so recently fled their native land to find it here in America. They threw themselves wholeheartedly into these celebrations. Czech immigrants also initiated festivals and contests. Their first sharpshooting contest was held at Washington, Missouri, in 1840 when they crowned the first United States King of the Sharpshooters.

Camping and Outdoor Education

Perhaps the earliest record of camping and an attempt at outdoor education for a school group is that of the Round Hill School where in the 1820s the boys were taken on weekly hikes and on an annual trip by horse and wagon when they "encamped."[3]

ACTIVITIES OF PHYSICAL EDUCATION

Rhythmical, gymnastic, and sports activities as they developed in the United States are discussed below, and the ongoing story of their further development in later periods is discussed in chapters that follow.

Dance

The dances of Colonial days were carried over into the nineteenth century, and practically all schools for girls advertised dancing as one subject to be taught to the young ladies. To most heads of these schools, this alone seemed a sufficient physical education program for girls. Mrs. Emma Willard (1787–1870), a famous educator of the day, set the thinking in that direction when, in a speech of 1819, she said: "Exercise is needful to the health and recreation to the cheerfulness and contentment of youth. . . . Dancing is exactly to this purpose. . . ."[4]

Just what form of dancing was used in these school programs other than the ballroom forms of the day is not made clear; but since the dance advocates suggested the use of dancing as a substitute for calisthenics the forms used for class work, no doubt, had some calisthenic type and content, probably the forerunner of the "fancy steps" of a later day.

Throughout the nineteenth century and into the early twentieth the Virginia Reel was an ever-popular "ice breaker" for social gatherings of mixed groups. Of unclear origins, it may have been a New World dance from the ballrooms of the plantations of the South. Or it may have been a modification of some French or English dance brought to the New World by the colonists and given this New World name. With many social groups it took the place of the squares and quadrilles, and was one of the earliest dances to be accepted as a sort of game and thus approved by the more liberal of the religious groups.

Gymnastics, Calisthenics, and Exercises

All three terms, *gymnastics, calisthenics,* and *exercises,* were used in this era to designate physical education activities other than sports or dancing. When the newly arrived German immigrants used the term *gymnastics,* they meant the German form so that the older settlers became accustomed to use the other two terms to designate exercises other than those of the German system.

German System. The great influx of German political refugees during the early part of the nineteenth century brought their love of gymnastics with them, giving this system a running head start in America. Among these refugees were three close friends: Friedrich Ludwig Jahn, Germany's famous physical educator of that day; Charles Follen, Charles Beck, and Francis Lieber, who were excellent teachers and devoted followers of Jahn. These three men interpreted to America the German gymnastic movement with its great fervor for freedom and its great hatred of oppression of every kind. In fact the coming of these men to America in 1824 and 1827 marked the real beginnings of a physical education program in the schools.

When a high school opened in New York City in 1825 it was announced that included in the school program would be German gymnastic exercises. In that same year four leading men's colleges—Yale, Harvard, Amherst, and Dartmouth—offered instruction in gymnastics under the leadership of these recently arrived German refugees. However, because of callings in other fields (as discussed in a later chapter) the three followers of Jahn went on to other important work, and their initial effort of the 1820s to introduce German gymnastics into America died aborning. However, the conviction that something should be done in the schools for bodily development endured in the minds of leading doctors and educators so that there remained some fertile ground ready for a revival in the 1850s and 1860s.

Swedish Gymnastics. Although little was heard of Swedish gymnastics in America before the closing years of the nineteenth century, there are a few scattered and vague reports of its being used here and there in the 1820s. But there seem to be no firm records, such as exist concerning the use of German Gymnastics, until the announcement of the offering of a course in the Swedish Movement Cure by the Dio Lewis Institute of Physical Education in 1862. Little is heard again of Swedish Gymnastics until the late 1880s.

Catharine Beecher's Calisthenics. The program of useful exercise through domestic duties that was set up at Mt. Holyoke Female Seminary in 1837 was copied in many schools, but it held no appeal to many educators as a real physical education program for girls. Nor did the German gymnastics get a favorable response from women educators who felt that they were too strenuous for most girls. So Catharine Beecher (1800–1878), a fighter in her day for the education of girls, devised a system of calisthenics of her own. Coining the word *calisthenics* from the Greek *kalos* meaning "beautiful" and *sthenos* meaning "strength" she devised a system of physical education built around twenty-six lessons in physiology and two courses in calisthenics, one for schoolroom use and one for exercises in halls.[5]

The exercises, made up of simple movements to be accompanied by music, acquired much popularity throughout the country and were accepted by many schools as a substitute for dancing. She preferred that they be practiced in a hall arranged for the purpose, but, where that was not convenient, the ordinary schoolroom would suffice. The aims were to produce grace of motion, good carriage, and sound health. This marked the first attempt of a native-born American to devise an exercise program for Americans.

In 1852 Elizabeth Blackwell (1821–1910), America's first woman graduate of a medical school, published a series of lectures, *The Laws of Life in Response to the Physical Education of Girls,* thus giving valuable backing to Miss Beecher's work.

Strength Seekers. Dr. George Barker Winship (1834–1876), a graduate of Harvard, became famous throughout the United States as the advocate of heavy gymnastics. His ideas appealed to all young men who sought to have bulging muscles and great strength. From 1859 to the early 1870s he toured the United States and Canada, lecturing on gymnastics and giving weight lifting exhibitions. The Winship Gymnasium in Boston became the most famous school for strength seekers in the country. Winship's exhibitions tended to confirm the popular idea that the gymnasium was a place for strong men, prize fighters, and wrestlers, and that great strength was the aim of gymnastic training and was synonymous with health and well-being. It has taken physical education almost a century to live down this concept that developed from these strength seekers.[6]

Because of the popularity of the strength seekers, Dr. Dudley A. Sargent (1849–1924) later called this period the "heavy-lifting phase of physical education" during which time every home and office had a "health lift." (When Sargent was being considered for the position of Director of Physical Education at Harvard in 1880, this phase was still enough in the public attention that his nearest rival for the position was a man who was running a health-lift establishment in Lowell, Massachusetts.)

Dio Lewis's System.[7] Dr. Dio Lewis (1823–1886), a well-known temperance and health lecturer, attacked vigorously the popular idea that great strength was the mark of well-being and that gymnasia were primarily for gymnasts. In his writings he strove to prove that light wooden dumbbells were better suited to the real practice of gymnastics than those of iron. He took pains to destroy the common belief that free, unsupervised play of children was sufficient to develop sound and properly formed bodies. He held that a gymnastics teacher was as essential to the proper development of the body as the ordinary school teacher was to the development of the mind. He called his system the New Gymnastics. Those who advocated military training for the schools, of whom there were many, found that Dr. Lewis believed that military training not only failed to develop the upper half of the body but was conducive to rigidity and to strained positions. Also, he maintained that athletic sports, as a means of physical education, fell far short of organized gymnastics because of their overexertion of certain parts of the body and neglect of other parts. The time was ripe for something new.

So he devised a system of exercises for America's schools according to his own ideas. He advocated the use of music or a drum to mark the rhythm of the exercises, which should be fast enough to increase the rate of heart beat and respiration. He also originated the idea of tossing beanbags as an exercise. He preferred the beanbags to balls because they were more easily grasped with one hand. The gymnastic crown, weighing from three to one hundred pounds, was one of his contrivances. It was worn to secure erect spine and good carriage. Many of his exercises were with wands, dumbbells, clubs, and hand-rings. He claimed to have invented 500 exercises and advocated their use in place of military drill, skating, riding, and dancing.

Dio Lewis was a good salesman and engendered much enthusiasm for his system of gymnastics. He was widely acclaimed all over the country. Many magazine articles were written about him and his system. Celebrated writer Thomas Wentworth Higginson (1823–1911) took note of him, saying in the *Atlantic Monthly* in 1861:

> Gymnastic exercises are as yet but sparingly introduced into our seminaries, private or professional, though a great change is already beginning. Until lately all our educational plans have assumed man to be merely a sedentary being; we have employed teachers of music and drawing to go from school to school to teach those elegant arts, but have had none to teach the art of health. . . . It is something to have got beyond the period when active sports were actually prohibited. It would be unpardonable in this connection not to speak a good word for the favorite hobby of the day-Dr. Lewis and his system of gymnastics; or more properly of calisthenics. . . . Dr. Winship had done all that was needed in apostleship of severe exercises, and there was wanting some man with a milder hobby, perfectly safe for a lady to drive. . . . It will especially render service to female pupils so far as they practice it; for the accustomed gymnastic exercises seem never yet to have been rendered attractive to them on any large scale and with any permanency.

Sports

The earliest settlers of Colonial days participated in many sports; these were played without organization and without universally recognized rules. But in the nineteenth century, rules were developing for certain sports, and organizations to formulate them were being established. Examples of these sports follow.

Baseball. Since its development in the latter eighteenth century, as a game apart from rounders, baseball (then spelled as two words) gradually spread throughout the settled part of the country. It is probable that the game was being played in most of the colleges by the 1830s, and there is a firm record that it was played at Dartmouth College in 1837.[8] This belies the claim of Cooperstown, New York, that the game originated there in 1839. It is probable, however, that the diamond-shaped field as used today may have originated there, thus partially legitimatizing that town's claim to baseball fame aside from the fact that it now possesses the Baseball Museum and Hall of Fame, which was established there on the basis of the earlier and now challenged claim.

Although Abner Doubleday (1819–1893) is named as the originator of the game in Cooperstown, this scarcely holds up in light of the facts of his life. In 1839 he was a student at West Point, and his home was not in Cooperstown. During the Civil War he was one of the commanding generals at the Battle of Gettysburg, and he devoted much of his later life to writing and lecturing on military topics. Never did he, in his writings or lectures, show an interest in the game of baseball or make any claims for himself as originator of the game.[9]

In the game as played in this era, base-running was done clockwise, the ball was pitched underhand, and the game was won by the team that first scored twenty-one runs. *The World Almanac* of 1966 states that the first baseball rule book was put out in 1858 by a man named Henry Chadwick (1824–1908), but the young Knicker-bocker Club in Hoboken, made up of business and professional men, put out rules in 1845. During the 1850s, however, baseball clubs increased rapidly. By 1858 there were twenty-five teams playing in and about New York City and in that year the National Association of Baseball Players was founded. This association agreed on the rules of the game and specified that the ball was to weigh $6\frac{1}{2}$ ounces and was to be $10\frac{1}{2}$ inches in circumference. The bat might be any length but must not be more than $2\frac{1}{2}$ inches in diameter. The pitcher, who pitched, rather than threw, the ball, might stand anywhere on a line 12 feet long placed 45 feet from the home plate. Only amateurs who had been members of the club for 30 days were permitted to play in the regular games. These were the first nationally recognized rules—the ones referred to in the *World Almanac*. During the Civil War, the clubs charged admission to the games, and the players received a share of the money, marking the beginning of professional baseball history.[10]

Bowling. Bowling as an indoor sport was underway at the Knickerbocker alleys in New York City in 1840; the floors of that day were made of baked clay. Hoyle's

1845 edition of his game book carried information on bowling, and the following year the Providence Bowling Club in Rhode Island published its constitution and by-laws and rules.

Cricket. Cricket flourished in the eastern part of the country until the popularity of baseball of the Civil War period pushed it into the background. As late as 1859 a professional cricket team from the United States toured both the United States and Canada. The University of Pennsylvania had a cricket team as early as 1843, and the University of Michigan had one by 1860.[11]

Football. It was not until the first half of the nineteenth century, when American collegians blended soccer with rugby and added other forms of play, that the game began to resemble the present-day game. Students at Yale University played football as early as 1807 on the public green of New Haven. Both Harvard and Yale universities used the game to haze freshmen. By 1827 Harvard, and by 1840 Yale and Princeton, were promoting interclass matches.

The great rivalry that developed over football at Yale between the classes of 1855 and 1856 resulted in such controversy that it was written up and published in New Haven, starting years of such records.[12]

Lacrosse. A game spoken of as "primitive," lacrosse was played throughout Colonial days by Choctaw Indians of Mississippi, and in 1829 forty players were taken on an eight-month touring exhibition of the game. But acceptance of the game at large did not come until 1860, when a Canadian lawyer developed rules for the game which turned the ancient disorderly Indian game into an orderly one.

Rowing. There are records of rowing clubs on the Hudson River as early as the mid-1820s, in Detroit as early as the 1830s, in Boston by the 1840s, and on the Schuylkill River at Philadelphia and at Charleston, New Orleans, St. Louis, and Pittsburgh, by the 1850s. By then there were sufficient clubs to put on a regatta in New York in 1851 and on Lake Michigan at Chicago six years later. Several colleges also took up the sport—Harvard and Yale as early as the 1840s.[13]

Soccer. This game was being played at Phillips–Exeter Academy in Massachusetts as early as 1800.

Swimming. In 1791 the first swimming pool in America was built in Philadelphia on the banks of the Schuylkill River at the foot of Race Street. Called a "plunging bath" it was formed by a building being erected around a portion of the riverbed. It was privately owned and had connected with it two showers. By 1800, Philadelphia boasted of floating baths, structures similar to houseboats with portholes through which the river waters ran in and out,[14] which were popular at the time in France and England. They were located in the Delaware and Schuylkill rivers and according to Watson, "lay upon the water like low houses with white and yellow sides and green Venetian shutters with boatmen at hand to convey bathers to the establishment."[15] Some were elaborate having galleries and several bath chambers.

Help for amateur swimmers was soon forthcoming from none other than Benjamin Franklin, whose *Advice to Swimmers* (published in connection with Newton Bosworth's *Accidents*[16] *of Human Life*), must have been the first published instructions on lifesaving. At that time there was an organization known as The Humane Society, whose purpose was to restore life in persons apparently drowned. These publications were timely for it.

In 1827 Lieber opened the first public swimming pool in America. It was connected with the Boston Gymnasium. John Quincy Adams (1767–1818) attended this school and became an excellent swimmer and diver.[17]

Aquatic activities even spread to the colleges, the first instance being when in 1848 Girard College opened in Philadelphia with four indoor swimming pools, one each in the basement of the four dormitories, and one outdoor pool—all of which were planned by Lieber and were in use for over fifty years.[18]

Track and Field Sports. Scotch immigrants brought the "Caledonian games" to Boston in 1853, and from there they spread throughout the country until by the 1870s they had become very popular. These games were the forerunners of today's track and field sports.

Sports Clubs

Aside from the baseball clubs mentioned earlier, other sports clubs came into existence in this era. The earliest recorded club is the Savannah, Georgia, Golf Club of 1795. Quoit clubs flourished, the game having been brought to America by the English soldiers. Chief Justice John Marshall (1755–1835) is reported to have been the champion of his quoit club. The United Bowmen's Club of Philadelphia was functioning by 1830. The Czech organization of sharpshooters held its first contest in Washington, Missouri, in 1840, and a Deer Hunters Association organized in Ohio celebrated its centennial in 1958. Yale students formed the first college boat clubs in 1843, and the first intercollegiate sports association was born in 1858 when Harvard, Yale, Brown, and Trinity founded the short-lived College Regatta Association.

First Intercollegiate Athletics

Although there are reports of the playing of intercollegiate games as early as the 1820s between schools located near each other, it was not until in the 1850s that contests took place for which specific reports are available. The earliest such record is of an intercollegiate rowing match held between Yale and Harvard on August 2,

1852, on Lake Winnipesaukee in New Hampshire. This first intercollegiate event received but little notice in the papers, although it was advertised by circulars distributed widely by the railroad company, which sponsored the event in the interest of bringing vacationers to the area, ran excursions trains for the contest, and hired a brass band to add a festive note to the occasion.[19] In 1855 the two schools held another rowing match, this time in Springfield, Massachusetts, and (again) Harvard won. In 1859 the four schools that had organized the College Regatta Association staged the first intercollegiate regatta on Lake Quinsigamond at Worcester, Massachusetts. By this time much public interest had arisen in these rowing matches. Over 15,000 spectators turned out for the event. *The New York Herald* gave three and a half columns on the front page to the story, and postgame enthusiasm got so out of control that a pitched battle between students and police ended in the calling off of all contests for the next five years.

The second sport to enter the intercollegiate arena was baseball. The earliest record of an intercollegiate match is of a game at Pittsfield, Massachusetts, in July, 1859, when Amherst won over Williams by a score of 66 to 32. There has been preserved at Amherst College a copy of an "Extra" of the *Amherst Express* of July 1st and 2nd, 1859, which proclaims: "Baseball and Chess! Muscle and Mind!" After a report of the many preliminaries undertaken to arrange the contest the paper goes on to report the events. The Amherst players had a 90-mile journey to Pittsfield which they made the day before. The Williams teams arrived at the rendezvous the following morning having only "20 miles to overcome." The two baseball teams were put up at different hotels, and the chess players were entertained by the Pittsfield Chess Club. The Williams baseball boys were dressed "in the club uniform . . . Amherst decidedly in undress." Each team furnished its own ball, Amherst's weighing 2¼ ounces and measuring 6¼ inches around, while Williams's weighed 2 ounces and was 7 inches around. The teams from both colleges were chosen by ballot from the student bodies. It was rumored that the Amherst "thrower" was the town blacksmith, hired for the occasion. So the first gun was fired that day at Pittsfield in intercollegiate athletics. And in that very first engagement rumor of unfair advantage lifted its ugly head.

4

Physical Education
Comes to America

EDUCATION IN GENERAL

The ideas of educational leaders in Europe had considerable influence in the young nation. In the early nineteenth century there were four physical educators at work in Europe in particular whose theories were strongly felt in American education circles, molding much of the first thinking on physical education. The four men, born in a period from 1759 to 1778, were all at the height of their careers from 1800 to 1850. They were Johann Friedrich Gutsmuth (1759–1839) of Germany, Per Henrik Ling (1776–1839) of Sweden, Franz Nachetegal (1777–1847) of Denmark and, as previously mentioned, Friedrich Ludwig Jahn (1778–1852) of Germany.

In America it soon became generally accepted in this period that exercise and games are necessary for the proper growth of children and that the schools are responsible for the physical as well as the intellectual education of youth, so that at last the idea of physical education in the schools was spreading, though not without setbacks provoked by three distinct groups: the overly ardent advocates of manual labor as sufficient for exercise needs, those still strongly influenced by the Puritan idea that play in any form is sin, and the many scholars who felt that, although play might not be a sin, it was most certainly a waste of time.

As far as physical education for girls was concerned, there was a fourth group to speak out against it—the many who felt that girls were too frail to be expected to exercise and, besides, should not be drawn into such unseemly conduct.

The many German educators who came to America brought an enthusiasm for

German gymnastics which, in its ebb and flow of popularity for more than a hundred years, greatly influenced physical education in the United States. Earlier, the English love of sports had set the pattern of physical activity, but from then on there developed the two interests—gymnastics and sports. By the close of the Civil War, gymnastics had such a strong hold that the term *physical education* (which was in use as early as 1859 according to reports of the New York State Department of Education) had come to mean to most people merely gymnastics, and there arose the custom of speaking of physical education *and* sports as if they were two different things.

Lower Schools

Many educational leaders of the day advocated that education for health, by means of regular exercise and instruction in hygiene and physiology, was necessary for complete education. The teachers, however, had no well-defined idea of the real scope and significance of the science of physical education. The popular concept was that the time for games and physical exercise was after school hours, and that special teachers were not necessary. Nevertheless, as early as 1821 the Latin School for girls of Salem, Massachusetts, was encouraging play for its educational as well as recreational value, using simple gymnastic and play apparatus; Emma Willard in her Female Seminary in Troy, New York, was requiring of her pupils two half hours per day for exercises; a year later, Catharine Beecher in her school in Hartford, Connecticut, was starting her classes in calisthenics; and in 1823 a school for girls in Boston was giving its pupils some calisthenics and exercises in hanging and swinging on bars and in running and jumping.

The Round Hill School. The first recognition of physical education as a real part of a school program came when the Round Hill School was established in 1823 in Northampton, Massachusetts, by George Bancroft (1800–1891) and Joseph Green Cogswell (1786–1871), two promising young scholars. (The former was later to become famous as the "father of American history," and as the Secretary of the Navy who founded the United States Naval Academy and as United States Minister to both Great Britain and Germany, and the latter was to become recognized later as one of America's brilliant scholars and as the founder of the Astor Library in New York City.[1]

In the Round Hill School, physical education became for the first time in the United States a regular part of the course of instruction, marking the first time a person specifically qualified for the task was hired to teach physical education—this in 1827 when the school added to its faculty Charles Beck, a German political refugee, to teach both gymnastics and Latin. This also marked another first—the earliest teaching of German gymnastics in America.[2]

From the very start, the school had given the boys a rich program of physical activities, which included archery, baseball, boxing, camping, dancing, football, hiking, running, skating, swimming, and wrestling; but these activities were carried on informally and not as a part of the school curriculum and without a specialized teacher to teach them. When Beck joined the faculty, he set up an outdoor gymnasium with apparatus such as was used in a German gymnasium, and the entire school was divided into classes, each meeting for an hour three times a week for gymnastic instruction. Beck was succeeded by Charles Follen, another German refugee.

Other Schools. Following this lead, about fifteen other secondary schools organized gymnastics classes for their students. When the Chauncy Hall School was organized in Boston in 1828, provision was made for exercises and games. The head master, being especially interested in the promotion of the physical welfare of the students, provided some crude apparatus for physical exercises and at recess periods took the boys to the Bostom Common to play games.[3]

An early record of the demands for school ground areas to be set aside for games and exercises is that of the state superintendent of schools for Minnesota in his first annual report of 1851 in which he called for at least one acre of land to be set aside for the physical development of the pupils.[4] A year later, the superintendent of schools of Boston, in his school report said: "In addition to the exercise allowed at the time of recess each half day, all the younger children need provision for some gentle exercise as often as once in every half hour, such as riding, walking, marching accompanied with such motions of the arms as would tend to give fullness and erectness to the chest." The next year a rule that every "scholar" should have daily some kind of physical or gymnastic exercise was passed but scarcely enforced. In his annual report of 1858, the superintendent again spoke out for physical education saying: "While the intelligence is in training, the conscience and the body must not be neglected. Liberal playgrounds ought to be provided for every school at whatever cost, and they should be used." After a brief lull in the establishment of more schools, Horace Mann (1796–1859), a noted educator of his day, aided by other interested parties, founded the West Newton English and Classical School, a private school called the Allen School, which opened for both girls and boys in mid-January 1854. This school is looked upon as the first school in America of actual secondary rank. It had a gymnasium building for exercises for both girls and boys and here Dio Lewis gave his first classes in "free gymnastics."[5]

In San Francisco schools, boys were being given exercises in 1856, in parallel bars and flying rings, and in swinging Indian clubs, wands, and dumbbells. That same year the school put on a festival to raise money to transform the schoolyard into an outdoor gymnasium, with plans to give the boys exercise for thirty minutes daily at the noon hour and some time at the morning recess period. The girls were to be given a daily drill in a school room in free exercises and the use of wands.[6] The time was ripe, however, for the enthusiasm and confidence of Dio Lewis, whose system of calisthenics was first taught in the Allen School in West Newton, Massachusetts in 1860. The superintendent of the Boston schools became interested in this system and secured instruction for his teachers, so that it could be introduced into the Boston schools. The teachers were to give not more than one-half nor less than one-quarter of an hour to the exercises once during every school session. By 1862 there were seventy teachers who had had training and were giving the work to the school pupils.

In the 1850s educators were also awakening in the Middle West and on the West Coast. Many school yards of St. Louis were equipped with play apparatus which was used at recess periods, and some schools were practising "manual exercises," whereas in Cincinnati there were a few parallel bars, horizontal bars, horizontal ladders, and circular swings in four school yards. In 1857 the superintendent of the Cincinnati schools proposed that all teachers employed in the schools should be instructed in a system of gymnastics adapted to the several grades of the schools from the first through the sixth. A year later a department of physical education was established with a special teacher in charge of the work. A daily program of calisthenics and free play was inaugurated in 1854 in the Rincon School of San Francisco, and two years later a public exhibition of the work of the pupils consisted of exercises on horizontal bars and flying rings, and with wands, dumbbells, and Indian clubs. Several other cities made efforts to organize a system of physical training for the public schools in the 1850s, but none was able to entirely overcome either the obstacles of lack of funds, facilities, and trained leaders, or the general skepticism regarding the value of the work.[7]

Girls' Schools. In this era many people deplored the health condition of young girls and urged that physical education be made a part of their school programs. The editor of the *Boston Courier*, after attending a girls' school festival in 1858, wrote that "not one girl in ten had the air or look of good health." Catharine Beecher in her two schools in Hartford and Cincinnati used the system of calisthenics which she had developed for girls in an effort to combat this state of affairs, and many schools adopted her system. In her *Reminiscences* there is preserved a speech which she gave in Cincinnati, in 1837, in which she said, in part:

> When physical education takes its proper place in our schools, young girls will be trained in the classrooms to move head, hands and arms gracefully; to sit, stand and walk properly and to pursue calisthenic exercises for physical development as regular school duty as much as their studies; and these exercises set to music, will be sought as the most agreeable of school duties.[8]

In 1825 William Bentley Fowle (1795–1865) introduced into his girls' school in Boston the use of bars and pulleys at recess periods, teaching the use of the apparatus himself and reporting that his participation in the exercises with his pupils did not lessen their respect for him and that the discipline of the school was not thereby impaired. He also admonished that the household labors and walking which some schools advocated should not be used as a substitute for gymnastic exercises. (This report of Fowle's physical education work given in the *American Journal of Education* in 1826 probably marks the first published record of physical education for girls.)

Some private schools for girls of this era gave their students a physical education program that was indeed rich for that day including skating, archery, riding sidesaddle, dancing, swimming, croquet, walking, and calisthenics. A few schools, notably Mt. Holyoke Female Seminary in Massachusetts, offered physical education as early as 1837 but substituted domestic duties for a large part of the program. Nevertheless they did offer the students walking and calisthenics, the latter consisting mainly of dance steps accompanied by singing. Rockford Female Seminary in Illinois offered its students a physical education program as early as 1849.

In speaking of his work with girls, Fowle said: "My chief difficulty was in the selection of proper exercises for females. You know that prevailing notions of female delicacy and propriety are at variance with every attempt to render females less feeble and helpless."[9]

Colleges

On the whole, college authorities evidenced little interest in the physical well-being of their students. They provided no gymnasiums and no facilities for sports. What little interest there was came from a small handful of individuals devoted to an educational ideal. A superintendent of the United States Military Academy resigned from the service in 1818 and began an agitation for the reform of the higher educational institutions of the nation, maintaining that one of the great defects of the educational system was the neglect of physical education in all the principal seminaries.

In 1826 Harvard gave permission to Charles Follen, who was then an instructor of German in the college, to organize gymnastics for the students although the activity was not recognized as a part of the educational program. On a piece of ground called the Delta, the students, directed by Follen, constructed some crude apparatus consisting of bars, ladders, wooden horses, and suspended ropes, and laid out places for running and jumping. It was a German "turnplatz" transplanted to America. The authorities also appropriated one of the vacant halls for indoor work. The student body showed great enthusiasm, and Follen had large numbers on the Delta and on the hikes and cross-country runs.[10]

At this same time the Dartmouth students set up an outdoor gymnasium "behind the college" and established cricket clubs which "covered the green during the summer."[11] Soon thereafter Yale, Amherst, Williams, Brown, and Bowdoin, set up outdoor gymnasiums. In many cases the faculty and students worked together to clear the ground and construct apparatus. Instructors were employed, and classes were held from two to five times per week. In addition to the outdoor gymnasium a room was usually provided for indoor work. The apparatus consisted of parallel and horizontal bars, ladders, ropes, mats, and wooden horses. Running and hiking were encouraged. In some institutions fencing and boxing were taught.[12]

First Thoughts on Health Education as a Partner of Physical Education. As early as 1818 Harvard University offered a hygiene course called Health Education, and in 1823 Amherst College started lectures on anatomy. By 1850, other colleges had followed their lead.[13] At that time mumps and typhoid fever were the main illnesses to be combatted on the college campus. In recognition of this health concern, the director of physical education (in those days usually a medical doctor) was also able to serve as the college physician.

Physical Education Through Manual Labor. Throughout the 1830s and 1840s the colleges of the manual labor movement clung to their theory that manual labor was the best form of exercise and would conserve the time that participation in gymnastics would waste. These manual duties, therefore, were a substitute for physical education in all of these schools in their early years. Hence there was little progress in the development of physical education in colleges in general until in the 1850s when a nationwide interest in the subject manifested itself and became felt in institutions of higher learning. However, this work was not given recognition as an official part of the education program.[14]

Amherst College Department. In his 1855 report to the trustees, William Stearnes, who had been a pupil of Follen at Harvard and had been inaugurated as the fourth president of Amherst College in 1854, remarked: "No one thing has demanded more of my anxious attention than the health of the students. The waning of the physical energies in the midway of the college course is almost the rule rather than the exception among us, and cases of complete breaking down are painfully numerous."[15] He called for a Department of Health and Physical Education, and outlined what came to be known as the Amherst Plan.

In 1859 the construction of Barrett gymnasium, a two-story structure, was begun at the total cost of $15,000, and the trustees voted to establish a department of physical education, the first such department in the United States. They set forth the following requirements for the person to be selected as its head: He must be "thoroughly educated, a doctor of medicine and he must know something of gymnastics and sports and adhere to the principles that (1) the object of the gymnastics was not to learn to perform difficult feats but to keep the body in health, (2) the exercises used should be suited to all who engage in them and (3) students should be guarded against overwork in exercising." This person was to be given full academic rank and the title of Professor of Hygiene and Physical Culture.

Dr. Edward Hitchcock, recently graduated from both Amherst and Harvard Medical School, was selected for the post, following a brief tenure in the position by John W. Hooker, M.D., who because of ill health did not remain long enough to get a department fully established. Hitchcock became the first officially recognized College Director of Physical Education in the United States. At the same time, he achieved the rank of Professor—the only physical educator to hold that title in any college in the United States for many years to follow. He took over his duties at Amherst in August, 1861, remaining in that post for fifty years until his death in 1911 at the age of eighty-three.

At first Hitchcock built his program around heavy gymnastics, but soon coming to the conclusion that light gymnastics, when executed rapidly, were more beneficial, he revised the program. He stressed hygienic living and regular strenuous exercise of a pleasant, recreative type, and early in his work there sponsored an intramural program of sports. The first program of physical education called for a half hour of exercise for each student, four days a week.

From the first year at Amherst, Hitchcock compiled statistics of measurements of the students and thus became the first physical educator in America to apply the science of anthropometry to physical education. Measurements were taken of each student upon entrance and at the close of each school year. From the findings, advice was given as to his physical education needs and special exercises were prescribed as needed. The records were kept so that the student might know how he compared with others and how he changed from year to year. It was over half a century before most physical educators caught up with Dr. Hitchcock in this phase of his program at Amherst. Also, from the very beginning of the first college department, Dr. Hitchcock called it the department of physical education, not physical training or physical culture-terms that were in popular use but which finally gave way to Hitchcock's original designation. Also from the very start, Dr. Hitchcock aligned all the physical education work closely with the latest thinking of those years on hygiene and healthful living. He ruled that there be no smoking in the gymnasium.

This department was not only the first of the modern type to be organized at a college, but for twenty years it stood alone, unequaled in efficiency and professional excellence—years ahead of its day.

First College Gymnasium. In 1820 Harvard University constructed the first college gymnasium. Although privately owned, it was maintained for the use of Harvard students. It was well equipped with German apparatus of the day. Other gymnasiums followed: Williams College in 1851—a gymnasium with baths, owned and controlled by the students; University of Virginia in 1852—a building destroyed during the Civil War; Miami University (Ohio) in 1857—a building renting for $60 a year. Harvard University, in 1859, constructed a building that cost $8000 including the cost of equipment. This new Harvard gymnasium, an octagonal building of brick, was a gift of the class of 1822. It had two bowling alleys and dressing rooms but no baths and was opened in 1860 to all students for a $2 fee per term. In that same year, 1859, Princeton University built a little shack painted red which it acquired after an uprising of students demanding a gymnasium; and Yale University at a cost of $11,000 built a gymnasium which had a bath and bowling alleys in the basement.[16]

In 1860 Amherst College built a two-story stone gymnasium; in 1861 Oberlin College built a men's gymnasium; in 1863 Bowdoin and Wesleyan followed suit; and in 1864 the students at Williams College raised $5000 and erected a stone gymnasium, which, like the one built in 1851, was completely owned and controlled by them.

Teacher Training

As early as 1827, Follen at Harvard University personally perpared a few students as monitors to teach gymnastics under his supervision. This is the earliest record of an attempt at teacher training in physical education in America. Although normal schools had by now come into the educational picture, none as yet offered special courses for the preparation of teachers of physical education. In 1837, Michigan's first State Superintendent of Public Instruction called on the teachers of the state "to know something of physical education and sound health," and in 1852, at the dedication of the Michigan State Normal School at Ypsilanti, he advocated courses in physical culture for all students. In 1859 the New York State Normal School asked for recognition of physical education in the schools and for the preparation of teachers to handle the subject. In 1860, the then State Superintendent persuaded the Michigan State Teachers Association to hold a series of institutes to prepare teachers to handle physical education classes. He was advocating that the training and care of the body should receive attention along with instruction of the mind. But plans for special schools for such a purpose did not materialize until 1861. Preceding this, however, at the Pittsburgh convention of the turners in 1856, it was proposed that a normal school be established as a means of filling the demands for trained teachers. Thereupon plans were made to open a school in Rochester, New York, in 1861, but it was not yet in operation at the outbreak of the Civil War when the entire teaching staff and all prospective students rushed to the defense of the Union, and plans for the school were abandoned for the duration of the war.[17]

In 1862, Mlle. Adele Parot was brought to San Francisco from the East by John Swett, the San Francisco Superintendent of Public Schools, to teach in the State Normal School which he operated to prepare teachers for the local public schools. Her assignment was to prepare teachers of physical education. A pupil of Dio Lewis, she taught his system of exercises, which is discussed in material that follows. In that same year, John Swett was elected California State Superintendent of Public Schools, and two years later he invited Mlle. Parot to lecture and demonstrate her work at the State Teachers Institute.[18]

Dio Lewis Normal Institute of Physical Education. Founded to train teachers of physical education, the Dio Lewis Normal Institute of Physical Education opened in the summer of 1861 at 20 Essex Street in Boston with such a distinguished faculty that it augured well for a tie with education in general. The president of Harvard University was the school's first president, and he had a board of directors of distinguished gentlemen and an imposing faculty of four medical doctors: one as professor of anatomy, one as professor of physiology, one as professor of hygiene, and Dio Lewis as professor of gymnastics. The school opened with fourteen pupils. It offered two full courses of ten weeks each and included two periods of gymnastics drills daily, covering a series of 200 exercises to be learned in a ten-week period. In the second year, elocution and a course in Swedish Movement Cure were added to the curriculum. By 1868 the school had conducted nine sessions and issued diplomas to 250 persons who went out to teach mainly in the large cities of New England, although some went to other sections of the United States.[19] His graduates were greatly sought by schools and colleges. By the early 1870s Dio Lewis had turned his attention to other interests, and the school closed its doors. (Various records indicate that the school closed in the late 1860s but the author has seen a certificate issued by this Institute and signed by Dio Lewis under the date of 1871, which indicates that the school must have been open into the early 1870s. There is also a record of a summer school of his in 1884 as mentioned later.

OUT-OF-SCHOOL PROGRAMS

The German turner groups with their ten thousand members by 1861, the private athletic clubs, the YMCA's, and the public gymnasiums that were established in this era furnished opportunities for large numbers to pursue physical activities outside the schools.

Turnverein Movement

After its popularity of the 1820s and its subsequent dying out in the 1830s, the German system of gymnastics again rose to a position of importance in the United States. In 1848 revolutionary movements again swept over Europe. In Germany, in particular, the government used a policy of reaction and suppression against those demanding a liberal form of government. As a result of this suppression, thousands of Germans migrated to the United States settling mainly in the north. They represented a high level of intellect and broad cultural interests. Deeply interested in both physical and mental development for a "chainless mind in a fetterless body" they soon, wherever sufficient numbers had collected, organized the Old-Country German gymnastic society—the turnverein.

The first such group was organized in Cincinnati, in 1848. At this time the

Germans in Cincinnati still wore German peasant costumes of black velvet with red vests and big silver buttons. In that same year the second society was formed in New York City. The turnverein held its first national turnfest (outdoor gymnastic meet) in Philadelphia in 1851. Its aims were to promote physical education, intellectual enlightenment, and sociability among the members. The turnverein building was always provided with a gymnasium where classes in the German system of exercises were conducted for men, women, and children. The teachers in the early period were men who had had experience in Germany. The Know-Nothing Party, which was against all foreigners, took every opportunity to oppose the turners and even to jeer and ridicule them. When the call came for volunteers for the Union Army the turners joined in such numbers that many societies ceased to exist, and their newly founded normal school closed.[20]

Young Men's Christian Association

In 1851 the first YMCA in the United States was organized in Boston, seven years after George Williams (1821–1905), a London clerk, had started the movement. The growing interest in athletics and gymnastics which swept the country in the 1850s led the YMCA's to favor their promotion as "a safeguard against the allurement of objectionable places of resort," in the phrasing of the leaders of that day as reported by both Eddy and Morse. At its third international convention of the YMCA's of the United States and Canada held in 1856 in Montreal, the question was raised "whether any means can be provided by the YMCA's for the physical development and promotion of the health of their members by gymnasiums, baths, etc.," but political and economic considerations of the day took precedence, and little was done in this direction until after the Civil War other than in the establishment of boys' departments. By 1861 there were two hundred YMCA's in the country, and most supported boys' departments where exercises and games of sorts were offered.[21]

Public Gymnasiums

Shortly after the two immigrants Beck and Follen arrived from Germany and began their teaching of gymnastics at the Round Hill School and Harvard University in the 1820s, prominent citizens of Boston began agitation for a public gymnasium. Dr. John C. Warren (1778–1856), Professor of Anatomy and Physiology at Harvard University, was a leader in the movement. The Board of Aldermen granted a request for a piece of ground for the purpose of establishing a school for gymnastic instruction and exercise. Money was raised by public subscription to guarantee a salary for a teacher and to provide apparatus. By September, 1826, the first public gymnasium, located in Washington Gardens, was ready, and Follen had been secured as the teacher. The gymnasium proved very popular and enrolled students until 1832. But even the expert gymnast could not keep the Boston Gymnasium alive. The novelty soon wore off, the participants became the target for the humorist and caricaturist, and the gymnasium closed its doors.

When the movement was revived some thirty years later Thomas Wentworth Higginson (1823–1911), noted writer of that day, commented as follows in the *Atlantic Monthly* in 1861:

> It is one good evidence of the increasing interest in these exercises that the American gymnasia built during the past year or two have far surpassed all their predecessors in size and completeness, and have probably no superiors in the world. The Seventh Regiment Gymnasium in New York, . . . is 180 by 52 feet in its main hall and 35 feet in height, with nearly 1,000 pupils. The beautiful hall of the Metropolitan Gymnasium in Chicago, measures 108 by 80 feet and is 20 feet high at the sides, with a dome in the center 40 feet high and the same in diameter. Next to these probably rank the new gymnasium at Cincinnati, the Tremont Gymnasium at Boston, and the Bunker Hill Gymnasium at Charlestown, all recently opened. Of college institutions the most complete are probably those at Cambridge and New Haven. The arrangements for instruction are rather more systematic at Harvard.

With the growth of gymnasiums in the schools, colleges, and YMCA's, the public gymnasium eventually died out.

PROFESSIONAL ORGANIZATIONS

Teachers' associations had by now come into existence, and, at their meetings, physical education became a topic for discussion. In August, 1830, a convention of "Teachers and Other Friends of Education" met in Boston and organized the American Institute of Instruction. At this convention, Warren gave a lecture, *The Importance of Physical Education,* speaking on the effects of poor ventilation, unsanitary school buildings, and improper seating, and on the relation of physical exercises to the problems of general education.

PROFESSIONAL LITERATURE

Several books and one periodical on physical activities came off the presses in the United States in this period. Most such books published in this era were on sports, but there were three books on gymnastics besides the 1831 book of Warren, *The Importance of Physical Education,* which might be called the first publication in the field of philosophy of physical education. From *Youthful Sports* of 1801 to *Medical Parlor Gymnastics* of 1859 a great variety of activities is covered. Foremost among these books are: William Turner's *Art of Swimming,* published in 1821, which included Benjamin Franklin's "Advice to Swimmers"; Charles Beck's translation of Jahn's *Treatise on Gymnastics,* published in 1828. William Clarke's *The Boy's*

Own Book, Boston edition of 1829, which contains the first published mention of the game of rounders in the United States with a "diamond" indicated; Catharine Beecher's *Course in Calisthenics for Young Ladies in Schools and Families,* published in 1831 and containing sixty-two illustrations and a discussion of teaching methods and course materials, the first American book on curriculum and methods; Robin Carver's *Book of Sports* of 1834, which is the first to give rules of baseball; Chandler Robbins Gilman's *Life on the Lakes* of 1836, which gives an account of a canoe trip to the pictured rocks of the Lake Superior Region of the Canadian Border Lakes; *The Sports of Childhood,* published in 1839, containing information on archery, cricket, and the art of walking on stilts; and *The Boy's Treasury of Sports, Pastimes, and Recreation,* published in 1847, containing around four hundred engravings in addition to information on archery, golf, and hockey. In 1857 Miss Beecher published her second book, *Physiology and Calisthenics,* and in 1862 Dio Lewis put out his book, *New Gymnastics for Men, Women and Children,* which had wide circulation and ran through twenty-five editions. Several of these books are owned by the New York Public Library, the Racquet and Tennis Club of New York City, and Yale University.

The first American periodical in the physical education field was established by Dio Lewis, named *Gymnastic Monthly and Journal of Physical Culture.* It was published in Boston, beginning in December, 1861, but it did not survive long.

LEADERS OF PHYSICAL EDUCATION

For the first time in the United States there now arose leaders who fully devoted some period of their lives to the cause of physical education-three men born in Europe and one man and one woman of American origin. They are discussed chronologically according to year of birth.

The first three—German immigrants of superior education—were, beyond their training in philosophy, law, the classics, theology, political economy, and history, deeply interested in physical education. In laying the foundations of physical education in the United States, they brought to the groundwork a scholarly approach. Some workers in the profession of physical education today express the thought that these German political refugees, Follen, Beck, and Lieber, have been given undue attention for their contributions to the profession in America. Some even labeled their period (1825–1830) in particular as a time of a fad, exploiting German gymnastics. But there is another view on this. It is true that all three men shortly left this field of work for educational work in other directions particularly suited to their superior intellectual qualifications. But to have the foundations of physical education in America laid by men of such caliber was to the everlasting credit of the profession. In a later period when wrestlers, weight lifters, and pugilists gained undue attention of the public, who mistakenly took their offerings as the foundation of physical education, the profession was well served and its place in education safeguarded by the memories of the work of these three men who were truly educators in the best meaning of the word.[22]

Charles Follen (1796-1840)

Born in Romrad, Germany, Charles Follen, as stated earlier, fled the country after Jahn's release from prison in 1820 when gymnastics were banned in Prussia by Royal Decree.[23] He went first to Switzerland with another of Jahn's disciples, Charles Beck. None too safe there, the two soon went to France where the Marquis de Lafayette, then a deputy in the French Chamber of Representatives, urged them to go to America. Armed with letters of introduction to Lafayette's friends, they arrived in Philadelphia in 1824. Follen, who held the degree Doctor of Civil Laws from the University of Geissen, soon found employment at Harvard University to teach German. Later he added the teaching of gymnastics to his schedule and soon took on the added responsibility of teaching at the first public gymnasium in Boston. In 1826 he was appointed Professor of German Language and Literature at Harvard University, and on the side established a gymnastics hall for the students and gave instructions in Jahn's exercises.[24]

Charles Beck (1798-1866)

Charles Beck was born in Heidelberg, Germany, and procured the degree Doctor of Theology from the University of Tubingen. He fled to America with Follen, and almost immediately upon his arrival the head master of the famous Round Hill School secured him to teach gymnastics and Latin. This marked the first time that German gymnastics was taught in the United States. Beck left the school in 1830 to assist in the establishment of Phillipstown Academy in New York. Two years later he became Professor of Latin at Harvard University. His last years were spent as a Unitarian minister and a leader in the fight for the abolition of slavery.[25]

Francis Lieber (1800-1872)

Born in Berlin, Germany, Francis Lieber was educated at the University of Jena, where he procured the degree of Doctor of Philosophy. As a friend of Jahn, he found life increasingly difficult in Germany and escaped to America in 1827. At that time Follen gave up his teaching at the Boston Gymnasium, and Lieber was offered the position there, where he opened the first swimming school in the United States and taught swimming while serving as editor of the first edition of the *Encyclopaedia Americana*. In the 1840s he was invited to make plans for the new Girard College which was opened in Philadelphia in 1848. Following this he took up the teaching of political economy and history and became known as America's "first academic political philosopher." His *Political Ethics*, published in 1838, and

Civil Liberty and Government, published in 1853, marked him as one of America's top scholars. Still later he became a legal adviser to President Lincoln.[26]

Catharine Esther Beecher (1800-1878)

Catharine Beecher born in East Hampton, Long Island, was the daughter of the well-known preacher, Lyman Beecher (1775–1863) and sister of Harriet Beecher Stowe (1811–1896), author of *Uncle Tom's Cabin,* and Henry Ward Beecher (1813–1887), the famous preacher and reformer. Reared in a home of unusual educational advantages, she was tutored at home by her father and did not attend her first school until she was ten years old. Twelve years later after the family had moved to Hartford, Connecticut, she opened her own private school for girls, the Hartford Female Seminary. It achieved such fame that she soon had over one hundred pupils. Sensing that they needed an exercise program, she investigated the German gymnastics that had come into prominence in the Boston area but rejected them as too strenuous for the average frail girl of that day. Becoming interested in physiology, she combined this interest with her attempts to devise a system of exercises advisable for girls. In 1831, she produced her first book, *A Course of Calisthenics for Young Ladies*-the first manual of physical education in America-and in 1858 her second book, *Physiology and Calisthenics.* A sustained effort of twenty-seven years was required to perfect the system of exercises which she developed to produce good posture and grace.

When her family moved to Cincinnati in 1832 she opened the Western Female Seminary there and soon thereafter launched upon a career of lecturing in an attempt to sell education, in general, and physical education, in particular, throughout the East and Middle West. In 1864, she joined the staff of Dio Lewis's new school for girls in Lexington, Massachusetts, but the two soon disagreed on fundamental philosophy concerning their two systems of calisthenics, and Miss Beecher resumed her educational promotion work. She organized women's educational societies in the East to raise money to send women to the Mississippi Valley as missionary teachers to start schools there. She may justifiably be claimed as the first American to originate a system of gymnastics and as the first woman physical education leader in America.[27]

Diocletian Lewis (1823–1886)

Dio Lewis was born in Cayuga County near Auburn, New York. Quitting school at the age of twelve, he began his teaching career three years later. When nineteen he embarked upon medical studies through a combination of a few courses at Harvard University and study in a physician's office. At twenty-eight he received an honorary degree of Doctor of Medicine from the Cleveland Homeopathic College, and shortly thereafter embarked upon a seven-year lecture career on temperance and health topics which took him all over the country.[28]

In his travels he encountered the German system of gymnastics, but, aside from its great popularity, he felt that it was not what the United States needed. Within this time he studied briefly at health clinics in Paris and became interested in devising a system of calisthenics of his own. In June 1860 he went to Boston and established evening classes in several suburbs and a school in West Newton where he introduced his system of gymnastics. Achieving immediate acclaim he was invited by the American Institute of Instruction to present his system at their convention in Boston in August. He was given two 2½-hour periods in their program.[29] Following this he organized his Normal Institute of Physical Education. Thus in Boston in 1861, began the first teacher-training work in this field.

In 1864 he established a school for girls at Lexington, Massachusetts, and brought Catharine Beecher to its staff. Within three years the school had three hundred pupils from various parts of the country, mostly girls of delicate constitution sent there for their health. Tiring of this venture, Dio Lewis renewed his lecturing, and shortly thereafter the school closed. He then organized The Woman's Crusade, which later developed into the Woman's Christian Temperance Union, and he added Europe to his lecture itinerary. He popularized physical education and sold the need for it to many educators who, through his influence, put it into the school programs.

PHYSICAL EDUCATION OF THE LATTER NINETEENTH CENTURY (1865–1900)

CHAPTER 5

Physical Activities of the Latter Nineteenth Century

By the close of the Civil War the population of the nation reached a total of 28 million. In their informal leisure the people still enjoyed quilting bees, cornhuskings, square dancing, hunting, and fishing. By the 1890s bicycling, athletic contests, and prizefighting had become popular. The great German immigration to the Middle West brought to that region the love of Sunday picnics and outings, much gay music and dancing-all frowned upon by the dominating Puritan stock throughout the Colonial period and early years of our national life. This post–Civil War period brought forth two new activities—basketball and bicycling—the former was to make a great impact on physical education in later periods, the latter springing up in sudden, brief, but great popularity and then dying down to a special niche in the ongoing life of the nation.

ACTIVITIES OF PHYSICAL EDUCATION

Gymnastics became the core of the physical activity program across the land in nonschool organizations as well as in the schools. The sports and games pursued by school children and college students under their own organization and management received but scant attention from the schools except in a few situations. However certain groups of adults began to promote athletics and games, foreshadowing today's rich sports heritage. Here and there dancing claimed some attention—it, too, presaging an interesting future.

Dance and Rhythms

The free exercise of Catharine Beecher were performed to music, and in some schools they developed into a sort of dance form which later replaced calisthenics, but they did not have the permanency of the dance forms now discussed.

Ballroom Dance. It would have been unthinkable in the nineteenth century to teach any form of ballroom dancing in a public institution. It was taught only in private schools and in dance studios. The minuet of Colonial days had about died out as a social dance by the time of the Civil War, but the Virginia reel kept its popularity. In the early part of this era the most popular ballroom dances were the schottische, polka, gallop, lancers, quadrille, mazurka, varsoviana, Newport, and gavotte. The waltz was not popular until later and then for quite some time was danced correctly only in the East. In the 1890s when the famous band leader John Philip Sousa (1854–1932), toured the country, his band music became so popular that its two-step rhythm popularized the new dance step, driving all other forms into the background.

Esthetic Dance. The earliest record of esthetic dance in America would seem to be a listing of this activity in the curriculum of the Normal School of the American Gymnastic Union when it opened in 1866. Just what form of dance this was is not recorded. The next mention is in 1894 of the "new esthetic dancing" taught by Melvin Ballou Gilbert (1847–1910), a famous dance master of Boston. He was the first well-known dance teacher to align himself with the schools to offer dance as a part of a physical education program. He based his work on a modified ballet form and first taught it at the Harvard Summer School of Physical Education in 1894 and a few years later at Vassar College and the Boston Normal School of Gymnastics. This form of dancing became very popular throughout the country, particularly with women.

Folk Dance. The early immigrants brought their various native dances to America, but they rarely displayed them publicly probably because, in their eagerness to become Americanized as rapidly as possible, they did not care to give others a chance to accuse them of trying to keep their homeland customs alive in the New World. Not until teachers of physical education went to Europe and collected the dances did they become known and widely used in the schools. However when Dr. Hartwig Nissen (1856–1924) came to America in 1883 as Vice Consul for Norway and Sweden he taught Swedish and Norweigan folk dances in Washington, D.C. Jane Addams (1860–1935), Nobel Prize winner of 1931, urged the people of various nationalities who flocked to her Hull House Settlement in Chicago to keep alive their native country dances and helped them put them on for the public. Thus a wealth of folk dances became known through her work there beginning in 1890.

When Senda Berenson (1868–1954), head of physical education at Smith

College, studied in Sweden in the spring and summer of 1897, she collected folk dances, and upon her return home introduced them to the Smith students. A year or two later Anne Barr (1868–1945) visited Sweden and also brought back folk dances which she introduced into her program at the University of Nebraska in the fall of 1898 and at the Chautauqua School of Physical Education in the summer of 1899.

Square Dance. As the frontiers moved ever westward the pioneers carried to their new homes a form of dance brought originally from England known as country dancing which had developed several American forms of its own-the Kentucky and Tennessee mountain form, the formal one of New England, and that of the plains and the cowboys. The new England form of square dance, derived from the stately quadrilles of French and English court life, never attained the national popularity of the "country" dance. Square dancing did not carry over into school physical education programs in the nineteenth century. Its popularity existed in pioneer communities as the recreational dance form of the people, and it was handed down from parents to children. Thus it persisted enthusiastically in the Middle West, South, and Far West throughout the century.

Gymnastics

In the nineteenth century there were practically no public school "exercise rooms" in the United States. Class work had to be carried on in the regular schoolroom or in a large hallway with large groups being served in a small space by teachers who were unprepared to teach physical activities. A class routine to be learned by rote had to be committed to a program of formal gymnastics in order to exist at all. In many places Old World formal gymnastics served well in this formative period of the physical education profession. It gave children as well as many adults excellent physical fitness training, albeit a narrow program.

German System. The German system of gymnastics had gained a strong foothold by the close of the Civil War, particularly in the larger cities of the Middle West. In the 1880s Chicago alone had fourteen special teachers in its public schools to teach German gymnastics. With another wave of German immigrants coming right after the war, German gymnastics took a still firmer hold and throughout the rest of the nineteenth century was very popular. The spectacular feats of the German gymnasts created such a sensation wherever they exhibited in public school or YMCA gymnasium that Dr. Sargent labeled this era the acrobatic stage of physical education.

Many people, though, refused to accept German gymnastics. Americans of other national strains were repelled by the intense German nationalism of the promoters of this system. Dr. Edward Mussey Hartwell (1850–1922), of Johns Hopkins University, felt it necessary to point out to these critics in his remarks at a conference in 1889 that "the fondness of the German people for gymnastics is as marked a national trait as is the liking of the British for athletic sports.'' Much misunderstanding has always existed about the German system which might have been avoided had the German immigrants differentiated between German gymnastics and the overall German physical education program. To them, the word *gymnastics* embraced the overall program, but to non-German Americans the word meant merely calisthenics and apparatus work. Americans in general do not interpret the word to embrace sports, games, and rhythms as well as free-standing exercises and apparatus work—hence the consternation of the German-Americans when the system was so bitterly attacked because it was accused of being so narrow. The true German system of gymnastics consisted of five types of activities, all evolved from Frederick Ludwig Jahn's work, namely: (1) tactics and marching; (2) free exercises with short and long wands, dumbbells, rings, and clubs; (3) ''dance steps'' for girls; (4) apparatus work using balance board, buck, horizontal bars, long and side horse, ladders, parallel bars, poles, ropes, round swing, suspension rings, and vaulting box; and (5) games and play-a graded set as developed in 1793 by GutsMuths.

Since both the German and Swedish systems held the serious attention of both the school and nonschool groups for a rather long period, a somewhat detailed description of what they actually offered as exercise is of historical significance. In the May 1894, *Mind and Body,* is a chart outlining the German system of gymnastics then in use in the United States. The main features of the program consisted of the following as arranged by the author from the chart:

1. General exercises of strength, acquired through:
   a. Wrestling, weights, and putting the shot.
   b. Straining a large number of muscles to the utmost, combined with the act of exertion thus increasing ''the strength and dimension of the muscle.''
2. Localized exercises of strength acquired through:
   a. Calisthenics with weights-the movements frequently repeated combined with long holding.
   b. Work on horizontal bars, parallel bars, rings, or pole vaulting.
   c. Straining a small number of muscles to the utmost.
3. Exercises of skill done through ''compound and flourishing calisthenics,'' balancing exercises, work on horse, buck, horizontal and parallel bars, far and high jump.
4. Exercises for quickness acquired through:
   a. Walking, marching, running, rope-jumping, dancing, hopping, climbing ladders or hills, swimming, rowing with moveable seat, bicycling, skating, sawing wood, mountain climbing.
   b. ''Rhythmically repeated movements distributed over a great number of muscles with intention of moving forward quickly . . . or as rapidly as possible straining the activities of the heart and lungs to the utmost and causing temporary exhaustion of these organs.''
5. Exercises of endurance acquired through:
   a. Exercises listed in numbers 3 and 4 above.

    b. Moderating the speed to preserve "equilibrium of different organic activities" so that the "motion may be continued for hours."

6. Exercises of attention acquired through tactics and "rhythmical motions as in May dancing, etc., where a single member is but a part of the whole."

7. Exercises of alertness acquired through:

    a. Wrestling, fencing, intricate running, and ball games.

    b. Mastering of the unforeseen and need of suddenly necessary motions on the impulse of the movement.

As this system became incorporated in our schools, track and field activities were gradually added as a start at Americanization of the program, although all parts of the offering suffered from lack of equipment, leaving calisthenics to receive the major share of attention.

Swedish Gymnastics. Although there is a record of Swedish gymnastics being taught in a girls' high school in Boston as early as 1874, it was not until the 1880s that the system of Per Henrik Ling received sufficient attention in America to challenge the German system. Great rivalry developed between the advocates of the two forms. In fact the famous Physical Training Conference held in Boston in 1889 concerned itself primarily with discussions of the relative merits of the two systems. At that meeting Dr. Edward Hitchcock, Director of Physical Education of Amherst College, threw the weight of his influence behind the announcement of the Boston Public Schools that they were going to try out the Ling system. But Dr. Luther Halsey Gulick (1865–1918) of the YMCA school in Springfield, Massachusetts, opposed the use of either system, saying that both demanded "too much attention to detail and too much patience for what it was worth." However, he approved of the Swedish system for school children who had to exercise in the school room, but not for adults nor for free hours out of school.

The Germans held that the Swedish method was too formal and uninteresting, that it failed to obtain recreational values and was very weak in social and moral training. The Swedish supporters claimed that the German system lacked scientific foundation, that too much music and rhythm accompanied the exercises and thereby prevented the maximum physical benefit from being derived, that too much emphasis was given to the recreational and not enough to the educational results, and that the system was unable to cope with problems of individual and specific weaknesses.

In light of all the arguments it is interesting to note that although a few women physical educators went to Sweden to study, no record reveals names of women as having sought foreign study or even local instruction so that they might bring the German system of gymnastics to the girls and women of America. The first American woman to study at the Royal Central Gymnastics Institute of Stockholm was Kate Campbell Hurd, M.D., the first medical director of Bryn Mawr College, who studied there in the winter of 1889–1890, followed by Senda Berenson of the Smith College faculty in 1897.

The Swedish Day's Order. Swedish gymnastics were characterized by: (1) the Day's Order, (2) progression of exercises day by day and week by week from easy to difficult, from light to strenuous work; (3) use of word of command for all movements; (4) stress upon correct holding of positions; and (5) corrective or remedial effects. In fact, out of the Swedish system grew the corrective gymnastics that have assumed so important a place in the school physical education program of the twentieth century. The apparatus work of Swedish gymnastics was quite different from that of the German system. In the Swedish form the following apparatus was used: high and low boom, swinging ladders, swinging and traveling rings, climbing ropes, bar stalls, rope ladders, and vaulting box. In the free-exercise part of the program no hand apparatus of any kind was used, nor was there any musical accompaniment. However, like the German system, the Swedish system included marching, rhythms, and games.

The advocates of this system of gymnastics claimed that the functioning of the heart and lungs was the fundamental function of the body and that Swedish educational gymnastics served to develop these organs. They were not concerned with the development of muscle strength or speed. As Dr. Claës J. Enebuske (1855-?), who held medical degrees from both Harvard University and the University of Paris and the Ph.D. from the University of Lund, Sweden, said to his pupils at the Boston Normal School of Gymnastics: "Get the heart and lungs right and the muscles will meet every reasonable demand." The Day's Order consisted of the following schedule of exercises.

1. Order movements
2. Leg movements
3. Strain bendings
4. Heave exercises
5. Balance exercises
6. Back exercises
7. Abdominal exercises
8. Lateral trunk exercises
9. Jumping exercises
10. Slow leg exercises
11. Respiratory exercises

Each lesson contained an exercise for each of the eleven items listed above and in that order. From lesson to lesson the exercises became more strenuous and difficult either by increase in the number of repetitions or by advancing to exercises requiring ever greater skill of execution. Enebuske's book *Gymnastic Day's Order According to the Ling System,* widely used throughout the United States in this era, gives three series of twenty-five lessons each, all progressively arranged from lesson one through lesson seventy-five.[1] To show the progression in difficulty in the Day's Order, Lessons 1 and 75 as given in Enebuske's book are aligned together here in the short-cut writing system used for Day's Orders at that time.

	Lesson 1	*Lesson 75*

Lesson 1

1. Order: Fund. std. and rest
2. Leg: Std., ft. placing sideways

Lesson 75

Order movements
Stret. ½ horiz. std., knee bending

3. Strain bend: Std., back bend hd — Stret. bow std., alt. leg raise and heel raise

4. Heave: Wing std. position — Std. 2 arm ext. and alt. arm ext. in various directions

5. Balance: Wing stride std., 2 heel raising — Stret. ½ toe std., arm sinking sideways downward slowly

6. Back: Cross std., 2 arm rotation — ½ stret. fall-out std., chg of arms and ft. with adv. in zigzag and about facing.

7. Abdomen: Std., back bending of tnk (gently) — Stret. horiz. ½ toe lean std., arm parting

8. Lateral trunk: Std., side bending — Stret. fallout twist std., side bending and strd prone falling, alt arm and leg raising

9. Jumping: Mark time — (a) Wing toe knee bend std., spring jump in place with alt. stret of knee.
   (b) Std., free jp in place with facing 360 degrees.

10. Slow leg: Wing std., 2 knee bend — Stret. walk toe std., 2 deep knee bend

11. Respiratory: Std., 2 arm raising with deep breathing — Cross twist outward fallout std., arm flg sideways with chg of ft in series, alternate with std. circumduction of arms with deep breath

Delsarte System.[2] During the early 1890s the Delsarte System of Physical Culture received much acclaim, and great numbers were converted to its theories. This system took its name from its founder Francois Delsarte (1811–1871), a French vocal and dramatics teacher. Finding that ideal poses and gestures could best be taught through physical exercises, he devised a system for use in his work. Some historians classed him with dancers rather than with gymnasts, but he found the ballet dance of his country not at all to his liking with its lack of expression of emotions and ideas. Although he had no thought of devising a system of gymnastics, many elocution and dramatics teachers accepted his methods and, adding their own ideas, evolved a system of exercises which they claimed would produce poise, grace, and health. These claims gave the Delsarte system a universal appeal to women as neither dance nor gymnastics but as culture exercises. Elocution teachers were in demand to teach this system in many girls' schools and a few coeducation colleges where it was accepted as a physical education program. This system was characterized by a series of relaxing, "energizing," and deep-breathing exercises augmented by poses to denote various emotions. Related as it was to voice and speech culture, as these courses were spoken of at that time, the term *physical culture* now came into common usage in America stemming from the Delsarte system of exercises. Without sound principles behind it, this system proved but a fad, and it soon died out although it enjoyed much acclaim in its day.

Sports and Games

The post–Civil War period brought new sports to the national scene and changes to others, as is discussed in the material that follows.

Archery. Archery as a sport came to the American scene in the late 1870s, and from its very beginnings women were included in this activity. Very soon a national archery tournament was developed and twenty women came out for it in 1879.[3] However, information about the sport in its early days is difficult to come by.

Baseball. The game of baseball was popular in many army camps during the Civil War, particularly among the northern soldiers. After the war it quickly became the number-one sport in the South and West. By the mid-1870s all young America was playing the game in school yards, home playgrounds, empty lots, wherever children could find a fairly good-sized spot and something to use for bats and balls. With the coming of electric lights and the many great regimental armories in the larger cities, indoor games at night became common.[4] In 1866 the ball was made smaller, the pitchers began to throw curves, and the distance and force of the batting and throwing increased to such an extent that padded gloves and masks became necessary. The overwhelming popularity of baseball hurt cricket, which had heretofore been popular particularly in those parts of the country with large settlements of English descendants. Now cricket became almost an unknown game in the United States.

In the Middle West as early as 1866 a four-state baseball tournament was held at Rockfort, Illinois. Teams were entered from Detroit, Michigan, Milwaukee, Wisconsin, Chicago and Rockford, Illinois, and Dubuque, Iowa. This sport as a game for women was frowned upon and when the first Female Base Ball Club was organized in 1880, the players were spoken of as women tramps.[5]

By 1886, the Michigan Central Railraod was connecting many cities from Boston, New York, and Philadelphia, with Chicago, Kansas City, and St. Louis, and *Spalding Official Baseball Guides* carried advertisements of the railroad, informing baseball clubs of the connections. However, it was not uncommon for clubs of smaller towns having no railroads, to walk four or five miles to play a neighboring village club and walk home after the game.[6]

Basketball. Basketball is exclusively American in its origin. Invented in 1891 by James Naismith, M.D. (1861–1939), then a young teacher at the YMCA Training School in Springfield, Massachusetts, it claimed immediate popularity both as an indoor and outdoor game and as a sport for both men and women. In the first tryout game, played at the YMCA school in December 1891, using peach baskets for goals, Naismith and Amos Alonzo Stagg (1862–1965), another young teacher, who later became a famous football coach, were captains of the two teams, and George L. Meylan, M.D. (1893–1960), a visiting YMCA director, who later became Medical Director of Columbia University and a foremost leader of the camping movement, played on one of the teams. C. Ward Crompton (1877–1964), then a schoolboy, later to become a well-known physician, was captain of the third basketball team to be organized in New York City.

In this first game a soccer ball was used and there were nine players to a team, for the simple reason that there were eighteen members of the class that was being used as the "guinea pigs" as the game was being developed. Boys from California, North Carolina, and Montreal were on those first teams. The first public game was played at the Springfield School on March 11, 1892, with seven teachers playing against seven students. Gulick, Stagg, and Naismith were three of the teachers playing. Stagg was constantly fouling, calling forth Naismith's oft-repeated saying: "I wish Lonnie wouldn't play so rough."[7]

Later, in 1894, the free throw for fouls was added to the rules. The peach basket was attached to the railing of the gallery running track, whereby the height of the basket was established, with an attendant on a ladder nearby to retrieve the ball after a successful throw. This clumsy set-up soon gave way to a hoop and netting, out of which the ball was poked by a long pole, and in 1906 the bottom of the netting was opened to let the ball drop through after losing its momentum. The first time the rules of this new game appeared in print was in January, 1892, when they were published in the YMCA Training School paper, *The Triangle,* with a repeat in October 1892 when Gulick reported that the game was being played all over the country. Then for a January 1894 edition, Dr. Gulick, head of physical education at the Springfield YMCA School, collaborated with Naismith for an edition called the Official Guide. Thus the game became known by high school boys in Y's all across the country. The game's sudden popularity created serious problems for many YMCA's caught unaware and poorly prepared to handle such an outpouring of boys wanting almost full use of the Y gymnasium for this game alone. These schoolboys took the game into the high school and later into college. Thus the game made but little impact on the world of college men until the coming of the new century.

When Naismith left the YMCA School in 1895, Gulick found it too consuming to carry on alone in the work of promoting the game and getting out the revised rules yearly, so in 1896 he turned over full responsibility for the game and the rules to the Amateur Athletic Union of America. In 1897 the number of players on a team was officially set at five. Now the rules were published by the American Sports Publishing Company for the Spalding Library Series.

When Stagg, at the University of Chicago, and Henry Kallenberg, at the YMCA in Iowa City, brought together enough graduates of Springfield Training School for a game, it chanced that Stagg's men were all at the University of Chicago and Kallenberg's were all attending the University of Iowa. Later this match game played January 18, 1896, was officially declared a bona fide intercollegiate game— the first.[8]

Naismith, trained for the ministry and later to acquire both Doctor of Divinity and Doctor of Medicine degrees, lived to see his game used by gamblers for their own ends. Not only did this grieve him, but maintaining always that basketball was a game to be played, not coached, he was ill at ease in the world of intense training and coaching that grew up around the game.

The rules of the game as created by Naismith were published by the American Sports Publishing Company for the Spalding Athletic Library series and were unquestioningly accepted as the official rules of the game for boys and men. (In the early years of the game, the name was spelled as two words-*basket ball*-not one as today.)

Basketball for Women.[9] In the spring of 1892 Senda Berenson at Smith College with Naismith's consent and advice modified his rules for the use of girls. Carried to their various home states by Smith graduates, her modified form spread rapidly throughout the country. Within the first year the girls' game had reached the University of Chicago where Stagg, at the University of Chicago, who had played in the first public tryout game at the YMCA Training School,[10] was setting up a physical culture department. Also in th.. year, women's basketball had reached the Pacific Coast where, as well as in the Middle West, the game was at first looked upon merely as a game for girls and grade school boys.

One of Miss Berenson's first changes was to divide the playing space into three courts, with each player to be confined to her assigned court. This gave the modified game the name *line basket ball* by which it was known in its earliest years. After a brief trial period, Miss Berenson made further modifications, such as allowing a player to hold the ball no longer than three seconds and to bounce the ball no more than three times. The rules, put out in some copy-machine form of that day, were sent throughout the country on request.

Shortly after Miss Berenson's modified rules became known across the country, other women produced their own modifications of the game for the use of girls, and as these various modifications differed widely from each other, confusion arose as to which set of rules was most approved by the profession.

Feeling the need of official backing of some sort for the rules, Miss Berenson (as related in the first printed guide of 1901) asked at a conference on physical training being held at the Springfield School of Christian Workers, in June 1899 under the auspices of Luther H. Gulick, that a committee be set up to study the rules of the game for girls. Dudley A. Sargent, then President of the American Association for the Advancement of Physical Education (AAAPE) was present at this conference, and he immediately appointed a committee to function under that national organization. Alice B. Foster (1866–1937), then of Oberlin College, was named chairwoman of the committee, with Ethel Perrin (1871–1962) of the Boston Normal School of Gymnastics, Elizabeth Wright of Radcliff College, and Senda Berenson as the other members of the committee with Miss Berenson to serve as editor of the rules. Thus was born the first official committee on girl's sports-the Woman's Basket Ball Rules Committee of AAAPE. This move in 1899 was the first step toward what is now, many decades later, the National Association of Girls' and Women's Sports of today's American Association for Health, Physical Education, Recreation, and Dance.

The rules drawn up by this committee were made available in duplicated form, but shortly the demands for copies became too great for this method of distribution, and when James E. Sullivan (1860–1914), Secretary of the Amateur Athletic Union, invited Miss Berenson to submit the rules to the American Sports Publishing Company for inclusion in the Spalding Athletic Library, the Committee accepted this offer, although the first printed guide did not come off the press until 1901.[11]

Bicycling.[12] There was an early attempt in France in the 1760s to develop a velocipede (derived from the French words for *swift, footed*), which was a two-wheeled machine with the wheels set up in tandem with a rider's seat between them. The rider would propel the velocipede by his feet running along the ground. But this attempt did not catch on. The Germans took up the idea and in the early 1800s developed what it called the hobby horse with the rider still propelling the machine with his feet running along the ground. But this also proved unsatisfactory. By the 1860s the idea of working the machine by pedals attached to the front wheel axle proved to be the solution to the propulsion problem. In the United States alone, over a thousand patents on bicycle parts had been issued by 1869. All this in turn led to the high front wheel of the 1870s with the saddle over the high wheel, which lead in the 1880s to the small-wheeled machine with chain and gears, devised by an Englishman, and called the safety bike. By 1888 the development of pneumatic tires revolutionized the early problem of tires for bicycles, sulkies, and later for automobiles. It was the bicycle craze that started the movement for good roads in America. With the coaster brake added in the 1890s the bicycle craze was on in both Europe and America. In 1893 a million bicycles were sold in America, each costing around $16. "The Bicycle built for two" led to "triplets, quads, quints" and even to wheels with eight and ten saddles. Cycle racing soon became the sport sensation of the world, and the top racers were *the* athletic heroes of the day.

Women in their long, voluminous skirts of the early 1890s took to the sport, but the skirts had to be shortened. They receded to ankle length causing consternation in many communities, but that was nothing compared to the uproar that arose in every village all over the country where the bolder of the young women, abetted by liberal parents, adopted the dress reform sparked in an earlier day by Amelia Bloomer, a prominent writer, lecturer, and champion of women's rights and dress reform. The cities less stormily accepted the shortened skirts and the "bloomers" along with the bicycle riding for girls and women.

Everyone of all ages took to wheels. On weekdays the streets were full of people going to work on "bikes" and on the weekends they were full of bicycle club members who were on their own outings or following bike races somewhere nearby. By 1900 bicycling was the fashion of the day among all classes of people-it was, indeed, the biggest sports craze of the late nineteenth and early twentieth centuries. So many people took to wheels that bicycle speeders became a menace in the large cities, and police were mounted on bikes to catch these speeders who were endangering the lives of the other citizens at 20 miles per hour. Then, with the coming of the electric car the fad ended almost overnight-ending almost as suddenly as it arose. Bicycling then fell into its twentieth-century niche as a means of recreation for children and youths and as a means of transportation for school children and, in the earlier years of 1900, for the working man. But while this fad lasted, in the 1890s and the first decade of the 1900s, bicycling brought splendid physical developmental exercise to the great masses of the population.

Bowling. It was not until the 1860s that bowling, popular from Colonial days on, developed into a ten-pin game and became a well-regulated sport. In the 1870s bowling clubs were organized in great numbers all over the country. In 1895 the American Bowling Congress, successor to the National Bowling League of 1875, revised the rules and standardized the equipment. In 1892 there were more than a hundred clubs in New York City alone.[13]

Fencing. In the 1880s and 1890s, fencing became a fashionable sport, especially for women, although by 1892 men had taken up the sport sufficiently to support a men's national championship tournament. Most of the fencing was taught by French fencing masters.[14]

Football. Since 1873 football has been the most popular sport connected with college life and the most opposed and condemned; it has caused more college conferences and agreements than all other games combined. The earliest games of football were so rough and so devoid of rules that for a while the "class rush" was substituted for it as a safer activity. As the game grew it was more like "association" football (soccer) than the present style of game.

When Columbia and Yale played a match in 1872 they used twenty men to a team. In 1873 Princeton, Rutgers, Yale, and Columbia met together to draft a football code. The following year Harvard students organized a football team using a form of soccer rules and challenged the students of several colleges in the United States. When none accepted, they challenged the students of McGill University of Montreal, Canada, who accepted, and the game was played in May 1875. McGill was playing rugby rules, kicking, catching, and running with the ball, which were unfamiliar to the Harvard players. The Harvard men asked them to explain their rules, and the two teams agreed to play the first half of the game by McGill's rugby rules and the second half by Harvard's soccer rules. One year later (1876) Harvard and Yale played their first match with Yale the victor. The Harvard men asked the Yale students to play by some of McGill's rugby rules to which they consented. In 1876 several colleges, not satisfied with the rules adopted in 1873, met in Springfield, Massachusetts, to revise and standardize the game. Yale and Harvard delegates insisted that some rugby rules be incorporated, and the group acquiesced. At this time the American Intercollegiate Football Association was organized with Columbia, Harvard, Princeton, Rutgers, and Yale as members. The following year (1877) they revised the rules again, setting fifteen as the official number of players to a team.[15]

Dr. Dudley A. Sargent, then Director of Physical Education and Athletics at Harvard, writing in *Outing* Magazine in 1885, declared that football had no peer as a physical developer but had degenerated into a brutal contest, although, as he said, it could be conducted so as to be a credit instead of a disgrace to a school.

Golf. As mentioned previously, Golf was played in colonial times. However, what is generally considered to be the first golf course in America—a nine-hole course—was laid out in Greenbrier County, West Virginia, in 1884, by a man who had played the game in Scotland. He and a group of transplanted Scots living near him organized the first golf club in the country but it did not have a lasting existence. Later, a Scotch linen merchant coming to New York City brought golf clubs and balls with him and when he tried them out in Central Park he was arrested for disorderly conduct. Not discouraged he interested a friend from nearby Yonkers in the game and the two of them interested others and in 1888 they founded the St. Andrews Golf Club. Theirs was a six-hole course laid out in a member's farm. Four years later they moved to another location and laid out a second six-hole course. Then in 1897 they settled permanently in a third location, at Mt. Hope, near Yonkers.[16]

Earlier than that, golf clubs were organized in Buffalo (1879), and by 1891 in Philadelphia. Another golf club was founded on Long Island, near Southampton, the first to be chartered. The earlier St. Andrews Club was finally chartered in 1895. A Chicago golf club founded in 1893 was the first to have a full eighteen-hole course. The U.S. Golf Association was born in 1894 with five clubs as members. In 1895 the first public golf courses were laid out in Boston, Indianapolis, and New York City. By 1900 there were 400 clubs in the country.[17]

Women were not particularly welcome on golf links with men in these early years of the sport in America, but in 1891 the golf club at Southampton on Long Island was open to them. However American women did not take up the game in large numbers until the twentieth century. One sports writer of the 1920s and 1930s estimated that only around one hundred women in all in the United States were playing golf by the close of the century.[18]

There were enough women playing golf by 1895, however, to run off a women's championship tournament at Meadowbrook, on the East Coast, and by the close of the century there were thirty-eight Women's golf clubs from Boston to Chicago. By the mid-1890s the game had reached the Pacific coast, at Tacoma in Washington, at Portland in Oregon, and in a few California cities. By 1897 there were twenty golf courses on the Pacific Coast alone. The first public golf course in the United States opened at Van Cortland Park in New York City in 1896. By the close of the century there were an estimated 887 golf clubs in the country with 154 of them west of the Mississippi.[19]

Rowing. The sport of rowing took on new life after the Civil War. When the New York Athletic Club was founded in 1868, it built a boathouse on the Harlem River and took up the sport. In 1873 Yale built a $15,000 boathouse to replace its smaller one of 1862. William Blaikie (1843–1904), a former Harvard crewman, became interested in the English style of rowing, which used the back and leg muscles as well as the arm muscles, and developed a style for the Harvard crews that became known as the Blaikie plan and soon produced a series of Harvard teams. Rowing is the sport that introduced to the college world the first hired coaches. This was in the 1870s.[20]

Skiing. Scandinavians introduced skiing into the California Sierras in 1867, but the sport was slow in catching on in other parts of the country.[21]

Softball. This game was invented in 1887 as an indoor game for the winter season as was the game of basketball four years later. But it never got a real start nor enthusiastic followers until school girls discovered it for themselves during the first World War.

Swimming. From Frances Lieber's swimming school of 1825 grew the popularity of the "floating baths." However Boston established its first of eleven baths only in 1866 and in 1870 New York City built their first of twenty-seven baths, five of which were in use up to 1904. Some of Boston and New York City's pools were for men and boys only, some for women and girls only, and some for both sexes but at different periods for each. Some had both deep and shallow pools for adults and children. Gradually, because of the changing sanitary conditions of the rivers, these pools changed to "fill and draw" type. Some converted to the use of city water and emptied into the rivers. Many of this type were in use as late as 1939.[22]

Following the lead of Girard College of 1848, Harvard University put in the second college pool in 1880, a wooden affair. The year 1885 brought the first YMCA pool (in Brooklyn) and the first municipal pool (in Philadelphia), and the year 1888 brought the first pool for women, installed at Goucher College (in Baltimore). These pools had no showers, no water sterilization, and no hot water. They were open only in the summer and with no instruction offered. About 1896 word came from Germany that the spread of diseases could be traced to swimming pools. In the 1890s Milwaukee, Utica, San Francisco, Chicago, Newark, Brookline, and Boston put in municipal pools. Of these cities, San Francisco was the first to offer instruction and Milwaukee was the first to have its pool open all year and to have warm water and showers. After 1896 showers became a common requirement for all pools. The size of these first pools ranged from 11½ to 150 feet in width and from 20 to 300 feet in length.[23]

Tennis. The game of court tennis, played since Colonial days, gave way to lawn tennis when an Englishwoman, Mary Outerbridge, brought the new form of game and a net, rackets, and balls from a regimental store in Bermuda[24] to America in 1874. It was first played in the New York City area, with the Staten Island Cricket and Base Ball Club being the first organization to give the game attention. From there it spread to Nahant near Boston, and then to Newport, New Orleans, and Germantown. As the game spread, attempts were made to establish uniform rules and equipment, but it took many years to accomplish this.[25] Within a year the girls at Mt. Holyoke Female Seminary were playing the game. Since women took up the game so enthusiastically, it was at first ridiculed by many as a game fit only for frail girls and women. Nevertheless, a tournament was held in Philadelphia in 1880, and the next year the United States Lawn Tennis Association was organized.

Track and Field. From the Scottish Caledonian Games, brought to America in the early nineteenth century, developed the track and field sports of today. However, track and field sports had been popular in England since the mid-nineteenth century when the British Amateur Athletic Association established their first championships in 1866. These and the famous Sheffield Handicaps for professionals held annually from 1869 on attracted many American sportsmen who frequently won top honors there after 1880. Following closely after the first Modern Olympic Games in Athens in the summer of 1896, which introduced the marathon race to the modern world as a sports event, a first American Marathon was held in September, 1896, running from Stamford, Connecticut, to New York City.[26] The boys at Princeton were introduced to the Caledonian Games in 1873 by their Scotch physical director, George Goldie (1841–1920). The popularity of the games then spread into other colleges and down into the lower schools. The colleges of the Middle West took up this sport in the 1880s, but it never became a popular sport in America until the revival of the Olympics in 1896.

Other Sports. Badminton was first played in this country in 1888; the first ski club was organized in Red Wing, Minnesota, in 1886; softball was invented in 1887 at the Farragut Club in Chicago, and in that same year the first United States skating competition took place in Philadelphia; handball was first played in this country in 1888, with the first tournament put on by the Amateur Athletic Union in 1897; and volleyball was invented in 1895 by William Morgan, a YMCA physical director of Holyoke, Massachusetts, using a basketball bladder for the ball, which was exchanged shortly for the basketball itself, today's ball not coming into use until several years later.[27]

SPORTS CLUBS AND ASSOCIATIONS

The poor physical condition of the soldiers drafted for the Civil War called for greatly increased sports in national life. This gave impetus to the rise of sports and favored adoption of physical education in the schools and colleges. Leagues of amateur and professional athletes, athletic clubs, and similar organizations contributed to the wave of enthusiasm and promoted athletic games and contests. This upsurge brought the first permanent sports clubs and intercollegiate associations.

Nonschool Sports Organizations

Although baseball clubs existed as early as 1845, the post–Civil War period brought a vastly increased interest in the game in all parts of the country. By 1867 there were fifty-six baseball clubs in Illinois alone and forty-two in Iowa, and many in other states. In that year the National Association of Base Ball Players was organized, and shortly after that intersectional contests sprang up. In 1869 the Red Stockings of Cincinnati turned "pro" and toured the East, winning all games. The Chicago White Stockings, Philadelphia Athletics, and Washington Nationals were formed, and in 1871 ten such clubs played championship series. So much gambling, drinking, and corruption came to be attached to the games that professional baseball was no more than started when it became threatened with extinction. Out of efforts to lift the game to a respectable position came the National League of Professional Baseball Clubs in 1876. Other leagues soon followed, such as the American Association in 1882 and the American League in 1900.[28]

By 1879 participation in sports had grown to such proportions that a need for standardization, control, and nationwide promotion was felt, and the National Association of Amateur Athletes of America was organized. Its aims were to check the evils of professionalism, keep athletics on a respectable level, promote legitimate sports, define rules, and conduct competitions in an orderly and fair manner. From this organization developed the Amateur Athletic Union, which held its first meeting in 1888 in Detroit. With about 125 member clubs, it was completely reorganized in 1891, becoming a union of amateur athletic assocations, rather than an organization of individual clubs.

From its very start, AAU set itself up as the sanctioning authority for all amateur sports contests and demanded that any amateur athlete wishing to compete in any sport register as one of its members. Then it barred all amateurs not registered with it from taking part in any sport under its control and all its own member athletes from playing in any contest not sanctioned by it. Thus it quickly gained almost complete control of most amateur sports and most amateur athletes in the country.[29] The leading nonschool sports organizations were born in this era, as follows:

1866—First thoughts of organizing sports nationally

1867—National Association of Base Ball Players

1871—Rowing Association of America

1874—American Rifle Association

1875—National Bowling League

1876—National League of Professional Base Ball Clubs

1879—National Association of Amateur Athletes of America (today's AAU)

1879—National Archery Association

1880—League of Amateur Wheelman

1880—National Canoe Association

1881—United States Lawn Tennis Association

1882—American Association of Base Ball Clubs

1884—National Skating Association

1890—Pacific States Tennis Association

1891—Fencing League of America

1894—U.S. Golf Association

1895—American Bowling Congress

1895—Athletic League of the YMCA's of North America

1900—American League of Professional Base Ball Clubs

Intercollegiate Sports Associations

The earliest intercollegiate associations were established as follows:

1870-Rowing Association of American Colleges (organized at the suggestion of the Harvard Rowing Club, with Bowdoin, Brown, and Massachusetts Agricultural College-today's University of Massachusetts-participating).

1873-Intercollegiate Association for Football (organized by Columbia, Pennsylvania, Rutgers, and Yale).

1875-Intercollegiate Association of Amateur Athletes of America (The ICAAAA, today's National Collegiate Athletic Association, organized to promote track and field in the college field; the earliest association to survive).[30]

1876-Intercollegiate Football Association [organized by Columbia, Harvard, and Pennsylvania to replace the 1873 association; at first a student group, but when Walter Camp (1859-1925) graduated from Yale in 1880, he continued to attend the meetings and it accepted graduate representatives from then on].

1883-Intercollegiate Athletic Conference (the first attempt at faculty control of college sports).

1893-American Football Rules Committee (organized to replace the Intercollegiate Football Association of 1876).

1895-Intercollegiate Conference of Faculty Representatives (from which grew the Western Conference, today's Big Ten).

Shortly after the NAAAA (today's AAU) came into existence (in 1879), it came into conflict with the ICAAAA of 1875 (today's NCAA) as it attempted to draw college athletes under its control. Thus began a feud between the two groups which more than a century later still was unresolved.

Interscholastic Sports Associations

There was no control of high school sports until 1896 when a group of teachers in Wisconsin set up a committee to control their contests. Schools in the states of Michigan, Illinois, and Indiana soon followed suit. These efforts marked all that was done in this direction in the nineteenth century. Before organizations arose to control these sports, teachers, principals, and even janitors played on high school teams.

Women's Sports Organizations

Sports associations and clubs for women above the local level were practically unknown in the nineteenth century, and the local ones that did exist were mostly organizations of college women. As early as the 1880s, some sports clubs were in existence in some of the women's colleges, and by the 1890s in a few large universities. These were mostly bicycle, boating, tennis, and walking clubs. Bryn Mawr College united its various sports clubs into one organization in 1891, giving birth to the first college Woman's Athletic Association. In 1895 Mt. Holyoke College was presented the gift of an ice-skating rink, and the students immediately organized an ice-hockey club.

SPORTS COMPETITION

The spread of railroads throughout the nation meant much to the overall national economic growth of the nation, and no segment of national life prospered more from the growth of railroads than did the sports life of the people. With the driving of the Golden Spike at Promontory Point, Utah, on May 10, 1869, the final formal link between the Union Pacific and Central Pacific Railways, one could travel by rail "from sea to shining sea." Baseball players and other ardent sporting men of that day and their followers took quick advantage of it.

By 1766 the Atlantic Cable had been laid and sports news to and from Europe became common and quick. Heretofore it had taken at least two or three weeks to get news either to or from Europe. By the 1870s the telegraph and newspapers were expanding across the nation, and they carried sports news. By 1882 United Press had been established, and five years later the Associated Press had become a rival company. By 1896 *The New York Times* brought out its first illustrated Sunday supplement, giving a big boost to sports in general.

Goodyear's development of the vulcanization of rubber in 1830 opened the way for the manufacture of elastic and resilient balls of various kinds. Edison's invention of incandescent lights in 1879 was a great boon to the development of indoor games at night; and Eastman's invention of the kodak in 1888 revolutionized the newspapers' coverage of sports.[31]

After the National League of Professional Baseball Players was established in 1876, A.G. Spalding, by then a famous pitcher for Boston and Chicago teams, began publishing the official rules for baseball and other popular games. The series, called the Spalding Library of Athletic Sports, was destined to serve the country for many years. He soon turned to the manufacturing and merchandising of sports equipment. In the 1880s and 1890s he absorbed other athletic goods companies, becoming quite a monopoly for a while. He made baseball uniforms and own brand of bats, advertising his goods in his *Sports Guides*. In 1887 he prevailed upon sports leagues and conferences to adopt his Spalding baseball as the official "league" ball, which cost from $.5 to $1.50 at that time, depending upon whether it was a practice ball or championship game ball.

Another early promoter of sporting goods was Sears Roebuck and Company, which devoted more than eighty pages of its 1895 catalog to sports equipment. (Sporting goods stores as such were as yet unknown to retail districts.)

From all the great advances of the later nineteenth century in national life, the free enterprise system of the new nation was proving to be a great boon in every way.

NonSchool Competition

With the coming of railroads to all parts of the country in this era, making travel easier and less time-consuming, the several national sports associations born after the Civil War (as discussed earlier in this chapter) began to promote out-of-school competition. Intertown, intercity, even interregional and national championship contests arose. The early 1870s brought on the first great baseball matches, which at first were limited to the larger cities of the East and Middle West. At this same time, many rowing matches developed between cities, as far west as Chicago and as far south as New Orleans. In 1879 the first national archery tournament was held in Chicago; in 1881 the first national lawn tennis match for men was held, and in 1887 the first for women was held; the 1890s brought much intercity bicycle racing; and in 1895 the first United States golf tournament was held—a one-day, sixteen-hole contest. Yet, sports did not hold the general public attention enough for the development of the special sports page in the newspapers of the land. This awaited the coming of the twentieth century although all these events brought about the beginnings of professional sports in the United States.

Early Baseball Competition. It was baseball that claimed the greatest and earliest attention of the sporting public in post–Civil War years. As early as 1867 the

Washington Nationals toured the Middle West; a year later the Philadelphia Athletics, the Brooklyn Atlantics, and a New York club traveled as far as St. Louis to play clubs there; the year after that the Cincinnati Red Stockings made a transcontinental tour stretching from Maine to California; and a New Orleans club traveled by river boat to play Memphis, St. Louis, and Cincinnati teams, creating a great sensation wherever they went.[32]

Intercollegiate Athletics

The first intercollegiate contests in the United States involved baseball and rowing and took place just before the Civil War as discussed in Chapter 3. Following the war, intercollegiate sports grew rapidly, and the first intercollegiate football match and the first regattas opened the door to over a century of intercollegiate matches which today have surpassed any dreams of the years of their beginnings.

The First Intercollegiate Football Game. In 1869 Princeton and Rutgers played the first intercollegiate football game in America. The game was played at New Brunswick on November 6 with twenty-five players on each team. At this game yelling was introduced by the Princeton players, using an imitation of the Confederate rebel yell-a bloodcurdling cry of Civil War days. In this first match the Princeton players used the yell to frighten their opponents, but it took so much breath from the players that in the second game they asked their fellow students on the sidelines to give the yell for them. Thus started the United States custom of organized sideline yelling at games. Following this game, Columbia, Yale, Cornell, Pennsylvania, and Harvard were soon playing against each other.[33]

Other Early Colleges Take up Football Competition. Columbia University was playing football by 1870, Yale by 1872, and Harvard (also McGill University in Canada) by 1874. The University of Michigan was playing Harvard, Yale, and Princeton by 1881; West Point and Annapolis were playing each other by 1890, and at the same time the universities of Iowa, Kansas, Missouri, and Nebraska had created a Western Intercollegiate Football Association.[34]

In the 1880s Walter Camp (1859–1925), a Yale graduate and a New Haven businessman, became a volunteer adviser to the Yale football team. In 1889 he started the selections for an All-American honorary team (one of his Yale players who made that first All-American team was Amos Alonza Stagg. Camp wrote much about the game of football for newspapers and magazines of that day. Finally he became Yale's football coach serving for many years and becoming known as ''the Father of American Football.''

By 1884 a crowd of at least 3000 had attended a Harvard–Yale game. ''Spectatoritis'' was being born in America, leading to a gradual growth in America of the Roman sports ideals over the Greek ideals. The dawning of the day of great football coaches was beginning to emerge. Glen (''Pop'') Warner went to Georgia in 1890 and developed the game in the South. John Heisman at Clemson became an early famous coach.[35] Also in the late 1890s Woodrow Wilson (1856–1924), then a young professor at Princeton, assisted with the coaching of football at that university.[36]

In 1892 when the University of Chicago was established, it immediately set up a department of physical culture and athletics. The record of its first varsity teams offers interesting study. The acting captain of both its first football and baseball teams and a winner of the coveted "C" was Amos Alonzo Stagg who played right halfback on one team and pitcher for the other, and at the same time was head of the department. Also Joseph E. Raycroft (1867–1955), the university physician, played quarterback on the first football team. But then only nineteen students came out for sports that first fall of the new university.[37]

By the close of the nineteenth century, universities across the land could boast of having a football team.

The First Organized Restrictions. The first organized efforts at restrictions in college sports took place in this era. In 1882 a three-man faculty committee was set up at Harvard after the faculty complained that students were missing too much school work because of their games. Dr. Sargent was a member of the committee, and the following year he called a conference of other colleges for December 1883, in New York City to consider faculty control of athletics. Nine colleges were represented at the meeting with three college presidents present.

In 1884 a committee representing twenty-two of the leading institutions attempted to secure the agreement of the college authorities to the following propositions: that athletic and gymnastic instructors shall be appointed by the faculty and not by the students; that college teams must be confined to games with college teams; that a standing committee of college representatives shall pass on the rules and regulations for conducting the contests; that no student may play on a team more than four years; and that games shall be held on college grounds only. However, these principles were not generally accepted.

Football was abolished at Harvard following a report by the president in 1885 stating that his investigating committee was "convinced that the game of football as at present played by college teams is demoralizing to player and spectators and extremely dangerous." In 1890 play between Yale and Harvard was revived, and that year Harvard won its first victory over Yale. This was a stupendous event for its day with 20,000 at the game and a special train to bring in the "fans."

With but little improvement in the contests, the President of Harvard University, following his earlier denunciations of 1885, again protested in 1894 and made proposals that stirred up great dissent among the students. The three main proposals were: no freshman to play in intercollegiate contests; no one to play in more than one contest a year; and intercollegiate contests to be held only once every two years. Following this, serious quarrels took place. Harvard University severed athletic relations with Yale University in 1894 and abolished its "flying wedge" play. Not to be outdone in sports warfare, the U.S. military and naval academies broke athletic relations with each other in 1893 and again in 1899. Harvard again broke athletic relations with Yale in 1897 and that same year with Princeton. The 1890s were quarrelsome years for football—the Greek ideals were completely neglected.

Early Regattas.[38] The first intercollegiate regatta following the Civil War was held by the three schools making up the Rowing Association of American Colleges— Harvard, Brown, and Massachusetts Agricultural College—in 1871, near Spring- field, Massachusetts, with the Agricultural College winning. A second was held in the following year, with Amherst, Bowdoin, Williams, and Yale added to the contestants, and Amherst winning. In 1873 eleven colleges entered, but such con- troversy arose over the race, which Harvard won, that at the insistence of Harvard, future employment of professional coaches was forbidden. Gradually such publicity arose in connection with the regatta that college officials came to look upon these contests as great prestige builders. They drew large crowds, various localities bid for the contests, and leading newspapers and weeklies gave much attention to the sports, with frontpage headlines that presaged the national publicity that would later embrace other college sports. It was rowing that first claimed such public attention for the college world.

The regatta of 1874 on Saratoga Lake, with nine colleges entered, was man- aged by a promoter who raised funds from railroad companies, a large hotel, and members of the Saratoga Rowing Association. It turned out to be a great social event, such as characterized the Oxford–Cambridge matches in England, and among the over 30,000 spectators was President Ulysses S. Grant. The winning Columbia team received a great welcome home in New York City. The next year's regatta, also held on Saratoga Lake, was an even greater success. Two well-known publications constructed a 30-foot tower overlooking the Lake and manned it with reporters, photographers, and telegraphers who reported the contest in full detail as it took place. At the same time, crowds gathered in hotel lobbies, in telegraph offices, and on the streets outside newspaper offices in cities and towns over a wide area for the running account of the race at Saratoga Lake. This must have been the country's first sports broadcast, foreshadowing the beginning of radio broadcasts of sports events a half century later. By the late 1870s, first Yale and then Harvard dropped out of the Rowing Association of American Colleges, and gradually row- ing gave way to football as the prestige college sport.

Other Firsts. Football, baseball, and rowing were not the only sports used in intercollegiate contests. As early as 1874 the first intercollegiate track and field meet was held at Saratoga, New York, and in 1893 the long-famous Penn Relays were established. In 1897 the first intercollegiate swimming contest was held be- tween Pennsylvania, Columbia, and Yale Universities.

Intramural Sports Competition

The term *intramural* as applied to sports was not generally used in this era. The word *sports* alone sufficed for all, in the lower schools referring to intramurals only, and in the colleges usually meaning only the varsity.

What few sports were carried on in the lower schools before the twentieth century were almost entirely intramural, but records of even this are scanty. Exceptions are reports in the old files of the Scholastic Bulletin of the New York City Public Schools, which tell of baseball, football, and track and field teams of the public high schools of New York City, in action in the 1890s, sponsored by a games committee made up of representatives from each high school. The Barnard Games staged each year in mid-September by the New York City Public Schools were the great athletic event of the school year. But as everywhere else, sports for the New York City elementary school children were neglected, although organized efforts were made to meet the needs of the high school boys. Now and then some school would offer some track or field event for the elementary school children. This was the extent of their sports even in New York City where many elementary schools had fine gymnasiums and excellent playgrounds.[39]

There was much intramural sports competition going on among college boys. Most of it, as in earlier periods, was organized, coached, financed, and managed by the boys themselves. However in the leading colleges, by the closing years of this period, there were physical education departments to assist the boys in their sports. Such assistance meant including more boys than the earlier informal sports programs involved. Even in these schools organized intramural programs as we know them today were but a dream to be fulfilled only in the years ahead.

Interscholastic Competition

There was but little of interscholastic athletics in the country in the nineteenth century. What little there was came almost entirely in the closing decade of the century and was largely pupil inspired, pupil controlled, and pupil coached occurring mostly in the schools of the smaller towns where there were no physical education teachers.

International Competition

The little international sport there was in the nineteenth century came only after the Civil War. International intercollegiate contests were ushered in by the great boat race between Harvard and Oxford universities, which was held on the River Thames near London on August 7, 1869. The course covered four miles, two furlongs. Oxford won by a half length in the time of 22 minutes and 20 seconds. This first international college contest received much acclaim both at home and abroad.[40] One of the famous Currier and Ives prints is of this race.

This race was managed from the United States by William Blaikie (1843–1904), the young Harvard graduate who had developed the training plan for the Harvard crews. (Ten years later Blaikie, then a well-known attorney in New York City, gained nationwide fame for his promotion of physical fitness and for his book, *How to Get Strong and How to Stay So*.) He stroked the Harvard crew that had defeated Yale in 1866. In 1869 he went to England as manager of the "Harvard four." He was invited by the English hosts to referee the Harvard–Oxford match but declined upon which he was asked to select the referee. He chose Tom Hughes, who later became author of *Tom Brown at Rugby*. Finally Blaikie served as starter for the contest.[41] Seven years later (1886) he had so identified himself with the one-year-old American Association for the Advancement of Physical Education that he was elected its second president.

In 1875 the one-year-old American Rifle Association sent a team to tour Ireland, Scotland, and England. Captained by Henry A. Gildersleeve-father of Virginia Gildersleeve (1877–1965), long-time dean of Barnard College-the American team won all its matches and on its victorious return was given a tumultuous welcome and a parade up Broadway.[42] Albert G. Spalding (1850–1915), one of the earliest nationally known baseball pitchers, took two baseball teams called an "All-American team" on a grand tour of the world in 1888, introducing the American game to fourteen countries on five continents.

United States Participation in the Modern Olympics

France's Baron Pierre de Coubertin (1863–1937), founder of the modern Olympic Games, set up the first games of the revival to be held in 1896 in Athens, Greece, rather than at the site of the ancient games. A special stadium was erected in Athens for this event.

Although there was no such thing as an official U.S. team entered in the first two of the modern games a few individuals from the United States entered on their own initiative or on that of some sports club. For example, James B. Connolly (1869–1957), a student at Harvard, dropped out of college to train for the 1896 games, and entering as an independent contestant won the hop-step-and-jump event to become the first American to win in the Olympics. Other Americans won in the 100-yard dash (the winner being the only entrant in that event using a crouch start), the discus throw (although the winner had never seen a discus until he had one made to practice with a few weeks before leaving for Athens, which turned out to be heavier than the one used by the Greeks), and six other events for a total of nine wins out of twelve track and field events.

From Connolly's own report of the games, the United States athletes were the only ones who had trained for the contests, the athletes from the other countries knowing but little of such procedures. Also they were the only ones to set up a training table and keep early hours for retiring. Three Greek youths who entered the Marathon with no training and attempted to keep up a pace of eight miles an hour for a three-hour stretch died in the attempt.[43]

Twelve nations were represented in these first modern Olympics Games. Although no records were broken, the games were considered an unqualified success. There were twelve bands on hand and an audience of around 80,000 until time for the finish of the Marathon race when an extra 20,000 people surged into the stadium, since this was the one event above all that held the attention of the Greek populace.[44]

The rebirth of the ancient Olympic Games, as conceived by Baron de Coubertin, following the ancient ideal of sports was of a high spiritual order, aiming at a world brotherhood of man. The Baron offered an Olympic Creed—*The important thing in the Olympics is not winning but taking part. The essential thing in life is not conquering but fighting well.* He also offered an emblem (five circles entwined representing the five major continents of the world bound together in fellowship through sports) and a motto: "Swifter, higher, stronger."

The sports offered in the first modern Olympics were: covered court tennis, two events; cycling, four; gymnastics, eight; lawn tennis, two; shooting, three; swimming, one; track and field, twelve; and weight lifting, two.

The Americans exceled in track and field, the French exceled in cycling; the Danish and British in weight lifting; the Germans in gymnastics; the British in tennis; and the Greeks in the Marathon and shooting.

The second Olympics was held in Paris in 1900, the closing summer of the nineteenth century. Again the United States athletes scored high in track and field events, the other countries scored high in the other sports. Again there was no official United States team, but the U.S. athletes who entered, were almost as many as from all the other countries put together, each going independently or sponsored by some organization, each contestant or sponsoring group making its own arrangements and providing its own coaches independently of the others. Yale, Princeton, the University of Pennsylvania, Syracuse, Georgetown, Michigan, and Chicago universities sent representatives, each financing its own group.

In the second games no new sports were added, but swimming, tennis, and weight lifting were dropped with all cycling except the 1000-metre race. On the other hand, ten events were added to track and field, making a total of twenty-two events for that sport alone. Also four shooting events were added, and two dropped. The total events offered were thirty-one. Since the opening ceremonies and first sports events occurred on a Sunday, all U.S. athletes (each on his own, not united as a team) refused to take part in any activities on that day.

In these closing years of the old century, the United States—a young nation of the New World—had, through the skills of her young athletes, much more than held her own alone against the athletic feats of all the nations of the Old World combined. Through its young athletes, the United States had won worldwide acclaim, a dramatic ending for the first full century of its nationhood.

Sports Competition for Women

From their beginnings, the women's academies and colleges favored participation of their students in sports and games as well as in gymnastics and dancing. By the 1870s American college women in particular were skating, riding sidesaddle, forming walking clubs, and playing tennis. The girls at Vassar were even playing baseball. By the 1880s Wellesley College had its crews and competitive rowing on its campus lake, and Goucher and Vassar colleges had swimming pools of sorts. By the 1890s the girls at Mt. Holyoke had an ice-skating rink; at Wells, a golf course; at Bryn Mawr, riding stables; at Vassar, an athletic field; and everywhere everyone was bicycling. With the exception of baseball, team sports were beyond the experience of girls and women until 1892, when Smith College offered basketball for women. Also the closing years of the century brought track and field sports to schoolgirls, no doubt inspired by the revival of the Olympics.

The periodical *Mind and Body* in its November 1895, issue reported Vassar as offering the first women's field day held in any college in the United States, roundly condemning the innovation as a sport for girls and women. Also at this time, gymnastics demonstrations and gymnastic-drill contests became popular, especially with college women.

For the out-of-school woman, there had long existed walking, riding, and tennis clubs and since the early 1890s bicycle clubs, but it was basketball that opened the door of team competition to women out of school. In many cities, and also in small towns, young married women and young business women organized basketball clubs, some playing in armories and some in the few YWCA or YMCA gyms available by then.

Intercollegiate Competition for Women. Soon after the game of basketball was created, several women's colleges in the East that were near each other began playing the game in interschool contests, but Miss Berenson, the originator of the women's game, held out against such contests. Quoting from her biography:

> Soon there came challenges . . . from all over the East and West, and at this point Miss Berenson again proved herself a leader. With a long look ahead she foresaw that intercollegiate athletics might well become a menace to real physical education for women, she answered each letter politely, but firmly explained her reason for refusing all offers. By this stand, steadfastly adhered to, she dissipated the fear which had been at the bottom of much faculty hostility to her department.[45]

By 1896 intercollegiate sports for women had reached the West Coast, where the University of California (Berkeley) and Stanford University were playing intercollegiate basketball. As to the situation in the Middle West, little is known, which probably means that little intercollegiate playing was going on before the turn of the century. Since there were few colleges in the farther reaches of the country that supported departments of physical education before the close of the nineteenth century, it is quite probable that there is little along this line for research workers to discover. Of the little that is known of Middle West contests, the earliest record is of a match game played at the University of Nebraska between the University girl's basketball team and a town team from Council Bluffs, Iowa, played March 4, 1898. In 1898, women students in five Kansas colleges were playing intercollegiate basketball with each other—University of Kansas, Baker and Ottowa universities, Emporia Normal School, and Washburn College.[46]

There are records that the girls at Northwestern University were playing basketball in the late 1890s against Armour Institute and several nearby suburban high schools. The girls at the University of Missouri may have been playing intercollegiate basketball before the close of the century, but the available records are not clear.

Interscholastic Competition for Girls. Since team sports were so new for girls and women, competition between teams was chaotic at first; college teams, high school teams, and out-of-school women's teams all played against each other indiscriminately, perhaps not so much because of a failure to understand the need for discrimination as from inability to find teams of one's own age group to challenge. If one community had a college girls' team, another had only a high school team, and yet another had only a business or leisure women's team. Except in the colleges, practically all teams were coached by men, showing the great lack of women physical education teachers of this era.

Judging from the numerous photographs of high school girls' teams displayed in the first printed basketball guide of 1901, depicting teams from Alaska and California to the East Coast, there was widespread competition going on in this sport, involving, however, only a few of all girls in high schools of those years. The very thought of girls in team sports was as yet too recent an idea for it to have affected any but the most enthusiastic sports women.

6

Organized Physical Education in the Latter Nineteenth Century

From the end of the Civil War until the close of the nineteenth century over 13 million immigrants were admitted into the country. Nationalism had become the great emotion of the world, and the United States, because of her particularly strong belief in the equality of men and in the dignity of the individual, came to feel that to be worthy of the new nationalism all children must receive an education.

EDUCATION IN GENERAL

Whereas in 1850 there had been but eleven public schools—an American innovation—in all of the United States by the close of the Civil War most states had established public schools, and an estimated 50 percent of the children of the nation were attending them. Although public schools and colleges in both the North and South were impoverished, almost all educational work had to start anew because of the Civil War. The war also brought to the people a realization of the need to wipe out illiteracy, and compulsory education was born as an expression of the firm belief that every child has a right to an education. But with so many children taking advantage of the opportunity, it soon became apparent to leaders of educational thought that although all children should receive an education not all require the same kind of education.

In the 1890s business and labor were both demanding that the schools give apprentice training; social workers were insisting that hygiene, domestic science, and manual arts be offered in the schools; agricultural groups were asking that courses in farming be offered; and a body of physical educators had arisen to demand that physical exercise programs be established as a part of the regular school curriculum, not only to substitute for the out-of-school lack of exercise, because of dwindling home chores of the new era, but also to meet the now recognized social needs of the child.

EVENTS AFFECTING PHYSICAL EDUCATION

In the post–Civil War era, three events occurred that had a marked effect on the development of physical education in America: enthusiasm for military drill in the schools, state legislation for physical education, and the birth of the Progressive Education Movement.

Military Drill in the Schools

In 1862 Congress passed the Morrill Act creating the land-grant colleges of which the universities of Cornell, Purdue, and Illinois were the earliest. To secure the land as an endowment, the schools had to agree to teach military tactics as a part of the regular course and to require it of all male students. Following this lead scores of other colleges and universities adopted military training, too, using it as a substitute for, rather than a supplement to, physical education. Moreover, during the Civil War the military leaders of the Union took note of the excellent training and discipline of the Southern troops and ascribed it to the numerous military academies of the South. This resulted in an irresistible movement to introduce military training in the schools of the North, as soon as the war was at an end. Also, reports of the poor physical condition of over a million men recruits from sixteen to forty-five years of age who were examined during the Civil War resulted in a renewed drive for military training in the schools sparked by leading military men and statesmen-a combination of influences that gave physical education a setback felt in some schools as late as the mid-twentieth century.

State Legislation

In 1866 California passed the first state physical education law under the state superintendency of John Swett, an ardent believer in the value of physical education as a part of general education.[1] It required that physical exercise be given to pupils ''as may be conducive to health and vigor of body as well as mind.'' From then on things rested until the State Teachers Associations, the American Association for the Advancement of Physical Education, the Women's Christian Temperance Union, and the turnvereins of Ohio and Pennsylvania threw their organizations support to efforts in several states to procure such laws. Ohio's law, the second, was passed in 1892, and North Dakota followed in 1899. In 1897 Wisconsin passed a permissive law.

The Birth of the Progressive Education Movement

When Francis Parker (1837–1902) became Superintendent of Schools of Quincy, Massachusetts, in 1875 and found the children trained by rote unable to apply their knowledge to anything beyond their textbooks, he began questioning the conventional curriculum and methods of teaching. He put aside the old textbooks and devised a schooling for the children based on observation of life about them, reading of current materials, nature study at first hand, and experiences in doing original writings. With a basis of learning established, he then brought back the use of the textbooks. He developed his theories still further as Supervisor of the Boston Schools and still later as principal of Cook County Normal School in Chicago. Before the 1890's his ideas were not widely recognized, but once they were made known through articles in magazines and newspapers, a growing number of educators, unhappy with the old formalism, seized upon his theories, and politicians and reformers, as well as parents and teachers, began pushing for reforms in education. Thus as Cremin points out (see references), began the Progressive Education Movement. Later John Dewey, who was so markedly to affect physical education as well as all other parts of education, was to acclaim Parker as "the Father of Progressive Education."

STATUS OF PHYSICAL EDUCATION

Physical education, as well as education in general, was neglected during the Civil War, and the advocates of physical education had to wage battle anew on every front, especially against the military leaders who were working to introduce military training into the schools. In the 1870s the argument of the day among educators was that of military drill versus gymnastics. Dr. Dudley A. Sargent, then head of physical education at Yale University, led the battle for gymnastics against the principals of the Boston schools, who held out for military drill. When Bowdoin College gave its students the privilege of voting between gymnastics and military drill for a requirement they stood almost unanimously for gymnastics.[2]

The calisthenics of Catharine Beecher and Dio Lewis, popular just before the war, soon began to lose their hold, but not without a last effort of Miss Beecher, who now was promoting exercises for boys as well as for girls. In an address on *Female Suffrage* given in 1870 in the Music Hall of Boston, Miss Beecher made a public appeal for trained teachers of physical education for girls in which, speaking from a need for substantial change, she said:

> The department of the physical training of all the institutions should be committed to a woman of good practical common sense, of refined culture and manners and one expressly educated for this department. By the aid of both parents and teachers, she would study the constitution and habits of every pupil, and administer a method of training to develop healthfully every organ and function, and to remedy every defect in habits, person, voice, movements, and manners.[3]

The German system of gymnastics was receiving increased attention in many parts of the country, and by the close of the century the Delsarte and Swedish systems had put in their appearance. Throughout the nineteenth century sports and athletics still had no place in the official school or college programs. They were recognized only as the students' own after-school projects.

The 1880s and 1890s brought a period of great expansion for physical education not only in the schools but also in nonschool organizations. Many gymnasiums were built, and the schools began to demand teachers who were professionally trained. However, full-time positions were scarce, and most teachers took on two or more positions in schools, athletic clubs, or YMCA's, or coupled teaching with some other work in order to make a living. Many who had a medical degree practiced medicine on the side or, as some of the leaders did, established private schools which they maintained along with their other positions.

Although the formal physical education programs borrowed from the Europeans played a major role in schools during the second half of the nineteenth century, a new attitude toward physical education began to gain momentum. The desires of people for recreation, the popularity of organized field sports, college athletics, and a changing educational philosophy gave concern to the staunch proponents of the traditional formal program. The 1880s were years of struggles between scientific training and classical culture. It was a period of growth and expansion following the slump after the Civil War. Physical Education rode in on this wave and got a good start at that time.

The office of the U.S. Commissioner of Education reported in 1891 on the status of physical training in the schools of 272 leading cities of the United States. The figures showed that 83 cities had a special director of physical education for the entire school system, 81 others required the schoolroom teacher to teach exercises, and 108 permitted teachers to offer exercises if they so wished; 10 percent of the schools had established exercise programs before 1887, and of those offering physical education, 41 percent used the German system of gymnastics, 29 percent used the Swedish system, 12 percent used the Delsarte system, and 18 percent used a combination of these. At this time there were reported to be 31 gymnasiums in the schools of eleven cities of the 272 investigated.

Terminology

The term *physical culture,* used widely from the 1860s on, continued in use in some quarters as late as the 1910s with its use at its height in 1895. The classics predominated in higher education in the nineteenth century, and the word *culture* was used generally by the classicists. When the University of Chicago was founded in 1892, it named its physical education department the Department of Physical Culture and Athletics. In 1895 the University of California called its arts and science college the College of General Culture. Many colleges offered courses entitled Religious Culture and Social Culture. Also, physical education came to many schools in those early days through the elocution departments, which called their course Voice Culture; so it was natural for them to call the physical activity courses Physical Culture.

The word *training* crept in when military departments were assigned the responsibility of the physical activity courses, and it was natural to make the two terms *military training* and *physical training* conform. When the social and psychological objectives came into the picture, also when the Ph.D. degree began to replace the M.D. degree in a large way among the leaders of the profession, the word *education* naturally came to the front, and the term *physical education* came into its own. It must not be forgotten that when Hitchcock in 1861 set up at Amherst College the first department in any school in the United States it was officially designated as the Department of Physical Education and that many of the physical education leaders used this term in the 1890s. By the 1920s *physical education* had become the universally accepted term. Throughout the nineteenth century and the first decade of the twentieth, the terms *physical culture, physical training, physical education,* all referred to but one thing—gymnastic exercises, whether called calisthenics, exercise, or gymnastics.

Elementary and Secondary School Programs

Gradually a physical education program was being accepted as a "must" and introduced into the large city schools. In 1867 the Board of Controllers of Philadelphia made provision in the budget for two or three well-trained physical-exercise teachers with the class work to begin in all primary and grammar grades the following year. The teachers were required "to devote in each school room ten minutes during the course of each school session to such physical exercises as the size of the room and other circumstances might permit." Two years later they established a department of physical education with its own special teachers in a girls' high school—the first department of physical education for girls in a public school in America.[4]

In that same year there is a record of a two-county institute held in Minnesota where faculty members of the Winona Normal School offered physical education courses to help regular school teachers bring physical education to the schools.[5]

At the same time the female seminaries, all of which were of secondary school level except Elmira, were adding physical education in some form to the curriculum, and Miss Beecher renewed her campaign in behalf of physical education in these schools. Whereas in the era preceding the Civil War the emphasis of the school physical activity program for girls was on the cure of physical defects which were supposed to be brought on by too much study, in this era it became apparent that girls could stand the stress of attending school and needed, in physical education, not so much cure as prevention of ills.

The great amount of physical activity which children undertook on their own during recess periods was, except in schools with unusual teachers who assumed responsibility "beyond the call of duty," completely unsupervised. The recess periods were great fun with much physical activity wherever a few natural born leaders and a lot of lively children got together. But the timid and less venturesome were neglected, and the sort of citizenship training that came out of this play was dependent solely upon the naturally good leaders or the "bullies," as chance dictated, who would "rule the roost."

As to physical education, schools soon divided into two camps—those using the German system of gymnastics and those using the Swedish system; only a few schools departed from the pattern. The development from the 1870s on is discussed under these two headings.

Adoption of the German System. The following cities established physical education in their schools using the German system: Cincinnati, 1855; Cleveland, 1870; Milwaukee, 1876; Omaha, Kansas City, and La Crosse, 1885; Chicago, 1886; Davenport, 1887; St. Louis, 1888; Los Angeles, Oakland, Moline, Detroit, and Erie, 1890; Indianapolis, San Francisco, Spokane, and Dayton, 1892; and St. Paul, 1894. They procured their teachers from the Normal College of the American Gymnastic Union (NCAGU), which was the revived school started by the turners in Rochester, just preceding the Civil War.

The story of the founding of the department of physical education in the Kansas City schools depicts the part played by the turners in the establishment of the system in the schools of America. Carl Betz (1854–1898), a graduate of the four-month training course of the NCAGU, then located in Milwaukee, was appointed instructor in the Socialer Turnverein in Kansas City, Missouri, in 1885. That same year he accepted an invitation to demonstrate with a class of girls wand and club drills before the teachers' institute. His work was well received, and all agreed that something of that kind should be a part of the schoolwork. Betz offered to direct the exercises for a few months without pay in order to demonstrate their practicability. The school board accepted his offer, and before the end of the year (1885) he was employed as director of physical education of all the schools of Kansas City, which position he held until his death in 1898.[6]

Adoption of the Swedish System. Dr. Hartwig Nissen (1856–1924) introduced the Swedish system of gymnastics to America when he came to Washington in 1883 as Vice-Consul for Norway and Sweden. Immediately upon his arrival in Washington he began to acquaint the physicians with the value of medical gymnastics and massage and opened the famous Swedish Health Institute. Among his "patients" were prominent men such as Benjamin Harrison and Ulysses S. Grant. Next he introduced Swedish gymnastics and folk dance into the Franklin School and, in 1887, among students at Johns Hopkins University. When Baron Nils Posse (1862–1895), the son of a prominent family of the Swedish nobility and a graduate of the Royal Central Institute of Gymnastics of Stockholm, arrived in America from

Sweden in 1885, he first visited Nissen and then went to Boston in the hopes of establishing himself there in the practice of medical gymnastics.

Mrs. Mary Hemenway (1820–1894), the widow of a prosperous Bostonian shipping merchant, was deeply interested in the advancement of education. Her son had given the magnificent Hemenway gymnasium to Harvard in 1879, and she was prepared to give financial aid to projects in behalf of the public schools. Seeing in Swedish gymnastics possibilities for bettering the health of school children, she offered to finance the teacher training of over a hundred teachers per year provided the school board would give Swedish gymnastics a place in the school program for all pupils on an experimental basis. They consented to the project, and Mrs. Hemenway provided the services of Posse to train the teachers. By 1890 over four hundred teachers were prepared to give instruction in the Swedish system. The superintendent thereupon ordered "that the Ling or Swedish system of educational gymnastics be introduced into all the public schools of this city." Dr. Edward M. Hartwell, formerly of Johns Hopkins University, was elected to the position of Director of Physical Training and began his duties in 1891. This title was an innovation for that time. Shortly Nissen was persuaded to come to Boston as Hartwell's assistant.

Following Boston's lead, many schools and colleges adopted the Swedish system for their physical education programs. This was made possible by the Boston Normal School of Gymnastics, which was established to prepare teachers to offer this system of gymnastics to the schools and colleges of America. Thus Swedish gymnastics gained a firm hold in the schools, particularly in the New England area and in the women's departments of colleges, as the graduates of this school took positions all over the country. Within a year of its introduction in the Boston public schools alone, over 60,000 children were taking Swedish gymnastics. Until the War of 1914 to 1917, this system of gymnastics enjoyed great popularity in the non-German population areas of the country.

Adoption of Other Systems. Despite the flurry of excitement over the relative merits of German and Swedish gymnastics, some schools installed physical education programs built around exercises devised by their own teachers or composed of their own revamping of the calisthenics of Catharine Beecher and Dio Lewis of an earlier day, perhaps even using the Delsarte exercises which had become popular in the 1890s. Still other schools, particularly those in small towns, occasionally had teachers who had heard of exercise programs in the city schools and, wanting to give their pupils something but knowing nothing of any of these systems, contrived some drills that produced activity even if not founded on anything of a scientific nature.

One "independent" school system of the period was Brooklyn, which set up its own school program in 1895 with Jessie H. Bancroft (1867–1952) responsible for organizing the work. Miss Bancroft devised her own set of exercises and built up a program for all the schools of Brooklyn. She was soon given the official title of

Director of Physical Education of Public Schools-the first woman in the United States to hold such a title.

Facilities, Requirements, and Staffs. Although the 1880s were an active period for building gymnasiums and establishing physical education, the U.S. Commissioner of Education reported that in 1885 not one city in America had a gymnasium in its lower schools; in 1887 of 419 public high schools in the country only 89 offered physical culture programs; of 172 academies, seminaries, and private high schools for girls, only 50 had such programs; of all private schools for boys or girls or coeducational counted together, only 151 offered physical education programs; and by 1890, only 94 out of 2526 public high schools had gymnasiums.[7] Certainly the lower schools were slow in supplying gymnasiums. For example, by the end of the century there was in Chicago but one elementary school that had a gymnasium, although 205 principals were requesting them. However, seven of the fifteen Chicago high schools had gymnasiums; and the others used hallways for classes with wands, dumbbells, and Indian clubs in racks on the walls. This was, no doubt, typical of the situation throughout the country.

Athletic fields, unlike play space for recess hours, were not as yet considered a necessity for schools, since sports were not considered a part of a physical education program. They were desirable adjuncts for recreation for out-of-school hours but they were the responsibilities solely of students themselves. Recess areas could be used for team sports in after-school hours if they were large enough and pupils had permission from the school authorities, but school athletic fields were luxuries as yet generally unknown.

By the end of the century many schools were requiring at least five minutes of exercise of each pupil daily or twenty minutes, two or three times a week, or a half-hour, two times a week. Most schools averaged fifty minutes per week. This was, indeed, quite the accepted requirement in schools that had a program at all.

In Chicago, typical of conditions in large cities, there was as late as the 1890s only one special physical education teacher assigned to an elementary school, but there were seven other specialized teachers to supervise the physical education work given by the regular classroom teacher in the other elementary schools. These handled 30,000 pupils in thirty-four schools. Each school was visited three or four times a year by a supervisor, and those schools where the hallways were outfitted with exercise equipment were visited as often as every four or six weeks. In the seven high schools with gymnasiums each had a special teacher of "physical culture."[8]

Physical Education for College Men

With the close of the Civil War, physical education began to develop in earnest in many colleges. Dr. Hitchcock, at Amherst College, was setting the example for all other schools. By now the students there were having intramural athletics, but according to Hartwell, Hitchcock was firm in his denunciation of "hot and violent contests with professional gamesters," and he gave but lukewarm acquiescence to games with other colleges. Early in his work there he had instituted corrective work for those needing it.[9]

In 1869 George Goldie, then a professional gymnast in New York City and before that a well-known athlete in Montreal, Canada, was appointed Director of the new $10,000 gymnasium at Princeton University. (He had learned gymnastics and circus stunts at a private gymnasium in New York City which was the rendezvous of professional gymnasts.) He built his program around both gymnastics and sports. According to the Princeton Alumni Weekly his gymnastics teams "could perform acrobatic stunts . . . which might have aroused the envy of P. T. Barnum." In 1873 he inaugurated the first college track meet, which was immediately named the Caledonia Games in honor of Goldie, the Scotsman, who held the Caledonian championship for all-around athletes. Also in that year, he organized the first college amateur athletic association.

In the early 1870s, Dudley A. Sargent established a physical education program at Bowdoin College while he pursued work for the bachelor's degree. He gave all the boys free exercises varying the program: the freshman year with dumbbells, the sophomore year with Indian clubs, the junior year with chest weights, and the senior year with wands and pulley weights—training in all of which he had "picked up on his own." All gymnasium classes were dismissed in the spring for military drill so Sargent went to Yale University each spring from 1872 on and established a program for that college while he pursued his medical studies. In 1875 the Yale authorities gave the students their choice for requirement between Greek and gymnastics, and all but two selected the latter. William Howard Taft, then a student at Yale, destined later to become a president of the United States, was one who elected gymnastics, and he became one of the class leaders.[10]

Program At Harvard University. As Hitchcock's program at Amherst College was an example of excellence of the pre–Civil War period, Sargent's program at Harvard University is an example of excellence of the post–Civil War era, both far ahead of their times. The Hemenway Gymnasium, costing $110,000, was ready for occupancy in 1879, replacing the old gymnasium of 1859. This new gymnasium contained a wooden swimming pool.[11] At that time Sargent was appointed to take charge of the physical education work with the title of Assistant Professor of Physical Training and Director of the Hemenway Gymnasium. He relates in his *Autobiography* that many faculty members considered the new gymnasium as a vast waste of money and resented having a college graduate placed in charge of physical education—work which they considered unworthy of a college-trained man. Sargent was charged with the task of equipping the new building, determining the policy of the department, and arranging the work. Believing that the difference in the physical makeup and physical needs of the students was too great to allow uniformity of exercise he began building a program around the individual needs of the students. He took bodily measurements of all students and also gave them strength tests that he devised. Then he prescribed exercises for each, using the many different pieces of apparatus that he invented to meet specific physical developmental needs. For many years he worked on his mechanical contrivances which came to be called "Sargent machines." They included foot, ankle, wrist, leg, and back machines, rowing and lifting machines, chest expanders, chest weights, quarter circles, and short and long inclined planes. He also used some German and some Swedish apparatus, and. at the same time, he developed a more detailed system of measurements than was being used at Amherst College. His studies along that line added greatly to anthropometric knowledge.

Dr. Sargent used photography as early as 1889 in his work, taking photographs of each student in three positions (front, back, and side) upon entrance and repeating after a period of training. This is the earliest record of the use of such a device in physical education work, almost a half century ahead of the times.

Program in Other Colleges. It was many years before other schools caught up with Hitchcock at Amherst and Sargent at Harvard. However, in 1876 Princeton organized the first college athletic association and the University of Chicago in 1893 became the first to set up a faculty committee to adminster intercollegiate sports. Of the private coeducational colleges, Oberlin was the first to establish a department of physical education (1885). The University of Chicago opened in October of 1892, and its Department of Physical Culture was one of the many departments established from its very first days. Amos Alonzo Stagg was the first head of the three-fold department, which encompassed physical education for men, physical education for women, and athletics, possibly the first such tie-up in the American college world. When Clark W. Hetherington (1870–1942) established the department of physical education at University of Missouri in 1900, he also was head over all three divisions of work. Of the state universities the University of Wisconsin offered the first classes in physical education (1870), although this date does not mark the establishment of a department. For some years before an actual department of physical education with its own staff materialized, in practically all schools, physical activity classes of a sort were offered either by the students themselves or by some teacher in an academic department. The following list shows dates for the actual establishment of departments for men in state universities:

1888-California	1893-Utah	1896-Minnesota
1890-Wisconsin	1893-Illinois	1897-Ohio
1890-Texas	1894-Kansas	1899-Iowa
1891-Indiana	1894-Washington	1900-Missouri
1891-Nebraska	1894-Michigan	

(Such dates as the ones given above are difficult to determine with any as-surance of accuracy, since many school records do not differentiate men's and women's departments. In most universities, however, departments for men were established ahead of those for women, so that when two conflicting dates are offered, the earlier one probably represents the men's department and the later, the women's.)

Facilities. Many gymnasiums were erected after the Civil War, starting with the Dartmouth building of 1867 which cost $24,000. Following that Princeton replaced its earlier red shack with a $38,000 "gym," the finest of its day. Bowdoin's gymnasium had no heat, and the men dressed for class even in zero weather, changing to cotton shirts and tights and cloth slippers. Jerseys and woolen sweaters were as yet unknown.

Gymnasiums were built in the Middle West in the 1870s at Washington University (St. Louis) at a cost of $7000, at Beloit College (Wisconsin) at a cost of $5000, and at the University of Wisconsin at a cost of $4000, this last being the first gymnasium building in a state university. The Yale gymnasium of 1875 had eight long bathtubs lined with zinc, which the students used only on payment of a special fee. Then 1879 brought the wonder gymnasium of the age—Harvard's $110,000 Hemenway gymnasium—followed shortly by the University of California's modest $12,000 Harmon Gymnasium and Vanderbilt's $22,000 building. During the 1860s and 1870s many colleges that could not afford gymnasiums fitted up vacant rooms as drill halls.

The 1880s and 1890s brought many more college gymnasiums, most donated by wealthy alumni and ranging in cost from $10,000 to $40,000. The usual plan consisted of one large exercise floor, an examining room, a running track that could be used also as a visitor or spectator's gallery, bath, dressing and locker rooms, and offices. A few of these later gymnasiums included a bowling alley and a small room for fencing or sparring. An indoor swimming pool was still a rarity. The U.S. Commissioner of Education reported that in 1885 there were only thirty-five colleges known to have some sort of facilities for physical education but by 1887, seventy-seven colleges had gymnasiums. When the University of Chicago opened in October 1892 and the gymnasium was completed in November, the students, under the supervision of Stagg, built the fence around the athletic field with lumber contributed by local merchants. The first football game was played on Thanksgiving Day of 1893. There were as yet no seats on the athletic field, and the students set up wooden horses with planks borrowed from buildings under construction.[12]

In 1890, the University of Nebraska in Lincoln built a combination armory and gymnasium with a bowling alley in the basement, and nine years later added on a large wing for a combination woman's gymnasium and university convocation hall. In 1876, Ohio State University completed a new gymnasium at a cost of $100,000, containing a pool for women as well as one for men. When Columbia University opened its new gymnasium in 1898 it was hailed as the largest in any educational institution in the world. The main floor was 170 by 130 feet and the swimming pool 100 feet long.

Staffs. Yale University listed in the catalog an instructor in physical training for the school year 1860–1861 and again for 1867 through 1872. In 1867 Harvard University acquired its first teacher of gymnastics, a pro boxing teacher. Although listed as Instructor and Curator of Gymnasium, his name was not included in the list of regular faculty members. Amherst College gave Hitchcock the faculty status of professor from the date of his first appointment. Later Harvard University conferred upon Sargent the rank of assistant professor. When Stagg went to the University of Chicago in 1892, he was given the rank of professor and director. The woman under him, Alice B. Foster, who was head of women's work and held the M.D. degree, was given only the rank of tutor. But in most colleges the earliest appointees to be placed in charge of the gymnasium were ex–prize fighters, weight lifters, and janitors. In those days there were no schools in the United States preparing teachers of physical education.

Gradually men with some semblance of training in physical education became available and, taking on two or more part-time positions, managed to find full-time employment. By the close of the century, a fairly good supply of professionally trained teachers was available for the positions that did exist. The YMCA Training School at Springfield, Massachusetts, furnished most of the teachers for YMCA's and the leading colleges and universities.

Salaries. Hitchcock started full-time work at Amherst in 1861 at $1000 per year, and was raised to $1200 his second year. Sargent, at part-time employment, was paid $5 per week when he first went to Bowdoin College in 1869. Two years later the salary was raised to $500 per year. In 1872 he was paid $50 a week at Yale University on special assignment. In 1875 he asked Bowdoin for $1200 per year from which he would pay the janitor and his assistants, purchase the apparatus needed, and pay all other expenses except heat, light, and building repairs. The college refused this salary request, and he resigned.[13] By the end of the century, Hetherington received a salary of $1800 at the University of Missouri for his full-time employment as head of athletics and physical education for both men and women.

Physical Education for College Women

As a rule physical education fared better in this era in the women's colleges than in coeducational schools. The establishment of several of today's leading women's colleges meant much to the advancement of physical education; Smith and Wellesley colleges opened their doors in 1875, Bryn Mawr, 1885; Randolph–Macon,

1891; the Women's College of the University of North Carolina, 1892; Radcliffe, 1894; and Barnard, 1899. All took an important place in the promotion of physical education. From their very founding the women's colleges offered physical activity classes to their students whereas in most coeducational schools such classes came most belatedly long after the establishment of the schools.

First Departments of Physical Education.[14] Vassar was the first college in the United States to offer physical activity classwork for women as a part of the school program. This was in 1868. Mt. Holyoke and Rockford colleges had been offering work since 1837 and 1849, respectively, but niether achieved collegiate rating before the 1880s. Wellesley established its department in 1881. Oberlin College was the first coeducational college to organize a department of physical education for women (1885). A few state universities recognized departments for women before those for men: Indiana, Kansas, Utah, Michigan, Ohio State, and Texas. In three state universities it was the military department that brought about the establishment of a department for women: California (Berkeley), Nebraska, and Wyoming. State University departments for women were founded as follows:

1889—California (Berkeley)	1894—Illinois	1894—Wisconsin
	1894—Michigan	1896—Iowa
1890—Indiana	1894—Nebraska	1896—Minnesota
1890—Washington	1894—Oregon	1897—Ohio
1893—Kansas	1894—Washington	1900—Missouri
1894—Utah		

The story of the beginnings of one department of physical education for women in two coeducational institutions during this era follows.

The University of Wisconsin Department for Women.[15] The catalog of the University of Wisconsin at Madison of 1863–1864 announced that the women students would be trained in the Dio Lewis new system of gymnastics, but there is no record of a teacher being assigned or classes being held. However, in 1872 concern was expressed about the physical training of the women, and it was announced that a room would be set aside in the Ladies Hall for "calisthenics and light gymnastics with music." But apparently no teacher was assigned for this work.

In 1874 the women students, seeking some rights, demanded the use of the school gymnasium twice a week in the fall and this was granted, but apparently without a teacher assigned. In 1878 William G. Anderson (1860–1947), then a senior student at the University who had taken physical education work during his high school years in Boston at the YMCA under the much talked of Robert J. Roberts, M.D. (1849–1920) offered to teach a volunteer class of women students, and gave them calisthenics and work with barbells. This lasted one year, and for the next ten years the women were on their own once more. But they managed to get in a varied program of croquet, hiking, and tennis as all volunteer, unofficial class work.

In 1889 a young women who had taken work in Boston at the Allen School of Gymnastics (a short-lived school of that day) was granted permission to teach the women for a small fee. The following year the Board of Regents appointed her as an instructor in physical culture for women. She gave an eight-month course for the women, who came to her class twice a week. This developed into a four-year offering of "Swedish movements," apparatus work with physical examination required, and a prescription of exercises for each student as needed for the correction of defects. At last this was a serious beginning. For all the years of optional work the women had been granted space on one floor in Ladies Hall for a gymnasium. The year 1894 marked the real birth of the beginnings of a department of physical education for women at Wisconsin. The Regents at that time made a ruling requiring two hours per week for a one-year course in physical culture of all women students with a one-hour credit allowment toward graduation. At the same time they brought to the faculty Abbie Shaw Mayhew (1864–?), a graduate of both Wellesley College and the Sargent School of Physical Education, to put the requirement into effect. She immediately went into plans to enlarge the space heretofore granted in Ladies Hall for women's gymnastics. Within two years this space was enlarged to the use of two stories, with a running track, gallery, lockers and showers—quite a wonder for its day. For costumes they wore a "divided skirt" (as bloomers were often spoken of), and they had a wealth of Swedish apparatus to work on, such as ropes, stall bars, window ladder, and vaulting boxes.

Swedish gymnastics made up the content of the class credit work, and for their informal recreation the women now organized tennis, bicycle, and bowling clubs, and a boat crew. They also organized a Girls' Boating Association, which was an activity apart from the boat crew club. No doubt Miss Mayhew's four years as a student at Wellesley College, where American college women first enjoyed boating, as a class activity, meant much to her in this teaching career, since the location in Madison offered two lakes.

Before the close of the century the University of Wisconsin women students through their physical education department were enjoying cycling, bowling, golf, tennis, rowing, skating, and basketball. (The article used in this reference (see Footnote 15) adds field hockey and volleyball to this list but this has to be in error for neither of these sports was known to America before the turn of the century.)

The University of Nebraska Department for Women.[16] In the late 1880s, at the University of Nebraska, a group of women students urged the Military Department to give them military drill, and this it consented to do provided the girls would be content to drill indoors. In 1891, Wilbur P. Bowen (1864–1928), a mathematics teacher at Michigan State Normal School, who had attended Sargent's Summer

School of Physical Education at Harvard for a couple of summers, was brought to the University to set up the Department of Physical Education for Men. The women pleaded so persistently for classwork, too, that Bowen and the new Commandant of the ROTC—Lt. John J. Pershing (1860–1948) recently graduated from West Point, who had, also, come to the university faculty in the fall of 1891—decided to do something about it. Pershing offered to teach the girls fencing and marching and Bowen to teach them dumbbell exercises and Indian-club swinging.

At the insistence of Pershing, who felt strongly that "ladies" should not be doing military drill at all and that in their physical activities they should be taught by a woman rather than a man, the Chancellor finally capitulated and the next school year (1892–1893) he employed a local woman, Anne Barr, who had learned some Indian-club swinging at the local YMCA, to take over classwork for the women students on an hour-pay basis. Becoming interested in her teaching, Miss Barr went to the Harvard Summer School of Physical Education the following summer and there began actual professional training (which she pursued from then on at the Chautauqua Summer School of Physical Education) for the position which she held for several years—first as class leader and by 1894 as Directress of the Women's Gymnasium and later as Director of Physical Education for Women. In 1894 physical education became a requirement of all young women for the first two years with four hours a week of activity and one of hygiene.

Program. The core of the college program for women was calisthenics or gymnastics with some sports hanging on as fringe activities without official college sanction.[17] Mt. Holyoke College added to its requirement in calisthenics a daily walk of one mile in good weather and a three-quarter-hour walk in bad weather. The Dio Lewis system of gymnastics was the favored form for college women in the 1860s. In the early 1880s most women's colleges changed to the Sargent system; in 1888 Goucher College took up the Swedish system. The other women's colleges except Vassar swung over to this system, also; in 1890 Elmira and Rockford colleges adopted the Delsarte system; but not one of the women's colleges accepted the German system.

However, as with men students, women organized sports activities for themselves, sometimes with faculty help but most frequently without. As early as the 1870s there were rowing, tennis, croquet, bicycling, and baseball clubs in action. In the 1890s golf and basketball were added to the list of activities.

The programs for women in coeducational colleges followed somewhat the pattern set by the women's colleges but the men's programs and men teachers on the same campus introduced forms of activities and a type of emphasis on methods and philosophy that differed somewhat from that originating in the women's colleges.

Facilities. In the women's colleges, physical education classwork got under way in this period by using the out of doors, corridors, assembly halls, and storerooms. One school used a privately owned gymnasium in the local community—Radcliffe at Sargent's gymnasium. Vassar was the only college that started its physical education work with a special building constructed for it. In 1860 it built a "Hall for Calisthenics" with footprints painted on the floor to indicate where students should stand during their exercise periods. Mt. Holyoke had a gymnasium by 1865 (that cost $1900), Smith College by 1875, Bryn Mawr by 1885, Goucher by 1888, and Mills College and the University of California by the end of the century.

The coeducational colleges lagged far behind the women's colleges in procuring physical education facilities for women students. As a rule the women were permitted to use the men's facilities on occasion, and in many schools some large room in the women's dormitory was set aside for a women's gymnasium.

Goucher College constructed the first swimming pool for women in 1888, although it did not list swimming as an activity for students until 1904; Vassar built the second pool in 1889; Smith installed a "swimming bath" in 1892 which could be used by two to five students at a time and was used for over thirty years; Bryn Mawr built its pool in 1894, and by the end of the century Radcliffe College had built one. There were no pools for women or men in any coeducational college or coeducational university of this era.

Costumes. In the 1860s the girls at Mt. Holyoke College wore for their exercise classes the Zouave trousers introduced into America by Dio Lewis for exercise periods. The Vassar girls wore a costume of gray flannel with the blouse high necked and long sleeved and the skirt ankle length with bloomers underneath. Elmira College girls in 1872 wore a costume of black alpaca, lined throughout, with a "Garabaldi" waist and a skirt reaching to within ten inches of the floor with Turkish drawers underneath with elastic leg binding and falling to the length of the skirt, with skirt and blouse trimmed in scarlet "Gilbert opera flannel."

By the 1880s shorter costumes appeared with a divided skirt; but when the bicycling craze of the 1890s brought out a new version of the costume first introduced by Amelia Bloomer in the 1850s as a measure of dress reform for women, bloomers became the universally accepted costume for sports and physical education work for women.

These bloomers of a new era were made of woolen materials and were worn for all seasons of the year. They were very full, and although caught up at the knee by an elastic the folds of the material hung down to mid-calf. The blouse of the same material was long sleeved, high necked, and usually trimmed with a large sailor collar.

Staffs. Physical education in these early years was taught by teachers of other subjects who read a book or two on exercise and, from this, undertook to teach calisthenics or some dance-like activity called "fancy steps." As early as 1862 the Mt. Holyoke College catalog listed a teacher of calisthenics. The Smith College prospectus of 1874 announced that "regular gymnastic exercises in the gymnasium will be prescribed under the direction of an educated lady physician."

In the 1860s and 1870s women's departments were able to procure as part-time teachers pupils of Dio Lewis who offered the first teacher-training in physical education to women in America. Wellesley College was the first to employ a full-time teacher of physical education for women, in 1881. Following its lead, other colleges began employing full-time teachers for this work: Vassar, 1883; Bryn Mawr and Oberlin, 1885; Smith, 1887; Goucher, 1888; and the University of Chicago, 1892. From then to the close of the century, many other colleges fell into line on this practice. After professional training schools for women opened in the 1880s, women teachers who were prepared for this special work became available, and schools were no longer dependent upon those who had just "picked up some superficial training on their own or had had some elocution courses that offered a smattering of training in exercises of sorts. Oberlin, the first coeducational college to appoint a woman to teach physical education, selected for the position in 1885, Delphine Hanna (1854–1941), a graduate of the Sargent School of Physical Education, who three years later procured the medical degree. Following that, Goucher College appointed a physical education teacher from the Central Gymnastic Institute of Stockholm. Mt. Holyoke had two women teachers with the Ph.D. degree teaching gymnastics along with their special subjects, most obviously women not trained in this field. However, when these women teachers of academic subjects no longer taught gymnastics "on the side" and women trained in the field did come upon the scene, it was several decades before a Ph.D. degree again graced the women's physical education ranks. No woman physical education teacher in any women's college received recognition in academic rank of any sort in the nineteenth century. The coeducational colleges were more advanced in this respect.

Salaries. Information on salaries paid to women working in physical education in the late nineteenth century is difficult to find. What little is known has been for the most part discovered in autobiographical sketches or in reminscences of close personal friends of various women. But even this is rare. Until women found a real niche in the work of the world and in large numbers, salaries were seemingly a deep and dark subject not to be openly discussed. We do know that a woman graduate of the NAGU School of Milwaukee was paid $450 per year in 1883 to teach in that city. When Delphine Hanna went to Oberlin College in 1885 to establish physical education there she was to be furnished room and board by the college and $300 with which to purchase necessary class equipment.[18] How she financed herself beyond room and board is mere conjecture. We also know that Anne Barr at the University of Nebraska was paid by the hour for her first few years of work there in the early 1890s. In 1893, Jessie Bancroft became Director of Physical Training for the public schools of Brooklyn at a salary of $1200 per year, apparently very good for that day. Until both the Victorian and Edwardian eras were over, it seemed to be "not quite nice" to discuss money in reference to women.

However, there are some studies that show without doubt that no matter what a woman was paid in salary for teaching, it was far less than a man would be paid for what seemed to be the same type of work. One study reports that women who did teach were paid the nearest to what men teachers were paid in 1835 (the women drawing one-half of what the men drew), and paid the worst compared with men's salaries in 1875, when the man was being paid two and one-third times the amount paid a woman.[19] There are records that women graduating from the Boston Normal School of Gymnastics were receiving in the 1890s salaries from $1000 to $1800 per year—unusual for that period even for work in a specialized field.

Research

This period was one of great interest in anthropometric testing, which started in the United States with Hitchcock's work, at Amherst College in 1861, based on his deep interest in ascertaining the physical-developmental needs of the students as individuals. From the very start, he used data from eight items in his research work: age, weight, height, chest girth, arm girth, forearm girth, lung capacity, and pull-up. For forty years he published annual anthropometric tables of Amherst men, which fill two large volumes. In 1873 Sargent, then a young medical student at Yale, started work on strength tests and later as a teacher at Harvard University carried it forward. From 1880 to 1886 he collected data on Harvard men, from which he devised his first anthropometric charts. Following this lead, charts were made by Jay W. Seaver (1855–1915) from the measurements of Yale men and YMCA men from 25 to 35 years of age, while research into the anthropometric measurements of women was carried on principally at Wellesley and Oberlin colleges and the University of Nebraska. In the late 1890s the three women heads of physical education in these colleges made anthropometric charts from the measurements of 1500 college women. Sargent's data through 1892 for both men and women college-age students was published in percentile tables, and from these, plastic figures were made and exhibited at the Chicago World's Fair in 1893, arousing much interest from the general public.

In 1890 the first athletic achievement test was born—the Pentathlon test of the Athletic League of the YMCA's of America devised by Dr. Luther H. Gulick. This is the earliest record of the use of elements of sports and games as test forms. It was the forerunner of many such tests which at the turn of the century, so markedly motivated the promotion of physical education in the schools. As developed further in the early 1900s by Gulick for the Public School Athletic League of New York City, these tests consisted of throwing for accuracy and speed, running for speed, and jumping for distance.

Teacher Training

This era marked the serious beginnings of professional training in physical education in America. Immediately following the Civil War, there were but two schools in all the country that offered training in this field of work—the Normal School of the North American Gymnastic Union, then located in Chicago and turning out only men teachers, and the short-lived Dio Lewis School training women teachers. In 1878 a woman named Mary Allen opened a private woman's gymnasium in Boston, and in 1881 she offered teacher-training courses. By 1889 she had graduated seven "instructresses." From then on, she and her school are lost to the records.

In the 1880s other training schools were established. These offered a seven-month course, which soon developed into ten months. By the 1890s all these schools offered at least two full school years of training. According to Hartwell's research, from the early 1860s to the close of the nineteenth century thirty-four normal schools of physical education were established. None, however, was of collegiate rank.[20]

Before teacher-training schools were established, the leading teachers of physical education were men and women trained in the field of medicine, the men being mostly Harvard, Yale, and Johns Hopkins graduates. Before the twentieth century, the M.D. degree could be acquired without a bachelor's degree, since that degree stood only for education in the liberal arts. The medical schools gave their students the foundation courses in the biological sciences. Therefore, the curriculum of the early normal schools of physical education, manned by men and women trained in medicine, lacked the social sciences and emphasized biological sciences and medical gymnastics.

As far as the professional training of women physical education teachers in America is concerned, there was one school in Europe that interested them deeply— The Royal Central Institute of Gymnastics (RCIG) of Stockholm, Sweden, founded in 1814 by Ling, the fountain head of Swedish gymnastics. Authentic records of attendance of Americans at that school are difficult to come by.

However, we do know that Mathilda Kristina Wallin, a graduate of RCIG of 1885, was head of gymnastics at the Women's College of Baltimore (today's Goucher College) in the late 1880s, and that Alice Tripp Hall, M.D., an 1881 graduate of Wellesley College and 1886 graduate of Women's Medical College of Philadelphia, "visited" the school in the spring of 1889.[21] For many years the Baltimore College employed on its physical education staff only graduates of the Royal Central Institute or graduates of Madame Bergman Osterberg (an 1881 graduate of the Royal Institute) of the Physical Training College of Dartford Heath, England.

Kate Campbell Hurd, M.D., the first medical director of Bryn Mawr College, spent the winter of 1889–1890 "visiting" the Royal Central Institute and the spring of 1890 "observing" physical education work at Madame Osterberg's school near London.[22] In the spring of 1897 Senda Berenson of Smith College "observed" work at RCIG, and the following spring Anne Barr of the University of Nebraska was there briefly just before the school closed for the summer.[23] These schools taught a variety of systems, some favoring German gymnastics, some Swedish, some an offering of both, and some offering a combination of Dio Lewis exercises and their own systems, with Sargent's own creation of calisthenics and apparatus work gaining favor as the Sargent System as the years went by. The facts about these schools have been verified insofar as is possible from the official early records of the schools concerned. The most notable of them are listed in the order of their founding as follows:

1866—Normal School of NAGU
1881—Sargent Normal School of Physical Education
1886—Anderson School of Gymnastics
1887—Harvard Summer School of Physical Education
1887—YMCA Training School

1888—Chautauqua Summer School of Physical Education
1889—Boston Normal School of Gymnastics
1890—Savage Physical Development Institute
1890—Posse Normal School of Gymnastics

Normal School of the American Gymnastic Union.[24] The Civil War disrupted the plans of the German turners to establish a teacher training school in Rochester, New York, in 1861.

Following the 1848 political revolution in Germany, several hundred thousand Germans fled their native land and settled in the United States. Many of these were Jahn gymnasts and it was they who hoped to establish a normal school of gymnastics. The threat of war aroused deep sympathy for the Union cause and hundreds of these men volunteered for service, enough that plans for a school had to be abandoned for the time being. A group of these German-Americans made up a special bodyguard for President Lincoln in 1861 and later joined the Eighth Battalion of the Union Army.[25] With the war at an end, the school was finally opened in New York City in 1866, open only to members of the turnverein. After three years there, it moved to Chicago with George Brosius (1839–1920), one of the foremost leaders of the turner movement, as superintendent of the school. Compelled to close because of the great fire in Chicago, the school moved again to New York City in 1872, and then in 1875 it moved to Milwaukee where it remained throughout the rest of the nineteenth century except for a two-year interval (1889–1891) when it was located temporarily in Indianapolis.

During these years the course had been lengthened to require ten months of study, and it included the history and literature of physical education, anthropology, anatomy, physiology, hygiene, first aid, principles of education, the German and English language and literature, fencing, swimming, Jahn gymnastics, esthetic dancing, observation, and practice teaching. Graduates of this school taught in public schools throughout the country although most located in the Middle West. In 1878 the school graduated its first woman student, Miss Laura Gerlach, for whom there is a record that she was teaching in Milwaukee Schools in 1883 at a salary of $450 per year.

Sargent School of Physical Education.[26] Dr. Sargent, having become head of physical education at Harvard University, was so importuned by young women of the town of Cambridge and of Radcliffe College who desired some training in the art of teaching exercises, and by heads of schools who desired teachers trained to teach this type of exercises rather than the German system, that he took over an old carriage house, converted it into a gymnasium, and set up such a course in 1881. He offered the courses at first gratis with the stipulation that the students would actually go out to teach. At that time most people felt that if they knew a dumbbell drill, a few exercises with Indian clubs, and a list of chest-weight exercises they were really professionally trained in physical education. By 1891 he had thirty pupils in his private school, and the course had developed into a thirty-two-week session for a $100 fee. Then he extended the course to a two-year course, the attendance doubled, and the school took on the title Sargent Normal School for Physical Education. It was primarily a women's school.

Anderson Normal School of Gymnastics.[27] In 1886 Dr. William G. Anderson, then Physical Director at Adelphi Academy in Brooklyn, established a teacher-training school in physical education and named it the Brooklyn Normal School of Gymnastics. When he became Associate Director of the Yale University Gymnasium in 1892, the school was moved to New Haven and renamed the Anderson Normal School of Gymnastics. In 1896 E. Herman Arnold, M.D. (1865–1929), became the director. This was also a women's school.

Harvard Summer School of Physical Education.[28] While attending Chautauqua in 1879 (which had been established at Lake Chautauqua in New York in 1874 as a summer outing institution at which lectures were given for lay church workers), Sargent conceived the idea of offering summer courses in physical education to attract teachers during their long vacation periods. Four years later he offered the first such course in the United States in a five-week session at his then two-year-old Normal School in Cambridge. This venture developed into the Harvard Summer School of Physical Education when Sargent obtained permission from Harvard University in 1887 to offer a six-week summer course in teacher training, open to women as well as men. In his *Autobiography,* he relates that although Harvard was not too happy about opening classes to women and the granting of teacher's certificates, the authorities finally gave permission provided he would assume all financial responsibility for the project. So intense was the local feeling against Harvard's being a party to such a venture that Radcliffe College discouraged its students from attending the course and the *Boston Medical and Surgeon's Journal* opposed it and denounced Harvard for allowing such a course. In spite of the initial storm of criticism the summer school prospered and carried on for thirty-two years under Sargent's expert direction. The very first session was so successful financially, because of the unexpectedly large enrollment of fifty-five pupils, that he cleared $1500, and beginning with the second session, Harvard officials took it over, relieved Sargent of the burden of collecting the fees and paying the bills, and named him Director of the Harvard Summer School of Physical Education, with salary.

Among the pupils attending the first session were several from leading colleges: Delphine Hanna of Oberlin, Helen Putnam of Vassar, Caroline Ladd of Bryn Mawr, Anna Bridgeman of Rockford, and Booker T. Washington of Tuskegee Institute. Of the 55 pupils enrolled for this first session of 1887, 37 were women and 18 men. In 1890 it became a two-summer course with 204 women and 98 men in attendance. The next year it became a graded four-summer course. By 1898, 653 women and 329 men registered for the course. It was very popular and growing fast.[29]

YMCA International Training School.[30] The YMCA International Training School in Springfield, Massachusetts (called the School for Christian Workers until 1890), was founded in 1887, establishing from its beginnings a two-year course in professional training in physical education, with Dr. Luther Gulick as its director. He immediately inaugurated a summer course as a refresher for teachers already in the field. In 1891 he set up a graduate course in physical education, the first in America, but it was short-lived. From 1891 to 1895 he also conducted a correspondence School in Physical Education, another first, but short-lived. In 1888, Robert J. Roberts, who had just completed twelve years of highly successful work as the director of the gymnasium of the Boston YMCA, joined the teaching staff. In 1895 James Huff McCurdy, M.D. (1866–1940), Director of Physical Education, New York City YMCA, succeeded Gulick in the directorship of the physical training department and extended the course to three years.

In 1886 the YMCA opened the Western YMCA Secretarial Institute in Chicago and four years later added a summer course for the training of teachers of physical education under the auspices of the Springfield School—the first summer courses in this field offered west of New York State. Also in 1890 the Institute was incorporated as the YMCA Training School of Chicago, offering a two-year course. At the same time the YMCA established another training school in Nashville, Tennessee, offering training in physical education.

Chautauqua Summer School of Physical Education.[31] The Chautauqua Summer School of Physical Education of 1888, was the second school to be founded by W. Anderson of Adelphi Academy. In the summer of 1886 when Dr. Anderson was attending the popular Chautauqua Summer Courses at Chautauqua, New York, he was importuned by three young women to offer them some training to handle exercise classes with school pupils. He accepted and this proved so successful that he was urged to repeat this for the summer of 1887, leading to an arrangement with Chautauqua management for a course to be recognized in their list of courses offered. This was so successful for the next two summers that in 1890 a company was formed to finance the building of a gymnasium and to take over the business management of the summer school with Jay W. Seaver, M.D. (1855–1915), Director of Physical Education at Yale University, serving as president of the Chautauqua Physical Education Institute, which would offer the Summer School of Physical Education with Dr. Anderson as the principal of the school. By the following year, the course had developed into a two-summer offering leading to a certificate.

In 1892, Anderson left Adelphi Academy for the position of association director of the gymnasium at Yale under Dr. Seaver, and in 1895 he was given the title of Dean of the Chautauqua Summer School of Physical Education under Seaver's presidency. Throughout the 1890s the school enjoyed much popularity among teachers seeking refresher courses in a summer resort setting as well as among teachers seeking help so that they might handle gym classes along with their other work. The school offered work in German, Swedish, Delsarte, and "American" systems of gymnastics. Methods of teaching each system were offered.

Boston Normal School of Gymnastics.[32] Mrs. Mary Hemenway, the Boston philanthropist, had financed the first sewing and cooking classes in the Boston public schools and then she financed the introduction of Swedish gymnastics and the training of classroom teachers to handle the work. In 1889 she founded the Boston Normal School of Gymnastics, to assure a continuing supply of professionally trained gymnastics teachers. This school should not be confused with the Boston Normal School, which is an older school established to train teachers in the field of general education. Mrs. Hemenway installed her secretary, Amy Morris Homans (1848–1933) as the director of the school and Baron Nils Posse (1862–1895), a noted Swedish emigrant who had recently come to America, as head of gymnastics. He was followed the second year by Claës Enebuske, M.D. (1855–?), who in turn served in that capacity for several years. From the very beginning, this school was the stronghold of Swedish gymnastics in America. Wherever its early graduates went, Swedish gymnastics became the cornerstone of their programs. The school was essentially for women but in its early years it did graduate a few men, chief among them being William Skarstrom, M.D. (1869–1951), who was on the faculty of Columbia University and Wellesley College for many years, and Walter Truslow, M.D., who became a nationally known orthopedic surgeon.

Through the years there has been handed down the erroneous statement that Baron Posse was the first director of this school, no doubt derived from Fred E. Leonard's early published history of physical education of 1915, which does carry such a statement. This error is readily understood when one realizes that before World War I it was difficult to accept the thought that a mere women would be head of a school. The Baron's position as head of gymnastics was easily and readily interpreted in most peoples' minds as head of the school, and since Miss Homans had for many years been Mrs. Hemenway's private secretary, people thought of her as the secretary of the school. In fact, of all the early leading teacher-training schools in the physical education field of that day, BNSG is the only one that had a women as the director.

In 1891 the school graduated its first class of twelve from its two-year course. Two years later it graduated forty-three with thirty others receiving a one-year certificate. The starting salary of these graduates ranged from $1000 to $1800, considered excellent in those days.

From the beginning the school maintained a distinguished faculty, numbering in its ranks in its earliest days the Professor of Philosophy of Harvard, the Dean of Harvard Medical School, and the Professor of Biology of Massachusetts Institute of Technology. Continuously until the school merged with Wellesley College in 1909 there were Harvard and Massachusetts Institute of Technology professors and heads of departments on the staff on a part-time basis, and, even after the transfer of the school to Wellesley College near Boston, many of these teachers were retained as special lecturers.

In its second year the school increased its staff and expanded its curriculum to include general anatomy, applied anatomy and physiology, histology, hygiene, and supervised teaching in the public schools of Boston. In the third year it added anthropometry, emergencies, general psychology, pedagogy, and voice training. To augment the activity program it added dance. In its fifth year it added to the curriculum physics, chemistry, comparative anatomy, embryology, and sanitation, all taught by Massachusetts Institute of Technology professors.

Savage Physical Development Institute. Watson L. Savage, M.D. (1859–1931), teacher of physical education at Columbia University, established his institute in 1890. Eight years later he changed its name to the New York Normal School of Physical Education, and shortly after that it became known as the Savage School of Physical Education (acquiring the title officially in 1914). This school prepared many teachers for the New York City public schools.

Posse School of Gymnastics.[33] After serving one year as head of gymnastics at the Boston Normal School of Gymnastics, Baron Posse founded his own school in Boston. Before coming to America he had been declared the skating champion of the world. He was also an excellent horseman and gymnast. Born into the Swedish aristocracy, he had been a lieutenant in the Royal Army, and up to that time had been the youngest man to be honored by the King of Sweden with the Order of VASA. He gave up the advantages of his family connections and position to come to America to pioneer in the field of medical gymnastics.

As head of his own school, he leaned heavily in his teachings upon the medical aspects of gymnastics and the principles of health education advocated by the Royal Gymnastic Institute of Stockholm. When he died in 1895, at the age of thirty-three, his widow, an American women whom he had met in Boston, carried on the school until her retirement, after which it had a succession of directors until its demise in 1942.

Colleges and Universities.[34] The earliest claim of a teacher-training course in physical education offered in a college in America seems to be that of Wayne

University, where a course to prepare elementary school teachers to handle physical education was offered in 1881. However, this may be contradicted by the fact that this institution was at that time known as the Detroit Normal School, which may not then have been chartered as of collegiate rank. In this case it would appear as far as records are now known that Oberlin College was the first institution of collegiate rank in which courses were offered to prepare teachers to handle physical education in the schools. In 1886, Delphine Hanna at Oberlin College offered such a one-year course, the first in a private college. By 1892 ten women had earned the certificate of this course, a special award offered by the teacher, herself. Then this course was expanded into a two-year normal course, and the college recognized it by offering the certificates in its own name. By 1900, thirty-five women had earned this two-year certificate.

Also in 1892 the University of Indiana, in 1894 the University of Nebraska, in 1897 the University of California, and in 1899 the University of Wisconsin started short teacher-training courses leading to a physical education certificate. In 1898 an Oberlin two-year certificate student also received the bachelor's degree, but with specialization for the degree in fields other than physical education. However, it was an innovation for a student to earn a two-year physical education certificate and acquire the bachelor's degree at the same time.

The 1890s brought the first offerings of the collegiate world toward an academic degree based on specialization in the field of physical education. In 1891, George Wells Fitz established a Department of Anatomy, Physiology, and Physical Training within the Lawrence Scientific School of Harvard College.[35] The first academically prepared professional physical educator in the United States was James F. Jones, the first to graduate from the Harvard program, receiving the B.S. degree cum laude in 1893. He returned to Marietta College in Ohio, where he had been a student, now as instructor in physiology, hygiene, and director of the gymnasium. Three years later he procured a medical degree at the University of Cincinnati.

In 1892, Thomas D. Wood, M.D., (1865–1951), at Stanford University, instituted plans for a major in physical education leading to the B.S. degree, graduating its first student, Walter Wells Davis, in 1897 who four years later earned a Ph.D. degree at Yale.[36] He was director of physical education at Iowa College (Grinnell), and Lehigh University in Pennsylvania, and later was supervisor of physical education for the public Schools of Seattle, Washington, from 1916 to 1942. In 1899, Stanford graduated the first woman in the United States to earn a bachelor's degree with a major in physical education, Miss Stella Rose, who later returned to teach in the physical education department to women at Stanford.[37]

Whereas the earlier certificate short courses were aimed at preparing classroom teachers to handle physical activity classes during school hours and at recess, the new full college course leading to a bachelor's degree was designed to prepare graduates to go into schools, colleges, YMCA's, YWCA's, and like organizations to teach physical education full time.

While Robert Clark, M.D. (1862–1945), a former member of Dr. Gulick's staff at the Springfield Training School, was head of physical education at the University of Nebraska (1894–1897), succeeding Wilbur Bowen, he planned and procured official recognition for a major in physical education leading to a bachelor's degree. This was one of four professional courses then offered at Nebraska: law, teaching, medicine, and physical education. The last was put into effect in the fall of 1897. By then Clark had rejoined the staff of the Springfield School, and W. W. Hastings (1865?-1961), a Springfield graduate and holder of the Ph.D. degree from Haverford College, succeeded him in the position at Nebraska so that it was he who put the new major into action. A young woman, Alberta Spurck (1878–1954), graduated from this course in June of 1900. The official university records show that this young woman had completed 52 semester hours in specialization including 24 hours in chemistry, zoology, physiology, and hygiene, and 28 hours in special physical education courses.

The first three institutions to offer an academic degree with specialization in physical education were Harvard, a private men's college, Stanford, a private coeducational school, and Nebraska, a state university, which in June 1900 graduated its first such student just as the nineteenth century was coming to a close.

In 1903 Dr. Hanna made a survey of the private normal schools of physical education, and her published report named three colleges offering specialization leading to a degree. She listed the University of California as starting its course in 1898, the University of Nebraska, 1899 (1897, however, is the correct date), and Oberlin College, 1900.[38] (Checking in the 1950s the University of California registrar found no record of such a course in Berkeley before the close of the first decade of the twentieth century.)

Early Summer Courses. As noted earlier, the first summer work offered in teacher training in this field was that of Dr. Sargent in 1881, a five-week course in his newly established private school. In 1887 Dr. Gulick at the YMCA School and Dr. Sargent at Harvard started summer courses. In 1888 came the summer courses offered by Dr. Anderson at Chautauqua; in 1890 came the summer courses at the Chicago and Nashville branches of the YMCA School; and in 1895, the summer courses of the Normal School of the NAGU in Milwaukee were begun. In 1898 and for several succeeding summers, Clara Baer of Newcomb College sponsored summer courses in physical education at the Monteagle Assembly at Monteagle, Tennessee.[39] In 1899 the University of Wisconsin advertised in the *American Physical Education Review* a summer school in physical education to be open to both men and women. If the course materialized, it was the first such for a state university and was short-lived.

First Talk of Standardization of Schools. In the late 1890s it was suggested in *Mind and Body* (a magazine published by the turners) that a national placement office be established to help teachers of physical education. This suggestion Dr. Hartwell hailed as novel but he proposed instead that a commission made up of experts be set up to examine all professional training schools, especially their science courses, in order to insure conformity in fundamental knowledge and permit each school to teach beyond that whatever system of gymnastics it prefered. But at that time nothing came of either suggestion.

Nonschool Organizations

Several forces besides the schools were at work in the last half of the nineteenth century to bring physical education to all the people. The turners and the YMCA's, born in an earlier era, now materially increased their physical education activities. The Sokols and YWCA's now joined the other groups in offering activities to still more people. Private athletic clubs came into existence, bringing sports to an ever increasing circle of citizens. The earliest of these clubs were the Olympic Athletic Club of California, born in 1862, and the New York Athletic Club of 1868, with a building of its own erected in 1885.

North American Gymnastic Union.[40] The 150 turner societies with their 10,000 members of prewar days and their Normal School at Rochester, New York, had been disbanded while the men fought in the Union army. With the Civil War at an end the NAGU was revived, and by 1872 there were 187 societies functioning. Before the 1880s little was known about the work of the turnverein in America outside German–American circles. The membership of the societies and the participation in the turnfests were confined to those of German origin. The German language was used, to a great extent, in all the activities, and no effort was made to interest other Americans in the educational, social, or gymnastic work. Throughout their history the turnverein met with vigorous hostility in some communities, for the turners were abolitionists, free-soilers, and opponents of prohibition.

During the 1880s their membership grew to 36,000 in 277 societies. They now began agitation for physical education in the public schools and contributed moral and financial support, material, publications, and leadership to that end. In some communities they purchased apparatus and placed it in the school yards. Some served as teachers free of charge in order to convince reluctant school boards of the value of their work. Their normal college demanded that its graduates be able to give instruction in the English language, that they might be prepared to enter the schools.

From 1881 on, the turner societies held turnfests every four or five years with 1200 to 3400 participants in the competition. At the World's Fair in Chicago, 1893, they gave daily exhibitions of their work and distributed thousands of pamphlets. In 1894 the organization began publication of *Mind and Body*.

By 1890 the turners had over 30,000 members with 160 gymnasiums in use, reaching over 400,000 participants in their physical activities alone, at the very time when the average USA tax payer was complaining that gymnastics in the schools was but an idle luxury.

Sokols. Bohemians (later to become known as Czechoslovakians) as well as Germans came to the United States in large numbers in this era, and the gymnastic's enthusiasts among them organized Sokol clubs, similar to the German turnverein—democratic, patriotic organizations for the practice of voluntary discipline aimed at both moral and physical fitness. The first American Sokol was established in St. Louis, Missouri, in 1865. Never as numerous as the German immigrants, the Bohemians did not become so widely known although the first of them came to America with the earliest Dutch settlers, having fled to Holland to escape religious persecution. The late-comers of the nineteenth century settled mainly in the Middle West and there enthusiastically pursued their physical activities—gymnastics, folk dancing, and sharpshooting.

Young Men's Christian Association.[41] Shortly following the Civil War, the Young Men's Christian Association pushed its prewar plans to offer opportunities to its members for physical development and promotion of health. It immediately put in the first free public baths and the first vacation schools offering carpentry, singing, and nature study, to keep children occupied during vacation periods. That same year (1866) the president of the New York City YMCA proposed a four-fold program—physical, mental, social, and spiritual—which was adopted. Three years later the first YMCA buildings with gymnasiums were erected in New York City, San Francisco, and Washington D.C., with the Boston building and gymnasium coming in 1872. G. Stanley Hall, famous psychologist, then but twenty-three years old and always an ardent champion of physical education, was a member of the New York City YMCA when it opened its first gymnasium.

In 1885 the Brooklyn Central Branch YMCA put in a swimming pool-the first YMCA pool in the United States. Until the YMCA school in Springfield began training teachers for the YMCA gymnasiums, the YMCAs had to use circus performers, weight lifters, and professional athletes as part-time teachers. With the training work under way, an International Committee was established to supervise the physical education work in the YMCAs throughout the country, with Gulick serving as head of this supervisory work.

The 1890s brought historic events to the YMCA. In 1890 Gulick devised the YMCA emblem, the equilateral triangle known today the world over. In 1891 and 1895 the games of basketball and volleyball were developed in YMCAs, as previously discussed, and in 1896 the Athletic League of the YMCAs of North America was founded.

By 1900, the YMCA had 294 physical directors and 22 assistant directors for 507 gymnasiums with nearly 80,000 men and 20,000 boys registered in their classes.

Young Women's Christian Association.[42] The Young Women's Christian Association was established in the United States in this era, the first branch being founded in Boston in 1866 by the wife of Henry Durant, the founder of Wellesley

College. In 1882 the first association, which was established in Boston, set aside a nearby park for calisthenics classes and installed chest weights in the hallway of the building with a female member of the association leading in classwork in these activities. Two years later Boston erected a new building which was the first YWCA in the country to include a gymnasium as part of the facilities, and, in 1887, the first classes in calisthenics were offered using a combination of Dio Lewis and Delsarte work.

In 1886 a national association of YWCAs was organized at a conference at Lake Geneva in Wisconsin, and in 1891 the eleventh conference created the International Board of YWCAs to send general secretaries and physical education teachers to YWCAs all over the world.

The physical education program generally in the 1890s consisted of Indian-club swinging, dumbbell drills, wand drills, "esthetic marching," and basketball. As early as 1895 the latter had become a very popular activity in the YWCA.

MOVEMENTS RELATED TO PHYSICAL EDUCATION

Although the great mass of the population still worked long hours six days per week and had but little leisure, a concern was growing in this era for the welfare of children in their out-of-school periods. Out of this concern developed two important movements—the recreation and the camping movements.

Recreation Movement[43]

As happened in so many movements in America which were for the enrichment of life, it was Boston, with its sand gardens, that started the ball rolling in the development of the playground and recreation movement. Brookline near Boston was the first town to vote public funds for a playground. This was in 1872. Chicago, in 1876, opened the first public park in America (the present Washington Park) and offered recreational facilities, although without supervision. In 1888 Boston designated seven schoolyards as playgrounds and the following year added eleven more to these, all open to children of all ages. Also, in 1888, New York City opened its school buildings in the evenings for recreational use by the citizens, and, in 1889, Boston established several so-called outdoor gymnasiums for older boys and men to spend leisure hours brought on by the shortened workday. A few years later sections were set aside in the parks for older girls and women.

Citizens of New York City organized The Outdoor Recreation League and secured from the municipal government an appropriation of about $30,000 with which twenty school yards were operated as play centers. The city then began the purchase and equipping of tracts of land at a very great cost. Seward Park alone cost $2.5 million. Jacob A. Riis (1849-1914), the leader of the Anti-Slum Movement to get children off the city streets and Secretary of the Committee on Small Parks, did more than any other person to secure adequate space for play in New York City. He was identified with the playground movement throughout his life.

The playground system of Chicago began with a vacant-lot play center managed by Hull House in 1893. Six years later New York City opened several school yard playgrounds modelled after that of Hull House, and the establishment of this type of facility quickly spread to all other parts of the country. Ten cities set up playgrounds between 1890 and 1900. In nearly all the cities the work was begun by philanthropic and humanitarian organizations; in some cases the city gave financial support, and in some it gave no encouragement whatever. The playground movement was definitely identified with the antislum and the social service movements. And it greatly affected the play life of the children of the cities.

Camping Movement[44]

Although camping was organized to some extent in isolated situations in earlier years, as for the boys at the Round Hill School in the 1820s and at the Gunnery School for Boys in Washington, Connecticut, in 1861, the camping movement did not get a real start until after the Civil War. The first camp on record was established by a Wilkes Barre, Pennsylvania, physician at North Mountain in Luzerne County in 1875; the first church camp, by a West Hartford, Connecticut, minister on Gardner's Island in 1880; and the first YMCA camp (Camp Dudley), by the Newburg, New York, YMCA on Grange Lake, the only one of these early camps still in existence.

The first private camp—a boy's camp on Burnt Island on Asquan Lake near Holderness, New Hampshire—was established in 1881 for the specific purpose of meeting educational needs of young boys of well-to-do families who were wont to idle away their time at summer resorts with their parents. This first camp started with a program built largely around physical activities, thus setting the pattern conformed to by the camps that followed and establishing for the camping movement objectives closely akin to those of physical education itself.

Family camping became popular, particularly in the Middle West in the last decade of the nineteenth century, but it usually meant a camp site along some river or creek within horse-and-wagon reach of home.

The National Park Service

During the administration of President Grant, the government created the first National Park-Yellowstone-in 1872. Yosemite, General Grant, and Sequoia parks were created in California in 1890, and Mt. Rainier Park in Washington in 1899. This marked the beginning of the vast national vacation and recreation areas of the United States.

PROFESSIONAL LITERATURE

Literature in the field of physical education began to increase materially in this era. For the first time not only books but periodicals and reports of surveys became available from the presses of the United States and from local authors. No longer were workers in the field of physical education dependent almost solely on foreign publications. Publishing companies were now flourishing in America and many of them were interested in manuscripts on physical education and sports.

Books

Several books achieved prominence in the field of physical education in this period. Foremost among them were: William Blaikie, *How to Get Strong and How to Stay So* (1879), which influenced several people who later became prominent leaders to take up the study of physical education and which, highly popular in both Europe and the United States, ran in many editions up to 1902; DuBois–Reymond, *Physiology of Exercise* (1885), a translation of a Berlin edition published in *Popular Science Monthly;* Carl Betz, *Free Gymnastics* (1887); Robert J. Roberts, *Classified Gymnasium Exercises* (1889); Nils Posse, *The Special Kinesiology of Educational Gymnastics* (1890); Claës J. Enebuske, *Progressive Gymnastic Day's Orders According to the Principles of the Ling System* (1890), which sold over 5000 copies; *Basketball Rules,* first edition mimeographed (1894); Jay W. Seaver, *Anthropometry and Physical Examinations* (1896); W. G. Anderson, *Methods of Teaching Gymnastics,* (1898); and Senda Berenson, *Basket Ball Rules for Girls,* first edition mimeographed (1899).

Five years before the translation of *Physiology of Exercise* reached America, Hartwell wrote his doctoral thesis at Johns Hopkins University on this subject. This is the earliest record of an American writing on this topic.

Periodicals

As in the period preceding the Civil War there were several periodicals that frequently contained articles on physical education activities, but none were in any sense periodicals of the profession. But in the 1880s there appeared the *Reports of the Proceedings* of the annual conventions of the American Association for the Advancement of Physical Education covering ten years from 1885 to 1895. Then in the 1890s came an awakening, and four professional magazines were born: *Physical Education* (March 1892–July 1896), in four volumes with Gulick as editor (preceding this he started a YMCA magazine called *The Triangle* in June 1891, which carried much of interest to physical education); *Posse Gymnastic Journal,* which started with the issue of December 1892 and ran for ten years after Posse's death in 1895 still carrying articles supposedly written by him; *Mind and Body,* a monthly magazine published by the North American Gymnastic Union, starting with the March 1894 issue (destined to last for forty years); and *The American Physical Education Review*, the official organ of the AAAPE starting in the fall of 1896 with Hartwell as Chairman of the Magazine (issued quarterly from 1896 through 1907, when it became a monthly periodical, and surviving today as the *Journal of Physical Education, Recreation, and Dance*).[45]

As to the first magazine, there is some confusion. Careful scrutiny of the four volumes of *Physical Education* gives no clue as to what organization, if any, backed this magazine. There is not even the mention of the editor's name, but Gulick's biographer states that he edited a magazine named *Physical Education*. It may have been the private venture of Gulick alone or of him and a group of his friends. The subscription price was $1 a year, and it was published by the Triangle Publishing Company of Springfield, Massachusetts. It listed an Advisory Committee made up of the profession's most distinguished leaders of that day. Hartwell was in charge of the Current Topics Department, and G. Stanley Hall, America's leading psychologist, was a frequent contributor.

Apparently the sponsorship of this magazine puzzled the people of that day for the editorial in the April 1895 issue says:

> *Our Purpose.* There are some of our readers who have received the impression that this magazine was, or desired to give the impression that it was the official organ of the physical education department of the International Committee of the YMCA. We wish to state clearly that *Physical Education* is not the official organ of any body whatsoever, neither the International Committee Association Training School at Springfield, Massachusetts, nor American Association for Advancement of Physical Education. It stands merely for a subject—Physical Training—in its relation to the development of all-round character for manhood and womanhood.

Organizations and Leaders of Physical Education of the Latter Nineteenth Century

Although general educators before the Civil War had formed organizations to pool their interests and ideas and to promote educational standards and objectives, there was not a sufficient number of physical educators nor a profession of physical education sufficiently recognized to sustain such organizations in the physical education field until in the 1880s. By then a group of leaders had been developed, and professional organizations arose out of their coming together for mutual aid.

ORGANIZATIONS OF THE PROFESSION

The few professional organizations that existed before the turn of the century are discussed here in the order of their founding.

The American Association for the Advancement of Physical Education (AAAPE)[1]

The national group known today as the American Alliance for Health, Physical Education, Recreation and Dance was founded November 17, 1885, as the American Association of Physical Education. The organization meeting was called by Dr. W. G. Anderson, then a young teacher at Adelphi College in Brooklyn, who earlier approached various influential persons interested in the advancement of physical education and found them enthusiastic about the idea of a meeting. It was a gathering of such distinguished persons as the Reverent Henry Ward Beecher, William

Blaikie, the New York City attorney who had written a popular book, *How to Get Strong,* Reverend T. De Witt Talmadge (1832–1902), the popular lecturer and writer, Charles Pratt (1830–1891), prosperous merchant of Brooklyn who two years later founded Pratt Institute, and leading educators, physicians, and newspaper men of New York City and Brooklyn, besides the best known physical educators of the day. At its organization meeting forty-nine members joined. At the second meeting (the first convention) in 1886, enough others joined to bring the membership to 114, and the official title of the organization became officially adopted as the American Association for the Advancement of Physical Education.

In 1892 the National Education Association, desiring to sponsor a meeting dealing with physical education, then a much talked of topic in educational circles, organized a Physical Education Conference to be held in July, 1893, in connection with the World's Fair in Chicago and invited Edward M. Hartwell, who was at the time of the planning President of the AAAPE, to serve as Chairman of the Conference. The AAAPE thereupon gave up its own plans for a convention in 1893, and newly elected president Dudley A. Sargent and his group threw their influence to the NEA meeting. This marked the first official recognition of physical education as a growing profession by the NEA. At the ninth annual convention held at Yale University in 1894, professional members were listed from California, Canada, Illinois, Iowa, Louisiana, Missouri, Oregon, and Wisconsin, as well as from all the Eastern States. In 1895 at its tenth annual convention held at Teachers College, Columbia University, in New York City it voted to reorganize along the lines of the North American Turnerbund, which functioned through a federation of local groups. At the same time it named Boston as the national headquarters and for the first time accepted representatives of a district, the New England Society, as members of the national council.

The destiny of the organization was in most capable hands. Five men served as president in the first fifteen years to the close of the nineteenth century-first, Dr. Edward Hitchcock, of Amherst College, then William Blaikie, New York City attorney (the only president in the history of the organization whose vocation was not in the field of health and physical education), and Drs. Dudley A. Sargent of Harvard University, Edward M. Hartwell of Johns Hopkins University and the Boston public schools, and Jay W. Seaver of Yale University. Dr. Anderson, the founder of the organization, served as the first Secretary–Treasurer. Photographs of all presidents from 1885 through 1960 are shown in the *Journal of Health and Physical Education* of April 1960. Also, all from 1885 through 1983 are listed with their years of service in the appendix.

The founders of AAAPE were men and women who had studied Greek, Latin, and philosophy, besides medicine. Their speeches reflect their intimate acquaintance with the best literature. They brought the theories and ideas of the great thinkers of the world to bear upon problems of the late nineteenth century. Never in the entire eighty and more years of history of this organization have there been leaders of broader intellectual and cultural background than these founders. The first presidents were close friends of United States presidents, Supreme Court judges, college presidents, and leading educators and ministers of the day. Through their great breadth of interests, Hitchcock, Hartwell, Sargent, Mosher and Gulick, in particular, were nationally known outside the profession. They were members of boards of trustees of several colleges and recognized leaders in many well-known movements.

The problems that claimed their greatest professional attention in the early years were testing and measuring, promotion of the profession, gymnastic systems, and the place of physical education in education. Anthropometric measurements, military training, and whether John L. Sullivan was the "typical" man were the topics most discussed. One delegate reported that 1300 school boys of Boston were drilling with eight-pound muskets and were rapidly developing spinal curvature. Brosius of the NAGU School in Milwaukee told the group how 500 boys could be drilled in a gymnasium at one time by one teacher. A questionnaire survey of physical education in preparatory schools was reported that showed that about 80 percent of the schools surveyed supplied exercise rooms, but a little less than one-third had gymnastics instructors. Although men predominated in the membership, women were cordially accepted into the association and from the first held elective office. At the first meeting Miss Helen Putham of Vassar was elected one of four vice presidents.

First District and State Organizations within AAPE.[2] In 1895 professional workers in New England were called together at Clark University, and at that meeting the Physical Education Society of New England was organized as a combined several-state section of AAAPE. (At this organization meeting, G. Stanley Hall, President of Clark University, addressed the group, and Sargent gave an illustrated lecture.) This marked the first effort to organize by districts. In that same year the leaders of Ohio organized the first State Association of AAAPE, followed by one in Connecticut in 1896, which at first lasted for only two years and was not to be revived until twenty years later. A year later W. P. Bowen, then of the Normal School at Ypsilanti, Michigan, and Dr. Eliza Mosher (1846–1928) of the University of Michigan called a first meeting of physical education teachers of the state to organize a Physical Culture Section of the State Teachers Association. This section died after three years, but it marks a first attempt to develop a physical education section within a state teachers association.

NEA Department of Physical Training

In 1894, the National Education Association set up a Department of Physical Education within its own organization, which functioned primarily to put on programs about physical education at its conventions. Through the years, individual leaders in AAAPE gave leadership to the NEA Department, which however was entirely without the jurisdiction of AAAPE. Dr. Edward Hartwell of the Boston public schools was this group's most notable leader in the 1890s.

Society of College Gymnasium Directors[3]

In October 1897, Anderson and Hartwell called all male college directors of physical education who were not using the German or Swedish systems exclusively in their work to come together at New York University to talk over where America stood in regard to gymnastics. Twenty-three directors responded to the invitation and they founded the Society of College Gymnasium Directors, which through the years has wielded strong influence in physical education in the United States. This organization, for many years known as the College Physical Education Association for Men, was founded to "promote the physical welfare of the students in the institutions of higher learning, to make surveys and conduct research and to promote a professional spirit among its members." Hitchcock, who had served as the first president of AAAPE, now took over as the first president of this new organization. (An interesting photograph of this group assembled in convention at Yale, December 1899, is shown in the February 1944 issue of the *Journal of Health and Physical Education.*)

Physical Training Conference of 1889[4]

In this period there occurred the first conference on physical education to be held outside the framework of an organized group. Known as The Conference of 1889 on Physical Training it was destined to be the forerunner of many equally notable conferences to follow in the twentieth century. (This first conference, fully reported and long out of print, is now available on microcard.) The conference, financed by Mrs. Mary Hemenway of Boston, was called by the Secretary of the Massachusetts State Board of Education, the Superintendent of Schools of Boston, the Presidents of Massachusetts Institute of Technology, Boston University, and Colby College, the members of the Boston School Commission, and an imposing array of leading citizens of Boston. The United States Commissioner of Education presided at the conference.

Among the thirty-four speakers at the four sessions were sixteen medical doctors, one general of the army of the United States, one earl from England, two barons (including Baron Pierre de Coubertin of France, who was touring England and America to study the sports activities, from which observations he soon thereafter developed his idea of establishing the modern Olympics), one doctor of laws and one a doctor of philosophy. Of these thirty-four speakers, five were women. The discussions and demonstrations centered around the German and Swedish systems of gymnastics. Two thousand people attended the conference, which was considered to be the most notable educational event of the era. Its success was a great boon to the advancement of physical education.

LEADERS OF PHYSICAL EDUCATION

The story of the rise of the profession of physical education is the story of its leaders who shaped the profession and advanced its cause. The list of those who materially advanced it following the Civil War is surprisingly long, considering the paucity of opportunity to prepare to work within this field and the lack of incentive in the meagerness of facilities and in the ignorance of the many educators and citizens regarding the merits of this branch of education. Most of the foremost leaders of their day were educated in the field of medicine and picked up their knowledge of physical education on their own, building on their science studies. In this period, for the first time, several women leaders came into prominence. Considering the difficulties during these years for a woman to procure an education, it is surprising how many fine and capable women dedicated their lives to this branch of education. Of the several women born before 1860 who markedly advanced the profession during this era, two, like several of the men, were not trained in this field; but, unlike the men, they did not actually teach physical education although they used their talents, influence, and administration ability for the advancement of the profession. Amy Morris Homans, through her organizational and administrative talents and flair for guidance of young women, served the profession well in setting high teacher-training standards; and Eliza Mosher, a famous physician of that day, aligned herself closely with physical education. Both Miss Homans and Dr. Mosher are listed in early editions of *Who's Who in America,* an unusual achievement for a woman in those years. Delphine Hanna had both the medical degree and some training in the field of physical education, also a rare combination for a women in that era.

For this era only those leaders born before 1860 are discussed in this chapter, with the exception of W. G. Anderson an ''early bloomer'' who was born in 1860, but belongs with this group. All people discussed in the biographies that follow who were still living in 1931 were in the first group to receive the Honor Award of the American Physical Education Association (as the national professional organization was then called), a ceremony as a new and long-deferred recognition to the still living pioneers of the profession.

Edward Hitchcock, M.D. (1828–1911)[5]

Edward Hitchcock was born in Amherst, Massachusetts, where his father Edward Hitchcock, Sr., was a professor at Amherst College and was later to become its third president. The younger Edward graduated from Amherst in 1849, and after two years of teaching chemistry and natural science at a seminary nearby, he went

Figure 1. Edward Hitchcock, M.D. (1828–1911). (Courtesy of AAHPERD.)

to Harvard University, acquiring his medical degree in 1853. He then resumed his teaching until 1860, when he went to London to study comparative anatomy under the famous Sir Richard Owen, then Curator of the British Museum. In the following year, he was called to Amherst as Professor of Hygiene and Physical Education, to head up the newly organized department, in which he served for fifty years until his death in 1911 at the age of 83. Although he was still nominally the head of the department, a member of his staff, Paul Phillips (1865–1941) carried on for him for the last few years and after his death succeeded to his position. But Dr. Hitchcock was there to advise and counsel. In his long directorship at Amherst, Hitchcock blazed such an excellent trail that his department set a fine example for all that were to follow. His work in establishing the first collegiate department of physical education in America has been discussed earlier in Chapter 4 under the heading Amherst College Department. He was greatly beloved by the students and alumni, who affectionately called him "old Doc" even when he was in his middle years. He was a genius at organizing and at seeing in the physical-exercise program a means to an end which transcended any system of gymnastics or calisthenics. He had no training in any form of gymnastics so he used the Dio Lewis ystem in the early days of his directorship as something tangible to start with, but he soon settled into a pattern of informal offerings of exercise and apparatus work which called for every student to be on the move all the class period—no standing around awaiting turns, no watching others perform, everyone exercising at something alone or in squads. He immediately embarked upon research into physical measurements, thus starting the first anthropometric studies in America, which he carried on throughout his entire professional career.

In 1865 he started to demand bathing facilities. As college physician he made a first request in 1875 for a college infirmary, following the deaths on campus of two students from typhoid pneumonia, and finally got his wish in 1877. In that same year he started a campaign to get the college outdoor toilets heated night and day in the winter. Sanitation was a constant problem in the years before it was possible to have running water in either homes or common-use buildings, and Edward Hitchcock tackled the problem, considering anything that had to do with the health condition of students as a part of his assignment.

As college physician, he treated students and called on those who were ill in their dormitories and rooming houses. As health counsellor, he gave students much of his time in conferences. Dr. Raycroft of Princeton University in later years spoke of Dr. Hitchcock as the country's first college psychiatrist.[6] He was the organizing chairman of both the American Association for the Advancement of Physical Education and the Society of College Gymnasium Directors and served as the first president of both. He took the lead in the research work of both associations and was a frequent speaker at their meetings. His genius lay in his insistence upon a sound scientific basis for all his work and upon accurate and truthful observation. In this he left the profession a valuable heritage. He is an Honorary Fellow in Memoriam of the American Academy of Physical Education.

On the fortieth anniversary of the founding of the Department of Hygiene and Physical Education at Amherst College, a complimentary dinner was given in Dr. Hitchcock's honor in New York City, on April 20, 1901. In the collection of congratulatory letters from co-workers presented to him at that time were letters from the great and near great of the profession as well as from the U.S. Commissioner of Education and from presidents of several colleges and universities such as Clark University, Harvard University, and the Massachusetts Institute of Technology. Following his death, through the generosity of an Amherst graduate, a Hitchcock Memorial Room was established in one of the buildings on the Amherst campus to house his professional memorabilia collection. The plaque to the room is headed:

In Memory of

Edward Hitchcock

1828-1911

and following a lengthy inscription ends: "pioneer leader in physical education in our country and affectionately known as 'Old Doc' to generations of students."

Twenty-one years after his death, a certificate was sent to Amherst College which said:

THE AMERICAN STUDENT HEALTH ASSOCIATION
AWARDS THIS
CERTIFICATE OF HIGH MERIT
TO
AMHERST COLLEGE
FOR INITIATING IN 1861 UNDER THE DIRECTION OF
EDWARD HITCHCOCK, M.D.
A COMPREHENSIVE PROGRAM PROVIDING FOR MEDICAL
EXAMINATIONS—PHYSICAL EXERCISE—CLINICAL CARE
FOR THE
PROTECTION AND PROMOTION OF THE MENTAL EFFICIENCY
AND PHYSICAL WELL BEING OF THE STUDENTS
UNIQUE   IN   CONCEPTION—EFFICIENT   IN   ADMINISTRATION—
SCIENTIFIC
FOR MANY YEARS IT STOOD ALONE AND MEITED THE TRIBUTE
OF PRESIDENT ELIOT:
"IT IS TO AMHERST COLLEGE THAT THE COLLEGES OF THE COUNTRY
ARE INDEBTED FOR A DEMONSTRATION OF THE PROPER METHOD OF
ORGANIZING A DEPARTMENT OF PHYSICAL TRAINING"

1932

Eliza M. Mosher, M.D. (1846–1928)

Eliza Maria Mosher was born in 1846 in Cayuga County, New York, and in her early schooling was educated in Friends Academy of Union Springs, New York.[7] After taking the medical degree in 1875 at the University of Michigan, she spent a year in study in London and Paris medical clinics and practiced medicine until Vassar College appointed her resident physician in 1883. There she had the additional responsibility of organizing their department of physical education for women. She introduced physical examinations of women students—a first in America. She also ushered in the divided skirt, a forerunner of the bloomer of the 1890s, thus

Figure 2. Eliza Mosher, M.D. (1840 -1928). (Photograph used by permission of Vassar College.)

breaking down barriers to acceptance of a costume that would permit women to participate freely in physical activities. After three years at Vassar and ten more of private practice she went to the University of Michigan (1896) as its first Dean of Women and first Director of Physical Education for Women, where she organized a physical education program for the newly erected Barbour Gymnasium for Women. Immediately, the University granted her the rank of professor, the first time that any college or university conferred this rank on a woman physical educator. (The University of Chicago had four years earlier—1892—been the first to so recognize its Dean of Women.) After three years there, she returned to private practice, where she gained international recognition. For twenty years she was editor of *The Medi-*

cal Woman's Journal. Through her deep interest in posture training, she became a recognized authority on the subject and with Jessie Bancroft was a co-founder of the Posture League of America.

She was frequently called upon to lecture on hygiene and posture at various colleges and at the Chautauqua Summer School of Physical Education. She was a prolific writer for medical journals from the 1880s on, authoring a long series of articles, particularly in the 1910s and 1920s. In 1912 she authored a book *Health and Happiness—A Message to Girls.*

She was one of the founders of the International Medical Association and served as honorary president of the Medical Woman's National Association. When the medical profession decided in the early 1920s to publish a series of biographies of American Medical Women, hers was the first to be published and was available at the International Medical Association meeting in Geneva, Switzerland, September 4–7, 1922.

There is no wonder that she came to be known nationally as the Dean of American Medical Women. She died October 16, 1928 in Brooklyn at age 88. New York City and Brooklyn papers announced her death in headlines.

Amy Morris Homans (1848–1933)[8]

Although not trained in the specialized field of physical education, Amy Morris Homans was one of the profession's great leaders. Born in Vassalboro, Maine, Nov. 15, 1848 she was educated at Vassalboro Academy by private tutors, as were most young girls of that day who received serious schooling. At the age of nineteen she became preceptress of a girl's seminary in Maine, and two years later went to North Carolina to become principal of two schools, one a normal school. After ten years of teaching and administrative work she became secretary to Mrs. August Hemenway of Boston. The two of them organized, and Miss Homans directed, the Boston Normal School of Household Arts which the State of Massachusetts took over later as the Department of Domestic Science of Framingham State Normal School-the first such school department in the country.

In 1889 Miss Homans conducted and Mrs. Hemenway financed the Conference on Physical Training of 1889 (discussed earlier in this chapter) which was a great topic of conversation in professional circles for many years to follow. Even today, almost one hundred years later, it is still frequently called to mind by workers in the field and spoken of as the famous conference of 1889.

Also in 1889 Mrs. Hemenway founded the Boston Normal School of Gymnastics and installed her secretary as director of the school. Under Miss Homan's skillful direction and farseeing educational philosophy the school quickly achieved leadership in the training of women. Under her management the school took the lead in acquiring collegiate status when, in 1909, it became the Department of Hygiene and Physical Education of Wellesley College.

From the year of the founding of BNSG, Miss Homans took an active interest

Figure 3. Amy Morris Homans (1848–1933). (Photograph of portrait by DeCamp. Used by permission of Wellesley College.)

in the American Association for the Advancement of Physical Education and served with it for many years in a variety of capacities. In 1915 she founded the Eastern Society of Directors of Physical Education for College Woman which, joined later by similar groups in other parts of the country, developed in 1924 into the National Association of Physical Education for College Women.

In the years 1909 to 1917, Miss Homans brought the old Boston Normal

School of Gymnastics into collegiate status and finally into graduate status, the first of the early private schools of professional training to achieve the latter.

Upon her retirement in 1919 at the age of seventy she was granted the title of Emeritus Professor, the first woman in the profession to achieve this distinction. Shortly after her retirement the alumnae of the Department of Hygiene and Physical Education had a portrait of her painted as a gift to the department. It now hangs in her memory in Mary Hemenway Hall at Wellesley. In 1967 the National Association for Physical Education of College Women established the Annual Amy Morris Homans Lecture in her memory. Today this lecture given annually at the AAHPERD convention, is sponsored by the National Association of Physical Education in Higher Education.

The young women who graduated under her tutelage were sought for physical education staffs by presidents of colleges and universities as well as by boards of directors of the YWCA and by superintendents of schools. For many years into the twentieth century, the directories of physical education for women in colleges and universities all across the country seemed to be a listing of graduates of her school.

As an outstanding leader of the post–Civil War era still living in 1926, Miss Homans was elected into charter membership of the American Academy of Physical Education, the second of four woman so honored. In 1930 she received from Russell Sage College the honorary degree Pd.D. (Doctor of Pedagogy), the first woman of the profession to receive an honorary doctorate. Until the time of her death at the age of eighty-five her counsel was continuously sought because of her rare wisdom. A woman of marked culture and refinement, she insisted upon a liberal arts education coupled with professional training. A gentlewoman in every sense of the word, she set a pattern for all women working in the profession that brooked no compromise with femininity. A woman of high courage, she was unflinching in her maintenance of high standards, and she set for her students a professional code that also brooked no compromise. A woman of dynamic personality, of unusual administrative ability, and of superior standards of thoroughness of work, she was inexorable in her insistence that students make the most of their educational advantages. All these qualities marked her as an unusual leader who demanded near perfection for her pupils yet claimed their deep respect, sincere admiration, and devoted homage.

Dudley A. Sargent, M.D. (1849–1924)[9]

Sargent was born in Belfast, Maine. He was but seven years old when his father died, and he was sent to Hingham, Massachusetts, to live with relatives. In the three years there, he had his first experience with gymnastics and liked it. Back in Belfast he entered a private school well equipped with gymnastics apparatus, and there he found a book describing dumbbells and Indian clubs and how to use them. He made himself a pair of each and at the age of fourteen began in earnest his own physical

Figure 4. Dudley A. Sargent, M.D. (1849–1924). (Courtesy of AAHPERD.)

development program, as he pursued his studies; at the same time he helped support himself chopping wood, lumbering, and farming, up at 6 A.M. in the winter and at 4 A.M. in the summer. At the age of fifteen he was studying Cutter's *Anatomy, Physiology and Hygiene* which he considered the most enthralling of all his school textbooks. As he grew older he took up carpentry and plumbing work to support himself, while he kept up his own physical development with gymnastic exercises he invented for himself.

When he saw a gymnastics exhibition at Bowdoin College, it interested him so much that with his chums he formed a gymnastics club, using his uncle's barn for their gymnasium; he became so proficient that he joined a circus doing an act of some of his self-taught stunts.

At the age of twenty he was appointed Director of the Gymnasium at Bowdoin

College, where for a salary of $5 per week for the first year, and $500 per year for the second year, he did, besides his teaching, all the janitor work for the gymnasium, setting and lighting the fires, trimming lamps, carrying water, and sweeping out.

Seeing that the boys who worked on farms and in mills and lumber yards had superior physiques, he set out to devise a program of exercises and apparatus that would give the other boys similar development. Using the muscular movements of everyday labor and sports activities he originated a system of gymnastics that was indeed "natural" gymnastics, foreshadowing that movement of the twentieth century. After teaching two years he registered in the college to study for his own degree and at this time persuaded the college to make gymnastics a requirement for five days a week, with the class work to be graded as other school subjects were. The following year, when he had to drop gymnastics for military drill in the spring term, he went to Yale to introduce his program there and thus started its physical education program. This pattern of three months of each year off for a term at Yale persisted until he procured his bachelor's degree in 1875. Armed with his degree, he asked for a full-time position and salary of $1200 at Bowdoin.

Bowdoin's refusal of this request for a full-time position was an important turning point in Sargent's career, for he resigned his part-time position there and continued his work at Yale. This provided the opportunity to enter Yale Medical School. During this period, aided by his physiological studies in particular, his determination to enter upon a career in teaching physical education was strengthened and reaffirmed.

In two and a half years Sargent had completed his medical studies and also the work for the M.A. degree, and since Yale offered him only part-time employment he left and opened his own private Hygienic Institute and School of Physical Culture in New York City, working daily from 8:00 A.M. to 10:00 P.M. There he became acquainted with William Blaikie, a Harvard graduate, who was instrumental in his being appointed Director of the Gymnasium and Assistant Professor of Physical Training at Harvard University. Sargent developed a scientific program based on the individual needs of the students. This led to the invention of his own anthropometric and other apparatus, which by 1889 was in use in 350 institutions. Wishing his inventions to become educational tools free to all, he did not patent them, and when a manufacturer took out patents on them he caused Sargent serious trouble, which led him to regret that he had not at least "policed" his own inventions.

In the summer of 1879, before he went to Harvard, he was invited to lecture and teach gymnastics at the then one-year-old Chautauqua Summer School for Church Laymen, becoming the first of many physical educators who through the years were to teach there. In 1881 he founded his private school and in 1887 the Harvard Summer School of Physical Education, both teacher-training projects, turning out hundreds of teachers through the years, most of whom were heads of departments in colleges, high schools, and private schools in the United States and in Canada, England, France, China, and Japan. After World War I, he established a camp connected with the Sargent School near Peterborough, New Hampshire, and there he died July 21, 1924. He is an Honorary Fellow in Memoriam of the American Academy of Physical Education.

He was a self-made man—a man of learning and culture—a man of great dignity, yet he was frequently caught up in serious controversies, particularly in his efforts to "clean up" football and to bring intercollegiate athletics under faculty control. He more than any other person guided intercollegiate athletics into proper controls and regulations. He took an active part in professional organizations and was one of the early presidents of the AAAPE and also of the College Physical Education Association. Always a student of philosophy and the sciences, he based his work on sound scientific foundations. Willing to speak out publicly on behalf of physical education, and an excellent speaker, he advanced the profession materially through speeches and writings. At the famous conference of 1889, he gave public voice to his professional credo when he said:

> One-half the struggle for physical training has been won when [a student] can be induced to take a genuine interest in his bodily condition-to want to remedy his defects, and to pride himself on the purity of his skin, the firmness of his muscles, and the uprightness of his figure.

> It is more to the credit of a university to have one hundred men who can do a creditable performance in running, rowing, ball-playing, etc., than to have one man who can break a record, or a team that can always win the championship. [10]

At this same conference, when asked what he thought were America's needs in a physical education program, he replied, "the strength-giving qualities of the German system, the active and energetic quality of English sports, the grace and suppleness of French calisthenics, the poise and precision of Swedish free movements-all of these systematized and adapted to our peculiar needs."

In 1894 Bowdoin College conferred upon Dr. Sargent the honorary degree of Doctor of Science.

Today the National Association of Physical Education in Higher Education offers the annual Dudley A. Sargent Lecture in his memory. The Sargent College of Allied Professions of Boston University carries on the work he started one hundred years ago in his Sargent School of Physical Education of 1881, which has new ideas and new challenges worthy of this man who, like Hitchcock, Homans, Hartwell, and Hanna, also had far-reaching dreams.

Edward Mussey Hartwell, M.D. (1850–1922)[11]

Edward M. Hartwell was born at Exeter, New Hampshire, the son of a brilliant lawyer and the grandson of a surgeon. He earned several degrees—the A.B. and A.M. from Amherst, the Ph.D. from Johns Hopkins, in 1881, and the M.D. from

Figure 5. Edward Mussey Hartwell, M.D. (1850–1922). (Courtesy of AAHPERD.)

Miami Medical College of Cincinnati in 1882. He also studied at the Royal Gymnastic Institute of Stockholm and in Vienna and Bonn. In 1898 Amherst College conferred upon him the honorary degree, Doctor of Laws—the first such degree to be conferred upon a physical educator in America. As a pupil of Hitchcock, he became deeply interested in research, and he advanced the profession through both historical and biological research.

For seven years, 1883 to 1890, he was Associate Professor of Physical Training and Director of the Gymnasium at Johns Hopkins University. In the spring of 1883 and summer of 1884 he traveled from Maine to Tennessee visiting gymnasiums for a survey of physical education for the United States Bureau of Education, producing a manuscript, *Physical Education in American Colleges and Universities,* which has through the years remained a masterpiece of historical research. In 1886 he did a treatise on the physiology of exercise, which was published in two issues of the *Boston Medical and Surgical Journal*[12], a first for the profession on this subject. Following this, in 1890, he made a third trip to Europe visiting playgrounds and school gymnasiums (in his various trips he investigated physical education work in Russia, Scandinavia, Germany, and Great Britain), and the following year he became the first Director of Physical Education of the Public Schools of Boston, a position he held until 1898, building a program which served as a model for all public schools for many years. In 1897 he became Secretary of the Department of Municipal Statistics of Boston serving in that capacity until his retirement in 1919.

He served the American Association for the Advancement of Physical Education as its president for five years and was a regular contributor of reports and papers, all scholarly and scientific. He gave dignity to the profession through his scholarly approach to all of his work. He is an Honorary Fellow in Memoriam in the American Academy of Physical Education.

Delphine Hanna, M.D. (1854–1941)[13]

Born in Markeson, Wisconsin, Delphine Hanna graduated from Rockport State Normal School in 1874 and for ten years taught in the grade schools of Kansas and New York. Becoming concerned about the lack of physical stamina of most pupils and teachers, she enrolled in the Dio Lewis Summer School in 1884 hoping to learn how to remedy this condition. Disillusioned by the lack of scientific basis of Lewis's physical education theories, she transferred to the Sargent School, graduating in June 1885. That summer she worked with Boston orthopedic physicians to study the treatment of spinal curvature, and in the evenings she studied the Delsarte system at the Currie School of Expression. Later she incorporated the best of this system into her posture training work.

In the fall of 1885 she went to Oberlin College as Instructor in Physical Culture with the promise of living expenses but no salary and $300 to spend on equipment. She started classes in calisthenics, correctives, and ''fancy steps,'' but the president had to be persuaded that there would be no harm in the ''fancy steps'' before she could proceed with them. She also offered classes to male students, and inspired several to take up physical education work. Two of these students, Thomas D. Wood and Luther H. Gulick, later became distinguished leaders in the profession.

She continued her studies at Harvard Summer School of Physical Education and in 1890 procured the medical degree from the University of Michigan and after that the A.B. degree from Cornell University and A.M. from Oberlin. In 1893 she studied Swedish gymnastics at the Posse School, following that with orthopedic study in Zurich, Switzerland. Then she began giving physical examinations to her pupils at Oberlin, which led to her anthropometric research and her devising of charts for women which were widely used by other colleges and in teacher-training courses.

During a year's leave of absence in the year of 1895–1896 she introduced

Figure 6. Delphine Hanna, M.D. (1854–1941). (Photograph used by permission of Oberlin College.)

girls' basketball to Colorado Springs, Colorado, which probably marked its first arrival in the Mountain States area. In 1902 she graduated her first pupil from the major in physical education leading to the bachelor's degree, which she had planned and put through at Oberlin in the closing years of the nineteenth century. This was a decade ahead of Miss Homans's tie-up with Wellesley College leading to an academic degree for her students. In 1920 Dr. Hanna retired as Professor Emeritus and became the first woman working in the field of physical education to be recognized with a Carnegie pension.

In her thirty-five years at Oberlin she held the titles of Instructor in Physical Culture, Director of Physical Training, Women's Department, and, from 1903 on, Professor of Physical Education and Director of the Department of Physical Education for Women. She was the second woman in the field of physical education to be granted the rank of full professor by a private college, following Dr. Eliza Mosher's similar recognition by the University of Michigan in 1896.

In 1925 she was honored by election into the University of Michigan Hall of Fame. In 1931 she was among the first to receive the Honor Award of the American Physical Education Association (in her case in *absentia*). On April 16, 1941, she died at the age of eight-six years and four months.

Dr. Hanna was a trail-blazer for American women in the field of physical education. She was the first woman trained in the field to set up work for women founded on sound scientific procedures, to devise anthropometric charts for American women, to establish teacher's courses in a college leading to a certificate, and to set up a major in physical education leading to a bachelor's degree. (The majors in physical education at Harvard and Stanford universities and at the University of Nebraska were all founded by men.) Before her retirement Dr. Hanna dreamed of a swimming pool, an athletic field for women, and a modern gymnasium for women at Oberlin. All of these dreams came true before her death, carried to reality by one of her own graduates who followed her in her position, Gertrude Evelyn Moulton, M.D. (1880–1964). Dr. Hanna's influence has lived on through the many fine young women who majored under her direction and went out to head up departments of physical education for girls and women in lower schools, YWCA's, and colleges and universities all over the United States as well as in many foreign lands.

Other Leaders[14]

No account of the leaders in physical education of the latter nineteenth century would be complete without mention of several other men and women who helped blaze the trails though the professional wilderness.

George Brosius, M.D. (1839–1920). Known as "the Father Jahn of America," George Brosius, a teacher for fifty years, was the greatest leader in America of German gymnastics of his era. As the head of the Normal School of the NAGU for twenty-one years, he trained large numbers of teachers who were employed in public schools all over the country. Particularly was their influence felt in the Middle West.

Robert Jeffries Roberts, M.D. (1849–1920). Self-taught in private gymnasiums and libraries in Boston, Robert J. Roberts, as head of physical education at the Boston YMCA, developed a program for hygienic bodybuilding which came to be known throughout the country as the "Roberts Platform" and became the cornerstone of all YMCA physical programs. When Gulick organized the department at the YMCA Training School in Springfield, he took Roberts there with him to teach the activity classes. Shortly, however, the Boston YMCA persuaded Roberts to return there where he continued for another thirty years until his death at the age of seventy-one. He was recognized at the foremost YMCA physical director of his day.[15]

William G. Anderson, M.D. (1860–1947)[16]. Born in St. Joseph, Michigan, September 9, 1860, William G. Anderson attended lower schools in Quincy, Illinois, and Boston. At the age of fourteen, he became acquainted with circus men who wintered in Quincy, Illinois, and they taught him work on the horizontal bars and the springboard. Three years later, when the family was living in Boston, he attended the Roxbury Latin School and there acquired still more skills in gymnastics at the YMCA under Robert J. Roberts. The next two years he attended the University of Wisconsin and continued gymnastics training at the outdoor gymnasium maintained there for male students. Sometime during these years before 1880, he traveled in the summer with a circus in Illinois doing gymnastic stunts to help finance his schooling, (as he personally related to the author in the 1930s).

After two years in Wisconsin, he taught school in Clayton, Illinois, and then became head of the physical department of the YMCA in Cleveland, Ohio. While there two years, he studied in his free time and earned the M.D. degree at the Cleveland Medical College (1883). After that he taught in Columbus and Toledo, and in 1885 was called to be Director of the Gymnasium at Adelphi Academy in Brooklyn. There he founded the Brooklyn School of Physical Education and the Chautauqua Summer School of Physical Education, which he served for eighteen years. In 1892 he became Associate Director of the gymnasium at Yale, and in 1903 Director, a position he held until he retired in 1932, having served Yale a total of forty years and acquiring the academic rank of professor in 1905. Concurrently with his early work at Yale and the Chautauqua Summer School of Physical Education, he served as president of the Anderson Normal School of Physical Education, the former Brooklyn school. While at Yale, by 1909, he earned the A.B., A.M., and M.S. degrees and in 1916 the doctor's degree in public health at Harvard.

He was the founder of the American Association for the Advancement of Physical Education and served as its first secretary from 1885 to 1888, taking on the position of treasurer from 1888 to 1892. He also was one of the founders of the College Gymnasium Director's Society and served as one of its early presidents. He was one of the earliest writers in the profession, producing five books and numerous articles in periodicals, mostly on medical research. He invented the ergograph and several other pieces of equipment for Yale's department of experimental psychology.

The American Association for Health, Physical Education and Recreation has created the Anderson Award in his memory and conferred upon him the Gulick Award. Traveling widely in Europe, he studied research methods there and became a Fellow of the London Society of Sciences and Arts. He was a member of the American Academy of Physical Education. He died July 7, 1947.

PHYSICAL EDUCATION IN THE EARLY TWENTIETH CENTURY (1900–1930)

CHAPTER 8

Dance, Gymnastics, and Sports of the Early Twentieth Century

ACTIVITIES OF THE PHYSICAL EDUCATION PROGRAM

With the new century came a determined effort to bring athletics and dance into the physical education curriculum as an acknowledged part of education. This presented a challenge to the gymnastics devotees to protect their previously unquestioned monopoly of the program. The battle of the gymnastics systems gave way to a new battle of gymnastics versus athletics and dance. Let us look at the status of these activities as the twentieth century got underway.

Dance

Dance gradually became solidly entrenched as a part of the physical education program, particularly in the women's departments in the colleges. By the second decade, outdoor dance festivals, May fetes, and May pageants built around the dance became popular, but following the first world war these gradually gave way to dance interludes (programs of unrelated dances) and these in turn gave way to dance concerts, usually held indoors.

The "dance exercises" of the 1850s and 1860s gave way to the "fancy steps" of the 1870s and 1880s. They in turn gave way to the esthetic dancing of the 1890s, which gave way to such other forms of artistic expression as modified ballet and natural dancing, and then "modern dance." Social dance, too, had its vagaries, and various forms have come and gone with the fickleness of the other forms of dance.

The more important of these will be discussed in relation to their impact on physical education of this era.

Clog and Tap Dance. A form of dance that became popular in schools in this era was clog, or tap dance as the school version of it came to be known. Clogging was a popular stage form in the late nineteenth century; in the 1910s children, on their own, had picked it up and had been clogging in play activities, and physical education teachers introduced this activity into the schools.

Esthetic Dance. Melvin Ballou Gilbert, who had first introduced a modified ballet, "esthetic dancing," into the schools of America through his teaching at the Harvard Summer School of Physical Education, widened his contacts through other teacher-training schools and continued his work until his death in 1910. His students took this form of dancing to the schools with them, but by the close of World War I "Gilbert dancing" as it was frequently called had passed out of the educational picture.

Folk Dance. Although the girls at Smith College since 1897, and at the University of Nebraska since 1898, had been folk dancing, it was Luther Gulick whose un-yielding determination and foresight brought folk dancing into the public schools of America. In 1905 he persuaded Elizabeth Burchenal (1874–1959) to leave her position at Teachers College, Columbia University, to join his staff in New York City to organize school athletics and folk dancing for the girls. She immediately went to foreign groups in the city to gather their native dances; but this approach proved inadequate, and she then went to their original sources abroad.

Early in this period the Playground and Recreation Association of America organized a National Folk Dance Committee to promote folk dancing in the play-grounds of America, and in 1916 the American Folk Dance Society was organized, Miss Burchenal serving as chairwoman of both groups. The folk festivals which she staged with thousands of children in Central Park each spring for many years received national as well as local attention, and folk dance for school children became a recognized part of the school's physical education program. Also Miss Burchenal taught folk dance for many years at the Harvard Summer School, passing on her knowledge to teachers who gathered there from all over the country.

The teaching of folk dance has increased through the years until it has become entrenched in the physical education program whereas other forms of dance have come and gone. Folk dance was the one stable form of dance of this era—stable because it was rooted in the real culture of the people.

Natural Dance. As esthetic dance was coming "full circle" of the period of its popularity, a new form of dance was developing, referred to by some with the term *natural dancing,* by others with *interpretive dancing,* and by still others with *interpretative dancing.* It developed from the earlier work of Isadora Duncan (1874–1927), America's first woman dancer of note, who achieved worldwide acclaim. She made her debut at Daly's Theater in New York City at the age of seventeen. Five years later she started a revival of the study of the ancient Greek dance. Although she developed a dance form from the choric dance of the classic Greek theater, she was not interested in reviving Greek dance as such, merely using the Greek form for the expression of emotion. She did, however, adopt the classic form of dress and custom of dancing in bare feet. She tried to bring the dance back to the people and tried to get people to dance for their own pleasure of self-expression.

At Columbia University under Gertrude Colby (1880–1960), there developed a modification of Miss Duncan's work for use in the schools which by the late 1910s and the early 1920s had completely replaced Gilbert's esthetic dance. This new form of dance was characterized by costumes of flowing draperies and bare feet and by its divorce from all ballet forms of techniques substituting much running, skipping, and leaping.

Margaret N. H'Doubler (1889–1982) developed at the University of Wisconsin a form of dance based, no doubt in its beginnings, on this natural dance form. But it was peculiarly her own concept. To her pupils and followers it was merely "the dance" although in her book *A Manual of Dancing* (1925) she herself labeled it "interpretative dancing." She broke with former techniques and developed fundamentals of dancing as basic teaching forms. Her work won quick acclaim as her pupils presented it throughout the country. By 1926 she had organized the first major in the field of the dance to be offered by any college or university in the United States. She also founded at the University of Wisconsin in 1926 a collegiate dance organization, Orchesis, which shortly acquired national status.

Modern Dance. Following World War I esthetic, interpretive, and natural dance gradually gave way to a new form, which developed from a combination of home and foreign influences. In the United States Ted Shawn (1891–1972) and his wife, Ruth St. Denis (1877–1968), established the Denishawn School of Dance in 1915, and as they toured the world with their pupils from 1922 to 1933 they evolved a form of dance that, merging with dance brought to America in 1930 by Mary Wigman (1886–1973), developed into what for want of a better name to differentiate it from the earlier forms became known as modern dance.

Mary Wigman, a leading dance teacher of Germany, was a pupil of Rudolph von Labam (1879–1958), a famous European dance teacher, who was an exponent of "absolute" dance to the extent of discarding all musical accompaniment. Later Miss Wigman accepted the use of percussion instruments and primitive flutes and still later allowed the return of the piano to the dance studio, provided the music was composed for the dance—not the dance for the music. This dance offers no set forms. It requires merely that the movements of the dance express something. Fundamental techniques are concerned not with form as in the ballet, but with putting the body under the control of the dancer.

American students of Miss Wigman and others brought this style of dance to a high stage of development in the United States, modifying the European to suit America's own interpretation. Notably among them, several of whom had been pupils of the Denishawn School, were Martha Graham (1893–   ), Hanya Holm (1899–   ), Charles Weidman (1901–1975), and Doris Humphrey (1895–1958).

As Margaret H'Doubler's form of dance[1] gradually blended into the modern dance form, she and Martha Hill (1900–   ), both of whom worked in the field of education, the former at the University of Wisconsin and the latter at Bennington College and Columbia University, offered majors in the dance for the preparation of teachers.[2] The major at Wisconsin is still functioning, but at Bennington it lasted only from 1934 to 1942. Gradually other schools developed specialization in the dance through summer courses and finally through regular college majors.

By the close of this era, the old forms of dance as taught in the schools had completely vanished, giving way to modern dance.

Social Dance. Although ballroom forms of the dance were still taboo in most schools in the opening years of the new century, young people as well as adults engaged in the activity outside the school in increasing numbers as many churches eased their earlier prohibitions against it. As a craze for new forms of ballroom dance occurred just preceding World War I, interest in the standard ballroom forms, the two-step and the waltz, died out. The popular turkey trot led to an epidemic of other animal-named steps such as the bunny bug, the grizzly bear, the camel walk, and the fox trot. Shortly the fashionable ballroom dance leaders of that day, Irene (1893–1969) and Vernon Castle (1886–1918), brought order out of the chaos as their Castle walk, later known as the one-step, proved so popular that it became the cornerstone of all ballroom dancing and has persisted ever since. The Castles referred to their new ballroom dancing by the term *modern dancing*,[3] which they proclaimed in the title of their book of 1916 describing their new dances. The term was in use for over a decade before the disciples of an altogether different form of dance popularized it some years later, to which form the term still applies.

Square Dance. Following World War I, after several years of eclipse, square dancing was revived. In widely scattered areas of the South and Middle West, it had never died out where the elders at their "old settlers reunions" still danced the dances of pioneer days and handed them down to their children. As late as the early 1900s, in many communities where there still remained religious objections to the waltz and two-step, this was the only form of social dance known to the young people. But to the rest of the country, square dancing had become but memories of the past until the early 1920s when Henry Ford (1863–1947), the industrialist, financed a revival that grew with the years until it had taken a firm grip on much of the country.

Whereas Henry Ford's efforts of the 1920s and 1930s were directed toward a revival of the dignified New England form of the dance, Lloyd Shaw (1890–   ), a school superintendent of Colorado Springs, and many others of the South and West brought back the cowboy and southern mountain forms which were in common use in frontier days. Along with this revival came renewed interest in the old-time dances, the polka, schottische, mazurka, and Varsovienne.

Gymnastics

As the twentieth century opened, gymnastics was the backbone of the physical education program. Sports were beginning to be approved and desired but in most places were only a sideline—not a part of the formal program. A Health-through-Exercise Movement began after the slump in interest in gymnastics that followed the Delsarte popularity of the past era. By the 1900s many business and professional men had a growing awareness of a personal need for exercise. Without sufficient trained leadership available a host of advertising physical culturists arose to meet this demand. Announcements in the popular magazines of the period from 1899 to 1917 illustrate the point. At the same time women developed an interest in what Gulick so aptly spoke of in 1907 as "society gymnastics." This was a reaction to the Delsarte system and became very popular because of its renewed promise of Catharine Beecher's earlier dream of teaching women how to sit and stand correctly, how to ascend and descend stairs efficiently, and how to perform daily activities effectively. In the latter part of this era some schools still using gymnastics took up forms of exercises, that held the interest of women students, with hoops, balls, and ropes, which were a mixture of ideas from Finland, Denmark, and England.

The National YMCA, by 1907, had developed a gymnastic program distinctly its own to meet its interpretation of the needs of American boys and men not reached by the schools. Their program was built around light gymnastics followed by a run, bath, and rub-down. They used very little heavy gymnastics in this program and gradually worked in exercises aimed toward athletic skills.

Up to 1915, 95 percent of the colleges and universities included gymnastics in the physical education program.

Attacks on Gymnastics. The controversy of the 1890s and the early 1900s as to which system of gymnastics, German or Swedish, was better for America had by 1900 developed into a controversy as to whether either should be used. Gulick dealt gymnastics a setback when he compared the gymnastic-trained man with the athlete. The former he described as a man of overdeveloped muscles, great shoulders and chest, weak legs, and heavy carriage; the latter as erect, graceful, and fleet with splendid endurance.[4] These statements made a deep impression, for Gulick was popular with both the professional and lay public. In 1910 Wood, of Columbia University and formerly at Stanford, advocated a program of exercises built around natural activities, sports, and games, which started a movement for what came to be called "natural gymnastics." A decade later G. Stanley Hall, noted psychologist and friend of physical education, in his book *Adolescence* had said:

> On the whole, while modern gymnastics have done more for the trunk, shoulders, and arms than for the legs, it is now too selfish and ego-centric, deficient on the side of psychic impulsion, but little subordinated to ethical or intellectual development. . . . Its need is radical revision and coordination of various cults and theories in the light of the latest psycho-physiological science.[5]

But Sargent of Harvard, then near the end of a long and distinguished career in physical education, cautioned in an address at the 1920 National Physical Education Convention:

> To condemn a thing simply because it is old or to recommend it simply because it is new, is not the best way to advance our cause. Read into physical education everything you can of the slightest value but don't read out of it the most fundamental thing of all— that is all-round *muscular exercise*.[6]

With the general acceptance in the 1920s of the educational philosophy that the schools should educate the child for adjustment to life in general, many educators, including some physical educators, charged that gymnastics was too subjective to meet the needs of education. Exponents of physical fitness persisted in maintaining some gymnastics in the program, but the activity held a firmer place in girls' programs than in boys' programs, no doubt because of boys' more intense interest in sports. The forms of gymnastics in use in this era are discussed in the material that follows. (The effect of the Progressive Education Movement on gymnastics is discussed later.)

German System. The turners were still the most successful agents in promoting German gymnastics in the early 1900s, making their appeal chiefly to the people of German origins. Other Americans did not stay with them long, perhaps because practice to become skillful requires patience, thoroughness, hard work, and continued effort. Americans of English origin wanted games in place of gymnastics in the physical education program. By 1909 the turners who were practicing German gymnastics numbered 40,000, but this marked the popularity peak, and from then on the numbers participating decreased continuously. Mills College was the first women's college to adopt German gymnastics (1902); Elmira College soon followed; but this system never achieved the popularity among American college women of the Swedish and Danish forms.

Swedish System. Since the Swedish system of gymnastics carried with it the theories of medical and corrective gymnastics, it increased considerably in importance, largely as a result of its tendency to be concerned with individual needs. It was taught in practically all college women's departments until Danish gymnastics came in the 1920s to challenge its hold. It was also used largely in the public schools except in the strongholds of German stock. The chief exponent of Swedish gymnastics of this era was Dr. William Skarstrom (1869–1951) who was born in Stockholm, Sweden, and came to America as a young man. After graduation from the Boston Normal School of Gymnastics and subsequently procuring the M.D. degree at Harvard University, he modified the system to meet America's needs as he saw them. He reached large groups of teachers in training through his work at Columbia University and Wellesley College.

Natural Gymnastics. A new term, *natural gymnastics,* arose in the first two decades of the new century from an attempt to formulate a system of gymnastic exercises for class use built on the fundamental skills of occupational, athletic, and dance forms of movements. Wood originated and fostered the movement, and later Dr. Jesse F. Williams (1886–1966) of Columbia University, Clark W. Hetherington then of New York University (who as a student had worked with Dr. Wood at Stanford University), and Rosalind E. Cassidy (1895–1980) of Mills College popularized it through their writings and teaching.[7] This form of gymnastics was a return to the theories of Locke and Rousseau of the seventeenth and eighteenth centuries, which stressed recognition of individual differences and sought to measure a child's progress in terms of his or her own growth. It was also a return to GutsMuths and Jahn whose programs of play, sports, and outings had apparently been forgotten by the overly ardent advocates of German gymnastic exercises and apparatus work. And it was a return to Hitchcock and Sargent of the previous era who before Wood had advocated the use of exercises adapted to the needs of the individual.

This new form of gymnastics proposed by Word, when properly devised, consisted of movements aimed at the acquisition of not only physical strength and endurance but also of physical skills that would be useful in play and sports activities and in the ordinary tasks of life. The movements of the exercises therefore had definite aims to be atttained and were not to be mere ends in themselves. There was to be no uniformity required of the pupils. Instead of responding to the teacher's word of command, the pupils were to follow the age-old natural desire of children, to chase each other, to leap over ditches, to vault fences, climb trees, swing on tree branches, and throw and catch objects.

Danish Fundamental Gymnastics. The Danish system came to the United States in the 1920s sponsored chiefly by Americans who had studied under Niels Bukh in his school in Ollerup, Denmark. This system retained some of the formalism of the Ling Swedish system, but it substituted rhythmic action for sustained positions and precision. It offered greater mobility and strength than the Swedish system, having eight divisions to its "day's order" (legs, arms, neck, lateral, abdomen, dorsal, marching, and vaulting), omitting the old Swedish span bendings, balance, and breathing exercises. It has largely replaced the old German and Swedish forms.

Designed for the Folk Arts Schools of rural areas of Denmark, it stresses flexibility to relieve the muscle-bound condition found in the Danish youth. In the late 1920s Helen McKinstry (1878–1949), then Head of the Central School of Physical Education and later President of Russell Sage College, was the representative in America of Niels Bukh. She promoted several summer sessions for American teachers who went to Ollerup to take instruction from Bukh. These teachers brought back this activity to school and college programs. Although it is a strenuous form of exercise it made a greater appeal in the United States to women than to men. It enjoyed great popularity in women's departments in colleges during the 1920s and 1930s.[8]

Corrective or Individual Gymnastics. Interest in medical gymnastics brought to this country by the Swedish experts of the 1880s and 1890s broadened into a highly specialized program of exercises, stemming from the Swedish system, which could be readily adapted to the school programs for correction of postural and other kinds of defects. As schools employed trained personnel for this work, special classes developed in the school programs for the benefit of pupils needing this special attention. For this, as in much of physical education, the colleges led with the development, and then adoption by the lower schools followed. A survey made by the United States Office of Education revealed that by 1931, out of 460 schools investigated 50 percent were offering this work. A shortage of teachers trained in this specialized activity, however, was a factor in its lack of support, and there was also a lack of understanding of its values by parents and general educators.

Sports

Wherever sports were given a recognized place in the departmental offerings for boys and men, the department was usually spoken of as one of physical education *and* athletics. Even now this distinction holds in many schools, although women have never accepted this dual terminology. It was 1910 before sports were generally accepted by school authorities as a legitimate part of the school program although some physical educators recognized their value in the education program and had been quietly including them in their class-hour activities for some time previous to this date. As part of the school curriculum, sports developed more rapidly in the colleges than in the lower schools.

New sports activities that came into the program in this era were hiking and other such informal activities usually supported by outing clubs which had their birth at Dartmouth College in 1910, shuffleboard introduced in Florida in 1913, and speedball created in 1921 by Elmer D. Mitchell (1889–   ) of the University of Michigan. Judging by sales of sports equipment during this period, the ten fastest growing sports were, in order: softball, badminton, basketball, squash, football, table tennis, lawn tennis, handball, paddle tennis, and horseshoe pitching.

In this era came the first radio broadcasts of running accounts of important games, which caused much discussion ''pro and con.'' Time proved that the extent to which the broadcasts hurt attendance was not enough to discontinue baseball broadcasts.

Baseball. At the opening of the century, professional teams began to overshadow the amateurs and claim sectional loyalties that kept the populace in a frenzy of excitement when big league pennants were being won. In 1903 the National and the American baseball leagues met for the first time in what they called the World Series games. As an outgrowth of these games, a year later the two leagues adopted joint rules. In the first decade of the century, before safety measures were put into effect, baseball suffered many casualties. In 1908 alone forty-two players died from injuries received on the diamond, and in 1909, thirty died.

Basketball. After the turn of the century the game of basketball entered into a period of rapid growth throughout the country. Whereas in many sections of the country, notably in Middle West and on the West Coast, girls had taken to the game first, boys and men now took it up in rapidly increasing numbers. In 1906 the open basket net was introduced into the game so the ball no longer had to be retrieved from the basket. In 1908, NCAA took over the control of college basketball rules for men. In 1915, NCAA and AAU joined forces to form a joint Basketball Rules Committee. By the close of the era, it was played all over the United States and in many foreign countries as well. Although a few professional basketball groups were first formed in 1898, it was not until after world War I that the professional game became popular as a spectator sport. The famous Harlem Globetrotters—an all-black team—was organized in 1927.

Basketball for Women. The Women's Basket Ball Rules Committee established in 1899, put out its first printed official guide in 1901. Entitled *Line Basket Ball or Basket Ball for Women* it was published as Volume 12 of the Athletic Library Series put out by the American Sports Publishing Company. It sold for ten cents a copy and carried the name of Senda Berenson as editor. This first official guide carried articles by Theodore Hough, a well-known physiologist of the Massachusetts Institute of Technology, on the physiological effects of basketball; Luther Gulick, on the psychological effects; and Senda Berenson on the significance of the game for girls.

The 1901 rules called for five to ten players on a team. The second issue of the rules was published in 1905–1906 by A. S. Barnes and Company, the start of many years of cooperation between this publishing firm and the women's committee, and in this issue the name *Line Basket Ball* was dropped. Miss Berenson remained editor of the rules until 1917. By this time Elizabeth Burchenal, then of Columbia University, had joined the committee to begin several years of work with this group. The second edition carried many photographs of girls' teams, among them teams at the University of Minnesota, a high school in Nome, Alaska, a YWCA in Missouri, a turnverein group in Leadville, Colorado, and a business club group in Denver, showing the wide-spread and diverse groups that had taken up the game.

Bowling. In some parts of the country, bowling suffered by its close association with pool in pool halls, becoming "off limits" for women and children. When a YMCA became established in a community, it usually paved the way for this sport by offering facilities under its own supervision or by taking over public alleys on certain days and evenings and supervising them. Gradually this sport took on respectability and its popularity grew. In 1927, the American Bowling Congress was organized to promote the game.

Cricket. Although cricket had all but died out in the East, it was played by the women at Wellesley College throughout the first decade of the new century.[9] At the same time it had spread to San Francisco, and in the early 1920s Sir C. Aubrey Smith, famous British movie actor of that period, introduced the game to the Los Angeles area where it has flourished ever since, UCLA taking up the game in 1933.[10]

Field Hockey. Although there is record that field hockey was played in America as early as 1897 (by men at the Springfield YMCA Training School), it was apparently a short-lived effort, for never have American men taken to this sport. It did come as a sport for women, however, when an English woman, Constance Applebee (1874–1981) came to the United States in the summer of 1901 to attend the Harvard Summer School of Physical Education and demonstrated the game as played by her English sisters. Immediately Vassar College, followed by other leading women's colleges, adopted the sport and from them it spread rapidly to all parts of the country. It was many years, however, before high school girls played the game except in the large Eastern cities.

Football. With the coming of a new century, football began taking on importance as a sport for high school boys and college men. In the college world it gradually grew into big business, still remaining a rough game. In the 1905 season there were nineteen deaths and two hundred serious injuries on the gridiron. In the 1909 season fourteen players were killed before November. In 1908 the California colleges abolished football, substituting rugby, and reported a marked drop in injuries to athletes. President Roosevelt's outspoken criticism of the roughness of the game led the 1906 Rules Committee to eliminate hurdling and mass formations, such as the flying wedge, and to initiate and legalize the forward pass, though it was 1913 before the forward pass was generally used.[11]

A modification of the game, touch football, now became popular in boy's and men's intramural programs.

With improved know-how and equipment for outdoor lighting, night football, like night baseball, took on importance in this era, with the first night football games coming in 1928. The coming of night games brought greatly increased gate receipts to high schools and small colleges in particular. Perhaps the most spectacular pageantry of all night games of that time occurred at Haskell Indian Institute in Lawrence, Kansas, where as the night game was about to begin, all lights went off and a spot light picked up an Indian chief in full war regalia silhouetted against the night sky from his pedestal on top of the high entrance arch. From the darkness of the stands below came the spine-tingling Indian war cry of the Haskell Indian students. Then the flood lights were turned on the gridiron, and the contesting teams dashed onto the field.

Golf. Interest in golf was now countrywide. Even in small towns golf courses were constructed, at first all privately owned. In the early 1900s, the United States became a formidable rival of Great Britain in international matches. An American women's golf team captured the English women's championship tournament in Scotland in 1905. In the early years, due to the cost of the links, the game was confined largely to the members of private clubs. When national, state, and municipal authorities began to promote recreation and play, this movement resulted in securing the necessary land for golf courses, and placing the game at the disposal of the general public.

By 1910 there were twenty-four public golf courses in the United States and by 1930 there were 400 municipal courses and 5856 private courses, 2414 of which were eighteen-hole courses. Manufacturing and handling golf equipment and golf course architecture and building had become big business in the United States. Almost every state had a golf association, which held annual state tournaments.

Softball. In 1907 playground ball was developed in the Chicago South Park playgrounds. In 1923 rules for this game were standardized by the National Recreation Association, and by 1930 the game had evolved into the present game of softball.

Swimming. Syracuse in 1900, Kansas City in 1901, and Pittsburgh in 1903 joined the ranks of cities with municipal swimming pools. Until 1904, however, only a few offered instruction in swimming. In 1903 Chicago added to its older pools the new McKinley Natatorium, then the largest in America—50 by 300 feet.

The first bacteriological studies of swimming pool water were made in 1909. These brought about the early organization of the American Association of Hygiene and Baths in 1912, which established standards for pools (1915). The first indoor pool located above basement level (sixth floor) was at the 23rd Street branch of the New York City YMCA. It was in this pool that the first Red Cross life-saving courses were given in 1910 and where the first tests were given in 1914.[12]

Tennis. With the coming of the new century, Californians in large numbers took up the game. There, play was possible the year round. By 1912 the Californians had taken the game away from the ''Four Hundred'' back East, where the game had been considered exclusively for the elite.[13]

Track and Field. Track and field activities came into renewed popularity after World War I. In the early 1920s difficulties developed between the National Collegiate Athletic Association and the Amateur Athletic Union over the selection of the United States track and field athletes for the Olympic games. This brought about the establishment of the National Amateur Athletic Federation which forced better representation of college organizations and of the Army and Navy.

The first national NCAA track and field championship competition was held in 1921. After that many famous relays, such as the Drake, Kansas, Penn, and West Coast relays, were introduced. From 1922 on, indoor meets became popular.

Volleyball. The United States Volleyball Association was formed in 1928. Before World War I the game was played almost exclusively in the YMCA's and YWCA's, but, after its introduction into the recreation programs of the armed services by the YMCA physical directors during the world war, it spread rapidly in both school and nonschool groups.

The game was not accepted by girls and women as eagerly as by men, perhaps because it was looked upon at first as a game for men only, spreading over the country from the YMCA's to Army camps and then taken by the GIs back to their home towns. It was well into the 1920s before college women took up the game.

Women's Sports. Women in coeducational colleges now found doors opening to sports participation with the coming of basketball. For the average high school girl, doors opened considerably later, probably because the few trained teachers went to college positions. Public schools were slow in awakening to the need of trained teachers for this work. As the women of the coeducational colleges were catching up with their sisters of the women's colleges, the latter were forging ahead with new sports. In 1901 Wellesley College started lacrosse, and Vassar, field hockey. In 1907 Smith played the first women's volleyball, and Bryn Mawr, cricket, water polo, and soccer. After World War I, in the 1920s, swimming for women took on new dimensions in colleges when water pageants and water ballets were introduced, which ultimately led to synchronized swimming.

Other Sports. The American Bowling Congress held its first championship competition in 1901. Badminton, a sport popular in Canada, did not mature in the United States until in the 1930s, when the sixty-five badminton clubs then in existence organized the American Badminton Association. Practically all the playing of this period was confined to the large Eastern cities and Detroit, Chicago, and Los Angeles. Douglas Fairbanks, Sr. (1883–1939), famous moving picture star, popularized the game in California.

The National Ice Hockey League was organized in 1917. (The Canadians, who created the game, had been playing since 1860 and had established their league in 1890.)

After World War I skiing became a popular sport. Austrian skiers came to America as instructors, and ski trails and tows were built and ski patrols organized.

Soccer became popular after World War I among college women and in universities with large foreign male student enrollments. American men did not take to this game in this era.

Although the know-how of the early 1920s for building all-weather courts allowed tennis to become increasingly popular, the climate conducive to year-round play produced better players in large numbers. By the end of the 1930s there were thousands of tennis courts in the country, of all kinds: dirt, clay, grass, wooden, asphalt, and newer compositions of many kinds.

SPORTS ORGANIZATIONS

With the coming of the new century, athletics took on such prominence in both school and national life that many organizations came into existence for their promotion and control. The most important of these (listed in the order of their founding) are discussed in the material that follows.

Lower Schools

Public School Athletic League of New York City.[14] In 1903 Gulick, then Head of Physical Education of the schools of Greater New York City, set up the Public School Athletic League. Although it was not a part of the school program it was sponsored by the Board of Education and also by the President of the College of the City of New York and by the Secretary of the Amateur Athletic Union. Wealthy citizens gave it financial support so that the school budget did not have to carry it. None but boys of good standing in their schools could enter the activities, and an effort was made to interest all such boys, particularly those of only average ability. Early in its program the organization developed an Athletic Badge Test, and McKenzie, who had considerable skill as a sculptor, designed the first trophies.

In 1905, a Girls' Branch of the League, under Gulick's sponsorship, was organized by Elizabeth Burchenal with the help of prominent women in New York City. Miss Burchenal became its first secretary and was the official instructor of folk dance and athletics. From the very start, the League refused to sponsor interschool contests. It started as did the boy's organization as a volunteer group outside the school program. However the Board of Education acknowledged it as the arbiter for all girls' athletics in the schools. In 1909, Miss Burchenal was appointed Inspector of Girls' Athletics for the public schools of New York City, this organization became a branch of her department. Other cities that supported highly successful athletic leagues during this period were Philadelphia and Baltimore. The philadelphia schools put on their first annual field day at Franklin Park in 1908.

National Federation of High School Athletic Associations.[15] As early as 1896 several high schools in Wisconsin that sponsored boys' athletic associations came together and organized a state athletic association. It was several years before the idea caught on in other states, but a rush to follow suit finally started in 1903 with Indiana followed by Iowa, Montana and Rhode Island, 1904; Illinois and South Dakota, 1905; Ohio, 1906; Nebraska, Oklahoma, and Utah, 1910; Kansas, Pennsylvania, and South Carolina, 1913; California and Oregon, 1914; Kentucky, 1917; and New Jersey, 1918. By then much dissatisfaction had arisen over contests being sponsored for high school boys by various colleges and universities and by some sports clubs and promoters without attention to eligibility rules and high school regulations, and in 1920 representatives of the state groups in Iowa, Indiana, Michigan, and Wisconsin met in Chicago and organized the Middle West Federation of High School Athletic Associations. Two years later eleven other states joined the Middle West group and established the National Federation, whose one aim was to work for the common interest in control and direction of sports for all high school boys.

One of the Federation's earliest acts was to prohibit interstate competition at the highschool level other than as sanctioned by itself. By 1928 forty-two states had joined and were sponsoring their own state tournaments, as follows: basketball by all 42 states, track by 33, football by 33, baseball by 30, tennis by 20, swimming by 14, soccer by 8, wrestling by 6, volleyball by 4, and golf and skating each by 3. The work of the Federation grew, and by 1940 it was necessary to establish a national office with a full-time paid executive staff.

State Leagues of High School Girls' Athletic Associations. In the early 1920s the first State League of Girls' Athletic Associations was established in Illinois. Its purpose was to promote programs of athletics for all girls to offset the undesirable program of interschool athletics maintained in many schools by male coaches for the highly skilled few. Shortly after this leagues were set up in Colorado and Nebraska. These three state leagues advised local girls' athletic associations in high schools and helped them set up intramural programs for all girls. They established state point systems leading to local and state awards for athletic participation and achievement.

These state organizations were opposed to interscholastic competition for girls and worked instead for large scale participation of girls in their home-school intramural programs. The state organization assisted local groups with program plans, advised on local GAA affairs, and offered state awards for unusual achievement in physical education and sports activities.

Despite these state leagues, all school sponsored, there were ten states in 1928 supporting state basketball tournaments for high school girls, but most of these were outside school jurisdiction and were controlled and promoted by men. In the Ohio tournament that year, there were 5500 high school girls entered; in Texas, 4000 girls; and in Oklahoma, 2000.

Colleges

National Collegiate Athletic Association (NCAA). Because of the great number of injuries and the brutality that had developed in the game of football, serious criticism arose from many quarters at the opening of the new century.[16] Many universities, including Stanford and Columbia, and several colleges abandoned the sport altogether. Doctors, educators, and ministers, even the President of the United States, spoke and wrote against it. In 1905 a convention of delegates from thirty-eight leading colleges, called together by the Chancellor of New York University, formed the United States Intercollegiate Athletic Association. This was the first open challenge to the AAU's control of sports in the United States and it had the enthusiastic support of President Roosevelt. It was empowered to make rules and regulations governing all major sports played by colleges. At the 1916 meeting the name was changed to the National Collegiate Athletic Association, football rules were revised so that play became more open, and penalties for violation of regulations were provided. Later the organization undertook to develop rules of other sports and to control the eligibility of the players.[17]

Throughout this period the AAU, unwilling to give up control of any sports to any other group, caused constant problems to the NCAA. Their disagreements developed into a feud that lasted for many years. But the NCAA, like other groups, managed to ride out the various storms to keep control of college men's sports. General Palmer E. Pierce, the first president of NCAA, won his battle to keep intercollegiate sports within faculty control, thus setting the pattern for control of sports by the college authorities. He also won adoption of the rule that participation in all intercollegiate sports be for undergraduates only.[18]

Athletic Conference of American College Women.[19] Under the sponsorship of Blanche M. Trilling (1876–1964), Director of Physical Education for Women at the University of Wisconsin, the Athletic Conference of American College Women was begun there in 1917. Envisioned at first as merely a Middle West organization, Miss Trilling and the WAA girls of the University of Wisconsin had sent out invitations only to female physical directors and WAAs of colleges and universities of that area. Women student delegates from WAAs and their sponsoring women physical directors from twenty-three colleges and universities accepted the invitation and convened to discuss their common sports aims, objectives, and problems. For the next meeting, colleges from all parts of the country were invited to send delegates, and, from that second meeting on, this was a national group. From the beginning this organization took a stand against varsity intercollegiate athletics for women, promoting instead intramural programs for all. Throughout this period the organization held triennial conferences starting with the conference at the University of Indiana in 1921.

In 1933 the organization changed its name to the Athletic Federation of College Women (AFCW) and in its platform reaffirmed its aim to uphold the Standard of Athletics for Girls and Women as set forth by the National Section for Girls and Women's Sports.

Outing Clubs. Although many outing clubs flourished temporarily in colleges in the 1880s and 1890s, none achieved permanence. The first to claim that honor was the Dartmouth Outing Club, organized in 1910. In 1922 Smith College organized the first women's outing club to endure. From then on these clubs became popular in many colleges. They sponsored all forms of outdoor activities in all seasons of the year, many maintaining clubhouses. Also community recreation departments, YMCAs, YWCAs, and similar groups organized outing clubs, some specializing in bicycling (as with the American Youth Hostel Association that came into prominence in America in the 1930s) and some in skating, skiing, and other activities.

Nonschool Organization

Athletic Research Society. In 1907 a group of male leaders in the profession, led by Luther Gulick, Clark Hetherington, Joseph Raycroft, and Dudley Sargent, founded the Athletic Society for the improvement of physical education, recreation, and athletics and their interrelationships. In 1910 they took up the serious problem of professionalism in athletics and attacked the problem of control of amateur sports. In 1915 they set up a special committee to investigate the development of intramural sports. Following Sargent's death in 1924, this society faded away, but it had served a good purpose and had been a powerful influence for good in athletics, particularly in bringing them under the control of physical educators in the schools.[20]

National Section on Women's Athletics. The original Women's Basketball Rules Committee, set up under APEA in 1899, was reorganized and enlarged in 1905 under president Gulick into a National Women's Basketball Committee to set standards as well as to make rules. Senda Berenson served as editor of the reorganized committee from 1905 to 1917. Gradually the women of the profession became involved in rules for other sports and felt the need to expand into something more than a basketball group. Finally in 1917 under APEA president William H. Burdick (1871–1935), the National Committee on Women's Sports was formed to establish standards and official rules for athletics for girls and women. Elizabeth Burchenal was appointed chairwoman of the new committee, which kept the original basketball committee as one of two subcommittees, field hockey being the second one. A year later two more subcommittees were added—track and field and swimming. Also in 1917 the American Sports Publishing Company was given the contract to publish all women's sports rules for this committee. In 1927 the committee was advanced to the status of a section within the larger APEA, known as the Women's Athletic Section, and in 1931 its title was changed to National Section on Women's

Athletics. For the next twenty years it was familiarly known as the NSWA of APEA.

National Amateur Athletic Federation (NAAF).[21] Shortly after World War I, great dissatisfaction developed among parents, educators, playground leaders, youth group leaders, and the lay public in general over the trend of athletics in the United States, which were under a leadership that seemed to have no guiding principles other than to produce winning teams at any cost. National leaders in several organizations concerned with athletics came together to discuss these problems. The secretaries of the United States War and Navy departments, both deeply interested in the right type of athletic programs for servicemen, joined in the informal discussions. Out of this meeting developed the NAAF in 1922 with Col. Henry Breckinridge (1886–1960), a New York City attorney who was President of U.S. Navy League, as President and Mrs. Herbert Hoover (1878–1944), whose husband was at the time United States Secretary of Commerce and who, herself, was President of the Girl Scouts of America, as one Vice President and Dr. George J. Fisher (1871–1960), Executive Director of the Boy Scouts of America, as the other Vice President. Its stated aim was "to create and maintain in the United States a permanent organization representative of amateur athletics and organizations devoted thereto; to establish and maintain the highest ideals of amateur sport; to promote the development of physical education; to encourage the standardization of rules of all amateur athletic games and competitions; and to encourage the participation of men of this country in the International Olympic games." All leading organizations in the United States interested in sane sports for American youth joined the federation which lasted until 1930. In that year it dissolved, having accomplished its main purpose—to raise the standards of American sports and to break the hold of certain sports promoters who had seized substantial control of American sports and American athletes.

Many leaders of physical education were members of the first Board of Governors of this important organization: J. H. McCurdy, Dudley Reed (1878–1955), and William Burdick, representing APEA; Blanche Trilling, representing the National Committee of Women's Sports; H. F. Kallenberg and John Brown, Jr. (1880–1961), representing the YMCAs; William A. Stecher, representing the NAGU; J. E. Raycroft and Amos Alonzo Stagg, representing the NCAA; and George Fisher, representing the Boy Scouts of America.

Women's Division of the NAAF.[22] In April 1923, Mrs. Herbert Hoover called a meeting in Washington attended by over 200 women who were interested in the promotion of sports for girls and women, and they set up a Women's Division within the newly organized NAAF. Mrs. Hoover was elected Chairman of the board, which position she gave up in 1928, when her husband became President of the United States. The groundwork of the organization was laid by the following female physical educators who were elected to membership on the Executive Committee: Helen McKinstry of Central School of Physical Education; Dr. J. Anna Norris (1874–1958) of the University of Minnesota; Ethel Perrin, then Executive Secretary of the American Child Health Association; Blanche Trilling of the University of Wisconsin; and Agnes R. Wayman (1880–1968) of Barnard College. Within five months the new organization had 250 members made up of institutions, organizations, and individuals. At its first annual conference held at the University of Chicago in April 1924, the organization adopted a platform for the formation of sane and wholesome athletics for girls and women of the United States, and they worked to get acceptance of this platform in schools, in industry, in fact, in all segments of life promoting sports for girls and women. Miss Perrin served as the first Chairman of the executive committee, and Dr. Norris served as Chairman of the resolutions committee which drew up the first NAAF standards for the conduct of sports for girls and women.

International Organization

American Olympic Association (AOA). The American Olympic Committee (AOC) was created in 1911 to take charge of the participation of American athletes in the Olympic games of 1912. In 1921 it developed into a permanent organization called the American Olympic Association, with its membership made up of a federation of independent associations. It then set up the present American Olympic Committee (AOC) to control the U.S. Olympic teams. But it shortly developed that AAU held the greatest power of all these organizations, and NCAA, the U.S. Army and Navy, and National YMCA refused to join the AOC. This discontent brought about the establishment of National Amateur Athletic Federation to combat this AAU influence. When this new organization demanded equal voting power with AAU in the American Olympic Association, this request was granted. But when William A. Prout of AAU was elected president of AOA in 1926, the NAAF group withdrew from AOA. A year later, when Prout died and General Douglas MacArthur (1880–1964) succeeded him in the presidency, the groups rejoined AOA and its mission accomplished, NAAF went out of existence.

SPORTS COMPETITION

The twentieth century brought great increase in sports, both amateur and professional, promoted in all segments of national life through the schools, churches, industry, athletic clubs, sports associations, and all manner of such new organizations as the Boy Scouts and summer camps that were fostering activities for youth. Perhaps the greatest promoter of all of this period was the armed services which during World War I staged a tremendous recreational sports program with the leading male physical educators of the country working both at home with the soldiers in the Army Training Camps and in the European Theater of War with the American Expeditionary Forces.

Amateur versus Professional Sport

With the great increase in professional sports, there arose a tendency among many amateur sports groups to permit amateur sports gradually to take on characteristics of professionalism. This brought about a conflict between educators in general, physical educators, and true amateurs (of whom there were many in the early decades of the century) on the one side, and on the other those who, claiming to be promoting amateur sports, were pushing athletes to win at any cost, searching for loop holes in amateur sports rules to allow a semblance of professionalism, and winking at undercover subsidization and recruitment of athletes. This brought about a soul-searching that precipitated long-drawn-out argument as to the nature of amateur as differentiated from professional sports.

From the opening of the century the Athletic Research Society, made up of leading male physical educators of the day, had sensed the rising tide of mockery of the word amateur in the field of athletics for college men and had waged battle against it. But with the demise of that group in the 1920s there arose an ever-increasing cause for alarm as the debasement of amateur sports spread into other sports fields beyond the college world. This alarm aroused public concern, and popular writers, ministers, educators, and sports writers, as well as physical educators and sportsmen themselves, began to raise questions: What is an amateur? What is good sportsmanship? Frequent arguments now arose at professional convention over the English type of amateur sport of that day as representing the true amateur spirit, as compared with the American type with its ever-growing interest in championships qate receipts, and winning teams. A check of convention programs of this period of the American Physical Education Association, of its various districts, and of popular magazines of the day and books of this period on sports, reveals the frequency of this topic, and a review of the articles and speeches shows the deep public as well as professional concern over keeping amateur sports in America truly amateur.

John Tunis, an amateur U.S. tennis champion of the 1920s later turned sportswriter, in his book *$port$: Heroics, and Hysterics*[23] defined an amateur sportsman as one who "knows the thrill of real sport, of playing, not for championships, for titles, for cash, for publicity, for medals, for applause, but simply for the love of playing." Charles W. Kennedy, A professor at Princeton University, defined a sportsman as:

> . . . one who loves the game for its own sake; who has a scrupulous regard for the rules of fair play and strives under those rules to pit his best against the best of an opponent

whom he respects; who admires excellence in a game for its own sake and who pays an instinctive tribute of respect to excellence whether it be his own or that of an opponent; who in the stress of competition strives to the uttermost without descent to breach of rule or vindictive spirit; who hates a quitter, an alibi, or a boast; who in the course of a game preserves courage in the face of odds, and dignity, self-respect and good will in the presence of defeat; who wishes an amateur game to be played by amateurs and not by masquerading professionals; [and who acknowledges] that in the life of a great democracy he is the better man who can prove it.[24]

With the coming of the depression of the 1930s and its accompanying curtailment of sports activities, these concerns gave way to that of survival of any programs at all as physical education, along with other subjects in the school curriculum, was attacked as merely a frill in education. The various types of sports competition engaged in during this period are discussed in the material that follows.

Intramural Competition

The intramural form of athletics preceded the intercollegiate and interscholastic forms by many years. Indeed for almost the entire nineteenth century it was the only form of sports competition in the schools except in a few rare cases. But when extramural competition developed into a widespread movement near the end of the century, it grew to such proportions and to such neglect of all but varsity prospects that educators found it necessary to give special thought to the organization of intramurals for the mass of college students and school children.

In Lower Schools. The earliest record of organized intramurals on a large scale in a public school system seems to be that of the Grammar School Athletic League of Philadelphia, organized in 1900 just as the nineteenth century was coming to a close. Another early record of intramurals for elementary school children is that of the first New York City Public School field day specifically put on for elementary school children by C. Ward Crampton, then head of physical training and athletics of the High School of Commerce and held in the spring of 1904 on South Field at Columbia University. Some thirty schools sent entries, and the meet was so great a success that it led to the birth of the Public School Athletic League of New York City, which was discussed earlier in this chapter.

After starting with a spectator type of program that resulted in poor responses from the parents and public, the New York City League changed its emphasis to the educational aspects of sports. Team affiliations grew up around the four classes in high school and the home rooms at the lower grade levels. The intramural idea, however, was slow to catch on in the lower schools of the country before World War I, in general because of lack of professionally trained teachers.

In 1915 the Athletic Research Society set up a committee to aid in the development of intramural sports in the schools, and by 1925 the intramural idea had filtered down into the high schools. This form of competition soon became quite popular, particularly in the large high schools where participation in the extramural program reached but a small group of students. Shortly after World War I, a form of competition developed in rural schools called play days, in which the children from several schools were brought together and assigned to impromptu teams, played with and against each other with no team represnting any one school. This form of competition became popular in several states on a county basis and furnished much fun for hundreds of children who attended schools too small to support sports teams on their own.

In Colleges. The early intramural programs in colleges were built around class, club, and fraternity groupings.

A survey in 1910 of intramurals for men in colleges reported that 75 percent of Harvard students were coming out for these sports; 67 percent at Yale; 49 percent at the University of Virginia, and 10–12 percent at the University of California at Berkeley; and that of 142 colleges and universities surveyed, covering 111,000 male students, 10.6 percent were coming out for varsity sports and 40.3 percent for intramurals. In 1915, Cornell University reported that 8 percent of its male students were taking part in intramurals. Intramurals were given big acclaim during World War I, when the U.S. Secretary of War declared "The gospel of college athletics should be athletics for all."[25]

During World War I, colleges based their program on units within the Student Army Training Corps (SATC) located on the various campuses. In 1912 at the University of Chicago and in 1915 at both Michigan and Ohio State, a physical education staff member was appointed specifically to organize and administer a sports program for the many, apart from the program offered for the skilled few. According to the Athletic Research Society, by 1916, 114 colleges had such programs. The University of Michigan was the first to grant the title, Director of Intramurals; it went to Floyd Rowe (1884–1960), who later was to become Michigan's first State Director of Physical Education. In 1919 E. D. Mitchell succeeded to that position, and in 1924 he published *Intramural Athletics,* the first book on the subject. In 1928 the University of Michigan opened its Intramural Sports Building, a building devoted exclusively to these activities—the first such specialized building in the United States.

Interscholastic Competition

The story of interschool competition of the first decade of the twentieth century, in the great majority of schools, is largely the same as the story of intercollegiate competition of the late nineteenth century, namely a story of boys organizing and administering their sports for themselves, with help from interested townspeople rather than from the schools. It took the schools at least a decade into the new century to awaken to their responsibility. Once the schools responded, the story is largely that of the state high school athletic associations.

Intercollegiate Competition

For the earlier years of the twentieth century, football dominated intercollegiate sports, to such an extent that the story of these activities is largely the story of football. This era brought highly paid coaches, training tables, large expenditures of money for sports, and huge gate receipts undreamed of in the nineteenth century. The all-too-common attitude of the college authorities toward student athletic sports was that they were a necessary evil, to be tolerated and at times restricted.

At the turn of the century, the presidents of Stanford University and the University of Michigan and a professor at the University of Wisconsin among others raised the question of using paid professional coaches for student sports which were supposed to be purely amateur sports. This brought some soul searching but little came of it. The first decade of the new century also brought widespread criticism of football because of the many fatalities suffered on the gridiron, when several schools dropped football for rugby. Until 1905, Harvard, Yale, and Princeton had held virtual control of football rule making. With their authority questioned and challenged from then on, these "Big Three" in attempting to work independently later created their own Ivy League which ultimately resulted in isolation from the big leagues of the state universities and their satellites.[26]

At this time when $5000 was the top salary paid to a full professor at Harvard, and Harvard's president's salary was around $8000, a 26-year-old coach was being paid $3500 by the university and $3500 by the alumni. At that same time Dr. Sargent, head of physical education and athletics, who had been on the university faculty for many years, was paid $3500.[27]

Quarrels such as had occurred in the 1890s over football now increased between leading schools. Many schools broke off athletic relationship, not without cause. Hetherington's *Biography* cites typical situations of this first decade of the new century when athletes were paid cash "behind the door." Many coaches were men of no educational background whatsoever, and supposedly school teams were made up of townspeople and faculty members. He reported one college game in the Middle West where seven members of the team were the town blacksmith, a lawyer, a livery man, and four railroad employees.[28]

Theodore Roosevelt during his presidency of the United States (1901–1909) remarked that "when money comes in at the gate, sport flies out the window," and called a White House Conference of football leaders and coaches in the hopes of bringing some order out of the chaos. But even that helped for but a short time. Sargent at Harvard began a campaign to abolish gate receipts in an effort to eliminate much of the evil, but to no avail.[29] No school would even try giving up gate receipts. Soon quarrels were rampant again. In 1912 and again in 1916 Harvard and Princeton universities severed athletic relations. Many other schools were engaged in similar quarrels and breaks, but the news managed to be kept under cover. By 1914 when college sports had taken on the "win at all costs" aspect, a vocal segment among the citizenry began to speak out, comparing the English objectives of sports with our American aims built on nothing less than victory. By 1920 the condition was under such fire that the Carnegie Foundation for the Advancement of Teaching financed a survey of the situation to ascertain the facts and improve the situation. Their findings were published in 1929 in a bulletin entitled *American College Athletics,* and for a while it brought some improvement.[30]

In 1928 one contest at the Yale bowl drew a crowd of 80,000 with special trains running from several cities carrying the private cars of the affluent as well as long strings of coaches for the common herd. In that same year a sportsman journalist of the era voiced the disgust of a large segment of the citizenry over the decay of athletics when he wrote of "The Great Sports Myth"—the myth that football players are heroes of high moral qualities, "purified and made holy by their devotion to intercollegiate sports." He claimed that intercollegiate and international sports do not produce nobility of character and strengthen the bonds between nations and individuals, but produce instead "broken ankles, bad feeling, cursing, and revelry in the sanctity of dressing rooms; coarse accusations and cheap humor in the publications of a great university."[31]

By 1930 attendance at college football games had reached the ten million mark, and the new decade ushered in the first radio broadcasts of intercollegiate games. But once more subsidization of athletes and methods of recruiting were causing serious quarrels between colleges.

Postseason bowl games had their birth in 1902, when Stanford University played the University of Michigan in Pasadena's Rose Bowl. (Today's Rose Bowl was not built until 1923.) But the idea did not catch on as an annual event until 1915, when Washington State, that year's Pacific Coast Conference champion, invited Brown University to play off a regional championship in the Pasadena bowl. This game, played January 1, 1916, started the annual event.

Nonschool Competition

The YMCA national sports program reached thousands of boys, but the AAU was the main promoter in the United States of amateur sports outside the schools. Following this organization's founding in 1888, it became powerful in the athletic world. District and national championship meets and tournaments in several sports were held under its rules and its management. The first night baseball game was played in Des Moines, Iowa, in 1930.

International Competition[32]

United States Participation in the Olympic Games. With the coming of a new century, the games became worldwide in representation. The 1904 games were held in St. Louis; 1906, Athens[33]; 1908, London; 1912, Stockholm; 1920, Antwerp; 1924, Paris; and 1928, Amsterdam. Winter Olympics were added in 1924 in Chamonix and in 1928 in St. Moritz.

At the last of the Olympic Games of this period, 1928, the 43 nations represented competed in 121 events with 4000 athletes taking part—quite a change from the first games of 1896, with 12 nations and 285 athletes in 34 events.

Olympic winners from the very first games to the present have been determined only event by event. There never has been an official point system by which totals may be decided. However, the news media has, through the years, devised its own unofficial point system for these games, particularly for the track and field events, and it is because of their own unofficial pronouncements that a claim is made that any country has won the Olympics. Such claims are without official sanction.

At each Olympics, new events were added within the sports already in use, and now and then additional sports were added, so that the total events offered in competition grew with the years.

In the 1904 games, which were held in connection with the Louisiana Purchase Exposition in St. Louis, were largely a contest between rival U.S. athletic clubs.

Although the games were to be held only every four years, 1906 was made an exception, and extra games were held in Athens in honor of the tenth anniversary of the first modern Olympics. This was the first time the United States sent athletes as an organized United States Olympic team. There was now an American Olympic Committee with President Theodore Roosevelt its honorary president. This first official U.S. team consisted of thirty-five athletes who were competing against eleven other nations.

In the 1908 Olympics, bickering that arose over the many questioned decisions of the British officials brought about the establishment of an International Olympics Committee to govern, manage, and officiate the games from then on.

In the 1912 Olympics, twenty-six nations entered. This was the first games to claim front-page attention in the papers at home, also the first to use an electric timing system. The great athlete of the United States team was Jim Thorpe (1889–1953), a Carlisle Indian. An interesting ceremony in connection with these games in Stockholm was the presentation to King Gustave of Sweden of the plaque, *Joy of Effort* (four feet in diameter), sculptored by R. Tait McKenzie, who at the time was President of the American Physical Education Association. The shield had been commissioned by the American Olympic Committee and was presented as a gift to the Swedish people. It was installed in the entrance to the Olympic Stadium where it is on view today.

Because of World War I, the VIth Olympiad was omitted in 1916, and by 1920 the memory of the conflict was still so fresh that Germany and Austria were not invited to send teams to the games in Antwerp. This was the first U.S. Olympic team to which the army and navy contributed athletes. The leading U.S. athlete was Charles Paddock, then called the World's Fastest Human.

In 1924, over 2000 athletes from forty-five nations marched in the opening parade in Paris. Finland's famous runner Paavo Nurmi (1897–   ) won much acclaim. This year was the first that winter sports were added to the games. For the United States, John Weissmuller (1904–   ) starred in swimming.

For the 1928 games in Amsterdam, General Douglas MacArthur (1880–1964) was president of the American Olympic Committee. The United States team consisted of 285 athletes, among them 19 women. Paavo Nurmi of Finland and Lord Burleigh of England held the limelight in these games.

Controversies over National and International Sports Competition. Although there have been controversies through the years over domestic competition in many sports, none has been so prolonged as the one over the control of track and field sports in international competition, which for over sixty years has claimed the attention of high government officials as well as the sporting public. Since the first modern Olympic Games in Paris in 1896, track and field sports have held the special attention of the public and the major emphasis and publicity of all Olympic sports.

A review of the history of the control of this sport gives a picture of today's situation and of the contending organizations that claim jurisdiction over it. The first extramural track meet on record in the United States was an intercollegiate meet held at Saratoga, New York, in 1874. The following year several colleges banded together to organize the Intercollegiate Association of Amateur Athletes of America (IAAAA), which took over control of intercollege sports competition. In 1905 this organization gave way to the United States Intercollegiate Athletic Association (USIAA), which was founded through the auspices of several college presidents who were demanding reforms in sports competition. This organization in turn developed into today's NCAA.

In the meantime, the amateur sports clubs that existed in the 1870s outside the then very small world of college sports banded together and organized the National Association of Amateur Athletes of America (NAAA). This was in 1879, four years after the IAAAA came into being to control college competition. In 1888 the NAAAA developed into today's AAU, which by 1900 claimed jurisdiction over all amateur sports in the country, including college sports already covered by the IAAAA. This brought about disputes that flared up intermittently until in 1907 representatives of high schools (for by then athletics had developed in this field), colleges, YMCAs, and Boys Clubs came together to discuss how they could protect their athletes from the AAU's attempts to take them over. The AAU was demanding that for the privilege of competing in any amateur extramural contest an athlete must take out membership in the AAU, and pay the membership fee and an entry fee for each contest. The AAU was so well entrenched by then that it could enforce its dictums. To protect their own athletes from this management, the other group now added to their earlier group representatives from playgrounds, social centers, turners, and the U.S. military forces and organized the Athletic Research

Society. In 1910 it appointed an official committee to challenge the AAU. In 1912 the AAU became a member of the International Amateur Athletic Federation and as the first organization in that body from the United States, acquired the American franchise in that organization for all U.S. international competition, which it held for many years.

After fruitless years of meetings between AAU and the Athletic Research Society, the latter called for the formation of a federation of all groups of amateur athletes that through union might be able to break AAU's control of amateur sports. In 1921 the NCAA tried to interest the AAU in joining these other groups, so that all would work together, but the AAU was not interested. Thereupon the other groups went ahead without the AAU and organized the National Amateur Athletic Federation to place the control of amateur athletics on a democratic basis consistent with the ideals of our nation. At this same time the AAU had undertaken the promotion of women's amateur sports along its usual lines so that in 1923 the Women's Division of the NAAF was established to enlist the help of women physical educators and all women interested in the welfare of American girls and women in their sports experiences. Although these two groups (the NAAF and its Women's Division) were short-lived, they alerted the leaders and citizenry of the nation to the unfavorable situations then existing in sports competition of the youth of the land.

In 1928 the Western Track Coaches Association disagreed with the AAU over control of their own track athletes, as a result of which a movement was started to form a democratic organization that would speak for all track and field athletes of the United States. But matters drifted during the depression.

Sports Competition for Girls and Women

At the opening of the new century women's sports in colleges and high schools began gradually to come under the control of the physical education departments although at Bryn Mawr College students held out as late as 1929 in turning over their own control and promotion of sports to the physical education staff. With several national organizations coming into existence in this era to set standards for girls' sports competition, all adopting the slogan, "A sport for every girl and every girl in a sport," the intramural form of competition became the form approved by the profession for American girls. The principles for sports were drawn up by the leading women physical educators of the day, working through the Women's Division of the National Amateur Athletic Federation, which drew up a platform of standards, as discussed below.

Platform of the Women's Division of NAAF. Under the chairmanship of Mrs. Herbert Hoover, one of the first actions of the Women's Division after its founding in 1923 was to appoint a committee to draw up a platform of aims and principles as guides for all groups in the country promoting competitive athletics for women.

Under the leadership of Dr. J. Anna Norris of the University of Minnesota, the committee presented a platform which was unanimously adopted. Among its many provisions it included such items as the following:

1. Promote competition that stresses enjoyment of the sport and development of good sportsmanship and character rather than those types that emphasize the making and breaking of records and the winning of championships for the enjoyment of spectators or for the athletic reputation or commercial advantage of institutions and organizations.
2. Promote interest in awards for athletic accomplishment that have little or no intrinsic value.
3. Promote educational publicity that places emphasis upon sport and its values rather than upon the competitors.
4. Promote the training and employment of women administrators, leaders, and officials who are qualified to assume full responsibility for the physical education and recreation of girls and women.
5. Protect the athletic activities of girls and women from the dangers attendant upon competition that involves travel, and from their commercialization by interest in gate receipts.
6. Protect the health of girls and women through the promotion of medical examinations and medical "follow-up" as a basis for participation in athletic competition.
7. Promote the adoption of approved rules for the conduct of athletics for girls and women.[34]

The rules of sports for women as approved by this organization were those made by the National Section for Women's Athletics of APEA. As these two groups worked together, the Women's Division was looked upon as the standards setting body, the other as the sports rules making body. Both groups were working under the leadership of the profession's outstanding women.

Competition in Lower Schools. In the early years of the 1900's, girls in some high schools in all parts of the country competed in interschool activities, although the games were not organized or controlled by school authorites. Some played college teams; some, other high school teams, and some, boys' grade school teams. By 1910 girls' interscholastic basketball had become big excitement in many small towns of the Middle West and South and more than any other sport was causing "headaches" for physical education teachers and girls' leaders. Through it the girls were frequently exploited for the publicity of many small towns and a few groups of men. These groups used boys' rules and male coaches in most situations, and where female coaches were used, they were as a rule women who were not trained in the educational aspects of sports and in the care of girls in their sports participation.

Partly in imitation of the college women's athletic associations and partly to combat interscholastic games, girls' athletic associations sprang up, and, sparked by them, intramurals took the stage in most high schools. These GAA's found support and encouragement in the state leagues which arose in the 1920s.

Competition in Colleges. From a mild start in the 1890s in a few isolated places, intercollegiate competition for women now increased in the 1900s. In the East a few colleges played intercollegiate basketball occasionally from 1900 to the World War I period, but during the 1920s, intramural competition had almost completely superseded all such competition. In the Middle West the University of Nebraska started a program of varsity basketball in 1900 managed by a woman English teacher, playing high schools, YWCA's, and an occasional college team, but by 1906 on orders from the offices of the Chancellor and the Dean of Women this type of competition was replaced by an intramural program of interclass games to be under the control of the Department of Physical Education for Women. In the West, the University of California's Sports Past-time (*sic*) Association ran off intercollegiate matches with the University of Nevada, Stanford University, and Mills College from 1900 to 1903 when because of unfavorable publicity the school authorities put a stop to the games.

In the early 1920s about 22 percent of the colleges sponsored some form of intercollegiate sports for women, but by 1930 only 12 percent were engaging in intercollegiate competition whereas intramurals, sponsored jointly by women's athletic associations and the departments of physical education, gained in popularity.

By 1925 play days had become popular, the first held at the University of Washington as an intramural affair. The University of Cincinnati was the first to sponsor an intercollegiate play day in which girls from various colleges were scattered among many teams—no one school putting any one team into play in any activity. In other words the players played with other schools rather than against them.

This era was one of great activity in sports for girls and women. With the National Section for Girls and Women's Athletics of APEA, various state high school leagues, Women's Division of NAAF, and the Athletic Conference of American College Women all working for sports for all and play for play's sake, intramurals have become the organized form of sports for the great mass of American school girls and women.

There was but little intercollegiate competition in sports for women in this era.[35] In general, such sports were frowned upon by most college authorities, most physical educators, and most parents. As early as the late 1890s, Senda Berenson at Smith College had made public pronouncements against intercollegiate sports for women, and in her book of 1903[36] Lucille Eaton Hill (1858–1941) at Wellesley College had spoken out publicly against them. In 1906, Luther Halsey Gulick of the New York City public schools in his writings made public his stand against such sports. In 1929, Agnes Wayman at Barnard College took public stand through her book.[37]

A survey of the 1910s[38] of sixty-one colleges showed that 14 to 23 percent of these schools engaged in intercollegiate sports for women. Of these, some played only one such game a year, but in 1915 Radcliffe College played in six hockey matches and eight varsity basketball games. A survey of intercollegiate athletics for women made in 1923 was repeated in 1930 at the request of the Women's Division of NAAF. One hundred fifty-four colleges and universities were included in this second survey. The 22 percent of colleges reporting participation in intercollegiate athletics in 1923 had dropped to 12 percent by 1930 with only 7 percent using the varsity-team type of competition, the other 5 percent using only the interclass type. Fifty-three percent of the colleges reporting took part in play days with other schools in which the girls were mixed together in temporary teams with no team representing any one college.

In this era, there was no intercollegiate organization comparable to the men's NCAA to promote and manage sports matches for women. Whatever activity existed in this line went on under the auspices, supervision and management of the departments of physical education for women of the colleges involved—each contest an event by itself. A few interstate contests were held—not that they made claim to settle interstate championships, they were merely contests between a college in one state and a college in another state—interstate communication at a low level.

Known records exist of women's games of the early 1900s in the Middle West between the universities of Minnesota, Nebraska, and Missouri, and on the West Coast between the University of California and a college in Washington State. In 1910 women's intercollegiate sports contests were banned in Kansas in the state schools.[39] They had been banned at the University of Nebraska since 1906.

Nonschool Competition. Although YWCA's, recreation centers, and like groups offered women a varied sports program, it was in this era that there first arose exploitation of girls through athletics. School girls were exploited by men's sports organizations, industrial and business groups, chambers of commerce, and a number of men athletic coaches, who saw that skilled girl athletes made good publicity. The AAU took the lead in organizing girls in industry for such competitive sports. Its attempt to take over the management of girls and women's competitive sports after World War I aroused the women leaders of physical education and many prominent lay women as well, who tried to counter its influence by the organization of the Women's Division of the NAAF. Although this organization did accomplish much in awaking the lay public to the desirability of sane and wholesome standards for sports for women, it never succeeded in breaking the AAU's hold completely, for the AAU continued to control women's competition in several fields.

In the 1920s women's national championship tournaments sprang up across the country—all male inspired, male managed, male coached, and male financially rewarded from the prowess of the worthwhile athletic "finds." Of all sports, basketball played by women caused the most controversy between physical educators (both men and women), who would keep women's sports purely in the realm of education and recreation, and those sports promoters who would push women into spectator sports with their accompanying gate receipts, win-at-all-costs atmosphere, and championships at stake. By the late 1920s the Women's Athletic Section of the American Physical Education Association and the Women's Division of the National Amateur Athletic Federation and state leagues vigorously opposed these forces in behalf of what they called educational athletics for girls.

Women's Participation in the Olympics. There are reports that the first entrance of women in the Olympics occurred in 1900 in Paris, but tables of events and winners in the Olympics give the year 1904 for the first participation of women, the sport being lawn tennis.[40] But it was to be 1920 before the U.S. team included women, and that first entry was in swimming. Other countries had entered women in swimming events since 1912. At the next games in 1920, women from the United States joined the others and won four events out of five, for an auspicious beginning. In 1924 women tennis players were added to the U.S. team. Throughout these years, the International Olympic Committee resisted the entrance of women into the games, clinging to de Coubertin's early objectives, but it seemed "to see the handwriting on the wall" when the women swimmers won admission. For the 1928 games it relented to support five women's track and field events (100 and 400 meter relays, 800 meter race, high jump, and discus throw) on trial, and the U.S. Olympic Committee went along. At that time the AAU boasted of complete control of the women athletes of America for national and international contests. In 1932 women speed skaters were added to the team, who won two out of three events offered in that sport.

As with the male athletes, it was track and field that claimed the lion's share of the publicity for women. In the first offering of this sport for women, the U.S. team won one of the five events.

After their entry into the Games in 1920 the presence of women athletes in the five Olympics before World War II was questioned from many sources at home. The United States was not yet ready to accept its women in such a public role, particularly not in track and field sports.

An Olympic Protest of Leading American Women. As soon as it became known that track and field sports were to be opened to women and certain groups in the United States were pushing for a U.S. women's track team, vigorous protests were registered with the Olympic Committee by the Women's Division of NAAF, with the vigorous supporting protests of the foremost men leaders of physical education. In 1929 at its annual meeting, the Women's Division went on record as a national group of women leaders, both in physical education and the lay world, that was opposed to the entrance of American women in the Olympics of 1932, and it adopted the following resolutions arranged from the original materials:

I. WHEREAS, Competition in the Olympic Games would, among other things (1) entail the specialized training of a few, (2) offer opportunity for the exploitation of girls and women, and (3) offer opportunity for possible overstrain in preparation for and during the Games themselves, be it

RESOLVED, that the Women's Division of the National Amateur Athletic Federation go on record as disapproving of competition for girls and women in the Olympic Games,

. . . . .

III. WHEREAS, The Women's Division is interested in promoting the ideal of Play for Play's sake, of Play on a large scale, of Play and recreation properly safeguarded,

IV. WHEREAS, It is interested in promoting types and programs of activities suitable to girls as girls, be it

RESOLVED, That the Women's Division . . . shall ask for the opportunity of putting on in Los Angeles during the Games (not as a part of the Olympic program) a festival which might include singing, dancing, mass sports and games . . . demonstrations, exhibitions, etc.

V. WHEREAS, . . . a crisis is at hand whereby the Platform and principles of the Women's Division will be severely tested,

BE IT RESOLVED, That the members of the Women's Division and all who are interested in the Federation and its ideals . . . do all in their power to spread more actively the principles advocated by this Division and to work unceasingly toward putting on for girls a program of sports and games . . . which shall (1) include every member of the group; (2) be broad and diversified; (3) be adapted to the special needs and abilities and capacities of the participants; with emphasis upon *participation* rather than upon *winning*.[41]

The above resolutions were widely publicized and were later adopted by the National Association of Physical Education for College Women, the National Section on Women's Athletics of the American Physical Education Association, the Athletic Conference of American College Women, and the National Board of the YWCAs of America, and they were endorsed by the national Association of Deans of Women and the American Association of University Women. In April of 1930 the Women's Division sent a petition to the International Olympic Committee urging the exclusion of women from the 1932 Olympics, calling their attention to a speech by Pierre de Coubertin, founder of the modern games, made at the XIth Olympic Games in Amsterdam in 1928, in which he said:

As to the admission of women to the Games, I remain strongly against it. It was against my will that they were admitted to a growing number of competitions.[42]

But both the United States Olympic Committee and the International Olympic Committee turned a deaf ear to these appeals.

9

Organized Physical Education of the Early Twentieth Century

EVENTS AFFECTING PHYSICAL EDUCATION

During this era the terms *physical culture* and *physical training* gave way to *physical education,* a term long in use in a few isolated situations, such as at Amherst College, where Dr. Hitchcock had used it ever since the 1860s. Forces affecting physical education and aiding it in procuring recognition are discussed in the material that follows.

State Legislation

The movement for state laws requiring that physical education be taught in the schools, which started in the 1890s, lagged in the 1900s. Up to 1914 only three more states had acted: Pennsylvania in 1901, Michigan in 1911, and Idaho in 1913. During the war eight more fell into line. Then general educators joined forces with physical educators to hasten this process. Even President Wilson had spoken out in behalf of the needs for physical training of all children. Shortly, a Committee for the Promotion of Physical Education in the Public Schools was organized, with headquarters in Washington, to push for a model state bill for physical education. Dr. John Dewey of Columbia University served as chairman of the committee, and Mrs. Ella Flagg Young (1845–1918), Superintendent of the Chicago schools and the first woman to hold the presidency of the National Education Association, served on the committee, as did Dudley Sargent and the state superintendents of education of

North Carolina, California, Illinois, and Washington and two college presidents—a notable group. Sargent was commissioned to draw up a model bill, and in February 1917 it was placed before the General Assemblies of California, Indiana, and Connecticut with the following preamble:

> We believe the time has come when the public schools can, and should, enter deliberately and purposefully upon a definite plan for the preparation of our youth physically for the exigencies of life and for all the demands of citizenship. We need to spend more money and more time upon physical training intended to develop the body so that both boys and girls may be prepared equally for the pursuits of peace and the vicissitudes of war.

This committee started the ball rolling. By 1930 thirty-nine states had passed physical education laws. With state legislation came state physical education directorships set up in the state departments of public instruction. New York in 1916 became the first state to create such a position with Dr. Thomas A. Storey (1875–1943), of the College of the City of New York, in the directorship. California was the second with Clark W. Hetherington serving as state director from 1918 to 1921. By 1930 twenty-two states had state directors of physical education. (See Appendix.) The rising tide of state legislation which increased physical education work in the schools revealed the shortage of teachers in this field, and private schools, normal schools, colleges, and universities stepped up their teacher-training work.

Most of the early laws required the teaching of physical education in the larger schools and allowed it in the smaller ones. Later the laws carried provisions for time allotment and required physical education credits for graduation. Whereas the first laws specified the teaching of calisthenics and/or gymnastics, the later laws specified instead sports and rhythms. However, the crowded conditions and lack of facilities of many elementary and high schools encouraged the use of calisthenics rather than games and sports. The joyous acceptance of sports and dance into the program brought about a public awareness of and interest in physical education, which in turn brought about public support for the program.

World War I

The world-wide war of 1914–18 was spoken of as the Great War until a second one twenty-five years later, when the earlier one became known as World War I. In the conduct of this first world war, into which the United States was finally drawn after serious attempts to keep free of it, the Government recognized physical education in many ways as it turned to various national leaders for advice and help in special projects, thus advancing markedly and favorably public recognition of the profession. Also many private agencies called on physical education leaders to help in their specific endeavors related to the war. Joseph E. Raycroft, of Princeton University, was appointed commissioner of the Athletic Division of the War Department Commission on Training Camp Activities and was sent by the Secretary of War to Europe to study conditions affecting the morale of the American Expeditionary Forces. Following this the United States Navy set up a similar commission with Walter Camp of Yale at its head. He immediately appealed through the NCAA for the colleges to loan their athletic trainers to work with aviators. Dr. Edward C. Schneider (1874–1954), of Wesleyan University, was appointed a member of the Medical Research Board of Aviation with the AEF, and Dr. Thomas A. Storey, New York State Director of Physical Education, was made Executive Secretary of the Government Interdepartmental Social Hygiene Board.

Women physical educators were also drawn into top positions of war work. Jessie Bancroft, head of physical education in the Brooklyn Public Schools, was called to serve as Chairman of the Government Commission on Training Camp Activities and President of the War-Camp Service. Elizabeth Burchenal was appointed a member of the U.S. Department of Labor's Commission of Wartime Community Services and a member of both the U.S. War and Navy departments' commission on camp activities. Dr. Clelia Mosher (1863–1940) of Stanford University was Medical Director of the Bureau of Refugees and Relief for the American Red Cross. Lillian Drew (1874–1930) of Columbia University was appointed by the Surgeon General as Supervisor of Reconstruction Aides for the War Department, and many women physical educators served in that branch of work both in Europe and at home. On the regional level Blanche Trilling of the University of Wisconsin served as one of the regional directors for the Fosdick Commission of the National Recreation Association for their recreation activities for communities located near war-mobilization camps, and Wilma Haynes (1888–1977) of the Dayton YWCA, held a similar regional directorship for the National YWCA Commission on Recreational Services.

Athletic Program of the American Expeditionary Forces (AEF).[1] Several leaders of physical education under the sponsorship of the United States Army laid the foundation for the great athletic program of the AEF of World War I. They included J. H. McCurdy, M. D. (1866–1940) of Springfield YMCA School, George J. Fisher, head of the Physical Department of the International YMCA, A. A. Stagg of the University of Chicago; Paul Phillips (1865–1942) of Amherst, George Meylan of Columbia University; E. B. DeGroot of the Chicago Park System, and F. L. Kleeberger (1885–1942) of the University of California (Berkeley). These men, with 345 others serving under them as athletic directors, reached a peak in participation in sports at rest camps of 21,710,406. When General Petain asked the United States to furnish recreation leaders to produce a similar program for the French poilus, Meylan was put in charge of this work, and he set up 1300 recreation centers for the French armies.

The GIs were offered a varied program of sports: baseball, basketball, boxing, football, swimming, volleyball, and wrestling, most of them experiencing many of these sports for the first time in their lives. The physical directors had 326 athletic fields at their disposal and $182 million worth of athletic equipment. In this work many older men from the Knights of Columbus and the Jewish Welfare Board assisted the YMCA volunteers. Newspapers and schools at home carried on great campaigns for donations of sports equipment for the Army Recreation Centers and collected an estimated 17,500 sets of boxing gloves, 7000 basketball nets, 21,000 baseballs, 3000 footballs, 3500 volleyballs, and 1750 medicine (oversized) balls. The American Red Cross lent its services wherever possible to sponsor sports tournaments.[2]

After the close of the war and while the allied armies were still in France, the YMCAs, under the leadership of Dr. John Brown, Jr., organized Inter-Allied Athletic Contests—the Military Olympics—which were open to all soldiers of all allied armies. For these games the YMCA's built a 40,000-seat concrete stadium and presented it as the Pershing Stadium to the French Republic, with General Pershing himself making the presentation speech. These games, in progress as the Versailles Peace Treaty was being signed, did much to seal international friendships between the men of the armed forces of the Allies. Later when the Armies of Occupation moved into the defeated countries, sports recreational centers were established for the occupying troops and athletic contests among the Allied forces were staged frequently in various cities. At the army camps in Europe, one young marine who won the AEF boxing championship, Gene Tunney, got his start for his later boxing career. Sports activities offered by the group of physical educators became the one great diversion of the U.S. soldiers. Besides this work in European army camps, there were at home thirty-two great mobilization camps, each with four physical directors in charge of the recreation work for the men.

The After-Effects of Draft Figures. Thirty-three percent of the men drafted for the U.S. armed services for World War I were rejected as unfit to serve. Out of the ensuing accusations and recriminations came an awakened conscience. People were now ready to give backing to a real program of physical education in the schools. This postwar impetus brought greatly expanded facilities and increased staffs. Swimming pools, football stadiums, spacious gymnasiums, and large athletic fields sprang up all over the country. A growing consciousness that physical education and athletics were for the many, not just for the few, brought a great upsurge for intramural sports and increased required work in physical education in the schools and colleges.

The Progressive Education Movement[3]

Birth of the Association for the Advancement of Progressive Education. As John Dewey's ideas on educational reforms became widely known, there developed an ever-growing group of educators who accepted them and tried to change general educational procedures to fit Dewey's philosophy. It was not until after World War I, however, that there was, even in education in general, such a thing as a formally organized group openly committed to advance the cause of *progressive education,* as this movement came to be called following his conversion to Francis Parker's theories on education of children of the later nineteenth century, as discussed in Chapter 6. The Association for the Advancement of Progressive Education was born in 1919, when it named President Eliot of Harvard its honorary president and announced as its objective the reformation of the American school system. To attain this objective, it aimed to meet the needs of children, to give the child freedom to develop naturally, to attend to all things that affect a child in his physical development, and to make *interest* the child's motivation to work. This meant changing the teacher from the task-master of old into a guide.

Dewey did not join this organization, although upon Eliot's death in 1926 he accepted the honorary presidency.

Adjusting Education to the Child. The progressive education movement raised in the world of education talk of adjusting the school to the child, not the child to the school; teaching children rather than subjects; adapting the school to life situations; giving the child opportunity for creative self-expression; taking into consideration individual differences; and teaching "the whole child." Several of these concepts had long been recognized by a few educators. For example, in the field of physical education, Hitchcock since the 1860s and Sarget since the 1880s had been advocating attention to individual differences.

The Leadership of Thomas D. Wood. From the beginning of physical education in the schools of America, gymnastics had been, in most schools, the core of the program—in many, the whole of it. The changes demanded by the new philosophy seemed to many physical educators to call first of all for a complete break with the old forms of gymnastics. But this did not come about without much argumentation within the profession. A small group of physical educators, led by Thomas D. Wood of Columbia University, who also found merit in Dewey's philosophy began examining physical education in light of the new ideas. By 1910 Wood had published his book *Health and Education*[4], in which he acknowledged the influence of Dewey on his thinking and proclaimed that through physical education the child should acquire mental, moral, and social, as well as physical benefits. He pointed out that physical education had been given space and time in the educational program only begrudgingly and only with the aim of counteracting the unhealthful influences of the school day. He maintained that this was no longer enough and that the physical education program should be psychologically and socially as well as physiologically sound. Recognizing gymnastics as an activity that could still be taught readily in the space allotted for physical education in so many schools in those days and to the large-sized classes required at that time in so many schools, he did not advocate the abandonment of gymnastics but instead the substitution of a new form to be called *natural gymnastics*, a term he used as early as 1891 when he established the department at Stanford University to be built around sports and activities related to life situations. He would retain gymnastics for its physiological values; but he would replace the old forms done in response to formal commands with this new form which would embody social and psychological objectives that were lacking in the old forms.

There soon arose a considerable body of followers of Wood for the "new physical education," but unfortunately too many teachers without a realistic understanding of either Dewey's or Wood's philosophy and disliking the old forms of gymnastics gladly seized upon the idea of natural gymnastics as a way out of a dilemma, and, lacking creative skill to formulate procedures to fit the new ideas, became involved with class periods in which the pupils had little exercise and attained little in the way of social or psychological objectives and definitely no physiological ones. They had merely wasted their time. This vacuum of attainment most certainly had not been the intent of the originator and the leading promoters of the new gymnastics, and these early failures led to a division among physical educators. One group would retain the old forms of gymnastics for their own value. Another group would keep the old forms but rob them of their old formal and militaristic aspects. A third group would replace the old forms of gymnastics entirely with Wood's natural gymnastics. A fourth group would have no gymnastics at all in the physical education program but would instead build the program around sports and dance in their various forms. In the end, this last group was the one that prevailed, although the proponents of the other three groups had their way for a brief period, each in various parts of the country, with some diehards holding out into the 1930s. None of these groups were formally organized, and one never knew for sure to which group others belonged except for the few outspoken people of each group.

Attacks on Gymnastics. There never was within the profession of physical education a progressive education movement as such. Things were not as clear-cut as that. The profession, aroused by Dewey and Wood, was groping toward something new but was not sure what this new thing should be. But since gymnastics had been the main activity recognized as physical education in the schools in the century just closed, it was gymnastics that came under attack in this new day.

Upon Wood's retirement from Columbia, his mantle fell upon Jesse F. Williams; and just as Kilpatrick had not hewn to the line in following Dewey's philosophy, Williams, too, departed somewhat from that of Wood. Whereas Wood had been for retaining gymnastics in the program but in a new form, Williams in public speeches voiced disapproval of any school system that would tolerate the retention of any form of gymnastics in its program. In his book *Organization and Administration of Physical Education* he spoke of formal calisthenics and gymnastics as a deformity in physical education, for which a cure should be sought.[5] (In this period the word *gymnastics* meant the combination of gymnastic marching, free-standing exercises, and apparatus work.) As lines came to be drawn for and against gymnastics as a legitimate part of physical education, the chief adversaries seemed to be Williams on the one side and C. H. McCloy (1886–1958) of the University of Iowa on the other. At least they were the ones who most frequently and publicly debated the topic against each other and who spoke out most emphatically in speeches and in writings, each in defense of his own theories. Both had large followings—neither stood alone. Williams and his followers were for deleting gymnastics entirely from the schools, whereas McCloy and his followers though in agreement as far as getting rid of the old militaristic forms was concerned, were for retaining parts of the old which they claimed had been tested and were found to be still good for the new day. In McCloy's *Philosophical Basis For Physical Education,* he said:

> . . . the monkey in us would point toward apparatus work as being as natural as basketball, merely needing to be reorganized, purged of its "exercises," and to be properly taught. . . . I am convinced that the dropping of this type of activity is not at all complimentary to our professional intelligence.[6]

Williams berated even the setting-up exercises of the type of the Daily Dozen, popularized by Walter Camp and many others, whereas McCloy defended them as appropriate for certain people unable to exercise otherwise and insufficiently knowledgeable to devise their own forms, though he disclaimed them as a criterion for a physical education program.

As natural gymnastics developed, it soon became apparent that even this new form, as it was presented by many, was not really natural after all, since many of the exercises used did not come to children naturally, but were thought up and taught to the children by others. The old teacher-imposed, teacher-controlled exercises of the German and Swedish systems were merely replaced by new teacher-contrived, teacher-imposed exercises of a new form and with a new name, so that shortly natural gymnastics (which regretfully never had a chance to develop properly for lack of adequate teachers) faded from the program, to be replaced entirely by sports and dancing. Gymnastic apparatus of all kinds now vanished from the gymnasiums of the American schools that adopted the new philosophy, and most did adopt it. The great majority of teachers, as usually happens, avoided the extremes at both the left and right, trying out the new but not forsaking all of the old, and in the process formulated a new and greatly improved program of physical education.

Outcomes for Physical Education. Followers of the Progressive Education Movement did get rid of the calisthenics drill master, but when schools replaced him with the domineering type of coach many complained that this was not enough. As physical education sought a reply to this new tyrant, there arose much talk of benching the coach during games, which talk did cause physical educators and many coaches as well to reappraise the function of the coach as an educator, although the bench-the-coach idea never did get a serious following.

Another accompaniment of the Progressive Education Movement that went to absurd extremes at the hands of radicals was the changing concept about teaching democracy. There grew up the idea that any decision made by a majority was superior to one arrived at by a minority, regardless of how greatly the balance of wisdom might be in favor of the minority. This extreme notion of the value of majority opinion on all things called forth much protest from many leaders. In the realm of physical education, C. H. McCloy again took the lead and spoke out when he said in his article, "A Half Century of Physical Education":

> I hope that next fifty years will cause physical educators to . . . seek for facts, proved objectively; [and] to question principles based on average opinions of people who don't know, but are all anxious to contribute their averaged ignorance to form a consensus of uniformed dogma.[7]

Although much nonsense arose as to how to teach democracy and how to reorganize the school as a pattern of democratic procedure, in the end common sense did prevail in most situations; and much good came from the effort, although there still lingers in the minds of many educators and lay people the thought that too much permissiveness may not after all have been real democracy in action. Was education producing a generation that considered the rights of the individual to be above the greatest good of the greatest number? The arguments on this still rage in many aspects of national life.

The 1930 House Conference on Child Health and Protection

In November of 1930 President Hoover's White House Conference on Child Health and Protection was held in Washington, D.C. Its purpose was "to get a composite picture of this complex child, to find out how he rates physically, mentally, morally, what our rapidly changing civilization is doing to make or mar him, to determine where our social, educational, and governmental machinery is at fault in training him to his utmost capacities, and where it may be strengthened."

The conference's conclusions were embodied in a Children's Charter of nineteen aims for the children of America, one of which pledged "for every child from birth through adolescence promotion of health, including health instruction, and a health program, wholesome physical and mental recreation, with teachers and leaders adequately trained."[8] This conference led to greatly increased interest in physical education for the schools.

STATUS OF PHYSICAL EDUCATION

Whereas in the nineteenth century the chief consideration concerning programs was the question as to what system of gymnastics to teach, attention now turned to whether the program should be built around gymnastics, or sports and dancing, or a combination of the three. Also, where previously a goodly segment of citizens had advocated military drill in the schools in place of physical education, physical education had so effectively demonstrated its values during World War I that even the War Department came to recognize it as a valuable partner of military training and openly discouraged the idea of substituting military drill in the schools for physical education.

The death knell of gymnastics as an activity in the school program was sounded largely in 1910, when the National Society for the Study of Education published its *Ninth Year Book* in which Wood of Columbia took a firm stand for sports as a substitute for gymnastics. Psychologists, led by G. Stanley Hall, and sociologists, backed him in this stand, and school authorities began to accept the idea.

In 1916 Ernest H. Arnold, M.D. (1865–1929), in his presidential address before the American Physical Education Association, complained, "the plow of physical training has scarcely drawn a furrow in the virgin soil." But by the end of this era, that plow had made a wide swath across the land. Just how much of a swath is revealed in the many figures in the material that follows throughout the remainder of this chapter. If there seems to be a surfeit of dates and statistics it must be realized that only by dates can an item be placed in its niche in history and only by figures can one grasp the extent of growth.

Aims and Objectives

Educators, parents, and the public in general now began asking what were the aims and objectives of physical education. Although Hitchcock and Sargent in an earlier day had both voiced their own aims, the profession as an organized group had not faced up to the challenge. Now Hetherington, President of the Physical Education Department of the National Education Association, voiced for the profession the aims in this new century as: (1) organic education for vital vigor; (2) psychomotor education for power and skill in neuromuscular activities; (3) character education for moral, social, and spiritual powers; and (4) intellectual education acquired through free play or development of social thinking. These aims were a far cry from the single, narrow aim of the earlier eras, that of relieving the tedium of the schoolroom.

At the same time physical education added to its aims a broader base: (1) to share in the development and carrying out of the pattern of general education—in other words, to become an integral part of education; (2) to offer a program that would become an integral part of community life through its recreational aspects.

Much talk arose over the concomitant learning to be derived from physical education activities, particularly over character education from plays and games. Frequent topics at professional gatherings for many years centered about sportsmanship. What are the elements of true sportsmanship? What is an amateur? What is a professional? Much oratory, some eloquence, much debate, some wisdom, came out of all the talk. School essays were written on the topic. Professional association presidential addresses dealt with it, and the professional literature of the period abounded in articles on the subject. What leader in the profession did not present his own definition of a true "sportsman" to have it checked against those of his peers for long argumentation as to just how participation in sports could be made to produce this concomitant learning in children. Even clergymen across the country discussed from their pulpits this newly recognized objective of physical education and looked with hope to the profession to make true "sportsmen" of all school children now that emphasis was placed on play and games as a part of the school program.

What physical education teacher worth his mettle did not keep posted in a conspicuous place on the school bulletin board his or her favorite definition of *sportsmanship* for all to read and study. And all that were posted perhaps none enjoyed more acclaim than the definition on page 151 offered as given by the Princeton professor.

Lower Schools

Whereas practically none but the large city schools had organized physical education by the end of the last century and only a few small towns had added it after the turn of the century, the post–World War I period brought great and sudden growth in this branch of education. For example, Alabama, California, Ohio, and Virginia not only employed state supervisors of physical education but county supervisors as well; the entire state of Florida had but three full-time physical education teachers in 1924, but by 1927 it had 73; Indiana had few schools in 1900 with special teachers of physical education, but by 1930 it had 802 in 477 schools; and Minnesota had only 108 full-time and 63 part-time teachers of physical education in 1924, but by 1930 it had 301 full-time and 698 part-time teachers. These are typical examples of what was going on throughout the country.

Facilities. Although gymnasiums of this new era far outnumbered those of the 1890s, building did not keep abreast with the growth of the programs. The medium-sized towns made the best showing in facilities according to the findings of the White House Conference of 1930, which reported, for example, that Ohio had gymnasiums in 80 percent of its public schools; New York, in 62 percent; the Dakotas, in 51 percent; and New Hampshire, in 44 percent.

The National Education Association through its Committee on School House

Planning set up standards for physical education facilities in the schools calling for every junior and senior high school to have a gymnasium which "must be a Hall of Health with an abundance of fresh air and sunlight."[9] The Committee on Reorganization of Secondary Education went further and recommended for every school two gymnasiums, one for boys and one for girls, and many schools strove to meet these requirements. In 1907 Detroit opened a swimming pool in its Central High School—the first high school pool in the United States and a year later built the first public school gymnasium to be exclusively used by girls. As to playing fields the Society of State Directors of Physical Education called for a field of three to four acres for every 400 pupils, and the NEA asked for fields of at least ten acres for all rural high schools.

Programs. The College Physical Education Association spent nine years on the study of a national curriculum for all grades through college and from this study set up an approved program for the elementary grades which was accepted as a national pattern. It consisted of the following: athletic games, 25 percent of program; rhythms, 20 percent; hunting games, 15 percent; and 10 percent each of self-testing activities, mimetics, free exercises, and relays combined with stunts and tumbling.[10]

Requirements. Most state departments of education set a minimum physical education requirement in the schools, and many city and town schools set their own minimum above that. In the 1920s many schools set a minimum of 415 minutes per week of physical education classwork in the elementary schools and 300 per week in junior high schools.

The question of granting school credit for physical education classwork was fought out seriously in this era. A survey of 582 schools of New York State in 1924 revealed that 82 percent of the principals and superintendents were in favor of granting credit. Of the 17 percent opposed one said, "I am opposed to giving credit for digging potatoes, etc. in lieu of Latin"; another said, "Schools are for training the young to read and write"; and yet another said, "It would be as much out of the general scheme as giving credit for eating well-balanced dinners." So it was obvious that as late as 1924 many educators still held a narrow concept of both physical education and education. However, by 1930 credit was being granted in seventeen states. From a survey of 254 school systems it was shown that 70 percent were granting credit by that date.

Staff. In 1903 when Gulick became the first head of the physical education department of the New York City schools he inherited a staff of thirty-six physical education teachers, the largest group in any school system in the United States at that time. Before his coming, these teachers had gone their way alone. Now Gulick united and coordinated them into a department staff. When Ethel Perrin was appointed Supervisor of Physical Education for the Detroit public schools, she inherited a staff of three men and two women specialists. When she left that position fourteen years later, she left a staff of 360 specialists.

Most elementary schools followed the general pattern of placing the responsibility of teaching physical education upon the classroom teacher. The high schools tended to employ sports coaches for the boys, and then assign them the physical education class work; whereas they called upon the home economics or some other academic teacher to teach the physical activity classes for girls. But after World War I the situation improved considerably.

By 1931 Alabama, California, and Virginia were maintaining county directors of physical education as well as state directors. Indicative of the progress throughout the country are the following figures: Indiana schools from 802 physical education teachers in 1930 to 1037 in 1932; Massachusetts schools from 211 physical education teachers and 60 school gymnasiums in 1920 to 1100 teachers and 700 gymnasiums in 1932; and Pennsylvania schools from 153 physical education teachers in 1921 to 2200 in 1935. Indiana schools in 1932 required all coaches of interscholastic sports in high schools to hold certificates of training in the field of physical education.

Studies of this era showed the commonly accepted standard distribution for the forty-hour-per-week teaching load of a physical education teacher to be twenty-five hours of teaching, five hours for administrative work, five for extracurricular activities, and five for consultation with pupils.

There is little information available as to salaries of this era but there is a record that in the New York City schools in the early 1900s, men physical educators were paid $1300 to $2400, and junior assistants, $1000 to $1200 per year, while the women teachers were paid $1000 to $1900, and junior assistants, $700 to $1000. These represent top salaries for the opening of the century.

Physical Education for College Men

In the early 1900s much antagonism still existed within the college faculties toward physical education as a part of the educational program. Nonetheless those colleges that had not yet developed physical education departments before the end of the nineteenth century now began to carry on the programs heretofore carried on unofficially by the students themselves.

The state universities that had not established physical education before the close of the nineteenth century fell quickly into line, with Pennsylvania leading in 1904 and Idaho in 1908. Of the several universities that first established physical education departments, fifteen maintained separate departments of physical education for men and women with five of these completely separated in all respects and ten separated but coordinated under a Division of Physical Education.

Facilities. This was a period of gymnasium building and rebuilding: funds were made available, and many fine buildings were provided. A 1909 survey showed that

114 colleges had gymnasiums whereas by 1920 there were 209 colleges with gymnasiums.[11] William Ralph LaPorte (1889–1954) of the University of Southern California invented the self-service locker-basket system which added much to the efficiency of dressing rooms and facilitated classwork materially. The increased popularity of indoor intercollegiate athletic sports caused architects to increase the seating capacity of the structures. Gymnasiums with a gallery running track became popular at the turn of the century, but interest in this feature had practically died out by 1930. Not only fine gymnasiums but also great football stadiums were built in this era.

Early in this era when football was becoming ''big business'' in the colleges and universities, Harvard University built the first of the large stadiums (1904). It seated 23,000, an unheard-of seating capacity before this date. Yale followed in 1913 with its coliseum, so-called at first because it was not open at the ends but was enclosed like the Greek and Roman coliseums. Later it became known as the Yale Bowl. It seated 67,000. Other colleges slowly fell into line, but most stadiums of this era were not built until the 1920s. By 1920 the total seating capacity of stadiums in existence was 929,523; by 1930 the total had risen to 2,307,000. The stadium at the University of Michigan first seated 87,500 and was later enlarged to seat 97,000; the Ohio State University stadium seated 77,000, later increased to 85,000 capacity.

As to gymnasiums of that period, the most magnificent in the United States, no doubt in the entire world, was the $10 million Payne Whitney Gymnasium at Yale University, completed in 1932. Five stories high, with an additional four stories in the large tower, each level represents one phase of activity in the physical education program. Its beautiful entrance hall is decorated with reproductions of sculptures of athletes by R. Tait McKenzie. Its spacious quarters can accommodate 1200 students participating in activities simultaneously.

Requirements. The University of Pennsylvania was the first university to require all students to take courses in physical education for all four years. Beyond this, following the advice of their own Benjamin Franklin, given 150 years earlier, the authorities also made the ability to swim a requirement for graduation. The land-grant colleges lagged in their physical education offerings, because of their commitment to require military drill of all male students. By the close of the era in the other colleges and universities, physical education was quite generally required for both men and women for three hours per week for the first two years of college work.

Staff Rank. The University of Pennsylvania gave R. Tait McKenzie the rank of full professor when he was brought from McGill University in 1904 to become head of its physical education department. Following that appointment, several other colleges granted professional rank to heads of physical education departments. A study by Meylan of Columbia University in 1916 showed that out of 252 colleges surveyed, 100 granted the rank of professor to men directors of physical education, but only 30 granted this recognition to women directors.[12]

The College Physical Education Society reported that by 1927 27 percent of college physical directors had the M.D. degree; 8 percent, the Ph.D. or Ed.D. degree; 20 percent, the master's degree as top degree; and 38 percent, the bachelor's degree. Seven percent had no college degree.

As to salaries after World War I, a survey of 1922 showed that although the top salaries to heads of departments were one of $10,000 and two of $8000, 61 percent of the 227 colleges of the survey paid the top position $2000 to $3500; 8 percent, between $1500 and $2000; 27 percent, between $1000 and $1500; and 3 percent, less than $1000. It is quite probable that these lesser salaries were paid to men who carried athletic coaching positions on the side for which they received salary from the athletic funds.

Physical Education for College Women

By the time of World War I, practically all colleges and universities with female students had established departments of physical education for women. In the coeducational schools, some were placed under the men's departments, some were coordinated with them, and some were independent of them.

Many forceful women were at the helm at this time shaping the destinies of these college departments and setting the pattern of a philosophy for the physical education of women which materially affected programs in the lower schools and in nonschool groups as well as in the colleges.

Facilities.[13] In most coeducational colleges and universities the women's physical education facilities were quite meager compared to those for the men. The women used the men's gymnasium floor and playing fields when the men did not wish to use them. But in a few colleges women were fortunate and had their own facilities. In 1900 Hearst Hall, a gymnasium for women, was built at the University of California (Berkeley). Women of the University of Texas had their own gymnasium in the basement of the woman's Building early in this era, and the University of Washington had a small building for a women's gymnasium. The Mary Hemenway Gymnasium of Wellesley College of 1909 was then years ahead of the times in many of its details, such as having central-controlled showers and a costume-disinfection system. But all too frequently the women fell heir to the men's old gymnasiums when they acquired new ones.

However, it was not until the 1920s that women students really came into their own in physical education facilities. The new Hearst Memorial Gymnasium at the University of California at Berkeley, built in 1927 in semimonumental style of architecture, was particularly magnificent in its architectural design and in its scope of facilities.

Four well-designed and equipped gymnasiums were constructed for college women in the 1920s at the Universities of Oregon, Washington, California (Berkeley), and at Smith College. Other notable buildings of that decade were those at North Carolina College for Women built in 1923, and at the universities of Minnesota, Colorado, and Illinois.

For outdoor facilities Mills College built the first college outdoor swimming pool in 1924 to be followed shortly by the three outdoor pools for women at the University of California.

The novelty of electrically controlled doors to divide gymnasium floors came as early as 1930. One of the first was in the women's gymnasium at St. Catherine's School in St. Paul, Minnesota.

Athletic fields for the exclusive use of women in coeducational institutions were first developed in this era. In the fall of 1901 the women at the University of Chicago had a hockey field laid out in an open parkway at Woodlawn Avenue and 59th Street.[14] Since the game had come to America only that summer, this must have been one of the earliest hockey fields in the country, most certainly the first away from the Eastern college area. The women's colleges have always led all other schools in their playing space for women. In 1902 Wellesley College constructed a boathouse and bathhouse on the shores of its campus lake, and by 1929 boasted twenty-two tennis courts, several hockey fields, and a like proportion of other play areas. Smith College by 1930 led all other colleges in its outdoor facilities for women. This college maintained in one field twenty tennis courts, ten archery lanes, a running track, and in another field of twenty acres, four hockey fields, a soccer field, a baseball diamond, a golf-driving range, several badminton courts, and a bridle path. Smith College also had three outing cabins, a boathouse, a crewhouse, and riding stables.

Programs. Although women engaged in sports in colleges from the earliest days of their enrollment in these schools, they, like the men students, organized them on their own, quite apart from any officially recognized physical education classes. Wellesley College was the first of the women's colleges to accept activities other than gymnastics and rhythms as a part of the physical education required program. It was not until the 1910s that sports were accepted as a part of the all-year school programs by most colleges.[15]

In the 1920s there was a marked increase of emphasis on corrective work (individual gymnastics) for those needing special developmental or protective measures in their exercise program. A few colleges offered this work in the 1910s, and a rare few, influenced by the Swedish Movement Cure of the late nineteenth century, offered this work in the first decade of the 1900s. The women's departments in all eras have been far in advance of the men's departments in this field of work in the United States.

Throughout this era there was a constant increase in sports offerings, also the introduction of courses in body mechanics. A survey of 1930 made in connection with research on women's athletics covering 120 colleges in all sections of the country showed that the most commonly used athletic activities were the following: basketball used in 96 percent of the colleges; softball, in 90 percent; field hockey, in 87 percent; swimming, in 80 percent; archery, in 70 percent; track and field, in 60 percent; and soccer, in 58 percent. In the 1930s and 1940s, fieldball and speedball, badminton, deck tennis, and handball were added to the women's programs.

Staffs. In the 1890s a department of physical education for women was considered sufficient in size if it had one teacher with possibly one or two student assistants. By 1900, however, several women's colleges had as many as two or three full-time teachers, and by 1929 most had two or more full-time teachers. Wellesley College boasted thirteen. A few colleges employed women trained in Sweden and England but most used graduates of American schools of physical education. As to academic training, Oberlin College was the only one at the turn of the century that employed a woman teacher trained in physical education who also held a college degree. Gradually teachers with college degrees came on the scene, and by the end of this era practically all heads of women's departments in colleges held at least the bachelor's degree, and most of them had from one to two years of graduate work. The several women heads of departments who held the medical doctor's degree in this new era were trained in physical education as well as in medicine.

In the earlier century the only title recognized for a woman physical education teacher except in one or two rare cases was that of director or directress of the gymnasium. Even into the 1920s many colleges conferred upon their women physical education teachers no academic rank whatsoever. On the other hand, as early as 1885 and 1895 Oberlin College and the University of Nebraska accorded the rank of instructor to their women directors of physical education. In 1896 the University of Michigan conferred the rank of full professor on their Director of Physical Education for Women[16] Oberlin advanced their women's director to the rank of full professor in 1903—the first private college to grant this rank to a woman physical educator. Wellesley College, in 1909, became the first of the women's colleges to accord the head of the department of physical education the rank of professor.

Salaries for women physical education teachers ranged from $500 to $1500 per year in the early part of this era, and after World War I increased to range from $1000 to $4000 in the 1920s and 1930s. These figures are for the average positions.

Costumes.[17] The most universally accepted costume of the first part of this era was the long, full bloomers of three to five yards of woolen suiting, a middy blouse and middy tie, or a blouse of the same material as the bloomers worn with a stiffly starched dickey with complicated underarm harness to hold it in place, long, black cotton hose, heavily ribbed, and leather, orthopedic-style gym oxfords. By the 1910s a decided change came about, and in the 1920s still another so that by 1930 the woolen costume had given way completely to cotton, and the full bloomers had practically vanished from the scene replaced by scant bloomers with elastic well above the knee or by shorts.

Not until the 1930s were swimming suits of other than gray cotton permissible for school use. By this date special treatment of materials had been devised to protect against the shedding of lint and the running of dyes. Thus swimming costumes at last became attractive to women students. For girls' gymnasium suits, this period brought into use the short cotton, knicker-type, scant bloomer with sleeveless blouse, or shorts with tailored blouse. For dance, the leotards came into use—knitted material like that used in swimming suits—some with short sleeves, some long, some shortlegged and some long. Boys' costumes, too, took on a *new look* with trunks greatly abbreviated from those of earlier eras.

Research[18]

The interest in research of the preceding century grew with the years, and the new century brought new and wider interests in testing. Whereas anthropometrical measurements and strength tests held the main interest in the earlier days, physical achievement tests and tests of cardiac efficiency now took the stage of interest, motivating for improved programs.

By the opening of the new century it had become apparent to the medical people both within and outside the profession that children, for their protection, should be classified for exercise according to the functioning of their heart and blood vessels. In 1905 McCurdy at Springfield started work on adolescent changes in heart and blood pressure, and in 1917 Schneider at Connecticut Wesleyan developed his cardio–vascular efficiency tests, which were used by the aviation services during World War I.

From the first physical achievement tests for school children (devised by Gulick for the New York City Public School Athletic League in 1904 from his earlier penthathlon tests of the 1890s devised for the YMCA) to those given in 1928 by the National Recreation Association to 44,117 boys and girls of 450 cities, there was a great advance in testing techniques and standard setting. The American Physical Education Association produced its athletic badge tests with established standards of achievement in 1913, and its national committee, set up under McCurdy in 1922 to work on motor ability tests, developed a physical intelligence quotient. At this same time the Playground Association presented its Athletic Badge Test consisting of, for boys, (1) arm strength, (2) jumping for distance, (3) running for speed, (4) throwing a baseball for accuracy, and (5) throwing a baseball for distance; for girls, (1) balancing, (2) running for speed, (3) throwing a baseball for accuracy, (4) throwing a baseball for distance, and (5) efficiency in fundamentals of a game, either baseball, basketball, or volleyball.

In the college field, Meylan of Columbia University devised in 1919 the first achievement tests for college men using elements of sports in running, jumping, climbing, vaulting, throwing, etc., and in the same year Agnes Wayman of Barnard College presented the first such tests for college women. In 1921, Sargent first presented his Physical Test of a Man, which achieved much attention throughout the country. This test consisted of a vertical jump using the factors of height and weight with ability to overcome the force of gravity. The efficiency index for this test was arrived at by the formula of weight in pounds multiplied by height of vertical jump in inches divided by height in inches. In the 1920s Frederick Rand Rogers (1894–   ), of Boston University, started work on a physical fitness index (PFI), which although largely replaced by later tests was still in use in the 1960s. However, this test aroused much controversy among the research specialists in the profession. It seemed that one was enthusiastically for the Rogers test or enthusiastically against it; there was no middle ground. This index is the achieved strength index divided by the normal strength index for the individual's age and weight. Tables of norms for age and height were worked out for the formula.

Interest in testing and research, aimed at improvement of the profession in all of its aspects, had grown so remarkably by 1930 that 25 percent of the schools in a national survey were found to be using a testing program of some kind whereas practically none had testing programs at the opening of the century. Beginning in 1930 the American Association for Health, Physical Education and Recreation established a periodical on the subject, *The Research Quarterly*. The summer of 1924 was the first time that a course in testing in physical education was offered in a teacher-training department—Teachers College, Columbia University.

There arose such a deep interest in testing in this period that many schools plunged into it without teachers adequately prepared to do such work or to interpret it correctly. Harold Rugg, a leading educator of the time, spoke of this period as one when education "was consumed with a passion for precise measurement." As he said:

> We lived in one long orgy of tabulation. . . . Mountains of facts were piled up, condensed, summarized and interpreted by the new quantitive technique. The air was full of normal curves, standard deviations, coefficients of correlation, regressive equations.[19]

Yet out of it all, with much enthusiam well placed, some misplaced, there came improvements in physical education programs with standards of performance at hand for the measurement of growth and progress.

Teacher Training

Unlike most teachers of physical education in the nineteenth century many teachers of the early decades of the twentieth century had technical training, and judging from the numbers graduating from the various professional training schools more women than men had a good preparation. This factor no doubt resulted from the fact that there were more training schools for women than for men, also, the laity considered any man to be sufficiently prepared to teach the subject if in his own school days he had participated in sports.

An increasing demand for more teachers brought forth more training schools and more attention to this need by the colleges. The growing demand that teachers have at least a bachelor's degree brought about the movement within the private noncollegiate normal school for affiliation with some college, which meant marked changes in many of these schools and the demise of others.

At the close of the World War I there were approximately 10,000 men and women in the United States professionally trained in physical education. By 1930 ninety-three institutions of collegiate rank were offering teacher preparation in physical education, to meet the demand for trained teachers in the field. Not only schools and colleges were asking for trained personnel but also playgrounds, recreation centers, boys' and girls' clubs, YMCAs, YWCAs, all manner of youth-saving groups, hospitals, rehabilitation centers, and all branches of the armed services. This demand brought about greatly increased teacher-training offerings. But the day of the private noncollegiate school of physical education was coming to a close. Practically all teacher training in the field of physical education was, by the end of this era, established in the colleges and universities.

Private NonCollegiate Schools. Practically all schools preparing physical education teachers before 1900 were private noncollegiate normal schools. Early in the new century, several new schools were established—the Chicago Normal School of Physical Education (1905), the Battle Creek School of Physical Education (1909), Bouvé-Boston School of Physical Education (1913), the American School of Physical Education in Boston (1914), Columbia Normal School of Physical Education in Chicago (1915), the Newark School of Physical Education (1917), the Central School of Physical Education in New York City (1919), the YMCA Graduate School in Nashville, Tennessee (1919), the Marjorie Webster School of Physical Education in Washington (1920), the Ithaca School of Physical Education (1920), and the Bouvé School in Boston (1925).

The first of the private schools to achieve collegiate rank was the YMCA International Training School of Springfield, Massachusetts, which acquired authority in 1905 to confer the degrees of bachelor of physical education (B.P.E.) and master of physical education (M.P.E.). In 1912, the name of the school was changed to the International YMCA College and in 1953 to Springfield College. By 1916 it had lengthened its physical education course to four years. Dr. J. H. McCurdy was head of the physical education work of the school from 1895 to 1930.

In 1907 the Normal School of the North American Gymnatic Union moved to Indianapolis, Indiana, and was authorized by law to confer degrees. Under the leadership of Emil Rath (1873–1943), who served as dean of the school from 1909 to 1934, the school widened its curriculum, and in 1941 it affiliated with the University of Indiana.[20] The Boston Normal School of Gymnastics was the first of these private schools to seek collegiate affiliation. In 1909 it affiliated with Wellesley College, offering a five-year course for the bachelor's degree, and a two-year course in specialization open to those who already possessed the bachelor's degree. In 1917 it achieved graduate status, fulfilling the dreams of many years of Amy Morris Homans.[21] In 1913 the YMCA Training School in Chicago achieved collegiate rating and became George Williams College.

The Anderson School (originally the Brooklyn School of Physical Education), which moved to New Haven in 1900 and became known as the New Haven Normal School of Gymnastics, took on collegiate rank in 1921 as Arnold College. In 1924 the YMCA Graduate School of Nashville achieved collegiate rating, but it closed its doors in 1937. In 1929 the Central School of Physical Education moved to Troy, New York, aligning itself with Rusell Sage College. In 1902 the Sargent School lengthened its course to three years, and in 1929 it became a division of the School of Education of Boston University.

Colleges and Universities. A few colleges and universities, such as Detroit Normal School of 1881 (later Wayne University), Oberlin College of 1886, and the universities of California and Nebraska in late 1890, had offered isolated teacher-training courses before the turn of the century to aid classroom teachers, and three in the 1890s had offered professional courses leading to a bachelor's degree: Harvard, a private men's school, then Stanford, a private coeducational school, and then the University of Nebraska, a state university, all three graduating their first candidates before the century closed (as discussed in Chapter 6). With the new century many colleges and universities quickly fell into line. Oberlin College had started its major in physical education in 1898 and graduated its first candidate in 1902. Several colleges and universities established physical education majors as follows: Teachers College, Columbia University (1903), the State Normal School, Ypsilanti, Michigan (1907), California, Oregon, and Washington, men (1910), Wisconsin (1911), Missouri and Utah (1914), Iowa (1918), Illinois, men, Indiana, men, and Minnesota (1919), Kansas (1920), Michigan and Washington, women (1921), Texas and Illinois, women (1923), Ohio State (1924), and Wyoming (1925).

Training of physical education teachers fell to some liberal arts colleges, some teachers colleges, and some schools of education, especially the latter two.

By early 1920s a struggle developed in the colleges within the fields of physical education, health education, and recreation for the control of teacher preparation in these fields. The heavy requirement of so-called education courses demanded by the teachers colleges on the false assumption that all students expected to go into the public schools to teach, allowed little time for courses in allied fields, hence handicapping professional training. Under the professional school form of organization, preparation in physical education readily combined with preparation in the fields of athletics, dance, health education, safety education, and recreation, while preparing students to work in colleges, YMCAs, YWCAs, and like organizations, in municipal recreation departments and for private groups. Several universities established this form of organization, some setting up this teacher-training work in its own school and others putting it in a college of health, physical education, and recreation.

The earliest record of an attempt to set up such a school or college within a university is that of 1908, when Clark Hetherington successfully piloted through the board of curators of the University of Missouri a resolution calling for the establishment of such a four-year school offering a bachelor of science degree in physical education. For some reason the approved project was side tracked, and nothing came of it. Two years later Hetherington left Missouri, and it was twelve years later (1920) when the first school of health and physical education within a university was established at the University of Oregon. In 1924 a similar school was established at Stanford University. This era produced only one college of health and physical education—this at Pennsylvania State University in 1930.

Public Normal Schools. The first public normal school to offer specialization in physical education was at Ypsilanti, Michigan. The course started in 1907 under Wilbur P. Bowen. Soon many normal schools, spurred on by state legislation, provided for specialization in physical education.

Graduate Preparation. In 1901 Teachers College of Columbia University, inspired by Dr. Wood, became the first institution to offer the master's degree with specialization in physical education, and soon thereafter a few other schools followed their lead. However, Wellesley College was the first to set up a graduate curriculum in physical education which was open only to persons who had completed full undergraduate requirements for a major in physical education.

For many years it has been accepted that Columbia University and New York University were the first schools in the United States to offer a doctoral program with specialization in physical education, both entering upon this work in 1924. But recent research refutes this and offers the following facts concerning the conferring of doctor's degrees with specialization in physical education: in May 1925 Columbia University conferred the Ph.D. degree upon Frederick Rand Rogers; in August 1925 the YMCA Graduate School of Nashville conferred the D.P.E. degree upon Glenn Gentry,[22] in May 1926 Columbia University conferred the Ph.D. degree upon Ethel Saxman. These were the first doctorates in this field: the first Ph.D., the first D.P.E., and the first doctorate to a woman.

By 1930 twenty-eight institutions were offering graduate work in physical education, New York University starting its program in 1925. The University of Pittsburgh and Stanford University (1929) were the first institutions to offer the doctor of education degree for specialization in physical education; the first such degree conferred was at Pittsburgh in 1932.

Summer Schools. By 1909 the Harvard Summer School of Physical Education had developed into a specialized course covering three seasons of work to procure a certificate. Following the 1918 session it closed, although that summer it had 230 students and a staff of 48 lecturers, instructors, and assistants. In its thirty-one years of existence it had been a powerful force in the advancement of the profession. According to Sargent's own records it had trained 3652 persons, who came from 1082 different institutions, 53 countries, 232 colleges and universities, 245 secondary schools, 326 elementary schools, 72 YMCAs, 19 municipal gymnasiums, 30 athletic clubs, 27 state institutions, 4 voice-training schools, and 11 normal schools. These students were school superintendents, college professors, principals of public and private schools, lawyers, physicians, members of foreign embassies, school teachers, and athletes.

The Chautauqua Summer School of Physical Education continued for several years into the twentieth century before closing its doors. In 1903 the Savage School added summer courses for a few summers. In 1904 Yale inaugurated a summer school of physical education, but it lasted only four years. In 1909 Teachers College of Columbia University offered its first summer courses in this field. In 1912 the New Haven School of Gymnastics and the University of Utah joined the summer school group. After World War I, summer courses increased markedly in universities, particularly making an appeal to the classroom teacher who had been drafted to teach physical education part time.

Specialized Training. Correspondence courses in physical education were offered by Dr. Jay W. Seaver of Yale in the opening years of the century. When these course offerings started is not on record, but letterheads carrying the date of 1903 have been seen with Dr. Seaver's name listed as President and Medical Director of the American Institute of Physical Culture—a Correspondence School of Health and Exercise. The letterhead carried the address of 29 Beacon Street, Boston crossed out with New Haven substituted.

In 1914 the University of Illinois offered its first Coaches School, and this idea spread quickly to other universities. Also, special professional courses in physical therapy were offered in some schools during World War I to meet the current need of trained personnel in that field. Following the War this specialization grew into permanent courses offered by several schools in cooperation with the physical education major.

Physical Education In Nonschool Organizations

Physical education developed rapidly in the 1900s in nonschool organizations such as YMCAs, YWCAs, and various youth groups. Those reaching the largest number of participants are discussed in the material that follows.

Young Men's Christian Associations.[23] The YMCA expanded its program, working with all types of community agencies, to promote physical activities for young boys in particular, yet giving increased attention, also, to its offering for young adults and older men. The national organization now maintained two colleges and a graduate school: the International YMCA Training College in Springfield, Massachusetts, George Williams College in Chicago, and the YMCA Graduate School in Nashville, Tennessee. All three specialized in the preparation of teachers of physical education to man their so-called physical departments.

In 1906 Dr. George J. Fisher, then a YMCA director at Brooklyn, was named head of the Physical Department of the International Committee, and in 1910 Dr. John Brown, Jr., a former YMCA director at Montreal and New York City and just out of medical school, joined the staff of the National Board. When Dr. Fisher became Deputy Scout Executive of the Boy Scouts of America in 1919, Dr. Brown succeeded to the national YMCA directorship of the physical department which he held until his retirement in 1941. Under the management of these two men the international physical education program expanded remarkably.

Dr. Fisher originated the "Teach America to Swim" slogan, and in 1906 the YMCA under his direction inaugurated a mass swimming campaign, followed shortly by swim tests and awards. It cooperated with the American Red Cross in setting up the earliest first-aid classes and until 1925 the two organizations gave a joint certificate. In 1910 the YMCA interested the American Red Cross in establishing life-saving courses. In 1915 it set up its junior and senior hexathlons, and in 1916 its School of Aquatics.

Since 1896 the YMCA Athletic League, upon recommendation of the YMCA Physical Directors Society, had been affiliated with the AAU, but in 1913 it broke off relations, not to renew the alliance for eighteen years.

During World War I many YMCA physical directors beyond service age worked with the allied troops both at home and overseas. The program they offered to the servicemen was designed to occupy leisure hours through recreational sports participation aimed at developing morale and a sense of brotherhood with all other servicemen. They also worked with convalescents in hospitals, helping with muscle reeducation and recreational activities. Many others worked in Community Service Camps and organized recreation programs for civilian war workers.

Following the war the YMCA started the national volleyball and indoor swimming championships in 1922, national basketball championship in 1923, and handball contests in 1925. In 1937 it held its first aquatics conference; in 1938 a Sports Championships Congress; and in 1940 it launched its Learn-to-Swim campaigns. Throughout this period there was a marked increased in the numbers of gymnasiums and athletic fields available to the public under YMCA auspices, also in numbers of trained leaders to man the facilities.

Young Women's Christian Associations. In this new era YWCAs spread rapidly all across the country as the YMCAs had in the era before. And like them they quickly installed physical education departments and added swimming to activity programs, with the first classes being opened at Montgomery, Alabama, and Buffalo, New York, in 1905. In 1911 they organized the first National Conference of

YWCA Health Education Directors. The National Board uses the term *health education* in preference to *physical education*. The Centennial Report of 1916 stated that there were 65,000 women attending YWCA gymnasium classes, and 32,000 were in the swimming classes. In thirty years the enrollment in physical activity classes had increased to 380,965.[24]

Turners and Sokols. With the public schools assuming the responsibility for the physical training of children, the Turner and Sokol clubs now placed their emphasis on programs for adults. With the coming of World War I, so much feeling arose against Germany that it became highly advisable for groups bound together by their common German and Czech backgrounds to dissolve and to identify themselves exclusively with other Americans as Americans. This materially affected these societies and they waned markedly.

Movements Related to Physical Education

Many important movements related to physical education in various aspects of their programs originated in this era, such as the Boy Scouts of America, headed in this era by physical education's George Fisher, M.D., and the Camp Fire Girls of America, founded by physical education's Luther Halsey Gulick, M.D., both in 1910, the latter association a strictly American innovation built around the legends of the world of the American Indian; the Girls Scouts of America (1912); and the National Park Service (1911). The recreation movement co-founded by physical education's Doctor Gulick and the camping movement founded by physical education's George Meylan, M.D., grew every more important with the coming of the twentieth century.

Recreation Movement.[25] The playground movement of 1900 helped to sell physical education to the public, and the play activities, athletics, and folk dance which were now added to the recreation program, helped immeasurably to popularize it. The promotion of recreation had become an accepted part of American life in the large cities and the groups that had previously supported settlement yards and school playgrounds broadened their activities to include municipal, state, and national recreation areas. Sums of money which were enormous for those days were spent for these ventures.

In 1900 Chicago appropriated $10,000 for the equipment of playgrounds in densely populated districts. Congress began the annual appropriations for playground work for the District of Columbia in 1905. Chicago, in 1903, voted a $5 million bond issue for small recreation parks, and ten were opened in 1905. By 1910 the city was operating sixty-five playgrounds and bathing beaches, and its South Park system was regarded as the finest in the world. Boston, New York, and Philadelphia also made provision for playgrounds and parks. In all, more than 150 cities reported playgrounds before 1910, and many other cities had them in the planning stage. Los Angeles appointed its first Board of Playground Commissioners in 1904.

The increased interest in recreation that followed World War I brought greatly expanded facilities: play fields, swimming pools, bathing beaches, golf courses, day camps, and winter sports facilities. By 1925, 748 cities had community recreation leaders, and 688 cities had 5121 playgrounds with 17,177 leaders representing a yearly expenditure of $1 million.

Camping Movement. With the American Indian recognized as the earliest of American campers, Indian lore has been woven throughout much of the fabric of the camping movement. Also, legends of Kit Carson and Daniel Boone gave inspiration for much of the rituals, while interest in outdoor life aroused by Teddy Roosevelt, Dan Beard (1850–1941), and Ernest Thompson Seton (1860–1946), all great outdoorsmen, gave impetus to the cause. By the opening of this century, there were an estimated 50–60 organized camps established in the United States, and the movement grew rapidly from then on.

The first Boy Scout camp was organized by Daniel Beard and Ernest Thompson Seton shortly after the Boy Scouts came into existence, followed soon by the first Girl Scout Camp in northwestern Georgia, named Camp Lowland after their founder, Juliette Lowe. The first Camp Fire Camp was established by the Gulick family at Lake Sebago in Maine and named Wo-He-Lo after the words, *work, health,* and *love.*

In the first sixty years (from 1860 to 1920) the movement was largely a recreational one. During the 1920s it began its educational stage, when camping became an extension of the school. Many schools now established their own camps. Omaha, Nebraska, established its school camp in the early 1920s—one of the first such camps. The most notable of the early school camps were the Life Camps maintained by the New York City Board of Education.

The Camp Directors Association of America was founded in 1910, and the National Association of Directors of Girls' Camps in 1916, with the wife of Luther Halsey Gulick as its president. In 1924 these two organizations merged and became the Camp Directors Association, with George Meylan as president. By then, camping had become a big summertime business in America.

Health Education Movement. The medical profession was gradually realizing that there was much the schools could do to teach healthful living to children, not leaving the task to the home alone, and that parents could be reached through the children, even if only indirectly. There were serious problem of sanitation, schoolroom hygiene, the health of the teachers as well as that of the children, disease detection and prevention, the relation of physical education to health education, all clamoring for attention. Much could be done beyond a course in hygiene.

Most schools could not afford both health educators and physical educators on the staff and assumed (whether correctly so or not) that because the physical education teacher, even the coach (who was probably not a physical educator), had in preparation studied anatomy, kinesiology, physiology, and hygiene, he or she could handle both physical education and health education. Hence there began at the turn of the century a pattern of combining these two disciplines into one teaching assignment, or at least into one administrative assignment.

Soon joint departments of health and physical education became common throughout the country, reaching even into state departments of education and professional organizations. Frequently the tie-up existed in name only with health education concerns being neglected for physical education concerns or vise versa, or both health education and physical education being neglected for coaching.

To compound difficulties, by 1930 talk began of unloading the latest teaching fads—driver education and safety education—upon the already heavily overburdened twin or triplet educator of health, physical education, and coaching.

Professional Literature

As if to make amends for the dearth of professional literature of the earlier years, many writers in the field of physical education emerged early in the new century, and many "firsts" for the United States came off the press, such as: Jessie Bancroft's *School Gymnastics and Light Apparatus*, 1900; a city school manual by Gulick, 1903; Sargent's book on philosophy and principles, *Physical Education*, 1906; Gulick's book on the same topics, 1907; Elizabeth Burchenal's *Folk Dance Tunes*, followed in quick succession by several other books on folk dancing, with a total of fifteen by her between 1914 and 1941; Jessie Bancroft's *Games for School, Home, and Playground*, 1909, one of the professional all-time best sellers; Clark W. Hetherington's *Normal Course in Play*, 1909; and R. Tait McKenzie's *Exercise in Education and Medicine*, 1909.

The second and third decades also brought forth several firsts, such as Thomas D. Wood's *Health Education*, 1910, the book that started the modern natural gymnastics movement; Gulick's *The Healthful Art of Dancing*, 1911, which was used for over twenty years in the schools of America; the state of Michigan's *Physical Training for Public Schools*, 1912, the first state manual; Wilbur P. Bowen's *Action of Muscles*, 1912, the first on kinesiology; Fred Eugene Leonard's *Pioneers of Modern Physical Training*, 1919, and *History of Physical Education*, 1923; James H. McCurdy's *Physiology of Exercise*, 1924; and Elmer D. Mitchell's *Intramural Sports*, 1928.

It was in the 1920s that the first books by Dr. Jesse Feiring Williams came off press. For many years he was the profession's most prolific writer, producing books covering a wide range of topics, some of which came out in many editions. No one book of this era, however, ran into more editions or topped the sales figures of Neils Neilson and Winifred Van Hagen's *Physical Education in the Elementary School*, first published in 1929 as a California State Manual.

Many authors furnished many books on many subjects. Each succeeding decade brought forth many new authors who contributed notably to the advancement of the profession after the "firsts" on various phases of work had charted the way. A perusal of the publishers' lists in the various issues of the national organization's periodicals through the years will reveal the wealth of topics covered and the names of persons who in this way served the profession.

The two periodicals started in the 1890s, *Mind and Body* (1894) and *The American Physical Education Review* (1896), continued through this era, the former surviving until 1935. Edward Hartwell was the editor of the latter until 1900, then Luther Gulick took over and was editor from 1900 to 1902. He in turn was followed by Dr. George Fitz (1860–1934) of Harvard University, who turned the editorship over to James Huff McCurdy in 1905. The periodical had been a quarterly from 1896 through 1907, when it became a monthly. McCurdy edited the magazine through the year 1929 and in 1930 it became the *Journal of Health and Physical Education,* under the editorship of Elmer D. Mitchell of the University of Michigan. Mitchell had been editor of the *Pentathlon* (the official organ of the Midwest Physical Education Association, which had been established in 1928 and had been produced in eleven issues). When he succeeded to the office of Secretary-Treasurer-Editor of the APEA in 1930 the Midwest group gave up its own venture, throwing its influence and support to the new national magazine. At the same time the APEA began publication of the *Research Quarterly.*

Four new magazines were established in this era. *Physical Training* was started by the YMCA in 1901, with Gulick as its editor. In 1905 George Fisher took over the editorship; in 1924 it changed its name to *The Journal of Physical Education,* and in 1926 John Brown, Jr., became its editor. The magazine *Playground* put in its appearance in 1907 as the official organ of the Playground and Recreation Association of America.

A periodical called *American Gymnasia and Athletic Record* was started in September 1904. It was published by the American Gymnasia Company of Boston, and it claimed to be "The Only National Physical Training Publication Giving News of the Profession." The few issues available for perusal are full of interesting news of meetings, programs, and teachers—much that the other periodicals of that time did not carry. The periodical did not survive long, but while it lasted it maintained a book sales division and a teacher's exchange—both in the field of physical education.

In March 1909, another magazine entered the field, *Hygiene and Physical Education,* edited by W. W. Hastings of the Springfield YMCA School. This magazine had purchased the mailing list of the defunct *American Gymnasia.* It carried articles on health education and hygiene as well as physical education, and its first few issues gave promise of a brilliant future in the educational field; but it too soon vanished from the scene. It apparently took the backing of a national organization to keep a professional periodical on its feet in those days.

10

Professional Organizations and Leaders of the Early Twentieth Century

The new century brought increased interest in the promotion and control of athletics as well as advancement in the profession of physical education so that many new organizations came into existence in the early 1900s. Also, the number of trained personnel in the field increased materially, and a new group of leaders arose to carry on the work started by the stalwart pioneers of earlier days.

NATIONAL PROFESSIONAL ORGANIZATIONS

Interests had become sufficiently specialized by the coming of the twentieth century to support several different types of professional organizations. The continuing history of those already in existence at the opening of the century will be discussed along with the history of new organizations, listed in the order of their founding.

American Physical Education Association (APEA)[1]

The American Association for the Advancement of Physical Education, founded in the fall of 1885, changed its name in 1903 to the American Physical Education Association. By the turn of the century it had several affiliated city groups, three state societies—Ohio, Michigan, and Nebraska, and one regional group covering several states, the New England Society of Physical Education. Now it undertook to organize its workers into sections of interests. By 1904 it had three sections—one on normal schools and professional training, one on gymnastic therapeutics, and one on anthropometry—besides three affiliated organizations—the Secondary School Directors' Society, the Public School Directors' Society, and the Society for Research—all of which later developed into sections. In 1912 a group of workers in the profession in the northern states, stretching from the Alleghenies to the Rocky Mountains, dissatisfied with APEA's neglect of their part of the country, organized their own professional organization, the Middle West Society of Physical Education. Under the initial leadership of Clark W. Hetherington, this organization became a strong force in the profession and finally in the early 1930s joined forces with APEA to become one of its district organizations.[2]

By 1919, the eastern states had joined together to form their own district group, and by 1927 the southern states also, but unlike the Middle West group, both of those new district groups sought ties with the national association. By 1930 it had eleven sections and five affiliated organizations. Also, it had united its many local groups into district societies, with the Eastern, Middle West (Central and Midwest united), and Southern districts coming into the mother organization in the order named. (The presidents of this organization are listed in the Appendix.)

College Physical Education Association (CPEA)[3]

The Society of College Gymnasium Directors of 1897 changed its name to the Society of Directors of Physical Education in Colleges in 1908. Throughout the 1910s and 1920s it held its annual meetings in New York City during the Christmas holidays in connection with those of the National Collegiate Athletic Association and the American Health Association. During World War I the society offered the services of sixty men in fifty colleges and universities to the United States government, all experienced medical examiners and practical physical educators. It also gave serious study to the problem of the relation between the departments of gymnastics and those of athletics, which in many colleges had developed as two separate departments. The early presidents of this organization are listed in the Appendices.

Physical Directors Society of the YMCA

There were enough men working in physical education in the YMCAs by 1903 to found the YMCA Physical Directors Society to improve the standards and enlarge the field of service in physical education in the YMCA's of America. It sought early affiliation with APEA.

Playground Association of America (PAA)[4]

During this era many organizations important to physical education came into existence. In 1904 the Big Brother Movement, Inc., headed by Jacob Riss, leader of

New York City's anti-slum movement, was born to help underprivileged boys. From it came the idea of a similar organization on the national level, and in 1906, sparked by Luther Gulick, the Playground Association of America was organized in Washington with Gulick as its first president, and Jacob Riis as vice president; Theodore Roosevelt was Honorary President. At this time there were forty-one cities in the United States with playgrounds already established. The new organization started to work for the development of year-round programs and for municipal support. It sent out field workers to conduct campaigns in cities to get playgrounds organized, and it set up programs for playgrounds and started a drive to find leaders to man them. In 1911 it changed its name to the Playground and Recreation Association of America (PRAA) with Joseph Lee (1862–1937), a philanthropist of Boston known as "the father of the playground movement," taking over the presidency and continuing in that office until his death in 1937. In 1930 it changed its name once more—this time to the National Recreation Association (NRA).

National Association of Physical Education for College Women (NAPECW)[5]

In the spring of 1910 Amy Morris Homans invited directors of physical education in women's colleges of New England to meet at Wellesley College to discuss their mutual problems. In 1915, again meeting at Wellesley, the group grew to include all Eastern colleges, and they organized the Eastern College Women's Physical Directors Society. Two years later the college women physical directors of the Middle West met at the University of Chicago where they organized their district association. In 1921 the Western group organized at Mills College. Then in 1924 these three regional groups through representatives met together in Kansas City in connection with the annual conference of the Middle West group and united into a federation as the National Association of Directors of Physical Education for College Women. They clung to that word *directors* for these district groups had come together in the first place because of their great need of mutual help in their tasks of organizing and administering their departments. These women had received their professional training in the late nineteenth and early twentieth centuries—a period when the training schools had not yet awakened to the realization that women would be in positions of directorships and therefore had offered them no courses in organization and administration work. Now they were turning to each other for help, for advice, for guidance, and they did not want any of their staff members sitting in on these so very exclusive and private meetings where they could confess their ignorance and help each other.

These district groups immediately embarked upon discussions of "how to" do everything connected with their jobs other than the actual teaching of physical activities. Gradually training schools awakened to the need to offer courses for such work and there was no longer need for directors to meet alone to make up for the deficiencies of their professional training. By the close of this era membership was opened to all members of the staffs of physical education for women in colleges and the word *directors* dropped from the title. (Early presidents of this national group are listed in the Appendix.)

American Academy of Physical Education (AAPE)[6]

An early Academy of Physical Education was organized by Gulick in 1904. This was an informal group of physical educators who desired to get together for discussion free of formalities and red tape. They met annually for an entire week in early September at the summer camp of Dr. George L. Meylan on Sebago Lake in Maine. The group of eleven included the preeminent male leaders of that day. The meetings produced much fine thinking for the advancement of the profession, but with the interruption of World War I and the death of its guiding spirit, Gulick, in 1918, this organization broke up.

In 1926 a new group organized the present American Academy. Three of the five organizing members—Clark W. Hetherington, R. Tait McKenzie, and T. A. Storey—had been members of the earlier group. The other two organizing members were William Burdick, M.D. (1871–1935), of the Baltimore Athletic League, and Jay B. Nash (1886–1966), of New York University. These five selected five others to join them, and these ten selected five more the following year. This process was continued until 1930 by which time the charter membership list was completed. This group then proceeded to draw up a constitution and to get the organization work under way. Of the earlier group Dudley Sargent, Luther Gulick, and Fred E. Leonard (1866–1922) had passed away and were elected Fellows in Memoriam. The others of the earlier group were Wilbur Bowen, J. H. McCurdy, George Meylan, and Paul Phillips, who were taken into charter membership, and Dr. C. Ward Crampton who had by then left the profession to practice medicine. Later, however, he was elected to associate membership. Throughout this four-year organization period, Hetherington acted as organizing chairman of the group, and in 1930 McKenzie was elected the first President, serving in that capacity for many years. (Early presidents are listed in the Appendix.)

Society of State Directors of Physical Education[7]

In 1914, Thomas A. Storey and a group of New York citizens entered upon a project to persuade the New York State Department of Instruction to set up physical education work within the schools as a state function. In 1916, Dr. Storey became the first state director of physical education. Now the United States Commissioner of Education was asking for a national group to push for laws requiring physical education to be offered in all U.S. schools and for there to be a director of physical education in each state to work within the state educational organization. From 1916 to 1930 seventeen state departments of education appointed state directors of physical education, and for mutual aid they joined forces to create the Society of State Directors. As more states acquired directors, the group grew in size and importance, and as the profession widened its concerns, it became the Society of State Directors of Health, Physical Education and Recreation. This organization concerns itself with interests in the lower schools of the nation. (Early presidents are listed in the Appendix.)

CONFERENCES ON PHYSICAL EDUCATION

After World War I, many conferences were held and patterned after the famous Boston Conference of 1889. The most far-reaching in its effects on physical education was one held in 1918 when the United States Commissioner of Education called sixty leaders of physical education to Atlantic City for a conference. Out of this meeting grew the formation of a National Committee on Physical Education with Dr. Thomas D. Wood at its head. It immediately established the National Physical Education Service to promote state and federal legislation on physical education programs and playgrounds in all schools under their jurisdiction.

National Physical Education Service

The Playground and Recreation Association accepted the sponsorship of this service, and $10,000 was contributed to finance it. James E. Rogers (1885–1959), who had been on the National Staff of PRAA since 1911, was appointed head of the service, and from then on he traveled constantly all over the United States until his retirement in 1950, promoting state and federal programs of physical education. It is impossible to fully appraise the advancement which this work brought, to the profession.

Mandates of the White House Conference on Child Health and Protection[8]

Following the November 1930 White House Conference on Child Health and Protection many dedicated educators took to heart its mandates and began serious investigation of their schools.

The conference had produced *The Children's Charter*, with its nineteen requirements, printed in a large scroll in beautiful illuminated lettering. Copies hung framed for many years in school rooms and offices of superintendents and boards of education throughout the country, to serve as a sort of bible for all people responsible for the care and education of children. The bottom of the charter read:

> For every child these rights, regardless of race, of color, or situation, wherever he may live under the protection of the American flag.

Article 16 of the charter specifically called for protection of every child from all things that might deprive him or her of the rights of comradeship and play. This in particular was a mandate for physical education.

LEADERS OF PHYSICAL EDUCATION

Time has given prominence to six leaders of physical education of this period to whom comes acclaim far beyond the confines of the profession itself, namely Luther Halsey Gulick, who brought the profession to the notice of the lay public and R. Tait McKenzie, who brought recognition of the profession to the medical and art worlds, Senda Berenson who gave to girls of America their own team sport—basketball for girls and women, Clark W. Hetherington who sold physical education to general education, Ethel Perrin who was one of the earliest women of the profession to head a physical education department of the schools of a large city and from that went on to work in health education on the national level, and Elizabeth Burchenal who brought folkdance to the schools of America and in her later years was the U.S. international representative on Folk Arts Councils. In the material that follows these six leaders are discussed, chronologically by year of birth.

Luther Halsey Gulick, M.D., (1865–1918)[9]

Luther Gulick was born in Honolulu of missionary parents and as a child lived in several foreign countries, in Europe as well as in the Orient. At Oberlin College he came under the influence of Dr. Delphine Hanna, who aroused his interest in physical education. Thomas D. Wood was his roommate, and together they worked out a philosophy of physical education which in later years brought strength and advancement to the profession. After two years at Oberlin College, he went to the Sargent School to prepare to teach physical education. There he became acquainted with Sargent, starting a friendship and a professional tie that served the profession well. From there he went to a position at the Jackson, Michigan, YMCA, resigning after one year to enter upon medical studies at New York University, where he procured the medical degree in 1887. From there he went to Springfield, Massachusetts, where he established the department of physical education at the School for Christian Workers (today's Springfield College). At the same time, he prevailed upon the YMCA to establish the position of Secretary of the International Committee of Physical Education of the YMCAs, becoming the first to hold the position. After thirteen years at Springfield, he became Principal of Pratt High School in Brooklyn, which position he held from 1900 to 1903, leaving it to become Head of the Department of Physical Education of the Public Schools of Greater New York City. Previously there had been separate departments of physical education of the various boroughs of the city but all were united into one overall department with Gulick the first to hold the directorship.

Figure 7. Luther Halsey Gulick, M.D. (1865–1918). (Photograph used by permission of Spring-field College.)

In 1907 he left the teaching profession to join the staff of the Russell Sage Foundation to work full time for the Playground Association of America which he had founded. During this period he built his camp at Lake Sebago in Maine, which developed into the famous Gulick Camps where the Camp Fire Girls of America was born. In 1913 he left the Russell Sage Foundation to take up full-time work for the Camp Fire Girls, leaving that work in 1918 to devote himself fully to the War Board of the YMCA. In this last work he went to France early in 1918, heading the foreign war work of the YMCA. After a six-week stay, he left Dr. James H. McCurdy in charge of affairs for the board in France with six helpers—all that were then available instead of the 300 urgently needed—and returned to the United States to conduct a recruitment campaign for the YMCA overseas workers. And it was in his Lake Sebago Camp that he loved that he died in his sleep on August 13, 1918, having gone there for a brief rest from his arduous war work duties.

Foremost Contributions. His many important contributions to physical education, recreation, education in general, and to the enrichment of American life are unmatched in number by any other leaders in the profession. He was the founder of many important movements, such as the establishment of physical education in the YMCAs of America, the Playground Association of America, New York University Summer School of Physical Education, the Department of School Hygiene of the New York Academy of Medicine, the position of Secretary of the International Physical Education Committee of YMCAs (he being the first to hold the position), and the Camp Fire Girls. Besides this he was one of the founders of the American School Hygiene Association, the Boy Scouts of America, American Folk Dance Society, and American Camping Association. He was the creator of the inverted red triangle emblem of the YMCA representing "spirit upheld by mind and body," and the inspiration for the founding of the Mother's Club of Springfield, Massachusetts, which was the forerunner of the National Congress of Parents and Teachers.

Literary Production. He served as editor of five different magazines, four of which he founded: *The Triangle,* 1891 to 1892, *Physical Education,* 1892 to 1896, *American Physical Education Review,* 1900 to 1902, *Physical Training,* the organ of YMCA, 1901 to 1903, and *Wohelo,* organ of the Camp Fire Girls, 1914 to 1918. Besides his editorial work he published 217 articles on both popular and professional topics in fifty different periodicals and eight handbooks, nine pamphlets, and fourteen books. Perhaps his two best known books are *Physical Education* of 1904 and *The Efficient Life* of 1907.

Honors and Important Offices. The honors conferred upon Gulick and the high offices he held in important organizations are legion. To mention but a few he was a member of the International YMCA committee, President of AAAPE for five years, a member of the American Olympic Committee, the first President of the Playground Association of America, President of American School Hygiene Association, and the first President of the Camp Fire Girls of America. Three medals are awarded in his honor: The Gulick Award of the American Association for Health, Physical Education and Recreation (see Appendix), the Roberts–Gulick Award of the Society of Physical Directors of the YMCAs of North America, and the Gulick Medal of the Camp Fire Association of America. New York City, operates a playground named in his honor. He is an Honorary Fellow in Memoriam of the American Academy of Physical Education.

Appraisal. Gulick had educational ideas in advance of his time. Before John Dewey expounded his educational philosophy, Gulick was informing his teachers that they were to teach boys and girls rather than subject matter, and as early as 1891 he introduced the use of photography to analyze movement.

When he first began his career the YMCA physical activity teachers were expugilists, old soldiers, and excircus performers—most were nonChristian and not interested in educational ideals. He started the movement to have none but men of Christian character to teach in the YMCA's for which he was criticized as expecting too much.

He was a great individualist, essentially different from others, quick to take up new ideas and also quick to drop them, the executive type not interested in details. He had an enormous capacity for work, and his interests were wide. He had unusual drive, unusual leadership ability, unusual vision—hence, he accomplished a prodigious amount of worthwhile work in the fifty-three years of his life.

Robert Tait McKenzie M.D. (1867–1938)[10]

Born in Almonte, Ontario, Canada, R. Tait McKenzie achieved international fame as a sculptor, but no less noteworthy were his achievements in the fields of medicine, writing, and physical education. A delicate boy, he took up gymnastics to strengthen his physique, and he continued this training at McGill University. Becoming interested in physical education, he studied at Springfield and at the Harvard Summer School before completing his medical studies at McGill in 1892. In 1891 he was appointed Director of the Gymnasium there, succeeding James Naismith, a friend of boyhood years. In 1893 he was given the title of Director of Physical Training, serving as House Physician at the Montreal General Hospital. In 1896 he added Medical Director to his title and served one year also as House Physician to the Governor General of Canada. In 1904 he became Director of Physical Education at the University of Pennsylvania, which position he held until his retirement in 1931.

In the summer of 1907 Dr. McKenzie gave an address in London before the British Medical Association, and that fall took on the responsibilities of Professor of Physical Therapy on the medical faculty, in addition to his other duties at the University of Pennsylvania, the first such professorship in this country. Early in 1915 he offered his services to the British in their war effort and was commissioned Temporary Major in the Royal Army Medical Corps. In 1916 he became Inspector of Physical Training for Kitchener's armies.

Literary and Artistic Production. The best known of McKenzie's several books are: *Exercise in Education and Medicine* (1909), *The Treatment of Convalescent Soldiers by Physical Means*, and *Reclaiming the Maimed* (1918). Several of his sculptured pieces are world famous. His *Joy of Effort*, a 46-inch plaque set in the wall of the stadium in Stockholm, was commissioned by the American Olympic Committee and presented to Sweden at the Olympic Games of 1912, following which the King of Sweden conferred upon McKenzie the King's Medal for distinguished service as a sculptor. In 1914 he produced his large statue, *The Youthful*

Figure 8. R. Tait McKenzie, M.D. (1867–1938). (From a photograph presented to the author by Dr. McKenzie in 1932.)

Franklin, which occupies a prominent place on the campus of the University of Pennsylvania, founded by Franklin. On Harvard University campus in the stadium grounds is McKenzie's 1927 Percy D. Haughton Memorial of Harvard's famous coach of the turn of the century.

His 1932 *Olympic Shield of Athletes,* the only one ever made by a sculptor, five feet in diameter, was completed for the Olympic Games in Los Angeles in 1932 and there won the Olympic Art Award. The original is in the Mill of Kintail Museum, which is maintained near his birthplace in Almonte, Canada, and is a memorial to him. (A smaller copy of the shield was made for the Olympic Games in Tokyo in 1964 and is owned by the Japanese Amateur Athletic Association.) Through his many sculptured pieces he became famous in art circles as the first sculptor since the days of the Greek ascendency to use the athletic idea as his subject.

McKenzie's statues of athletes are numerous, the best known being *The Relay, The Onslaught, The Javelin Cast, The Plunger, The Icebird, The Pole Vaulter, The Discus Thrower, The Brothers of The Wind.*

Hussey's biography of him, *R. Tait McKenzie: Sculptor of Youth,* contains illustrations of his chief sculptured pieces. As early as 1904 his art work was exhibited in London at the Royal Academy. He held a one man exhibit of his sculpturing in London in 1921 and in New York City in the 1930s.

McKenzie achieved international reputation for his British war memorials, notably one in Edinburgh completed in 1927 in Prince's Street Gardens entitled *The Call,* one in Cambridge, England near the railroad station entitled *The Homecoming,* and one in his birthplace at Almonte, Canada. A copy of his *Blighty* of 1919 was a favorite desk ornament of King George V of England. Reproductions of many of his statues adorn the entrance hall of the magnificent Payne Whitney gymnasium at Yale. Altogether he produced over two hundred works of art, including twenty-five war and other memorials.

Honors and Important Offices. In 1904 McKenzie was selected as lecturer in artistic anatomy for the Olympic games held in connection with the St. Louis Worlds Fair. He served the CPEA as president for one year, also the Academy of Physical Medicine. Then he served the APEA, as President for four years and was one of the founders and the first President of The American Academy of Physical Education, serving from 1930 until his death in 1938. Three colleges conferred honorary doctorates upon him.

The American Academy created the R. Tait McKenzie Memorial Lectureship in his honor. The full issue of the *Journal of Health and Physical Education,* February 1944, was devoted to his memory, containing biographical material and tributes from his vast circle of admirers. In 1937 he completed what was probably his last large piece of work, his *Column of Youth,* which was unveiled that April in the ballroom of Hotel Pennsylvania in New York City at the APEA banquet in connection with its annual convention. A year later, Dr. McKenzie died. Later the AAHPER purchased from his estate the marble reproduction of his *Column of Youth* and placed it in the national headquarters building of the National Education Association in Washington as a memorial to him. In 1968, AAHPER established the R. Tait McKenzie Award in his memory.

Appraisal. No one of modern times has bound the profession of physical education to the glories of its ancient heritage as did R. Tait McKenzie through his art work. In this his contribution is unique. He was a gentleman of the old school, a man of culture, with a great capacity for friendship. He had a quiet dignity and a deep interest in a variety of concerns—a man of unusual personal charm and magnetism.

Senda Berenson (1868–1954)[11]

Born in the province of Vilna in Lithuania in 1868, Senda Berenson came to America in 1875 with her mother, her brother, Bernard (who was three years older than she and destined to become an internationally famous author and art critic), and a younger sister. Her father had come a year earlier and scouted out Boston as the city for their future home. Hoping to have a college education, Senda attended Boston Latin School but because of physical frailty she frequently dropped out of school for long periods, thus delaying her graduation from the school. She hoped to take up music at the New England Conservatory of Music in Boston but was unable physically to handle the long practice hours required there. Friends of the family called attention to the new school in Boston just getting underway in the fall of 1889 under the auspices of the wealthy Mrs. Hemenway—the Boston Normal School of Gymnastics which specialized in Swedish gymnastics and stressed healthful living in all its aspects.

Realizing that she must conquer her frailties, Senda asked for an interview with Miss Homans. Nothing was farther from her thoughts than to prepare to teach physical education. She wished only to avail herself of the intensive physical training of the Swedish system of gymnastics. Miss Homans was sympathetic with Miss Berenson's wish to correct her physical frailties but she stood firm that anyone entering her school must take the full course. So Senda made the big decision and in the fall of 1890 entered to take the full course. She later reported that she hated the study of anatomy, physiology, knesiology, chemistry, and physics, but at once became interested in the exercises she was put through, gained strength, and became a new person physically. She gladly returned for the second year. She threw herself wholeheartedly into the classwork for in the fall of 1891 she was sent twice a week to Andover to instruct teachers there on how to teach Swedish gymnastics in their schools. She must have made a good record in her practice teaching for when Smith College informed Miss Homans that they had at last completed their wonderful new building, Alumnae Hall, which contained both a gymnasium and a pool (unusual for that day, 1892) and that they wanted a teacher to organize a department of physical culture for them, Miss Homans offered the position to Miss Berenson. Miss Homans assured her that she could handle the work satisfactorily even if she dropped out of the school at midyear. So Miss Berenson, by then deeply grateful for what one and one-half years of work in Swedish gymnastics had done for her personally and also deeply interested by then in teaching physical education and all it stood for, accepted the offer.

Smith College had been offering physical activities to their students since 1875 but in inadequate facilities and sometimes combined with elocution courses. Their teachers had been pupils of Dio Lewis, and their exercises consisted of wand and dumbbell and Indian club drills. Now things were to change. The petite Miss Berenson in the new gymnasium was to modernize physical education. She proved

Figure 9. Senda Berenson (1868–1954). (Photograph used by permission of Smith College.)

to be an excellent organizer and administrator, and she gave the students a well-rounded program which meant not only Swedish gymnastics, physical examinations, and rhythms but also sports.

The freshmen and sophomores were required to report for physical education classes, but in Miss Berenson's second year so many juniors and seniors asked to join her classes that she was given an assistant to help with the class work. Now she could give attention to adding sports to her program, activities that were beginning to claim the interests of girls as well as boys and that had been completely neglected in schools. This was ultimately to become the major contribution of her career.

Foremost Contribution. Miss Berenson had been at work at Smith College only a few weeks when she chanced upon a copy of *Triangle,* the school paper put out by the YMCA Training School at Springfield nearby, which carried an article about a game called "basket ball", which a teacher there named Naismith had created for use in winter for the boys. As early as possible she asked for an interview with Mr. Naismith and asked his permission to try out the game as a possibility for girls. He gave her his blessing and suggested some adjustments for a girls' game.

She began at once to experiment with Naismith's thirteen rules of the game and by the fall of 1892 she was trying out the game in her physical education classes at Smith College. Although these were not the first girls to play this game (as related in Chapter 5), this was the first that the game was played as a part of an educational program. After several weeks of experimentation with her revised rules, the first match game was played March 23, 1893, at Smith College between the freshmen (1896 class) and sophomores (1895 class) under her tutelage. At the conclusion of this game with its nine players to a team, as in Naismith's game for boys, Miss Berenson and the girls determined that along with some minor changes in the rules the playing space should be divided into three equal courts and that it would be a foul to snatch the ball from the hands of another player. Thus basketball for girls was officially born at Smith College in the spring of 1893. That first official game had been literally a "howling" success.

From the very beginning of her speculations about the game, Miss Berenson thought it should be adapted to the particular physical, psychological, and social needs of the sex of the players. (However in the early 1890s, teachers and other leaders of youth did not talk in such terms—the studies of psychology and sociology were not as yet well developed for general educational knowledge.)

As the Smith College girls returned to their homes all over the country, where there were not as yet many YMCA facilities in any but the large cities with physical directors to introduce the game for boys, they spread word of this new game for girls. Therefore in the Middle West, South, and Far West, the girls' game became known before the boys' game, and it became an instant sensation. Almost at once Miss Berenson began receiving challenges for her college girls to play match games of all kinds all around the country and instantly she replied to all of these, "We do not play games away from home." Apparently there was never a moment's doubt about this decision that Smith College would not enter into any intercollegiate contests in sports. Never did she waver from this decision.

Birth of Official Rules Committee on Basketball for Girls. Soon there were demands for copies of the Smith College basketball rules and Miss Berenson put out some form of material that could be mailed to inquirers. Shortly a few other women across the country began offering to the public their own rules of the game, differing somewhat from each other's versions and from the Smith College rules, so that confusion arose. When Miss Berenson learned that there would be a conference of the American Association for the Advancement of Physical Education for its section on teacher training held at the Springfield YMCA School in June 1899, she asked for a hearing with the national officers attending. She asked that the AAAPE take over her rules for basketball for girls and make them official, as coming from a national educational organization. Favorably disposed to the idea, the President of AAAPE immediately appointed a committee of four women physical education teachers to serve as AAAPE Rules Committee on Basketball for Girls and Women. Ethel Perrin, then a member of the Boston Normal School of Gymnastics faculty and Miss Berenson were members under the chair of Alice Foster of Oberlin College. On that committee Miss Berenson became editor of the official rules, a position she held for many years.

As soon as this committee began work Mr. Sullivan of Spalding's Athletic Library, who was publishing the official rules for basketball for men, approached Miss Berenson for permission to publish the committee's rules.[12] With AAAPE's permission, the committee accepted his offer with the understanding that the rules would be accompanied by articles about the game, especially articles featuring the good sportsmanship the girls needed so very much as they were being initiated into the world of participation in team sports. The first official *Basket Ball Guide for Girls and Women* was off press in 1901.

In 1905 the Basket Ball Rules Committee became a Committee on Basket Ball for Women with Miss Berenson serving as chairwoman until 1917 when she asked to be relieved of all committee responsibility after twenty-five years of devotion to basketball.

Other Contributions. Shortly following Bryn Mawr's lead, Miss Berenson organized a Women's Athletic Association open to all students; following Wellesley's lead she organized boating; following Vassar's lead she put on a field day for all the students. But unlike Vassar's meet it was not a track meet. She never approved of track and field sports for women aping the men in these activities. Her field days were made up of all manner of contests stemming from all the activities she was offering her students, which proved so popular with the Smith College girls that forty years after her first field day the tradition was still being carried on enthusiastically.

Studying fencing in Sweden in the spring and summer of 1897 under a fencing master of the Swedish Army Officers, Miss Berenson introduced that sport to her students. At the same time she studied for four months, observing work at the Royal Central Gymnastic Institute in Stockholm preparing to introduce remedial gymnastics for the students needing special physical help.

Appraisal. Senda Berenson conquered her frailities of early life to become a Rock of Gibralter for all women who hoped to have a career and to carve a niche for themselves in the field of physical education. The broad lane leading to today's Scott Gymnasium at Smith College is named Berenson Place in her honor. She is America's first Miss Basketball.

Clark Wilson Hetherington (1870–1942)[13]

Clark Hetherington was born August 12, 1870, in Lanesborough, Minnesota. His father was a successful architect and builder and so moved about the country. As a result Hetherington's early schooling was acquired in several different places. From early childhood he was frail and suffered off and on from severe headaches that kept him out of school, with the result that when he finally graduated from high school in San Diego, California, he was three years older than the usual age of high school graduates. At the age of twenty-one he started his college education, entering Stanford University in its first year of operation in the fall of 1891.

At Stanford he came under the influence of Thomas D. Wood. Young Clark in his own efforts to overcome his physical frailities had become a skillful gymnast, and Dr. Wood immediately offered him an assistantship that was to last all four of his undergraduate years.

Although Hetherington always held to his firm belief in the values of gymnastics as a body conditioner he soon became interested in Dr. Wood's ideas that instead of formal exercises of the European gymnastic systems for general physical education, children should be given exercises natural to themselves which Dr. Wood came to call "natural" gymnastics. Graduating with the first graduating class at Stanford, in 1895, along with his good friend and classmate Herbert Hoover, Hetherington took a position for three years in a state school for boys where he built up a department of physical education.

In 1898 he received a fellowship to study at another recently established university, Clark University, a graduate institution located in Worcester, Massachusetts (which opened its doors in 1889). For his second year there he received an assistantship in psychology, working directly with G. Stanley Hall who was not only head of the psychology department but also President of the University. There Hetherington organized for Dr. Hall the laboratory for study of animal psychology. In these two years of graduate work he developed his keen interest in child study.

In 1900 the University of Missouri offered him a position unusual for that day—directorship of both men's and women's physical culture and of all athletics, both intercollegiate and intramural, which he accepted hoping he could put into practice his many theories about education. In his second year he was able to change the title "physical culture," feeling that it connoted a fad or cult, to "physical training." After four years he was granted a year's leave to study biological psychology at the University of Zurich in Switzerland.

Following this study in Switzerland he returned to the University of Missouri for another five years. In 1910 he resigned that position for two years' work in

Figure 10. Clark W. Hetherington (1870–1942). (Courtesy of AAHPERD.)

Chicago on a grant from the Joseph Fels Endowment Fund, traveling throughout the country from headquarters in Chicago, helping local and state groups to organize state Physical Education Associations, he hoped to get state programs established in state departments of education. In the summers of these years he taught physical education theory courses at various schools. In the summer of 1913 at the University of California (Berkeley) he organized the first Demonstration Play School and directed it for several summers. In 1912 the University of Wisconsin offered him a professorship in their Department of Physical Education which he accepted and where for the next five years he worked at laying firm foundations for their teacher-training program for majors in physical education for both men and women.

In May 1917, California voted in compulsory physical education for all lower schools and normal schools, calling for a State Supervisor of Physical Education under the State Board of Education, and in January 1918, Clark Hetherington became their first state physical education supervisor, the second such in the country following New York State. Here was his opportunity to put his educational theories into effect. At the conclusion of three years he resigned to return to the classroom but not until he had laid the groundwork for an unusual state program.

He went to Teachers College Columbia University as an associate to carry on educational research. The following year, 1922–1923, he was offered the Directorship of a department of physical education to be developed at New York University within the School of Education, which he accepted. There he set up a four-year undergraduate and a three-year graduate curriculum to prepare teachers of physical education. In 1927 he established the New York University Summer School at Lake Sebago in Harriman State Park, Sloatsburg, New York. Poor health plagued him and finally in late 1928, knowing that his curriculum plans were well established, he resigned refusing an offer of a year's leave of absence.

Meanwhile, Thomas A. Storey (who entered Stanford in its second year, developing a strong student friendship with Hetherington) had gone to New York State as its first Supervisor of Physical Education and in 1926 returned to Stanford where he established the first School of Hygiene and Physical Education. As soon as he learned of Hetherington's resignation at New York University he offered him a professorship on his staff and allowed him great freedom of time for his writing and research. In 1934, N. P. Neilson, Chief of the Division of Health and Physical Education of the California State Department of Education was brought to the staff to understudy Hetherington in order to take over the teaching of some of his courses and to assist him in his writing. Four years later with no manuscript as yet ready for release to publishers, Hetherington reached retirement age, and Neilson accepted the position of Executive Secretary to AAHPER which took him to Washington, D.C., thus bringing to an end the collaboration of Stanford University, Storey, and Neilson to get Hetherington's work ready to go to press. Hetherington retired a deeply discouraged man. Poor health still plagued him, his eyes had always troubled him, and doctors could give him little relief.

When his wife of thirty-eight years died in 1940, he began to fail rapidly but he clung to his work, desperately hoping to get at least one other book finished. But he was a perfectionist. He refused to consider any of his manuscripts as finished. He wished to go over each time and time again, seeking better ways to express his thoughts until finally on December 27, 1942, he died—most of his writings, a vast amount of material, still awaiting his permission for publication. However, *The School Program in Physical Education,* his only volume to come off press, was widely used.

Foremost Contributions. Clark Hetherington was essentially an innovator. He was the founder of the Missouri Valley Athletic Conference and one of the founders of the Athletic Research Society, the Joint Committee of the NEA, and the AMA on Health Problems in Education, the Middle West Society of Physical Education, the Pacific Coast Society of Physical Education (today's South West District of AAHPER), and the American Academy of Physical Education. One of the chief promoters of the natural gymnastics movement, he was far ahead of his times in his thinking about physical education's place in education. He greatly influenced the formation and organization of state departments of physical education and directly influenced the universities of Missouri and Wisconsin, and Columbia, New York, and Stanford universities, where he gave of himself unstintingly to shape their curricula in physical education at both undergraduate and graduate levels.

In the first decade of the 1900s, specifically while at the University of Missouri, Hetherington plunged headlong into the battle being waged on several fronts just then to clean up intercollegiate sports. They were under severe attacks from the President of the United States and many prominent citizens as well as from college and university presidents and faculties for false amateurism and brutalities. He was one of a small group of men in physical education who through the Athletic Research Society perhaps more than through any other organization, did the most to keep intercollegiate sports on a proper course worthy of an educational institution. From his post out in the Middle West he wielded much athletic power through the Missouri Valley Athletic Conference which he founded. Through this organization he tried to organize a campaign to ban all interscholastic sports for high school girls. He was however interested in the intramural type of sports for girls.

He was also one of the founders of the Boy Scouts of America, serving on its National Council for several years and one of the founders of the Joint Committee of the NEA and the AMA on Health Problems in Education, the Middle West Physical Education Society, the Pacific Coast Society of Physical Education, and the American Academy of Physical Education. He was one of the chief promoters of the natural gymnastics movement.

Honors and Important Offices. Hetherington served as a member of the Board of Directors of the PAA, and was president of the Athletic Research Society of the Department of Physical Education of the NEA, and of the Midwest Physical Education Association, and in the four years of its organization period he served as Chairman of the American Academy of Physical Education.

He also served as a member of the Board of Directors of the Playground Association of America, and was the first president of the Athletic Research Society, President of the Department of Physical Education of the NEA, and the first president of the Middle West Society of Physical Education, which consisted of today's Mid West and Central District Associations of AAHPER.

He was the recipient of the Posse Medal for distinguished service in the field of health and the Gulick Award for distinguished service to physical education. The University of Southern California conferred upon him the honorary degree of Doctor of Pedagogy. The American Academy of Physical Education has established the Hetherington Award in his honor.

Appraisal. As a child and young man Clark Hetherington continuously fought tuberculosis. Plagued with ill health much of his life, he triumphed over great odds. He was a stern man, uncompromising in matters of integrity, and he found much in the promotion of sports in particular that antagonized him. He was also a reticent man and to many seemed difficult of approach, yet to those who broke through the wall of reserve he offered friendliness and inspiration of a rare quality.

He was recognized as the foremost scholar and philosopher of physical education of his day. In the words of Charles H. McCloy of the University of Iowa, upon receiving the first Academy Hetherington Award: "Clark Hetherington's thinking laid the base, not only for an integrated philosophy of physical education, but also to point the way for much scientific research which was to follow, to establish facts upon which to base further constructive philosophizing."

Ethel Perrin (1871–1962)[14]

Ethel Perrin was born in Wellesley, Massachusetts, in 1871 and presumably attended school in that village. She was seventeen years old when she went to the Howard Collegiate Institute, a boarding school, in West Bridgewater, Massachusetts, for two years. She entered the Boston Normal School of Gymnastics in its second class in the fall of 1890. Upon graduation in 1892 she was offered an assistantship in that school which position she held for fourteen years. When her former classmate, Senda Berenson, was to have a leave of absence from her position at Smith College from 1906 to 1907, Ethel took her position as a temporary substitute. The following year, a like vacancy arose at the University of Michigan and Ethel went to that position as a temporary substitute. There, never before having been away from her native state, she became interested in and deeply pleased with the informalities of the Middle West and was delighted when she was offered the directorship of physical education for girls in Central High School of Detroit.

There she found to her dismay that physical education for girls consisted chiefly of basketball for those who were skilled highly enough to defend Central High School against teams from the other two high schools in the city. This she brought to an immediate halt and put into its place a program of intramurals open to all girls of the school. The superintendent (also other teachers and parents) was so pleased that at the end of her first year in that position he urged Miss Perrin to apply for the position of head of all physical education and sports for all Detroit public schools and used his influence with the Board of Education to see that she was elected to the post. Thus in the fall of 1909 she started a fourteen-year career as the

Figure 11. Ethel Perrin (1871–1962). (From a photograph presented to the author by Miss Perrin in 1937.)

second woman in the United States (following Jessie Bancroft in Brooklyn) to head all physical education work in the public schools of a large city.

When Miss Perrin took over this position, she inherited a staff of six physical education teachers—three men and three women—who supervised the classroom teachers who taught all the activity courses. When she resigned she left a staff of 350 physical education and health education teachers and fifteen supervisors. Her physical education department was the envy of all other cities.

Following this, in 1923, she went into health education work as Associate Director of the Health Education Division of the American Child Health Association, with headquarters in New York City. She held this position for thirteen years until in 1936 when because of financial difficulties of the depression the ACHA was compelled to close its doors. Since Miss Perrin was then sixty-five years old she decided to retire to enjoy her farm near Brewster, New York, not far from New York City. With a companion who also loved the out-of-doors and farm chores, she spent her last twenty-six years full of contentment, with much time to read and see old friends who came that way. Quietly in 1961 at the age of 91 she died.

Foremost Contributions. While working in the Middle West Miss Perrin took an active part in advancing physical education there. In the call that was sent out in 1912 for a conference on physical education to be held in Chicago, Illinois, April 26–27, to consider the establishment of a Middle West Society of Physical Education, Miss Perrin was listed as secretary of a proposed Section on Public Schools Physical Education and in the tentative program was announced as a speaker at the University of Chicago on girls' basketball. When the organization was perfected she became in 1917–1918 its third president, the first woman to be so honored. In fact from the records now available it appears that this was the first time in the history of physical education in the United States that a woman was ever elected to the presidency of any mixed-sex national or regional group in the field of physical education—the year 1917 when the national struggle to allow women to vote was not yet over. The example she set in Detroit for a public school program in physical and health education for the new century was a model long looked up to as unique.

When she returned to the East in 1923 she threw herself into the work of the Women's Division of NAAF which was just then being organized (April 6–7, 1923) under the leadership of Mrs. Herbert Hoover, and wife of the then U.S. Secretary of Commerce. Mrs. Hoover was elected permanent chairwoman and she invited Ethel Perrin to serve on the first executive committee with six other leading women physical educators. From 1929 to 1931 Miss Perrin served as Chairman of the Executive Committee, the fourth to hold that position. She was one of a small group of women physical educators who did valuable volunteer field work for the organization and for several years served on the Board of Directors. She wrote articles for publicity of the Women's Division which were published in various magazines.

When radio broadcasting came to the service of education in the 1920s and early 1930s and there was at last to be a national hookup for the American Health Association the voice of Ethel Perrin (speaking also for the Women's Division) rang out all over the United States on the subject of play days for girls, hoping to stem the tide of unfavorable interscholastic athletics for girls sweeping some sections of the country at that time.

Appraisal. Ethel Perrin's fine personal qualities and professional excellence were acknowledged in 1931 by APEA's Honor Award and again in 1946 by the Gulick Award conferred by the same organization but under its new title, the AAHPER. She gave rare distinguished service to the profession both in the fields of Health Education and Physical Education. In the latter she was a Rock of Gibralter in efforts to keep girls' and women's sports in the true realm of education and out of the hands of male sports opportunists. Her work at Detroit alone set an example of directorship of a large department that has scarcely been equaled since.

Elizabeth Burchenal (1876–1959)[15]

Elizabeth Burchenal was born in Richmond, Indiana, in 1876 and graduated from Earlham College in 1896, following which she attended the Sargent Normal School of Physical Training, graduating in 1898. The next few years she taught physical education in Chicago and Boston and in 1902 joined the staff of Thomas D. Wood in Teachers College, Columbia University. In 1905 Dr. Gulick persuaded Miss Burchenal to join his staff in the New York City Public Schools as Executive Director of the Girls Branch of the Public Schools Athletic League in which capacity she was to organize athletics for girls, and to establish folk dance for all school children.

In 1909 she became Inspector of Girls Athletics for the New York City Public Schools. In 1916, having become so deeply interested in folk dance and folk arts in general she resigned from her teaching and founded the American Folk Arts Society which she served as Executive Secretary. In 1929 she became President and Director in charge of the Folk Arts Center in New York City as a Resident Fellow of the Carl Schurz Memorial and a Research Fellow of the Oberloender Trust. In the late 1940s she retired and after a few years of invalidism in a nursery home passed away in 1959 at 83 years of age.

Work in Girls' Athletics. In her many years in charge of athletics for girls and of folk dance she staged many May Day festivals in New York City's Central Park where hundreds of girls from the various schools throughout the city staged May pole dances and a great variety of play activities of low organization for the enjoyment of thousands of parents and others who turned out for the great display. The city newspapers carried great spreads of photographs of her May Day activities in Central Park.

When in 1917 the earlier Women's Basket Ball Rules Committee of 1893, that became the Women's Basket Ball Rules Committee of 1899, became an overall Women's Athletic Committee under the auspices of the APEA, Miss Burchenal was the first person to chair this important group. (This committee of 1917 has developed into today's National Association of Girls' and Women's Sports of AAHPERD.) As its first chairwoman Miss Burchencal started the work of establishing standards on the national level for all sports for girls and women. During World War I she served as Assistant State Inspector of New York Military Training Commission and was a National Representative on the U.S. Army and Navy Departments' Commission on Training Camp Activities and also a member of the War Workers Committee of the U.S. Department of Labor.

Work in Folk Dance. Miss Burchenal's work in folk dance and folk arts in general was no doubt her most important contribution to the profession. When Dr. Gulick told her he wanted folk dancing put into the programs for both boys and girls in the lower grades and that he wished all dances taught to the children to be authentic, she immediately went to foreign groups in the city to gather their native dances; but this approach proved inadequate, and she then went to their original sources abroad. Summer after summer, from 1904 on she traveled in Europe, collecting folk dances first hand, and immediately began publishing her popular collection of books of the dances of many nations. From 1908 to the 1940s she furnished the profession a total of fifteen books covering the folk dances of countries of most of Europe and America.

Having become deeply interested in folk dance she soon began lecturing and conducting institutes of folk dance throughout the United States, Canada, England, Scotland, Ireland, and Germany. She was the official delegate of the United States to the Fine Arts Section meetings of the League of Nations at the Hague and later was again for several years an official United States delegate to meetings of the United Nations Educational, Scientific, and Cultural Organization (UNESCO) at Geneva, London, and Paris.

Honors. Miss Burchenal was one of four women who were charter members of the American Academy of Physical Education, and a recipient of both the Honor Award (1931) and Gulick Award (1953) of AAHPER. In 1943 Boston University conferred upon her the honorary degree of Doctor of Science in Physical Education and she was long listed in *Who's Who in America*.

Appraisal. Although a few others were advancing folk dance as a part of the educational curriculum, Miss Burchenal did more than any other one person of her day to advance its cause. Through the rich program of dance she established in the New York City Schools she set an example for the nation's schools and through her many books on the subject and the many institutes she put on across the country she taught teachers how to teach folk dance. Perhaps the greatest tribute that could be

Figure 12. Elizabeth Burchenal (1876–1959). (Courtesy of AAHPERD.)

paid her was the memorial service, planned by her close friend and co-worker, Ted Shawn, held in New York City shortly after her death in November, 1959. After all who attended the services and wished to pay tribute to Miss Burchenal had spoken, the floor was cleared, a pianist took over, and the audience burst into spontaneous dancing, joyously in her memory going through several of her favorite dances. Nothing could have pleased her more for she was herself a joyous, happy, blithe spirit.

Others Who Notably Advanced the Profession

It is not possible in a short history to give even brief biographical sketches of all the fine leaders of the early decades of the twentieth century, who meant so much to the profession. The work of many leaders who beyond active service age took an important part in Europe with the sports programs for the American Expeditionary Force (AEF) is described in newsletters to the profession.[16] Many others have been mentioned throughout this book in connection with specific activities, movements, and organizations in which they played an important part. Other outstanding leaders, born in the 1860s and 1870s, are discussed in the material that follows in the order of their birth.

James Naismith, M.D. (1861–1939). Both in Almonte, Ontario, Canada, November 6, 1861, Naismith received all his schooling in Canada through graduation from McGill University in 1887 and stayed on at McGill as Director of Physical Education for three years. He came to the United States in 1890 to attend the YMCA Training School to further his specialization in physical education, joining the staff of that school from 1891 to 1895. The next three years he was Director of Physical Education at the YMCA in Denver, Colorado, during which time he studied for his medical degree which he received from the University of Colorado Medical School. In 1898 he went to the University of Kansas where he remained for the rest of his career and where he died, November 28, 1939. During his five years at Springfield YMCA as pupil and staff member, he created the game of basketball in 1891 for which he is famous worldwide.[17]

Clelia D. Mosher, M.D. (1863–1940). Born in Albany, New York, Clelia Mosher was educated at Wellesley College and at Cornell, Johns Hopkins, and Stanford Universities. She was deeply interested in research and early in her medical career she challenged the all too prevalent ideas about the physical incapacities of women. As an assistant in hygiene at Stanford University she developed her studies that refuted the idea that women naturally breathe costally. Out of this study grew a deep interest in dress reform for women. From 1894 on she waged battle for abandonment of stiff corsets and the adoption of sensible shoes and light-weight clothing, and encouraged women's participation in sports. She organized girls' basketball teams and arranged game schedules for them. When she became physical examiner of women at Stanford University she developed her research in functional periodicity in women and disproved the theory that menstruation is an infirmity that must be suffered by women. Later she devised exercises for the relief of painful menstruation, which known as the "Mosher exercises" have been used for over sixty years in Europe as well as in America. Following this she was a co-inventor at Stanford of the schematograph as an aid in posture training. During World War I she went to France with the American Red Cross to work with refugee children and later became Medical Director of the Bureau of Refugees and Relief. All women owe Clelia Mosher a great debt for, through her studies, she set them free physiologically to pursue an active life.[18]

Thomas Dennison Wood, M.S. (1865–1951).[19] Thomas D. Wood was born in Sycamore, Illinois. As a student at Oberlin College, along with Gulick, his roommate, he came under the influence of Dr. Hanna who interested him in taking up the study of physical education. After graduation from Oberlin in 1888 he procured his medical degree at Columbia University. In 1891 he went to California as one of a small group who assisted David Starr Jordan in organizating the newly established Leland Stanford University. He organized and directed the physical education department, which was called the Department of Hygiene and Organic Training. At the same time he also served as the college physician.

Trying out his own theories, he set up the first physical education program at Stanford around games, sports, tumbling, and outdoor activities, calling it a program of "natural gymnastics"—first in the United States. After ten years at Stanford, with Herbert Hoover and Clark Hetherington in his first freshman class, he went to Columbia University as Professor and Director of Health and Physical Education and College Physician, which position he held for twenty-six years. At the age of sixty-two he rounded out five more years before retirement in 1932 as Professor of Health Education at Columbia.

At Columbia University Wood established the first professorship of health education, the first outlines for a school health program, and the first graduate work in both physical education and health education in the United States. He was the originator of the movement to replace foreign systems of gymnastics with natural gymnastics of American origins. An advocate of the study of child development, he fought to bring the attention of educators to the fact that physical education could help in the social, emotional, and intellectual development of the child as well as in physical development. He also championed the education of the child for democratic living.

Dr. Wood was a Fellow of the American Association for the Advancement of Science, of the New York Academy of Medicine, and of the American Academy of Physical Education. He was the third person to receive the Gulick Award. He served the profession through many important positions in many related organizations. He organized the Joint Committee on Health Problems in Education of the American Medical Association and the National Education Association and served as chairman of the committee for over twenty-five years. He also helped develop the American Child Health Association. As Chairman of the Committee on the School and the Child of President Hover's White House Conference of 1930 on Child Health and Protection, he put twenty-eight subcommittees to work under his direction and turned out a prodigious report.

As coauthor of many books and contributor of major sections of various yearbooks on health and physical education, his writings have greatly enriched the profession. His earnest seeking after a better life for all children and his educational philosophy advanced the professions of both physical education and health education to a marked degree.

James Huff McCurdy, M.D. (1866–1940). Graduating from the International YMCA School of Springfield, James H. McCurdy went to New York University where he procured the medical doctor's degree in 1893. In 1895 he returned to the school in Springfield and in 1900 succeeded Gulick as Director of the Physical Department, a position he held for thirty years. From 1930 until his retirement in 1934 he was head of the Division of Health and Physical Education of Pratt Institute in Brooklyn. During World War I he was on leave to serve as head of athletics and medical and social services of the YMCA in France. Deeply interested in physiological research he devoted his years of retirement to studies of organic efficiency, particularly for men past middle age, war veterans, and army and navy fliers. Throughout his teaching career he made significant contributions to the profession in the field of physiology of exercise and published much material of value to the profession. His book on the physiology of exercise was one of the earliest in America on that subject. He devoted his adult life to the establishment of sound scientific procedures for the profession. He was a charter member of the American Academy of Physical Education. As Executive Secretary of APEA and Editor of its magazine, *The American Physical Education Review,* for twenty-four years (1906–1930) he gave the national professional association the best of his talents and the best years of his life.[20]

Fred Eugene Leonard, M.D. (1866–1922).[21] Fred Leonard was born in Darlington, Wisconsin, June 2, 1866. His father a Congregational minister, the young boy received the first eight years of schooling in Illinois, Missouri, Minnesota, and Utah, in turn. For his high school years he attended a private school, Salt Lake Academy in Salt Lake City. He taught school for the first term of 1884–1885 in a small town in Utah and when the school closed because of financial difficulties at mid-term, he completed the year teaching in a small town in Idaho. The fall of 1885 he entered Oberlin College.

At Oberlin young Fred encountered Luther Gulick and Thomas Wood, a year ahead of him there, and he was soon admitted into a select group of students who were interested in specialization in physical education, taught by Delphine Hanna of that college faculty. In his senior year, with Gulick and Wood both out of college, Fred inherited Wood's position as senior student head of the men's gymnasium. In the spring of 1889 Leonard graduated at Oberlin and in the fall entered the three-year course in the College of Physicians and Surgeons of Columbia University, acquiring the medical degree in 1892. He spent the summer of 1892 at the Chautauqua Summer School of Physical Training to augment his physical education training, and in the fall entered upon the position of Director of the Men's Gymnasium, Professor of Physiology and Physical Training, at Oberlin College, which position he was to hold for the next thirty years until death overtook him in 1922 at age 58.

Early in his professional career Leonard became intensely interested in historical research. He attended summer work in 1893 at the Posse School in Boston, and in 1894 attended Sargent's Harvard Summer School of Physical Education. That fall, at Oberlin, he gave what apparently was the first course in the history of physical education ever offered in a college curriculum in America. Two years later (summer 1896) he began his many trips to research history of physical education in foreign lands.

Not content with secondary sources, he studied German and French intensively so he could work with primary sources in foreign libraries. In 1897 he began publication of his findings in a variety of periodicals. Also, for the summer of 1897 Sargent invited him to teach a course in the history of physical education in the Harvard Summer School. For the next twenty-two years, he taught in Harvard Summer School for thirteen summers, mixing this with summers in Europe pursuing his researches.

The first trip to Europe (1896) was confined to research in Germany. Four years later he spent the entire school year in Stockholm and Berlin in intensive research. In 1913 he spent five months in Germany, Switzerland, three Scandinavian countries, and Great Britain in research. In this work he collected hundreds of photographs of facilities and costumes used in physical education, and birthplaces and photographs of leaders from which he devised almost 600 lantern slides which he used for many years in his lectures, many of which later were used as illustrative materials for his books.

As to his publications he presented his first series of biographical sketches of modern leaders of physical education with portraits, beginning in January 1909 in various issues of the YMCA periodical, *The Triangle*. In 1915, he put out these combined biographies in book form. Finally he united his offering with several new chapters and gave it the title, *A Guide to the History of Physical Education*. It had been accepted for publication by Lea & Febiger and, before his death in 1922, Leonard had corrected the proof sheets. Lea & Febiger then turned the manuscript over to Dr. R. Tait McKenzie as editor to complete the work for publication for the author posthumously. It came off press in 1923. Since then there were two editions of the book under McKenzie's editorship, and, after McKenzie's death, a 1947 edition under the editorship of George B. Affleck of Springfield College.

Beside his writings, Leonard was involved in Ohio state organizational work (the first to establish a state society of physical education). In the early 1900s he was one of the eleven leaders who made up the first Academy of Physical Education, and in 1912 he served as president of the College Physical Education Association (CPEA). He is an Honorary Member in Memmoriam of today's Academy of Physical Education.

Jessie H. Bancroft (1867–1952).[22] Jessie Bancroft was born in Winona, Minnesota. After one year at Winona Normal School and one at Iowa Medical College, she took a few gymnastic courses in Minneapolis from a former pupil of Sargent. She then opened a school of her own and conducted "parlor classes" throughout Minnesota, Iowa, and Illinois before attending the Harvard Summer School in 1891. In 1893 she was appointed Director of Physical Training of the Brooklyn Public Schools at a salary of $1200 per year. Ten years later she became Assistant

Director of Physical Education of the schools of Greater New York City under Gulick a position she held until she retired in 1928. She produced many books and carried on much research, particularly in the field of posture. As a result of her measurements of school children she procured adjustments in school seats and desks, an unheard-of innovation for those days. She was a founder and President of the American Posture League, the first person to receive the Gulick Award, the first woman to be taken into membership in the American Academy of Physical Education, the first woman in the profession to produce a considerable body of professional literature, writing on posture, games, and anthropometry, and the first woman to head a large public school department of physical education. During World War I she was Chairman of the Government Commission on Training Camp Activities and President of the War Camp Community Service. Also she established the American Cooked Food Services for the American Expeditionary Forces.

From 1895 to 1937 she produced eight books mostly on gymnastics, games and posture, the most popular of which was *Games for Playground, Home, School and the Gymnasium,* of 1909—a classic for its day, the bible of years of teachers and youth-group leaders needing help. It was still being revised thirty years later and in great demand long after that.[23] Her *Posture of School Children* of 1913 also proved to be a best-seller in the profession.

Having learned to enjoy living in France during her work there with the AEF of World War I, she went to Paris to live in her years of retirement after 1928, but she was driven back to America during World War II where she kept up her old professional friendships until her death in 1952.

Julia Anna Norris, M.D. (1874–1958).[24] Familiarity known as J. Anna Norris, Julia Anna Norris was born November 29, 1874, in Boston, Massachusetts. Following the usual years of schooling in Boston, she graduated in 1895 from the Boston Normal School of Gymnastics. She taught physical education for two years at New York State Normal School at Cortland and then attended the Women's Medical School of Northwestern University in Evanston, Illinois, procuring her medical degree in 1900. She then became Supervisor of Physical Training for the public schools of Springfield, Massachusetts. In 1907 she became Associate Physician in the School of Education of the University of Chicago. In 1912 she went to the University of Minnesota as Director of Physical Education for Women, where she rounded out her career in 1941. In retirement she suffered severe visual difficulties and took up Braille to continue reading. She died September 15, 1958.

One of the founders of the Middle West Society of Physical Education, Dr. Norris later became one of four women charter members of the American Academy of Physical Education; she was one of the founders of the Middle West Association of Physical Education for College Women, and one of the prime movers in the establishment of the National Association of Physical Education for College Women. She served for three years as the second woman to hold the presidency of the

Middle West Society of Physical Education (1923–1926). But probably her most noteworthy contribution was her work in the Women's Division of NAAF, serving from its founding as a member of its Executive Committee—and beyond that as chairwoman of the committee that drew up its *Platform of Athletics for Girls and Women,* which developed into the most important pronouncement on that subject in the twentieth century thus far. Her skillful guidance and deep thinking on the subject produced a statement, which published in leaflet form, was distributed by the thousands by the U.S. Office of Education and other important groups throughout the country. It was J. Anna Norris's crowning achievement. In 1931 she was recognized by APEA among its first group to receive the Honor Award.

Others Who Should be Honored. No recital of the leaders of early twentieth century would be complete without mention of the following stalwarts who also were born in the 1860s and 1870s, such as *Amos Alonzo Stagg* (1863–1966), the profession's coach and physical educator, *Thomas A. Storey* (1875–1943), the profession's first state physical director, *Blanche Trilling* (1876–1964), the founder in 1917 of the Athletic Conference of American College Women (today's College Women in Sports (CWS), or *Marjorie Bouvé* (1879–1970), who filled the void in teacher training for women in physical education in Boston when BNSG left Boston for Wellesley College.

PHYSICAL EDUCATION OF THE MID-TWENTIETH CENTURY (1930–1960)

11

Events That Affected Physical Education and The Activities That Made up Its Program at Mid-Century

EVENTS AFFECTING PHYSICAL EDUCATION

Mid-century was a disturbing era. The entire world was in upheaval. It opened with a great worldwide depression and from then on was caught up in a second worldwide war and its aftermath. The greatly increased mechanization of life in this period robbed large segments of society of the opportunities for physical exercise that formerly existed in both the home and work places. The shorter work hours of this period increased leisure hours, largely taken up now by watching the new invention television, now generally available.

The Depression of the 1930s

In the economic stress of the depression of the 1930s, school boards, urged on by groups of citizens, ordered drastic cuts in education. The specialized subjects—music, art, home economics, and physical education—were labeled "fads and frills" and came in for undue and sharp criticism and attacks. In many towns and cities these subjects were forced to bear the brunt of cuts in budgets and staffs. But thanks to the efforts of educators and citizen groups who recognized the aims of physical education and put up a fight in its behalf, physical education, on the whole, suffered no more than regular school subjects.

The Progressive Education Movement

The late 1920s and the 1930s witnessed the height of the Progressive Education Movement. (Its beginnings were discussed in earlier chapters.) It was causing much controversy among educators and parents of school children. The extremists in the movement claimed that a teacher should teach only what a child inquired about; the teacher was to keep in the background and let the child figure out what to learn and to ask for help; discipline was not to be imposed. Much of the country was in an uproar over these pronouncements and many children were removed either to private schools that accepted the extremes of the movement or to private schools that denied the movement completely, their parents being unwilling for them to be exposed to it in moderation in the public schools.

In physical education classes much time was wasted with pupils arguing about what they wished to learn, with now and then one or two children doing something physically active as the others looked on and discussed what they were doing. Too few pupils got any worthwhile physical activity out of these class periods, and in far too many schools physical education was almost a complete loss if the top educators insisted upon following this movement. However, physical education, as all other branches of education, was deeply influenced by the Progressive Education Movement of the twentieth century, and when the movement, controversial as it was, died out, physical educators looked back and saw that it brought about many worthwhile changes, chief of which was an acceptance of sports and dance as a legitimate part of a physical education program and not merely as activities to be tolerated as a side issue promoted by pupils themselves.

World War II

Out of 9 million registrants examined for the armed services of the United States in early 1943, almost 3 million (one third) were found to be unfit for any form of military duty. However, because of improved techniques of examinations and diagnosis since 1917, many were rejected who would have been accepted in World War I. Indeed more men were rejected for World War II than were accepted for World War I. But those who were accepted were soft and flabby and in need of conditioning. The chief of Athletics and Recreation of the Services Division of the United States Army had this to say at the War Fitness Conference in 1943:

> Our physical programs in high schools have been a miserable failure. Physical education through play must be discarded and a more rugged program substituted. We must assume our share of the responsibility for the unnecessary loss of American lives. Many of our boys have perished because of the accumulation of fatigue, the lack of endurance, stamina, and certain abilities. You read about the men who struggled through swamps and jungles and over mountains for days and days before reaching safety, or survived in rubber boats for many days before being rescued. They had the strength and

stamina to survive such ordeals, but you don't read about the hundreds that did not have such strength and stamina. They did not live to make a report.[1]

The military called on physical educators and trained coaches to man the Armed Services' physical training and athletic programs and to head physical reconditioning programs with trained physical educators, both men and women, on their staffs.

Women in Military Service. On May 14, 1942, Congress passed an act establishing the Women's Army Auxiliary Corps (WAAC) and on May 16, Mrs. Oveta Culp Hobby (1905–   ), a Public Relations Executive with the War Department, was sworn in as Director of the Corps with rank of colonel. It soon developed that for greater efficiency the Corps should be a full-fledged section of the military, not an auxiliary, and it was changed, on July 2, 1943, to the Women's Army Corps—to become known familiarly as the WAC.

By 1943 there were 232,000 women wearing the uniform of our Armed Services—the first women in U.S. history to be accepted for military duty. In September, 1944, the Surgeon General's office reported to the National Civilian Advisory Committee of the Women's Army Corps an unusually large number of rejections due to excessive weight and a general lack of strength, flexibility, and endurance of those women who were accepted.[2] (At the same time the Harvard Fatigue Laboratory conducted a series of fitness tests on college women and found that of the group that was considered to be fit, only 22 percent had even average strength and endurance.) Those who were accepted for the WAC were given a rigorous program of conditioning as outlined in the *WAC Field Manual of Physical Training*.

Following this, American women rushed to enter other branches of the armed forces as fast as corps were established for them in the Navy (the WAVES), Women's Air Force Corps (WAFs), Marine Corps, Coast Guard, and the medical corps of the various branches of the military. Women trained in physical education were at a premium. Top officers in many of these branches were such women. But a great number of these enlisted women were found lacking in strength and endurance. Other women left their homes by the thousands to work in industry, to help replace the men called to the armed services, and to do their bit for the war effort. Their softness and general lack of physical fitness showed up at once. The Labor Department reported that there were 16 million women working in industry in the summer of 1943, working a ten-hour day for seven days a week. Some were working on night shifts, some were loading freight cars, others were driving heavy trucks or welding and walking cat walks in shipyards. American women in such large numbers had never before been called upon for such physically difficult tasks.[3]

Also during the war large numbers of American women and men entered the service of the American Red Cross and were sent throughout the world wherever our armed forces were stationed. The assignment of many of these was to organize recreational activities. Also the United Services Organization (USO) functioned in all communities where Armed Forces Camps were established. Other organizations took over the promotion of recreation for the war workers in industry. After the close of the war, many of these organizations became permanent, where armed forces were maintained in the world.

World War II demands on man power tended to deplete the recreation leadership force, but community recreation, nevertheless, realized the contributions it needed to make toward the total war effort and forged ahead. By 1946 over 1700 communities spent over $50 million annually and employed over 30,000 leaders, some 5000 of them full time. These advances continued into the period immediately following the war. By 1949 the paid leadership force increased to nearly 50,000 leaders, with nearly 6000 employed full time.

Physical Fitness Movement

John B. Kelly (1888–1960), a distinguished citizen of Philadelphia and a former University of Pennsylvania and Olympic athlete, who had been intensely interested in fitness from his early youth and was deeply shocked at the draft information of World War II, appealed to President Roosevelt for immediate action to correct this situation among civilians as quickly as possible. The President was particularly shocked at the report that 40 percent of the men entering the armed services in World War II could not swim as far as 50 feet and that drownings were second only to motor accidents in causing accidental deaths, with most occurring in the 15- to 20-year-old range.[4] In 1942 the President set up a Division of Physical Fitness under the Office of Civilian Defense (OCD) and appointed Mr. Kelley head of this new Division. District divisions were immediately set up along the lines of the nine Army Service Commands with two codirectors, a man and a woman, appointed as Regional Directors in each Service Command.[5]

The majority of these eighteen persons appointed as regional directors were physical educators. Under the OCD and Mr. Kelly, serious controversies developed, and the movement became a political football to such an extent that it lost its initial effectiveness and shortly was removed by President Roosevelt to function under the Federal Security Agency (FSA) with the armed services, the United States Office of Education, the American Medical Association, the AAHPER, and other related organizations taking an active role in the promotion of physical fitness. Mr. Kelly's organization became one of several carrying on in a nationwide, cooperative endeavor under the FSA.

Under the FSA a still larger number of physical educators was brought into active service in the movement. Frank Lloyd (1897–1957) of New York University was appointed Chief of the Physical Fitness Division of the Federal Security Agency with headquarters in Washington, D.C., and William L. Hughes (1895–1957) of Columbia University was appointed Chief Consultant. Dorothy LaSalle of

Montclair, New Jersey, public schools was appointed head of the work for women and children and she, too, was given an office in Washington, D.C.

This movement brought about a change in attitude in regard to athletics in both the armed forces and the schools. In the colleges eligibility rules were relaxed to permit freshman and transfer students to participate at once, intensive participation of all students in sports was encouraged. The United States Office of Education organized the Victory Corps for school children with achievement tests and insignia for physical fitness activities and held regional institutes to promote the work.[6]

With World War II at an end, the enthusiasm for fitness died down, but then people were aroused in the early 1950s by the publication of rejection figures of the new draftees. The head of Selective Service reported in 1952 that 1.5 million of the 18½-to-26-year-olds were rejected for the draft.[7] Then the Kraus-Weber test results of minimum muscular fitness of school children, first published in 1953, showed the poor fitness records of American school children compared with European children. These tests consist of six tests of key muscle groups which show up the abilities required for healthy living. They were developed from a fifteen-year study of patients with low-back pain made by Dr. Hans Kraus (1905–   ), Associate Professor of Physical Medicine and Rehabilitation of New York University. Designed to measure one's ability to participate effectively in activities required for everyday living, these are not supposed to be tests of high levels of muscular fitness. These were given to 4264 U.S. school children and 2870 European children from comparable urban and suburban communities and 57.9 percent of the U.S. children failed the tests compared to 8.7 percent of the European children.[8]

Once more Mr. John Kelly alerted the President of the United States to the need for a physical fitness movement. Immediately when President Eisenhower's attention was called to the Kraus-Weber report, he ordered a special White House Conference on the subject which was finally held in June, 1956. Following this the AAHPER held a Fitness Conference in Washington in September 1956, and President Eisenhower established a President's Council on Youth Fitness and a President's Citizens Advisory Committee on the Fitness of American Youth. Later President's Conferences on Fitness of Youth were held in 1957 at West Point and in 1958 at Fort Riehie, Maryland.[9]

ACTIVITIES OF THE PHYSICAL EDUCATION PROGRAM

The mid-twentieth century saw many changes in the physical education that make up the usual physical education program as discussed below.

Dance

The World War II period brought about a complete acceptance of modern dance in the lower schools as well as in colleges and the world of the performing arts. It also witnessed a big revival of square and folk dancing all across the country, attesting to the acceptance of dance in its various phases as a tool of education.[10]

Modern or Contemporary Dance. As the years passed, *modern* dance gave way to *contemporary* dance.

The old argument of the earlier era as to whether the department of dance belongs in the department or school of physical education or in that of fine arts was still debated.

With the boost given by Ted Shawn to the idea that dance is a worthwhile and challenging activity for men as well as for women, an increasing number of men in colleges joined modern dance classes. Also, men sport coaches came to recognize the fundamental techniques of dance as excellent body-building exercises and urged their athletes to join classes in this activity.

In the Post-World War I period Martha Graham, an early pupil of Ted Shawn, developed her form of modern dance around the concept that movement based on the strength and flexibility of the trunk muscles originates from the center of the body and from there flows outward to the other parts of the body. Doris Humphrey, also an early pupil of Shawn, developed her form of the dance around the idea that all movement is a continuous process of fall and recovery, of losing and regaining balance. Various other leaders developed modern dance according to their own concepts of movement, but all held that dance is the vehicle through which one expresses emotion and ideas by movement. Some teachers held that movement is an end in itself. It does not have to express anything but itself, in relation to time, space, and energy, as it explores the relation between sound and movement, between light and movement, between words and movement, and so on. In the early years of the development of modern dance, great emphasis was placed on the divorce of modern dance from all forms of stylized dancing, such as ballet. But, modern dance was taking a fresh look at such forms to acknowledge a concept that dance of whatever form is the art of movement with the body its sole instrument.

Dance majors had developed in several colleges and universities for students of the dance who wished to prepare in college to teach dance in educational settings, not for themselves to prepare to enter the world of performing arts as professionals. Pupils of Martha Graham, Doris Humphrey, Margaret H'Doubler and other leaders of modern dance in the 1930s and 1940s headed dance work in departments of physical education in colleges and universities all across the country.

Square and Folk Dance. The post–World War I revival of square dancing persisted in some parts of the country. Following World War II it still moved forward enthusiastically. The Nebraska revival is typical of that in many other states. Lincoln, a city of a little over 180,000 population, had twenty-three square dance clubs in 1956; Omaha, twenty-nine; and other localities supported thirty-one other clubs. All were united in the Nebraska Folk and Square Dance Association, organized in the 1940s, which held an annual state festival in Lincoln each spring with as many as 800 or more dancers on the floor at a time. In the 1950s it maintained a youth section which sponsored square dancing for young boys and girls throughout the state. Each year at its festival it featured some one nationality represented among the citizenry of the state and invited this group to put on an exhibition of its Old-Country folk dancing. This brought much pleasure to these groups in the way of friendly recognition of their Old-World culture and much of educational value to others.

Gymnastics

In the post–World War I era when sports were making so strong an appeal for a place in the educational world long denied them, a reaction set in against use of the old-world form of gymnastics in the schools. At the same time the much heralded new "natural" gymnastics failed to make a place for itself from lack of teachers trained to handle this new form. These two developments meant the almost total disappearance of gymnastics from the schools of America in this mid-century era. In a few places this activity persisted, especially in colleges where there were women teachers trained to offer the new to America Danish gymnastics to college women, and in a few colleges where enthusiastic men teachers kept the activity alive for the few men interested, and in some towns where descendants of the 1848 flood of German immigrants and the later flood of Czechs still banded together to practice their gymnastics. Otherwise gymnastics almost completely died out in the United States.

Following World War II there was a new appraisal of gymnastics, and once more this activity went back in the program, though in a new form. Whereas in earlier years the word *gymnastics* referred to a series of formal free-standing class exercises done in unison at a teacher's command, followed by apparatus work; it came to refer mainly, at least as far as women were concerned, to the apparatus work alone. With the introduction of such new pieces as the high balance beam, the uneven parallel bars, and the trampoline, even the apparatus work took on new forms, which offered training in creativity and opportunities in the development of self-realization, through the performer's own original creation of exercise forms both on apparatus and in free-exercise routines. For this latter the student used tumbling, acrobatic, and rhythmical forms somewhat similar to modern dance techniques. Some of the free-exercise forms as done by women came to be called gymnastic ballets.

The use of the high balance beam, popular with women in particular, came to America by way of Sweden, where it was introduced into the Swedish Lingiads of 1939 to 1949 by Madam Maja Carlquist, who was seeking a new approach to Ling's principles of gymnastic exercises and developed work on the balance beam as important in the training of women. The high balance beam is 16½ feet long and 4 inches wide and is adjustable in height up to 4 feet. Basic rules for exercise on it and a Code of Points for judging one's performance have been developed by the Federation of International Gymnastics, which governs gymnastics for Olympic Games and other international competition. Exercises on this piece of apparatus aim at the development of grace, poise, balance, coordination, and the ability to orient oneself in space. The uneven parallel bars seemed to older persons trained in earlier years on the Swedish boom to be a fairly good substitute for that old piece of apparatus which was popular in years gone by. The trampoline widely known and used in this era gave people opportunities to learn to handle the body in mid-air, and thus was a unique piece of gymnastic apparatus.

Some of the apparatus used in earlier years, such as the horse, buck, vaulting box, parallel bars, and flying rings, were retained, but gone were the Swedish boom, climbing ropes and ladders, and the horizontal and vertical ladders. As to hand apparatus, gone also were the wands, dumbbells, and Indian clubs of the late nineteenth and the early twentieth centuries, but in their place, at least for women, were loops, hoops, and balls used along with the free-exericse routines.

With the coming of these completely new forms of gymnastics, following a period of almost complete lack in the schools of gymnastics in any form, there was a dearth of teachers prepared to handle such work, so that there had sprung up gymnastics-training institutes to carry on until teacher-training departments caught up with the skills of teaching gymnastics in its new forms. This applied more to women than to men, for the latter never did abandon gymnastics in the 1930s, 1940s, and 1950s quite so completely as did the women.

Danish Gymnastics. Wherever gymnastics of the older forms was found in the schools of the mid-twentieth century it was probably Danish gymnastics or some closely related form. Especially popular with girls and women, this form was worked into the fitness program for the Women's Army Corps and was also used in civilian fitness programs during World War II. With the close of the war, however, popularity for this form of gymnastics gradually died out, to be revived temporarily here and there where touring Danish gymnastics teams aroused enthusiasm afresh. But Danish gymnastics, popular in America in the 1920s, 1930s, and early 1940s, especially with women, also underwent changes in keeping with the times.

Individual or Adaptive Exercises. Individual or adaptive exercises (formerly spoken of as corrective gymnastics) refers to the program of specific exercises formulated to meet an individual student's needs that are amenable to correction by specific exercises, and not to a program of restriction within the regular school work in gymnastics, sports, or dancing. This latter, usually spoken of as "restricted" class work, was designed for those who did not need specific correction of physical faults but did need, for various reasons that showed up in a medical examination, restrictions on their exercise which they could nevertheless pursue as a part of regular class activity. Many students assigned to correction needed restriction in dosage of exercise, but many did not, and the corrective program was not to be confused with the restricted one.

By no means did all physical education programs, even in the mid-twentieth century, offer corrective work, since this called for highly specialized and individual teaching. But where offered, it, too, had taken on a new look. With the return of gymnastics to the physical education program, brought about by the Physical Fitness Movement, came a return of interest in corrective work in order to take care of the deviations of children from the normal physique. According to Rathbone and Hunt (see References), the new correctives talked of progressive resistance exercises, "circuit training" isotonic exercise, geniometry, psychophysical wholeness but still held to the earlier objectives of reconditioning and neuromuscular reeducation.[11] The Veterans Administration now required their corrective therapists to be graduates of an approved course in professional physical education training. After World War II there was an awakening of interest in corrective gymnastics, stemming from the public interest in the rehabilitation program of the armed services. Hospitals adopted individual gymnastics in the treatment of many ailments.

Sports

Without question the sports program that developed slowly during the nineteenth had by the middle of the twentieth century crowded the traditional and formal required physical education program out of the schools. Despite efforts by many leaders to broaden the base of athletics in schools and colleges, football, baseball, basketball, and track and field remained the important sports for boys and men, basketball and volleyball for girls and women. Of these sports, football held the number-one position with the public, with basketball a close second. But judging by sales of sports equipment, the fastest growing sports of this era were skiing, fishing, bowling, softball, badminton, skating, bicycling, basketball, table tennis, and paddle tennis, in the order listed.

The same thing happened to sports with regard to television of post–World War II years as happened after World War I with regard to radio. At first the television broadcasts cut into gate receipts of games, and many sports managers denounced them as radio broadcasts had been denounced earlier, but once the novelty of television wore off the crowds attending the big games were larger than ever dreamed of in earlier decades despite television's pull to keep many at home to watch the games in comfort.

Interest in sports had become so keen that more publicity was given to them in the daily papers than to any other single activity. The tendency of sports to attract spectators gave rise to considerable concern by many who desired to see people actively engaged as participants. However, those so concerned gained satisfaction from the numbers who participated in bowling, fishing, hunting, golf, tennis, softball, swimming, and various other sports and games. In fact a government report of 1955 showed that since World War II, participation in spectator sports had fallen off 19 percent whereas participation in individual sports had increased 34 percent, and the sale of boats, bicycles, aircraft, golf clubs, and like sports equipment had risen 137 percent.[12]

Baseball. By 1936 baseball was no longer an important sport in colleges.

Basketball for Boys and Men. It was estimated by 1936 that there were 50,000 high schools in forty-two states supporting state high school basketball tournaments for boys.[13] By the 1950s basketball had spread throughout the world. Teams from many nations competed in the sport now in the Olympic Games. In 1949 the National Basketball Association was established, marking growth in the professional game. An estimated 20 million people played this sport throughout the world. The National Collegiate Athletic Association elimination contest, the National Intercollegiate championship, and the National Invitation tournament represented the major college play-offs held near the end of each basketball season. Crowds of 15,000 or more people often attended college basketball games in various cities throughout the country. On occasion, gambling had reached out to involve college basketball players, but even with accompanying poor publicity the game continued to grow in its appeal.

By mid-century the game had changed considerably from that of the early days when the tallest men were the height we today consider but average. In "pro" basketball teams, the centers ranged from 6 feet, 9 inches, to over 7 feet tall, the forwards from 6 feet, 6 inches, to 6 feet, 9 inches, and the guards from 6 feet, 1 inch, to 6 feet, 7 inches. In college basketball the University of Kansas in 1957 claimed the tallest man of all basketball history in their player who was 7 feet, 2 inches tall, and in the 1960s a California school boasted of a player 7 feet, 1⅜ inches tall. High school players of this era averaged 5 feet, 5 inches.

Because of this great increase in the stature of athletes over that of the early 1900s, the height of the basket, which had remained unchanged through the years, was in an altogether different ratio with the height of the average player. Some have advocated, although as yet in vain, that the basket be raised. However, there were several rule changes aimed at neutralizing the extra-tall man, such as widening the free-throw lane to twelve feet, prohibiting a player from guiding the ball to the basket, adding the center 10-second line and the bonus free throw rulings, eliminating the center jump after each basket, and giving the ball to the team scored upon. These changes in some measure neutralized the advantage of the taller players.

Basketball for Girls and Women. Throughout most of this era two main groups had been putting out rules of basketball for girls and women—the National Section on Women's Athletics (NSWA) of AAHPER (used almost exclusively in colleges and large city schools) and the Amateur Athletic Union (AAU) (used mostly by out-of-school teams and small towns, with men coaching girls' teams). There were a few other rules-making groups, such as the Iowa Girls' High School Athletic Union, but these were used only within their own groups. In the late 1950s the NSWA (by then renamed the Division of Girls' and Women's Sports—DGWS) and the AAU had joined forced to set up a joint committee to edit and publish the rules.

Bowling. More people engaged in bowling in the United States in the late 1940s than in any other sport. It was estimated that fifteen million people were bowling at that time with the sport holding its greatest popularity in the Middle West. By that date there were in the United States 25,000 bowling alleys with an average of eight lanes each. Since then the sport has grown to still greater popularity.[14]

The American Bowling Congress (ABC) and the Women's International Bowling Congress (WIBC) were attacked by many individuals and groups in the late 1940s for the racial discrimination clauses in their constitutions. Industrial recreation groups particularly felt this injustice and opened an attack on these groups which paid off, for in May 1950, the ABC at its annual convention voted overwhelmingly to remove the word *white* from their constitution and thereby opened their national tournaments to all the American people. Previous to this a judge of the Superior Court of Cook County, Illinois, found the ABC guilty of racial discrimination and fined the organization $2500 on the ground that its conduct was "violative of the provision of the Illinois Civil Rights Act." This opened the door, and the American Bowling Congress "saw the light." Immediately the women's group voted racial discrimination out of its constitution also.

Cricket. After World War II cricket became popular in some parts of the country, particularly on the West Coast,[15] although in club rather than in school situations. UCLA is the one college that maintained the sport, which no doubt was supported largely there by the foreign students from such countries as India, Pakistan, and the West Indies, where the game has long been popular from early British-mandate days. The game has been played at UCLA since early 1930s.

Field Hockey. From its beginning in the United States in 1901 field hockey has been popular in the women's colleges and prep schools in particular, with small groups in many coeducational colleges and universities, and in some high schools of the larger cities. It has never appealed to most American girls and women, but the groups that have participated in it are ardently enthusiastic. The game enjoyed great popularity among small groups of young women recently out of college, who have joined forces with similar groups from nearby cities. Several large cities and communities with many college graduates support active hockey clubs, which under the banner of the American Field Hockey Association play in tournaments and on occasion compete against visiting English, Scotch, and Irish Women's teams.

Football. The popularity of American football in colleges was tremendous—crowds between 90,000 and 100,000 people at a single contest were no longer rarities. The first Rose Bowl game (postseason and intersectional) occurred in 1902. In midcentury more than twenty other bowl games were promoted in a single season in various sections of the United States.

Six-Man Football. The 1930s brought a modification of the game, six-man football, that shortly came into widespread use in high schools of small towns. Stephen Epler (1909–   ), then physical director and coach at the high school in Chester, Nebraska, created the new form of game and first presented it to the public in a master's thesis in the field of education at the University of Nebraska in the summer of 1934. The *Lincoln Sunday Journal and Star* published the dissertation September 2, 1934, bringing the proposed new form of the game to the attention of the public. The first match game was played October 3, 1934, in a contest between the high schools of Chester and Hebron, Nebraska, in Hebron. This immediately opened the game to the thousands of small high schools of the nation that could not produce a regulation-size team nor the regulation-size field. With a six-man team and an 80-by 40-yard field and several changes in the rules, this game required less expensive equipment and reduced the danger of injuries. The six-man game took the small high schools of the country by storm, and most high schools of America are small schools.[16] Within two years, 1233 schools were playing this form of the game. (Epler later received from the American Academy of Physical Education a citation for this creative service to the profession.)

The Heisman Trophy. In 1935, a poll of sports writers and broadcasters initiated the Heisman Memorial Trophy presented annually by the Downtown Athletic Club of New York City, for the best player of the year. Jay Berwanger of the University of Chicago was the first winner. This trophy is now owned by the Department of Athletics of that school. In this mid-century era, the trophy was won five times by players of the University of Notre Dame.

Football—the Wealthy Uncle. The budget, the efforts to lure skilled athletes to colleges, the commercialization of football surpassed that of any other sport.[17] More coaches, in high schools and colleges were employed for football than for any other sport. Despite occasional scandals concerning the conduct of football, it continued to grow in importance. It was the "wealthy uncle" who supported practically all the other sports in colleges and high schools and built the magnificent stadiums and gymnasiums.

Golf. The 1930s brought a craze for midget golf and golf driving ranges, which proved a great boon to schools wishing to teach golfing skills but not having the facilities. Sports equipment firms reported sales of golf equipment of $29 million, in contrast to $12 million sales in the 1920s. Between 1935 and 1940, the Works Progress Administration (WPA) constructed 207 municipal golf courses in the United States. By mid-century there were 700 public golf courses in the United States, and the United States Golf Association by then listed 1124 clubs with a membership of over 2 million. Golf championship matches had grown from a one-day eighteen-hole event to the four-day seventy-two hole event.

Softball. The Amateur Softball Association was organized in 1932. In 1934 a Rules Committee made up of NRA, YMCA, NCAA, and APEA representatives drew up official rules. The game became tremendously popular in industry, in intramural programs in the schools and small towns, and with all ages and both sexes.

Swimming. By 1931, 25 percent of all high schools and 1.2 percent of elementary schools in cities of over 100,000 population had their own swimming pools. Cities of population from 30,000 to 100,000 had pools in 23.9 percent of high schools and 1 percent of elementary schools; towns of 10,000 to 30,000 population had pools in 14.8 percent of their high schools; and cities of below 10,000 had no school pools. By 1937 there were 700 YMCAs in the United States that had swimming pools with 98 percent of them built since 1900 and the other two percent built between 1885 and 1900 and still in use in 1937. Because of the depression, building came to a standstill during the 1930s.[18]

By 1940 there were in the United States 8000 pools, half of them outdoor and half indoor, with 50 percent of them built since 1925.

In this period, aquatic arts and synchronized swimming became very popular especially with girls' and women's physical education departments emphasizing group action in swimming together, performing as a group rather than engaging in competitive swimming and diving.[19]

Following World War II the construction of swimming pools took on new life. Indoor pools, previously considered a "must" only for the gymnasiums in the larger cities and in the larger colleges and universities, were now installed in the schools of many smaller towns, whereas outdoor pools became commonplace in practically every community of at least several thousand inhabitants. Thus swimming at mid-century beame a sport for all of America, old and young. In the 1950s scuba diving was added to swim instruction, and a feature called drown-proofing was added to life-saving courses.

Other Sports

Badminton. By 1939 Southern California had 10,000 courts, the Detroit area boasted 50,000 players and New York State around 70,000 players, and 400 clubs had joined the Association. Also in that year the first international tournament was held with a Dane winning the men's title and a Canadian the women's title.

Handball. This sport came into popularity during the depression of the 1930s when the Works Progress Administration built 1365 handball courts in various parts of the country, most of them of the one-wall type.

Ice Hockey. This sport came into prominence in the 1940s, especially in the professional field with the establishment of professional leagues.

Ice Skating. In 1930 Sonja Henie (1913–   ), the famous Norwegian skating star, made her debut in the United States, starting a wave of enthusiasm for this sport which had existed for years in the wintertime in the northern states. The development of artificial ice rinks brought it to all parts of the country in all seasons of the year. The Works Progress Administration of the World War II period alone built 691 rinks throughout the country. Many modern municipal auditoriums had an ice rink, and they were spreading gradually into the college world. The large rink at the Ohio State University was in constant use by both faculty and students.

Outing Activities. Many large lakes had been created behind the dams that had been built by the government in many parts of the country since the early 1950s. These opened up fishing and boating to millions of people. Also, there were 180 million acres of public land in national forests with 116,000 miles of trails for hiking. The National Park Service giving employment to thousands was developing roads, trails, and camps at the price of $476 million to accommodate millions of park visitors each year.

Paddle Tennis. This sport became popular in the 1930s. The National Recreation Association reported that by 1939 there were an estimated 64,000 players using the ninety-two courts at Manhattan Beach, New York alone. The American Paddle Tennis Association was born in 1934.

Skiing. It was estimated that in the winter of 1936 there were 60,000 skiers in the White Mountain area, 88,000 in the Utah forests, 44,000 in Oregon, 110,000 in Colorado, 106,000 in Washington, and 639,000 in California.[20] The year 1931 brought the first ski train, or snow train as it was then called. This was organized by the Appalachian Club of Boston. By the winter of 1939 ski trains running in as many as ten sections were leaving New York City on Saturdays and Sunday mornings for the Adirondacks and White Mountains. Grand Central Station in New York City posted news daily in the concourse giving temperature and snow data at ski resorts in New England and New York. The three lone ski clubs of 1904 grew to 100 by 1930 and to 171 by 1940. In 1936 the United States entered its first ski team in the Olympics.

Of all sports, skiing had the greatest participation record. In winter, hundreds of thousands of skiers filled the ski trails of the mountain areas of the country, and the sport had been added to the curriculum of many colleges and universities.

Soccer. Gradually American men were taking to soccer, which as played in the United States before mid-century was almost exclusively a college women's game.

Volleyball. This sport increased markedly in popularity after World War II. The International Volleyball Federation was organized in Paris in 1947. Since then there was a marked increase in participation in this game.

CHAPTER 12

Amateur Sports at Mid-Century

In the earlier years of competitive sports in this country, only a few organizations existed for their promotion and control, some for a combination of sports and a few each to cover some one sport. But at mid-twentieth century there were many associations, clubs, and leagues covering sports participation both in and out of the school, both amateur and professional, for all age groups, for both sexes, and at all levels—local, state, regional, national, and international. To discuss them all is beyond the scope of a book on history of physical education. The material that follows takes up briefly new amateur sports organization since 1930 and the on-going work of the few amateur organizations still functioning that have existed since earlier periods and have been discussed in earlier chapters.

Although some early organizations that served to promote and control professional sports have been discussed in earlier chapters of this book, as a part of the heritage of some sports, the number and variety of such sports organizations have grown so tremendously and are so far removed from the field of education that they are given no further consideration in this book.

AMATEUR SPORTS ORGANIZATIONS

Various groups of sports organizations and the competition peculiar to them are discussed in the material that follows.

Organizations for Nonschool Sports

Amateur Athletic Union (AAU). At mid-twentieth century, the AAU was the oldest and most powerful of the organizations that persisted from earlier periods to promote and control amateur sports outside the schools. From the mid-1920s on its authority was being challenged as never before by several other organizations.

It claimed jurisdiction over all amateur sports not under the control of schools, colleges, YMCAs, and a few isolated sports such as golf, tennis, and bowling, each of which was controlled by its own national organization, and a few team sports such as football, ice hockey, and baseball, each of which was controlled by its own league. With these exceptions it claimed control of basketball, boxing, gymnastics, handball, running, jumping, track and field, weightputting, hurdles, pole vault, swimming, tug-of-war, wrestling, weightlifting, and volleyball.

In the earlier decades of this century, girls' and women's sports were just beginning to attract the attention of AAU which for the most part confined its work to sports for boys and men. But in the 1930s it became active in its effort to get control of girls' and women's sports, as is related later in this chapter.

North American Baseball Association. In this new era, the North American Baseball Association was established to revive and encourage small town teams and to restore the rural baseball diamond to its old-time popularity. The Amateur Baseball Congress was established in 1933 with thirty-five state and regional associations and 2200 teams playing under its jurisdiction.

Summer evening amateur baseball came to America in a big way with the night lighting of athletic fields. The first night baseball game was played in Des Moines, Iowa, in 1930. By 1950, radio broadcasts of games were cutting into attendance at minor league games. However it was 1935 before a major league tried out the night lighting and 1940 before night lighting of diamonds was universally accepted.[1]

Little Leagues. Although groups of adults had in earlier periods promoted sports competition for young boys outside the school program, they were not as numerous or widespread as they became in the 1930s and 1940s. When the first of them came into existence, shortly before World War II, with sufficient strength to claim much public attention, the American Association for Health, Physical Education and Recreation and many leaders of the medical profession and the Congress of the Parents and Teachers Association registered vigorous protests over their exploitation of young boys by adults who, in order to produce winning teams, were disregarding all tenets, psychological and sociological as well as physiological, of the type of sports competition suitable for grade-school-age children. The protests improved the situation, although still disapproved of by many adults, there were many organizations promoting these sports, such as the Little League Baseball, Biddy League Basketball, and Pop Warner Football League.

These groups promoted state, regional, and national matches which called forth protests from the medical profession, many school administrators, and physical educators. At its convention in 1947, AAHPER adopted resolutions advocating the abolition of interschool competitive athletics for elementary school children. In spite of this open opposition, little league football, basketball, and baseball was sponsored by private organizations for the benefit of boys twelve years of age and under. In the summer of 1951, Little League baseball was being played in thirty-seven states. The national championship games attracted over 10,000 people. Thousands of elementary school boys were participating in these sports each year. Unfortunately, wise guidance was frequently lacking in the conduct of these programs.

Sports Organizations for the Handicapped. Several sports organizations for the handicapped were established in late mid-century, but they did not get well underway until after World War II and, therefore, are discussed in Chapter 15.

Intramural Sports

Although intramural athletics had grown tremendously at both the college and high school levels, it was reported in 1949 in the proceedings of the 54th Annual Convention of AAHPER that of 113 elementary schools surveyed, only 46 percent provided intramural sports programs for elementary school children. Practically all colleges, large high schools, and a high percentage of smaller high schools were offering a varied intramural program of sports. Most students in college were finding some opportunity to satisfy their desire to engage in athletic contests of a recreational nature. Many colleges were employing on their physical education or athletic department staffs teachers to head their intramural sports programs. But as yet there were no intramural sports organizations.

Organizations for Interscholastic Sports

The world of interscholastic sports had not yet developed a multiplicity of organizations to promote and control it, as had the world of sports for adults. Practically all high school sports organizations were for boys under the jurisdiction of the one overall organization, the NFHSAA, which in many states controlled sports competition for girls as well as for boys.

National Federation of State High School Athletic Associations. Following its birth in 1920, the National Federation of State High School Athletic Associations grew until by 1940 it had established a national office with a full-time executive staff.

After World War II the federation brought about a reduction in the size of the football and the baseball for high school use, set up less expensive equipment as standard, standardized officiating in high school contests, and materially raised the coaching and playing ethics. One of its chief objectives, as in its earlier years, was to protect high school boys from exploitation in their sports. A prime concern was to protect them from groups not related to the world of education that would use them for publicity purposes regardless of the best interests of the boys. Strict rules were adopted concerning the recruiting of high school boys by colleges—rules designed to protect the best interests of the high schools and the boys.

Organizations for Intercollegiate Sports

For the many years since the birth of the National Collegiate Athletic Association (NCAA) in 1905, it alone had controlled all intercollegiate sports competition for men in the United States. By mid-century it had divided into three main groups— the large college and university group to be controlled by NCAA, the smaller college and university group to be controlled by the National Association of Inter-collegiate Athletics (NAIA), and the junior college group to be controlled by the National Junior College Athletic Association (NJCAA).

National Collegiate Athletic Association (NCAA). In the early years of inter-collegiate sports in the United States, the ivy league colleges—the old schools of the early years of our nation—held the limelight of publicity but as the later schools of the Middle West and the Far West were established and took up sports, they formed new groups to challenge each other, so that gradually there grew up various leagues such as the Big Ten, the Missouri Valley, and the Pacific Coast leagues, the old schools of the East Coast becoming known as the Ivy League. By Mid-twentieth century, the Missouri Valley League had disappeared, taken over by the new grouping called the Big Eight.

In 1947 NCAA added baseball and in 1948 ice hockey to its wide coverage of intercollegiate sports.

As intercollegiate sports became big business, especially in the big leagues, many of the college and university stadiums that were built following Harvard's lead in 1905 were now enlarged or replaced by larger structures.

A Second Try for a Sanity Code. At the turn of the century, at President Theodore Roosevelt's urging that the colleges clean up their intercollegiate sports, a Sanity Code was drawn up but little came of it. Complaints of the evils of intercollegiate sports accumulated until in the late 1920s the Carnegie Foundation for the Advance-ment of Education set up an investigation group resulting in the 1929 report that quickly caught the rapt attention of the world of educators.[2] In brief it claimed that "big-time" college sports were not educational but were entirely financial and commercial. This brought about renewed determination by NCAA to "clean house," but by 1933 all efforts to curb excesses in subsidization of college athletes had failed to improve conditions. NCAA set up a new committee in 1946 which drew up a Sanity Code that was finally adopted in 1948. This code covered such matters as amateurism, institutional control, academic standards, financial aid, and recruiting.[3] However, when several colleges were accused of violating this code in 1950, and the necessary two-thirds vote to expel could not be procured, charges were dropped, and the Sanity Code became ineffective just as the first such code of the turn of the century had failed in its day.

Although there were still occasional accusations and violations of NCAA rules by some schools in the organization, and now and then some penalty declared, on the whole the NCAA maintained good order within its sphere of sports control—indeed excellent order compared with the constant bickering, charges, counter-charges between colleges, the frequent discontinuance of competition between various schools, and the constant complaints of college faculties about sports competition that had existed in the early years of the organization.

In 1932 the NCAA added boxing to its sports coverage, and in 1933, gymnastics, tennis, and cross country; in that same year it undertook to curb excesses in the subsidization of athletes and to improve methods of their recruitment. The first national basketball invitational tournament for colleges was held in Madison Square Garden in New York City in 1938. The following year the NCAA added basketball to its coverage and staged its own basketball championship tournament in Madison Square Garden. In 1940 it added golf, and in 1941, fencing.

Membership in 1945 was 210, in 1909 302. Throughout the 1950s the NCAA was deeply concerned about the problems of televised games. In 1956 NCAA set up a Committee on Infractions which accomplished nothing, and in 1958 it hired a full-time investigator to attempt to clean house.

The Birth of Athletic Scholarships. As the need (whether real or imaginary) to put out winning teams intensified as the twentieth century got underway and the need to keep all players in amateur standing (which meant for one thing no payment for playing) grew, and the pressure grew to find legitimate ways to help skillful players who could not afford to attend college, there arose the questionable habit of alumni or other interested "friends of the college" of finding all sorts of ways to slip money "under the table" or as "gifts," as it were to athlete students so that they could "register in" and play on the team. This questionable practice grew with the years and was "winked at" by otherwise seemingly worthy citizens, even by college presidents and many of the faculty, even by "gentlemen of the cloth." It was a questionable form of dishonesty "winked at" in the name of education.

Gradually this practice became so blatant that voices were raised in protest and enough had the courage to call an end to this sort of thing. Finally by the 1950s someone (or ones) came up with the idea of handing out money from gate receipts to players "above board," calling the payment an "athletic scholarship." The exact process that was gone through and by whom to procure a ruling and from whom so that this would not jeopardize an amateur standing seems to this day to be still a deep, dark secret. Or is it a seeming secret because no one has demanded an explanation. At any rate, Athletic Scholarships became legitimate in 1954–1955 and the "undercover deals" died out for the betterment of all concerned. However not all colleges consented to the use of these scholarships—only those of the larger schools who flourished financially on large gate receipts. The Ivy League colleges refused to accept this subterfuge in the gesture to preserve amateurism; hence, they do not deal in "athletic" scholarships. Also the University of Chicago refuses to deal in them. As at the Ivy League schools, athletes may be considered for scholarships on the basis of athletic achievement but they are awarded by the official school scholarship committee, not by the athletic department, and the athletes, as all other scholarship students, must meet all qualifications required of all candidates for scholarships, regardless of the discipline under consideration—chemistry, history, psychology, physical education, athletics—and the student athletes so honored are not required in return to "go out" for sports.

Not long after athletic scholarships became legal in college amateur sports, thus attracting increased numbers of athletes to various campuses, it became apparent that graduating seniors were ripe for the world of professional sports. College sports took on a new look. Professional football that got its start in 1895 established its National Football League in 1922 and by 1933 was offering a contest against an all-star team of football players all just out of college. This developed into an annual "All-Star" game. Shortly before World War II professional basketball followed suit in this bid for college graduates.

National Association of Intercollegiate Athletics (NAIA). In 1945 small colleges of the country that were not served in their intercollegiate athletics by the various large-institution leagues, such as the Big Ten and the Big Eight, came together and united their small-college leagues (many of which are as old as the NCAA itself) into the National Association of Intercollegiate Athletics for mutual help and benefit. Sports in the schools of this organization were in their educational goals more closely related to the goals of women in their intercollegiate athletics than to NCAA.[4]

Organizations for Girls' and Women's Amateur Sports

Although the AAU, some state high school athletic associations, some women's state basketball leagues, various groups such as the U.S. Women's Field Hockey Association, the Women's International Bowling Congress, and the U.S. Lawn Tennis and Golf Associations controlled various amateur sports for women, there were three national groups functioning exclusively for women on the overall sports level—Women's Division of NAAF, National Section on Women's Athletics (NSWA), Athletic and Recreation Federation of College Women (ARFCW, originally the Athletic Conference of American College Women), and the Women's Board of the U.S. Olympic Committee.

Women's Division of NAAF. The Women's Division of NAAF had in no sense attempted to establish sports programs for women. At its seventh annual meeting, held in Detroit in April 1931, it revised its platform and took a determined stand against women's participation in the approaching Olympics and in state tournaments for girls. At this time the National Board of the YWCA, the National Association for Physical Education of College Women, the Women's Athletic Section of APEA, and the Athletic Conference of American College Women joined the Women's Division to procure abandonment of all state basketball tournaments for girls. By 1938 it had 768 organization members.

Feeling, as did the Men's Division of the NAAF before it, that now its purpose had been accomplished and other existing organizations could carry on, it merged its interest in 1940 in the National Section on Women's Athletics of AAHPER. In its sixteen years of battling for correct standards of sports for American women it had distributed over $106,000 donated by individuals, foundations, and trusts for their work and had spent an additional $12,000 for three years in maintenance of a Field Secretary to travel to trouble spots to help correct unfavorable conditions in women's sports. Whereas the National Section on Women's Athletics had been mainly a rules- and policy-making body, the Women's Division had set itself up as a standard maker and a liaison group between physical educators and the lay public. Hampered seriously by the financial vicissitudes of the depression of the 1930s, it finally closed shop, turning over all its records and hopes to NSWA of AAHPER. But it did so with great pride in its efforts to educate the lay world to an understanding of what women educators and thinking women of all walks of life desired in sports for women—not a copy of what men promote for boys and men but a program built on the psychological, social, and physiological needs and desires of girls and women.

National Section for Women's Athletics (NSWA). The National Section for Women's Athletics within APEA had been functioning for many years. To review its many changes of title it started out in 1899 as the Women's Basket Ball Rules Committee of AAAPE. It gave way in 1905 to the National Women's Basketball Committee of the APEA and it in turn to the organization of a larger group in 1917 named the National Committee on Women's Sports. In 1927 this committee became the Women's Athletic Section (WAS) of the APEA. In 1931 it changed its name to the National Section on Women's Athletics and was known for the next twenty-one years as the NSWA. In 1952 it again changed its name, this time to the National Section for Girls' and Women's Sports (NSGWS). But this name soon gave way to another as the organization in 1957 took on the status of a Division of AAHPER, to become known as the Division of Girls' and Women's Sports (DGWS), with ever-increasing responsibilities in behalf of girls' and women's sports in the United States. This group, that started out in such a small way over eighty years ago to set standards and make rules for one sport for women, has advanced through its several stages to the responsibility of setting standards and making rules for many sports for girls and women. With the Athletic and Recreation Federation of College Women, it also maintained joint committees on golf and extramural sports. In cooperation with the Men's Athletic Division of the AAHPER, the DGWS conducted rating centers for riding throughout the country and explored the concerns of intramural sports. It also maintained official rating boards with local boards in most states. Another new development of the 1950s was its promotion of clinics in various parts of the country to develop better sports skills among American women in the individual sports, such as golf, track and field, gymnastics, tennis, archery, and swimming. It also held institutes around the country on girls' and women's sports in general.

After World War II NSWA added to its many undertakings the promotion of intercollegiate sports competition for women and set up special committees for this task. This came about through a changing attitude of the female leaders in the profession following World War II. Although the older generation of leaders who fought to keep women and girls out of highly competitive sports had passed from the scene of action, there was still a small body of young women working in the profession who clung to the old ideals of women's place in the world of sports, but they were a seeming minority.

However, informal appraisals from various sources revealed that it may well have been only a small minority that was clamoring for intercollegiate sports. Some physical education teachers with a flare for coaching rather than teaching and looking forward to an opportunity to make a name for themselves as excelling in the coaching of women were behind the little group of women students in various colleges who excelling at some sports were clamoring for ''a place in the sun'' to match the glory of male athletes in their highly publicized and commercialized sports. The great majority of college women had no interest in their own participation in such activities. Also, the small group of women teachers and college women athletes who were pushing for intercollegiate athletics were seriously handicapped by lack of funds for such activities.

As late as 1957, under Mabel Locke's chair, NSGWS, as it was then called, repeated its earlier stand against intercollegiate athletics for women.

State Leagues of Girls' High School Athletic Association. State leagues, born in the 1920s, existed for the sole purpose of promoting athletics for high school girls on the intramural level. Their state meetings were conferences at which the teachers could compare notes and discuss their common problems and triumphs, and the high school girls could come together in play days.

By the late 1930s there were eight states supporting state leagues for girls' athletics: Illinois, Colorado, Nebraska, Alabama, North Carolina, Kansas, Iowa, and Oklahoma, founded in the order listed. Illinois, the originator of the league idea, had the most effective organization, maintaining an executive secretary and a central office in Chicago and sponsoring summer camps for its member groups. The Alabama and Oklahoma leagues were closely related to their state departments of education; the others were coordinated with the boys' state athletic associations of their states.

Girls Athletic Associations (GAAs). Most large high schools, if they supported athletics for girls, had an organization made up of those girls who were interested and under which sports were organized and conducted with the woman who taught physical education as its sponsor. Lacking such a teacher, some woman on the faculty took over this responsibility for after-school sports. Most of such GAAs of this era were carryovers from the earlier decades of the century.

Athletic and Recreation Federation of College Women (ARFCW). The earlier Athletic Conference of American College Women of 1917 had changed its name in 1933 to the ARFCW and at the time reaffirmed its aim to uphold the Standard of Athletics for Girls and Women set forth by the National Section for Girls' and Women's Sports. Later, dropping its biennial conferences it affiliated with AAHPER through the NSGWS with the officers of that group taking over its official duties.

This however did not affect the WAAs of the various college members. They continued as before with their work at the local level.

Organizations for International Amateur Sports

In the 1930s the Olympic Games were the main international sports excitement every fourth year. However, in 1933, AAU proposed the establishment of Pan-American Games but the idea spread so slowly that it was many years before those games became a reality.

Olympic Governing Committee. The Olympic Games from their earliest days have been under the management and control of the International Olympic Committee (IOC) and under it is an Olympic Committee for each nation represented. The U.S. Olympic Committee (USOC) was established in the late 1950s, with the American Association for Health, Physical Education and Recreation holding one seat with Vaughn Blanchard of Detroit serving as AAHPER representative. He requested that its National Section on Women's Athletics (NSWA) be represented on the subcommittee on Women's Sports. In response a Women's Advisory Board was created with NSWA assigned a seat on it. In the mid-1950s the IOC made a study of the athletes entering the games, which showed the following report of U.S. representation:

1. By race: The black athletes excel in sprints, hurdles, jumping, and boxing, whereas the yellow–browns excel in swimming, and the whites in technically differentiated sports. (The U.S.S.R. used no yellow–brown athletes on their teams although many such are among their citizenry.)
2. By climate: The cold countries produce more high-class athletes although some "hot belt" athletes are superior.
3. By age: Age of an athlete means little in performance. The youngest and oldest seem equally good.
4. By sex: Men and women both reach top level capacity earlier and retain it longer in the post–World War II period than they did twenty, forty, or even one hundred years ago.
5. By size of country: In relation to size of population to draw from for athletic competition, the Scandinavian countries rank above both the United States and U.S.S.R. in athletic achievement.[5]

Although international competition in various sports, principally tennis, golf, yachting, and track and field sports, had by mid-century become common, especially track and field in the years between Olympiads, none aroused so much international interest as the Olympic Games. Since student athletes from many schools were becoming involved in the Olympic Games in ever-increasing numbers the games were claiming more and more attention of physical education.

AMATEUR SPORTS COMPETITION AT MID-CENTURY

Mid-century was a time of much activity in sports due to the second World War calling for physical fitness of all citizens and special sports programs for the armed services for both men and women and excitement over five Olympic Games.

Controversies over Sports

Men's Sports. In 1936 the NCAA urged the United States Olympic Committee to change its constitution to give better representation to athletes from the college world, who by then were beginning to dominate the track and field sports. But things still drifted, and World War II came and went. Throughout the late 1940s and 1950s controversies multiplied. But the world had been torn by military confrontations for so much of the period that the bickerings over sports contests seemed of little consequence and there is little on the record to report.

Girls' and Women's Sports. Women, however, were deeply involved in sports throughout the 1930s when the AAU became very active in this field and staged many district and national championships for women in basketball, swimming, and track and field. These tournaments were given great publicity and they brought in large gate receipts for their promoters. There are interesting stories of how the Women's Division persuaded the AAU to accept certain standards for women's sports, to place women chaperons and nurses in women's dressing rooms at championship tournaments, replacing male trainers and "rubbers," to prohibit male coaches from free access to women's dressing rooms, and to give up its pregame bathing suit parades of contestants on the streets of the tournament city. Women educators trained in physical education waged constant war throughout this era in favor of wholesome sports for all instead of intense participation for the few. In this battle they were supported by noted male leaders who gave them courage to stand up against groups of other men who wished to exploit girls and women through sports. In fact in the 1930s the AAU in making a great show of wishing to cooperate with the leading female physical educators of that day who were becoming a real challenge to them in control of women's sports, began a campaign to place some of these women on their committees for girls' sports. Leading male physical educators warned the women to avoid being drawn into AAU organization work. Men such as R. Tait McKenzie, Clark Hetherington, James Huff McCurdy, Amos Alonzo Stagg, George Fisher, and Frederick Luehring warned the women from their own earlier frustrating experiences with AAU, that once they accepted appointments on AAU committees they would not be able to make their voices heard, that their names would be used for publicity purposes as a front to convince the lay world that women of physical education were backing them and their management and promotion of women's sports.

A few of the leading women did accept places on some of their committees only to learn firsthand how truly these men had spoken. Others took their advice and refused to be drawn into AAU's trap.

By working through the Women's Division and the National Section for Women's Sports, both men and women deeply concerned about the educational values of sports for girls and women did present a bold front against AAU's efforts at their exploitation.

Interscholastic Competition

For Boys. The NFSHSAA was quietly on the job throughout this era, running off through their state organizations, local, regional, and state tournaments in a variety of sports engaging thousands upon thousands of high school boys in hundreds of schools throughout the nation and throughout the years.

For Girls. It was difficult to get even an intramural sports program going for most girls.

At mid-century ten states (Arkansas, Georgia, Iowa, Louisiana, North Carolina, North Dakota, Oklahoma, South Carolina, Tennessee, and Texas) were maintaining state tournaments for high school girls in basketball, supported mostly by the small towns of each state. Nine states (Alabama, Colorado, Illinois, Nebraska, New York, Oregon, Utah, Wisconsin, and Wyoming), through their State High School Athletic Associations, were prohibiting all interschool athletics for girls. Nine other states were prohibiting only interschool basketball for girls, and several others only discouraged such activities. In Kentucky interschool sports for girls were permitted only in swimming and tennis, and in Oklahoma only in softball and basketball.

Intercollegiate Competition

For Men. Before and after World War II, intercollegiate sports for men followed the routine pattern of NCAA, NAIA, and like organizations as various colleges played against each other within their own specified leagues. But the war years meant a cessation of normal sports activities with the college men and their coaches and athletic directors caught up in various branches of war service.

Before the United States was drawn into the war, NCAA adopted a code on recruiting and subsidizing athletes, studied the effect of radio broadcasting on attendance at games, and held the first National Boxing, Gymnastics, Cross-Country, Basketball and Fencing Championships. Following the war it offered the first Baseball, Ice Hockey, Skiing and Soccer Championships. Also it reported in 1949 that 265 colleges were active members, it set up a survey to study the effect of television on attendance at football games, it revised its Sanity Code, and it voted in 1952 for limited live television broadcast and transferred the national office to Kansas City, Missouri.[6]

Although the Rose Bowl games at Pasadena, California, started in 1902, it was not until 1933 that the Orange Bowl in Miami started a flood of postseason bowl games where a top-ranking team of one league was invited to play a top-ranking team of another league. In 1935 came the Sugar Bowl in New Orleans; 1936, the Sun Bowl in El Paso; 1937, the Cotton Bowl in Dallas; 1946, the Gator Bowl in Jacksonville; 1959, the Astro–Bluebonnet Bowl in Houston and the Liberty Bowl in Memphis. These postseason games produced much excitement during the Christmas holidays for the spectator sports enthusiasts but contributed little toward furthering educational interests through sports.

For Women. Little was going on in this period in intercollegiate athletics for American women. The depression of the 1930s and World War II of the 1940s inhibited the development of such activities. With civilian efforts, especially in the 1940s, largely aimed at getting as many girls and women as possible out for intramural sports there was no big push by college girls themselves for intercollegiate sports. Gasoline rationing and limited civilian rail travel in those years were also big deterrents of such activities.

Competition at the International Level

Competition in this period for both men and women at the international level produced so much controversy (even charges of athletes being drugged by coaches or managers to increase athletic power) that the word *amateur* connected with it became suspect. Such unfavorable accompaniments incited by international amateur sport are so far removed from the aims and objectives of education that the sport which calls forth such actions merits no attention as a part of education.

The Olympic Games of Mid-Century. There were seven Olympiads in this era, but because of World War II the games of 1940 and 1944 were not held. A brief summary of the high spots of the five that were held follows.

The summer games of 1932, held in Los Angeles, California brought only 2000 athletes from thirty-nine nations, presumably because of the worldwide Great Depression. But these Olympics were different from earlier Games with an International Fine Arts competition and an International Folk Dance Festival arranged to run simultaneously to present to the world competition other than in sports alone. These were not, however, put on by the Olympic Committee, but by organizations concerned with the need to present a better picture of world fellowship and competition than the Olympics, with its petty bickerings and jealousies among athletes and officials.

The International Fine Arts competitions and the International Folk Dance Festival, held a few days before the Olympics opened, attracted a large group of competitors and hundreds of foreign guests. The evening of the Folk Dance Festival brought out spectators that crowded the huge Rose Bowl at Pasadena to its limits. Folk dance groups had entered from nations all around the world. They danced with and for each other. No one won. It was a joyous outpouring of brotherhood which permeated the setting but which all too quickly vanished once the games got underway.

The 1936 Olympics in Berlin brought out 5000 athletes from 53 nations. The star athlete on the U.S. team was Jesse Owens (1914–1980) of Ohio State University, who won four gold medals in track and field, setting three new world records, whereas no other athlete won more than one.

Basketball, having been an Olympic sport in 1904 and then dropped, was on the program for the second time after a thirty-two year absence, and James Naismith, the creator of the game, was a special guest of honor of the International Olympic Committee.

Because of World War II, the twelfth and thirteenth Olympics of 1940 and 1944 were not held. Due to the intransigeance of U.S. sports promoters as much as to that of any other nation, the 1948 Winter Games were mostly verbal battles of charges and countercharges of unfair advantages being taken, which rendered the games a farce as far as the promotion of brotherly love was concerned. The Summer

Games in London went better. In the aftermath of the war, Great Britain, despite the wreckage of its major city and much of the countryside and despite its food shortages and transportation difficulties, was host to the athletes of the world. The English refused to permit any competition on a Sunday. Six thousand athletes took part in the games, representing fifty-nine nations, the largest number of athletes and the most countries ever entered. Of all the athletes, perhaps none won more acclaim than Bob Mathias, the seventeen-year-old youth from the United States who won the decathlon.

The Olympics of 1952 marked the first time an American held the presidency of the International Olympic Committee—Avery Brundage (1887–1975) of Chicago. The ceremony of lighting the torch at the opening of the summer games at Helsinki was unusual in that after thousands of relay runners had carried the torch (which had been lighted at the Temple of Zeus on Olympia) across Europe, over the Baltic Sea, across Sweden and into the Arctic Circle, Laplanders there with the use of magnifying glasses lighted a fire from the rays of the Midnight Sun to blend with the flame from the torch. Added to this bit of drama was the selection of Paavo Nurmi, the famous Finnish runner of thirty years before, to be the final runner to enter the stadium at the opening ceremony to light the flame on its high peristyle.

Patricia McCormick, a swimming champion, won two gold medals for the United States, tying the 1932 record of Mildred Didrickson in track and field and of Helene Madison in swimming. But Helene Madison, winning two more in 1956, was the first American woman to win four gold medals.

Again young Bob Mathais of the United States won the decathlon amidst great acclaim. At this time Russia proposed a point system to determine the winning nation of the Games, but the IOC refused to consider it.

The 1956 Olympics in Melbourne were a different story for both the Russians and the United States. The Russians and their 510 athletes were served notice that there would be no separate housing for them—all would be housed together in the Olympic Village. This was the fourth time in the history of the modern Olympics that the United States had not led all other nations—in 1906, at the extra unofficial Olympics, the United States tied with France; in 1908 Great Britain led; in 1936 Germany led; and now in 1956 Russia led. In the fourteen games including those of 1956, the United States had been top scorer ten times. Once more, as in London eight years before, no competition was held on a Sunday. Melbourne did not even allow newspapers to be printed on a Sunday.

By now other nations had improved in the sports-training techniques and had become a serious challenge to the sports supremacy of the United States. (One U.S. athlete who equalled the record set by Paavo Nurmi was not good enough in 1956 to win even a bronze medal.) The U.S. Olympic Committee now established the U.S. Olympic Development Committee, in the hope of stemming this tide of challengers from other countries.

American Women in the Olympics. The efforts of the Women's Division of the National Amateur Athletic Federation, the National Section on Women's Athletics of the American Physical Education Association, the National Association of Physical Education for College Women, and the many national women's groups of the lay world supporting them, proved of little avail in keeping U.S. women out of the Olympics of 1932. The United States did enter a small group of women and out of six events open to women won five of them, with the sixth going to an American woman of Polish parentage who had entered under the banner of Poland.

In 1936 work on the uneven bars and vaulting box were added to the women's gymnastics events. The earlier gymnastics events for women, performed with hoops and other such hand apparatus, had been unknown to American women gymnasts.

In 1948 the U.S. women athletes outshone all others, but the Russian, Hungarian, and Australian women outshone the Americans in 1952 and again in 1956.

13

The Status of Physical Education at Mid-Twentieth Century

A 1932 survey covering schools in forty-six leading cities in twenty-two states showed that 80 percent of the three-year high schools required physical education for all three years and 70 percent of the four-year schools required it all four years. Would that a like survey had covered the schools of the smaller towns and of the rural areas. As with all other disciplines offered in the schools, physical education struggled through the depression, but unlike some, it came out fairly well. Also during and following World War II there began a great population shift from the rural areas to the larger cities as the United States changed to a society that was largely industrial.

As a nation we became enormously wealthy, which affected all segments of society as the standard of living rose to heights little dreamed of only a few decades before. At the same time there was a great increase in population, affecting education in many ways. From 1930 to 1966 the population of children enrolled in the schools increased from 26,678,000 to 36,089,000.

These figures, however, do not represent population increase alone. Some of the enrollment increase has been due to an increase in the percentage of children seeking an education. Figures on the education of the draftees of World War I compared to that of the draftees of World War II show a marked increase in educational interest between the two generations as follows:

	WW-I Draftees	WW-II Draftees
Average number of years in school	7	10
Percentage completed high school	20	47
Percentage with one year in college	5	16

A larger percentage of youth is attending school than ever before in our country's history, more than in any other land of the world. The changed educational philosophy of post–World War I is now being still further changed by the Civil Rights Movement that arose in the 1950s. Equal educational opportunity for all became the new objective, which brought with it much turmoil in many communities as blacks backed by many whites began the struggle for their right to an education equal to that of whites, just as one hundred years before, women backed by many advanced thinkers among the men were waging the same battle for the right of girls to an education equal to that of boys.

STATUS OF PHYSICAL EDUCATION

Lower Schools

Requirements. A 1932 survey showed that 80 percent of the three-year high schools required physical education for all three years and 70 percent of the four-year schools required it all four years. This survey covered schools in forty-six leading cities in twenty-two states.[1]

After World War II, the U.S. Office of Education reported that despite the great increase in physical education in the schools of America in 1956 less than 50 percent of all secondary school boys and girls were receiving training in physical education. Ninety-one percent of the 150,000 elementary schools had no gymnasiums, and 90 percent had less than the five acres for playing area recommended by the profession in 1930. Also, only 1200 out of 17,000 communities had full-time recreation leadership, and less than 5 percent of the children were getting camping experience. A later survey claimed that only 23 percent of the lower grades surveyed were meeting the generally accepted requirement of 15 minutes of exercise each school day, exclusive of recess periods, and that California was the only state requiring of grades 7–12 one physical education class period daily. An AAHPER survey of the late 1950s showed that 80 percent of junior high schools and 60 percent of senior high schools were requiring physical education only two or three times per week.[2]

At mid-twentieth century the most common weekly requirement was still the old one of three periods per week, although many schools held to a daily requirement. River Forest Township High School at Oak Park, Illinois, with its separate gymnasiums for boys and girls, set the standard of five hours per week for all four years, a standard maintained by many of the best high schools.

Facilities. In the late 1940s a national movement developed for war memorials that would be living tributes to the war dead, such as community recreation buildings and youth centers, and many of these were constructed. The memorials in some communities took the form of playgrounds outfitted with equipment requiring no supervision and having no right or wrong way to be used, such as dodger mazes, pipe tunnels, jump platforms, and mounds of earth to dig into and climb over.

A new development of facilities of this era in large cities was the high school field house for interscholastic sports—a building apart from the school gymnasium. Also many high school gymnasiums were being constructed with special rooms for corrective gymnastics, and for the past many years open showers have been approved for girls' dressing rooms.

Programs. Mid-twentieth century programs of physical education were considered excellent only if they contained a wide variety of activities chosen from aquatics, camping, combat activities, body mechanics, equitation, dancing in various forms, festivals and pageantry, free play, games, hiking, stunts, and sports of all kinds— group, individual, and dual. Many schools also maintained programs of recreation for the student body. The usual plan was to place the responsibility for administering the recreation program in the physical education department.

Closely allied to recreation was school camping. The gains in school camping in the 1930s and 1940s were tremendous. In 1951 there were approximately ninety school districts including nearly two hundred schools which sponsored some type of school-camp program. Physical educators took great interest and much responsibility in this movement.

Colleges

Facilities. In the early 1930s several splendid gymnasiums were constructed for the women students at the universities of Texas and California (Los Angeles branch), Stanford University, and Wellesley and Oberlin colleges. These buildings set a new style of beauty with utility for women's gymnasium's in the United States.

Some magnificent gymnasiums for either men or women were built after 1950, and a few fine ones were built for the joint use of men and women. In this last group were the $2 million gymnasium at New York State University Teachers College at Cortland, dedicated in 1954, and the $1 million gymnasium completed in the early 1950s for the new Riverside Branch of the University of California. The University of Southern California built a coeducational gymnasium in 1925 which was still an excellent building, but it did not at that time establish a trend.

Since World War II a splendid addition to the women's gymnasiums was the gymnasium at the Women's College, University of North Carolina, Greensboro, completed in 1952 and named after Mary Channing Coleman (1883–1947), the second woman to hold the presidency of the AAHPER and for many years Director of Physical Education at that University.

Many fine stadiums also were built in colleges and universities and even in some high schools in mid-century. The ivy league schools boasted of stadiums seating from 15,000 (Dartmouth) to 71,000 (Yale). Many state universities enlarged their stadiums of pre-World War II years, most handling crowds of from 30,000 to 60,000.

Academic Degrees of Staffs. Graduate degrees had become the rule for physical education teachers in colleges and were common in high school faculties. The top degree, the M.D. of the early years of the profession, had given way to the Ph.D. and Ed.D. The year 1939–1940 marked the last time that a person was elected to the presidency of the national professional organization holding the M.D. degree. At mid-century it was obligatory in most colleges and universities for the head of the department of physical education to hold either the Ph.D. or the Ed.D. degree and for the other staff members to hold the master's, although in many institutions, particularly colleges offering professional training, several staff members held the doctor's degree.

Research

A constantly growing number of members of the profession were entering upon research work in this field, following the lead of the early pioneers who, holders of the medical degree, naturally turned to physiological research. This research far outstriped the sociological and historical research. Also there was great activity in the test and measurement field which was slowly developing in the opening decades of the new century and came to very active life in the 1930s. John Bovard of the University of Oregon and of UCLA, David K. Brace of the University of Texas, Frederick Cozens of the University of California, Anna Espenschade of the University of California, (Berkeley), Ruth Glassow of the University of Wisconsin, Neils P. Neilson of the University of Utah, Eugene Nixon of Pomona College, Frederick Rand Rogers of New York State Dept. of Education, and Agnes Wayman of Barnard College took the lead in this type of research. Their tests were used quite generally throughout the country in both the lower schools and colleges, and with both boys and girls. Particularly productive in cardio-vascular research were Edward C. Schneider of Connecticut Wesleyan, whose cardiovascular tests were used in the service of aviation during the World War II, and Charles H. McCloy, Research Professor, University of Iowa. Both men were special consultants to the U.S. Army and Navy during World War II and carried on much research work for them. Also Arthur H. Steinhaus of George Williams College and Peter Karpovich of Springfield College carried on much physiological research for the military services.

In this period the profession awakened to the use of written tests of knowledge about the activities that were offered for credited class work in college. A few teachers had written and tried out such tests in the 1920s but it was not until testing of all sorts became almost a fetish in some schools in the 1930s that such written tests came into general use. The great preoccupation with the ''true–false'' form of tests that hit the country in the 1930s lent itself splendidly to much of the physical education class activity knowledge tests in their initial trials.

Professional Preparation

At the turn of the century, as related earlier, there were only four institutions of collegiate rank offering professional preparation in physical education leading to a degree: Harvard University, Stanford University, University of Nebraska, and Oberlin College. By 1936, the number had changed to 93; and by 1955 to 532.[3]

Status of Old Private Normal Schools. In 1931 the Bouvé–Boston School of Physical Education affiliated with Simmons College as the Bouvé–Boston School. In 1942 this joint school transferred to Tufts University where it remained for the rest of this era.

In 1931 the Ithaca School of Physical Education, which had merged with the Ithaca Conservatory of Music in 1920, became Ithaca College. In 1933 the Sargent School became Sargent College of Boston University. In 1931 the Savage School closed its doors and in 1943 turned its records over to New York University.

The Chicago Normal School of Physical Education became Kendall College of Physical Education in the early 1930s and, closing its doors in 1935, turned its records over to George Williams College. The Posse School closed in 1942, ending a fifty-two-year career. In 1953 Arnold College (originally the Brooklyn Normal School of Gymnastics, later the Anderson School, later still the New Haven Normal School of Gymnastics) affiliated with the University of Bridgeport, retaining its status as Arnold College.

The Boston Normal School of Gymnastics, which had affiliated with Wellesley College in 1909 starting the move for ties with established colleges, came to the end of its long and distinguished career in 1953, when Wellesley College decided to return to the status of a pure liberal arts college, divesting itself of professional training departments. So after sixty-four years of service to the profession (1889–1953), the last thirty-four at graduate level only, the old school bowed off the professional scene. As it closed its doors, it could take great satisfaction in the fact that throughout its years of service the majority of the top positions for women working in physical education throughout the country had been held in earlier years and still were held in the 1950s by its graduates.

By the end of this era each of the old schools of specialization in physical education had either achieved collegiate rating on its own, or had affiliated with some college, or had closed its doors.

Collegiate Schools and Colleges of Physical Education. Since World War II, schools and colleges of health, physical education, and recreation within colleges or universities increased materially. Several new schools of physical education joined the few established in the previous era: Washington and Ohio State universities, the universities of Washington, Indiana, Connecticut, Maryland, Massachusetts, Minnesota, West Virginia, and Illinois State College at Macomb. Six new colleges joined the one of the previous era: the universities of Florida, Utah, and Illinois (its school of 1932 developed into a college in 1957), Brigham Young University, Texas Women's University, and Boston–Bouvé College of Northeastern University. The two last named colleges gave the profession its first two women to hold the title, Dean.

Specialization in the Dance. Following the lead of the University of Wisconsin in the 1920s and Bennington College, Sarah Lawrence College, and Connecticut College for Women of the 1930s, the idea of a dance major in the school curriculum slowly developed. Majors were established in physical education departments, fine arts departments, or their own schools. Outstanding offerings of this era are the Summer School of Dance at Connecticut College and the Dance Department of the Julliard School of Music. By 1947 seventeen colleges and universities were offering a major in dance.

Graduate Work. According to a report of the U.S. Office of Education, 37 percent of the institutions offering professional training in physical education in the 1950s were offering work at the graduate level; 28 percent at the master's level; and 9 percent at the doctorate level. A decade later, 70 percent of the institutions offering professional training in this field were offering master's degrees; and 20 percent, the doctor's degree.

Accreditation. Previously the American Association of Colleges for Teacher Education (AACTE) had been the accrediting body for departments and schools offering professional preparation, but in 1954 its accrediting functions were transferred to the National Council of Accreditation of Teacher Education (NCATE).

Trained Personnel. Whereas by the end of World War I there was an estimated 10,000 men and women in the United States professionally trained in the field of physical education, by 1950 the number had risen to 76,000. In the year 1952–1953, 6230 men and 2250 women received bachelor's degrees with a major in this field or in combination with health education and recreation; 1539 men and 650 women, the master's degree; and 60 men and 47 women, the doctorate.

Professional Literature

By the opening of this era the profession was receiving great impetus from the many publications that were coming off the press in this field. A perusal of publisher's notices given in each issue of the *Journal of Health and Physical Education,* year by year, from 1930 to 1960 gives an idea of the great wealth of material that had become available. With the January 1949, issue of the *Journal of Health and*

Physical Education the word *Recreation* was added to its official title. (The Association, itself, had added the word *Recreation* to its official title in 1938–1939.)

Outstanding books of the 1930s were Neilson and Cozen's *Tests and Measurements* (1930); Josephine Rathbone's *Corrective Physical Education* (1934); Agnes Wayman's *Education through Physical Education* (1934); Mabel Lee's *Conduct of Physical Education* (1937); and Frederick Luehring's *Swimming Pool Standards* (1939).

Films and Microcards. A new development of this era was the production of films and microcards. There were available through the Athletic Institute over 2000 16-millimeter sports films. The AAHPER had films for loan or purchase at its national office. Many schools produced their own film strips. The School of Health and Physical Education of the University of Oregon started a microcard publication project as a nonprofit service to the profession. The productions were for the most part, unpublished research materials and doctoral dissertations, scholarly books that were out of print, and periodicals of historical value which were no longer available. The school furnished, on request, a catalog of all their microcards with prices. Following Oregon's lead the University of Michigan began making available microfilms of professional materials.

Nonschool Organizations Concerned with Physical Education

At mid-century many agencies, such as recreation and camping groups, youth agencies such as the Boy Scouts, Girl Scouts, Camp Fire Girls, youth centers, and private agencies such as sports clubs and commercial establishments, were sponsoring various activities of the world of physical education. A few of these are discussed in the material that follows.

The Recreation Movement. Recreation in its various aspects was being sponsored by many agencies—public, private, voluntary, commercial, religious, the armed forces, and industrial. As to the last named, the UAW–CIO Recreation Department was established in 1937 with a trained physical educator at its head with the status of International Representative of the Union.

In the 1930s the Works Progress Administration came into existence to relieve the unemployment problem. It covered projects for recreation in every state but Maine. It built 13,700 parks, 22,000 playing fields, 670 golf courses, 1510 swimming pools, and built or repaired 7930 recreation buildings.

By 1935 the WPA had undertaken the training of leaders for group recreation and had organized recreational programs in many communities throughout the country, using the leaders they had trained. These programs covered sports and games, aquatics, dancing, drama, and musical activities as well as play centers for preschool children and therapeutic recreation for the physically disabled. By 1938 some 38,000 people were employed per month on WPA recreation projects alone, not counting those engaged in construction projects.

The Camping Movement[4]. The American Camping Association, organized in the 1930s, was made up of owners, directors, and leaders of various camps. By then the movement had moved into the stage of orientation and responsibility. Physicians, nurses, and dieticians were added to the camp staff and camp life became less highly organized than in the 1920s.

By the late 1930s the United States was dotted with a wide variety of types of camps, such as organization camps, school camps, public camps, private camps, labor union camps, specialized camps, day camps, and Civilian Conservation Corps (CCC) camps. The CCC camps were established during the depression of the 1930s by the federal government so that young boys could be housed, fed, and given employment in areas where they could, under supervision, help construct camps, state and federal parks, mountain trails, and recreation areas. It was a lifesaver for thousands of boys who would otherwise have been thrown onto the streets unemployed during those difficult years. Just preceding World War II, the Girl Scouts alone maintained 453 camps, with a total attendance of over 700 thousand girls. Also, eighty-nine cities were operating day camps.

By 1950, ten thousand camps of many kinds served from 3 to 5 million boys and girls and adults each summer in the United States and Canada. At that time there were 2000 camps registered as members of the American Camping Association, which set standards for camp organization and management. By the 1950s a few state departments of public instruction were maintaining summer camps for school children. The Kellogg Foundation assisted the Michigan Department of Public Instruction to establish its camps. Soon after that, labor unions organized camps for the children of both employees and employers, and many new types of specialized camps arose such as music camps, pioneer-life camps, cardiac camps, diabetic-child camps, problem children camps, and crippled children camps. World War II brought into prominence the day camp, which proved popular in the large cities, where much was available in way of facilities, furnishing low-cost camping to many children who could not hope to attend other type of camps.

American Youth Hostels[5]. This European Hostel movement for inexpensive outings came to the United States in 1934 but in its beginnings it was confined mostly to the New England states and localized areas surrounding a few metropolitan centers where several hostels were established in communities easily accessible to each other by foot or bicycle. A few physical educators threw their influence and enthusiasm into the youth hostel movement because of its possibilities of arousing interest for hiking and biking to American youth and adults.

The first hostel in the United States was opened in the summer of 1934 in Northfield, Massachusetts, where the national office of the American Youth Hostel Association (AYH) was established by Monroe Smith and his wife, both of whom had become acquainted with the movement in Europe in the summer of 1933. A second hostel, sponsored by Mt. Holyoke College, opened in early 1935 in South Hadley, Massachusetts. By late 1935 enough members had joined the AYH and enough hostels were in operation in the New Hampshire and Vermont areas to warrant publication of a handbook giving locations of hostels and advice on reaching them.

Gradually a few hostels opened in other areas. Several physical educators as well as recreation leaders, labor union social workers, and representatives from several youth organizations tried to throw their influence into the management of the AYH, but to little avail. From the ranks of physical education, Gertrude Moulton, M.D. (1880–1964) of Oberlin College and Mabel Lee of the University of Nebraska served as members of its Board of Directors from its early years on, and in 1943, Ben W. Miller (1909–) of the University of Indiana joined the Advisory Council, but all felt that the movement was hindered by a lack of practical leadership.

Within the decade of 1937 to 1947, 250 hostels were chartered in twenty-nine states. The movement was advancing despite an overabundance of idealism and impractical leadership.

In 1948, John D. Rockefeller III, always interested in movements for betterment of youth, accepted the presidency of the AYH in the hopes of bringing its initial, idealistic leadership down to earth to get the movement moving realistically. Dr. Ben Miller, then Executive Secretary of AAHPER was appointed Executive Vice-President with headquarters in New York City.

After three frustrating years Dr. Miller resigned to return to teaching (as head of physical education at UCLA). Attempts to transplant Europe's youth hostel movement to the United States have not flourished chiefly because of the great distances between possible hostels in western United States, in particular, and the hazards of the highways from heavy automobile traffic.

Young Men's Christian Association[6]. As in World War I, the YMCA through its "physical department" (as the YMCA called it) again rendered valuable services to the nation in World War II. It developed physical fitness programs for men drawn into the war effort outside the armed services, and both at home and abroad assisted in morale building through recreational programs. In peacetime as well as wartime, the YMCA promotion of athletic games in foreign countries tended to bring people of different countries together in informal situations so that they understood each other better. At home the YMCA was one of the most powerful forces working for racial integration. Its physical education program offered unusual opportunities in this direction.

This era, as the preceding one, saw great advances in physical education activity in the YMCA. Notable achievements were the following:

1944—National YMCA handball tournament in St. Louis

1946—National YMCA volleyball tournament in Chicago

1951—International YMCA Physical Education Centennial in Cleveland

1952—National YMCA amateur sports competition

1953—856 YMCA Learn-to-Swim campaigns

1954—Third National YMCA Aquatics Conference

1955—YMCA Research Committee assignment of $1800 for physical education research

1955—National YMCA Fitness Clinic in New York City

1956—Fourth World YMCA HPER Consultation in Melbourne

1958—YMCA Pan-American Physical Education Congress in Chicago

Young Women's Christian Association. A rapid growth of the YWCA physical education program was accompanied by a broadening of the activities to include recreation and social activities. In the mid-1950s, activities in canteens, lounges, swimming pools, and gymnasiums attracted over 380,000 participants.

Turners and Sokols. The turner and Sokol groups in the United States, mostly third, fourth, and even fifth generation Americans thoroughly assimilated into American culture, had turned their attention to the American recreation movement and were its ardent supporters. But they had preserved their deep interest in maintaining physical fitness and had little faith that America's experimental efforts in this direction would match the Old-World forms of body building physical activities. They clung to their traditional forms of disciplined formal gymnastics in training their offspring and indeed, this kind of training was too seldom not offered in American public schools. American Sokols were still holding a slet (Sokol Olympics) every six years when gymnasts and athletes of the United States and Canada of Sokol descent came together, as they spoke of it, "to reaffirm their faith in a free and democratic way of life."

Professional Organizations of Mid-Century

American Association for Health, Physical Education and Recreation. A somewhat detailed picture follows of an all-embracing professional physical education organization. Originally the American Physical Education Association, it added health education to its concerns in 1937 and became the American Association for Health and Physical Education. The next year recreation was included and the name became the American Association for Health, Physical Education and Recreation.

This organization is the one above all others within the profession of education that is open to all persons working in any aspect of health education, physical education, and amateur sports, and recreation, regardless of type of work, or rank, or position, whether in lower schools, colleges, or nonschool situations.

Reconstruction Years. With the continued prodding of the Middle West Society of Physical Education the APEA became more national minded. The APEA was ready by 1930 to make concessions demanded by the Middle West group in return for the Middle West Society's accepting the role of being a district of APEA, such as the West Coast, Eastern, and Southern districts had done in the 1920s (as related in Chapter 10). However, in the late 1920s the early West Coast group, attempting to cover too large a territory, had died out. But in 1930 the Northwest group professionals had reorganized as a permanent unit. With Dr. Frederick W. Maroney of the Atlantic City public schools in the national presidency in 1929 and 1930, the National Council, at his urging, decided the time was ripe for a long overdue overhauling of the national organization, taking under serious consideration the Middle West group's criticisms of the national setup.

By 1930 when the national organization was a strange mixture of a few local societies, several state societies, and two district societies (East and South), with eleven sections of interest, some functioning well to serve the profession, some trying to keep alive, some all but dead, the Executive Committee of 1930, backed by the Council, decided to overhaul the constitution completely. Setting the calendar years 1931 and 1932 for the experimental years, they decided to scrap the old constitution, start anew, rid itself of all local societies by turning them over to function under their own state groups, and bring all fifty states into the fold through state organizations and divide the entire country into districts.

Dr. Maroney had already been at work for the full calendar year of 1929 when this era opened. He had listened to the many complaints about APEA's monthly magazine, *The Review*, then thirty-four years old, comparing it with the Middle West's young periodical, *The Pentathlon*, then but a few months old and already attracting national attention. Dr. J. H. McCurdy, editor of *The Review*, at retirement age had offered his resignation and Elmer Mitchell of the University of Michigan, the *Pentathlon's* young editor who was well known for his leadership in the field of intramural sports, had been persuaded to take over as editor for APEA. The Middle West had consented to merge its infant periodical with APEA's *Review* and the merger resulted in a lively new up-to-date magazine, *The Journal of Health and Physical Education*, which made its initial bow in its January 1930 issue. Shortly, Dr. Maroney had maneuvered the creation of a new periodical, *The Research Quarterly*, of APEA, which made its initial appearance, also under Mitchell's editorship, in 1930. This move was to separate the research publications from the lighter material aimed at the rank and file of professional readers.

President Maroney named a Constitution Revision Committee under the chairmanship of Clifford Brownell of Columbia University and it set to work with great determination. The major change called for was that the national organization would function through its district organizations which should cover the entire United States. As work got underway and all parts of the country were canvassed for their criticisms of the old form of organization and for suggestions for changes, I succeeded Dr. Maroney as its first woman president, for the calendar year of 1931. This was an innovation after forty-five years of having men as presidents. With the men always holding the great majority of the votes on the governing and elective body (the Council) and with no discernible women's campaign in effect to push for the women's place in the sun, this recognition of women came as a great surprise.

For the year 1931, myself, a woman, a Middlewesterner, was at the helm. Although I was the first woman elected to this office, I was not the first Middlewesterner so honored. After thirty-five years of none but presidents from the East Coast, Dudley Reed, M.D., of the University of Chicago in 1920 and Charles W. Savage of Oberlin College in 1926, had been elected to this high office from the Middle West.

Elected in New York City, December 31, 1930, to take office January 1, 1931, the new national president pushed for and quickly won the long fought for change of annual business meetings (held for so many years in New York City during the Christmas holidays when so many men of the profession were called there for coaches meetings) to the spring convention time when the members of the Association were called together. The 1931 convention in Detroit in April witnessed a complete reorganization of the Association through the work of the Constitution Committee.

I was reelected for the short term, January 1, 1932, through that spring convention, to make the transition from December to spring elections.

During the two-year presidency of Frederick Maroney, the Association's first award in recognition of unusual leadership, the Honor Award, was established to be conferred each year upon two or more members. Since the 1931 ceremony was to be the first, and many pioneer workers in the field were still living, the first ceremony honored forty-eight persons. Twenty-four received the honor at the national convention in Detroit in April, and thirteen who could not attend the April meeting were honored at the Eastern District meeting in May in Newark. Eleven were recognized in absentia. It was a historic occasion that included W. G. Anderson, Delphine Hanna, Clark Hetherington, Amy Morris Homans, James Huff McCurdy, R. Tait McKenzie, James Naismith, Amos Alonzo Stagg, and Thomas D. Wood, to mention but a few.

Several new interest groups called Sections were created at the spring 1931 convention, all accepted for a year on trial, and all old Sections groups wishing to carry on were informed of the new basic qualifications and given the year 1931–1932 to make necessary changes and return to the 1932 convention in Philadelphia with a petition for acceptance. At this time a group of women peitioned for a Dance Section to be accepted as a new interest group within the organization on a year's trial. At the same time another group of women petitioned for the many-years-old National Committee on Women's Athletics (masquerading for the past four years as the Women's Athletic Section but without voting privilege) to be accepted also on a year's trial as a bone fide section. Both petitions were accepted.

During 1931 matters came to a head over the many years of effort that the notorious Bernard McFadden had been making to procure acceptance of himself and his questionable magazine, *Physical Culture,* by the APEA. It was a most unpleasant problem for the first woman president to have to encounter. The American Medical Association had also for years been fighting McFadden's brand of quackery. With the practical advice and concern of the Executive Secretary of the American Medical Association and the advice of one of the nation's most notable surgeons, Wayne Babcock, M.D. (1872–1964) of Philadelphia this bug-a-boo of years was finally laid to rest. As far as APEA was concerned, this was the final effort of McFadden to gain even seeming approval of the physical education profession.

By the time of the 1932 convention in Philadelphia the new constitution had been on trial for a year. It had been a real reorganization and after two conventions I left the presidency, turning it over to a man once more hoping that my election had actually established a trend, as it has turned out to be. Although no official ruling ever existed on the subject, men and women have for all these years since evenly shared this office.

My successor, a "status quo" president, was succeeded for the year 1933–1934 by the second woman president, Mary Channing Coleman of Women's College of the University of North Carolina, the first president from the South. She pushed vigorously and successfully for election reform, and that spring, Strong Hinman of the Wichita, Kansas, public schools, was the first national president to be elected after a Committee on Nominations had been at work. It had alerted all members of the Association to send in nominations; possible candidates had been consulted and their consent obtained; and their names were presented to the Council by the Nominating Committee; and then a call for nominations from the floor followed by a secret ballot. This last caused great concern among the Easterners but it too got final approval.

The next problem to be tackled was that of writing into the constitution some arrangement by which the person who would succeed to the presidency would have a year's advance training for the task. As matters had stood for over fifty years, the vice presidency, usually held by a woman, was not to be counted on as a lead to the higher office. So Miss Coleman presented the idea of establishing the office of president-elect with that person serving for a year on the Council and Executive Committee before taking on the top task. The Association had grown and the days when a president could take office in great ignorance of its tasks and even its recent history were gone.

With the ball rolling for this reform, Strong Hinman, succeeding Miss Coleman, put the plan through, and at APEA's Golden Anniversary Convention in 1935 in Pittsburg. Agnes Wayman of Barnard College was elected next president, the last president elected to succeed to the office immediately, and at the same time William Moorehead of the Pennsylvania State Department of Education was elected the first of APEA's president-elects.

In 1933 the large Middle West Society of Physical Education came to the realization that it was too large geographically. With the majority of the members working in the area east of the Mississippi River, the annual conventions were all too frequently held in their part of the district. For the sake of nourishing the professional roots west of the river, the district split in 1933 into what are today's Midwest District east of the Mississippi River and the Central District west of the river.

The year after that the South West territory was organized under APEA and at long last the entire United States was under the wings of the National Association. By then practically all states were organized within their own districts, and all states that were organized were represented on the national council.

The Golden Anniversary Year Opens New Doors. The 1935 convention in Pittsburg was the Golden Anniversary Convention. W. G. Anderson, M.D., then seventy-five years old, founder of the Association, was the guest of honor. The other leaders of the first twenty years were all deceased. At that time of all living past-presidents, R. Tait McKenzie was the earliest and he was then sixty-eight years old. At the 1937 convention in New York City, Dr. McKenzie's statue, the original of his *Column of Youth,* was on its first display in the ballroom of the Pennsylvania Hotel at the APEA banquet, and it was unveiled by Dr. Maroney and myself as the first woman president.

Also at the 1937 convention, APEA joined forces with school health educators and changed its title of the past thirty-four years to the American Association for Health and Physical Education and voted to affiliate with the National Education Association, uniting with its over-forty-year-old Department of Physical Education to now become that organization's largest department. With this it established national offices in the NEA building in Washington, D.C. and took on in September 1938 its first Executive Secretary, Neils P. Neilson of Stanford University, who had been elected president-elect the spring before and whose presidency was completed by Frederick W. Cozens of the University of Oregon.

At this same time with the old Playground and Recreation Association of America (PRAA) having changed its name to the National Recreation Association (NRA) and having handed over to the AAHPE its old recreation group within the public schools, the AAHPE now added the R to its title to become the AAHPER. By then the interest groups known as Sections had grown to twenty-three in number.

By 1939 the Association claimed 269 foreign members from twenty-five countries and it established its Foreign Relations Committee.

Highlights of the 1940s. Some of the highlights of the 1940s were as follows: In 1941 the Association had grown so that it turned its former Council into a Legislative Assembly; from 1943 to 1947 Ben Miller of the University of Indiana took over as Executive Secretary as Neils Neilson had returned to teaching, this time to the University of Utah.

In 1944 the Gulick Award, established in 1923 by the New York City Physical Education Society, the largest and most distinguished grass roots physical education group in the country, now came into the possession of AAHPER.[7] The award medal had been commissioned in the early 1920s, and Dr. McKenzie, the profession's well-known sculptor, had completed it in time for the first award ceremony in 1923. After the 1929 award was made, there was a break of ten years during which time the New York City Society's affiliation with APEA had been canceled as that mother organization was restructured, dropping all local groups and recognizing only district and state subdivisions. However the New York City group still functioned intermittently and conferred the Gulick Award in 1939 and 1940, after which the award medallion and the right to confer it upon outstanding physical educators came into the possession of AAHPER. Since then the Gulick Award has been given annually and is looked upon as the organization's most prestigious honor. (See the Appendix for a list of honorees.)

The entire issue of the *Journal of Health and Physical Education,* May 1944, was devoted to the memory of R. Tait McKenzie, an unprecedented action in honor of this great man, who had died in 1938. Three years later, the marble copy of his original *Column of Youth* was presented to AAHPER in his memory and given a permanent home in the NEA building in Washington, D.C.

During the war years the government asked all organizations to give up their regular conventions unless their work contributed to the war effort, in which case each group could apply for permission to meet. Since AAHPER's greatest efforts of those years were devoted to physical fitness of civilians, permits were readily granted. Indeed, all such conventions were attended by representatives of various branches of the armed services at government expense. Conventions took on an exciting aura with so many of the speakers in military uniform. Especially interesting were the uniforms of the WACs, the WAVES, the Women Marines, the WAFs, and so on. It was indeed a new sight in the United States to see women in military uniform—and top echelon ones at that as was case within the physical education profession.

In 1945 the Association recorded 10,585 members, an all-time high, and in 1949 it conferred its first W. G. Anderson Award.

The Fifties Bring New Horizons. The 1950s brought new horizons to the Association. In 1954, the *Journal* added *Recreation* to its title; in 1956 the Puerto Rico Physical Education Association became a part of the Eastern District Association, and two years later the Hawaii Physical Education Association became a part of the

South West District. In mid-century foreign membership increased markedly—from 267 in 1939 to 566 from sixty countries in 1958. A big effort to reach the grass roots organizations resulted in the first annual conference of presidents-elect of all state associations at national headquarters in 1955.

For the first thirty-eight years of the national organization, 1885–1922, all presidents held the M.D. degree except William Blaikie, the second one, who was an attorney-at-law deeply interested in physical fitness. For the next fourteen years (1923–1937) there were nine presidents, only two of whom held the M.D. degree, Frederick Maroney and Jesse F. Williams; the others held neither the M.D. nor Ph.D. nor Ed.D., but all had professional training beyond the bachelor's degree. This period marks the transition years within the profession when the Ph.D. and Ed.D. gradually replaced the M.D. C. H. McCloy was the first president with the Ph.D. degree. Beginning with 1937 and until World War II, there were eight presidents all holding the Ph.D., except one, Margaret Bell (1888–1969), who serving in 1939–1940 was the last president with the M.D. degree. This clearly marked the trend within the profession itself, the gradual change of the early twentieth century from the medical to the educational emphasis.

College Physical Education Association. The Society of College Gymnasium Directors, of 1897, changed its title to the Society of Directors of Physical Education in Colleges in 1908, and in 1935 to the College Physical Education Association. Exclusively a man's organization its membership in 1957 numbered 675 representing 45 states and 320 institutions. During World War II its membership was caught up in war work, filling important posts in all branches of the armed services and serving as consultants particularly to the Surgeon General and to the Air Force on special physical fitness problems of aviation. Also, as in World War I, the oldest members again served valiantly in the GI recreation areas.

National Association of Physical Education for College Women. From the small Association of Directors of Physical Education for Women in Colleges founded in 1924, the National Association of Physical Education for College Women (NAPECW) rapidly grew into an organization with much influence in the profession, particularly in regard to college programs for women and the professional training for those who wished to prepare for a career in this field. Shortly it changed to an association open to all women working in the profession at the college level.

World War II found many of its leading women involved in war work, not only in the armed forces but also in the American Red Cross, both at home and overseas, and in the United Services Organization (USO). When General Marshall's aides were setting up his Civilian Advisory Committee for the Women's Army Corps, they turned to AAHPER and NAPECW to furnish the representative of physical education for his Committee (I was the one selected, having served as president of both groups). As the war was winding to a close, I persuaded NAPECW to assume the task as a final war effort of helping to find positions for women trained in physical education returning from overseas assignments. Unable to get anyone to chair such a committee, I took on the task and with the help of Irene Clayton of Bryn Mawr College and the enthusiastic backing of the Association's president, Gertrude Manchester, got the project on the move. Colonel Orveta Hobby of the Women's Army Corps paved the way for the first step of seeing that the military placed posters in prominent places at all disembarkment centers informing all women physical education teachers to get in touch at once with this NAPECW committee if they wished help in procuring a position. This committee was in no sense an arm of any placement bureau. It scoured the country to learn of possible openings and put the women in touch with these sources. In its short existence this committee of NAPECW found openings for over one hundred grateful women.

The Academy of Physical Education. Conceived in 1926, developing for the next four years, and finally established in 1930, the Academy of Physical Education, an organization of leaders of physical education, concerned with serious research in behalf of the profession and the development of worldwide ties with leaders from other countries, slowly grew in stature to fulfill the earlier dreams of Hetherington and McKenzie, its founders. (See Appendix for a listing of its early presidents.)

American College of Sports Medicine (ACSM)[8]. For some time in the early 1950s, a small group of physicians and physical educators in the Philadelphia area had been discussing the idea of uniting the medical and physical education professions for the purposes of promoting scientific studies in relation to the effect of sports on health and fitness, and of encouraging cooperation with other groups concerned with human fitness. The prime movers in this were Joseph B. Wolffe, M.D., Director of the Valley Forge Heart Institute and Hospital, Grover W. Mueller, Director of Physical and Health Education of the Philadelphia Public Schools, Albert S. Hyman, a cardiologist, and Ernest Jokl, M.D., who before coming to America had been the first director of the professional physical education course of the University of Stellenbosch in the Republic of South Africa and following that had spent several years on the physical education staff of the University of Kentucky before joining Dr. Wolffe's heart institute. These four men had contacted forty-five prominent physicians and physical educators across the country, inviting them to attend a meeting in connection with AAHPER's annual convention in New York City, April 22, 1954, to discuss the establishment of a group for this special work. Also an invitation was offered at the convention for all interested parties to attend this open meeting.

At this 1954 meeting, eleven persons asked to join the list of four founders and it was agreed to organize. Dr. Wolffe was elected president, Peter V. Karpovich, M.D., of Springfield College and Neils P. Neilson, Ph.D., of University of Utah were elected vice presidents, and Grover W. Mueller, secretary. At a second meeting, in December 1954, of the administrative council, a constitution was drafted and Dr. Karpovich was appointed chairman of a research committee. Then in January

1955, at a council meeting the list of eleven founders was confirmed including the following physical educators not previously mentioned, all holding the Ph.D. degree: Clifford Brownell and Josephine L. Rathbone of Columbus University, Leonard A. Larson of New York University, and Arthur H. Steinhaus of George Williams College.

In June 1955, on the eve of the convention of the American Medical Association, the constitution and bylaws were adopted, and the American College of Sports Medicine was officially born. A year later it reported a list of 121 members and from then on it grew phenomenally, holding conventions annually in various parts of the country, at first in connection with AAHPER conventions.

International Associations

International Association for Physical Education and Sports for Girls and Women (IAPESGW).[9] Through the efforts of NAPECW under the presidency of Helen Hazelton of Purdue University and the enthusiastic support and promotion of Dorothy Ainsworth, at that time a recent president of NAPECW, and a few foreign leaders of women in physical education (chief among them Agnete Bertram of Copenhagen University), the IAPESGW was established in July 1949, at a Congress in Copenhagen. Women physical educators from many countries were invited to attend this exploratory meeting, and 250 women from twenty-four countries accepted the invitation. Her Majesty Queen Ingrid of Denmark served as patroness for the Congress and Denmark's leading physical educator, Madame Agnete Bertram, gave the opening address. The Minister of Education served as honorary President and the University of Copenhagen offered its facilities for the use of the Congress. Denmark, the first country in the world to pass a law making physical education compulsory in the schools—in 1814—was the logical place for such a gathering.

America's Ruth Bryan Rhode (daughter of William Jennings Bryan) who had served as U.S. Minister to Denmark from 1935 to 1936 served as Chairman of the USA Honorary Committee for the Congress, and USA's Lillian Gilbreth, a famous engineer and industrial consultant who was deeply interested in physical education and its place in the schools, was a special guest speaker. Women leaders in physical education from South Africa and India were on the program. The Congress closed with Dorothy Ainsworth being appointed to chair a Continuing Committee to draw up plans for a permanent organization and an agreement being made to meet again in four years.

At the next meeting which was held in Paris in the summer of 1953, delegates numbering 500 from forty-two nations were in attendance. The organization was officially born at this time with Miss Ainsworth of the United States elected President, Miss M. T. Eyquem of France, and Miss C. M. Welester of England as Vice Presidents, and Miss Helen Hazelton of the United States as Secretary–Treasurer. Although NAPECW in America limited its membership to teachers in colleges, as its title infers, this limitation was omitted from this international group. Also although to American women the term *physical education* included gymnastics, correctives, sports, and dance, this was not true in foreign countries so that at the second congress the word *Sports* was added to the title.

The third congress was held in 1957 in London at which time a constitution was formally adopted.

International Council of Health, Physical Education and Recreation.[10] In the late 1940s, twenty-two national organizations working in health, physical education, and recreation united their efforts in international affairs through the establishment of a Joint Council on International Affairs. The AAHPER office in Washington served as headquarters for the council. Its purpose was four-fold: (1) to serve as a clearing house for information, projects, and services; (2) to stimulate interest in international affairs concerning U.S. fields of endeavor; (3) to be an organized group prepared to act in international projects and conferences; and (4) to represent the profession as a whole in exchange of news and exchange of persons, publicity, and hospitality.

In 1952 the World Confederacy of Organizations of the Teaching Profession (WCOTP) was established and when it later decided to take into membership certain specialized groups, a committee of health, physical education, and recreation teachers was invited to meet with WCOTP at the 1958 Assembly of Delegates in Rome, to consider within its scope the establishment of an international group of such special teachers. About twenty members of AAHPER attended this meeting, chief among them Dorothy S. Ainsworth (President of AAHPER 1950 to 1951) and Carl Troester, Jr. (then Executive Secretary of AAHPER). Out of this grew an international meeting of the group in Washington, D.C., in 1959 to discuss the establishment of an International Council of Health, Physical Education and Recreation. WCOTP approved the action and accepted this as a new international member. Dr. Ainsworth from the United States was elected first president, Michael Mela of England the first vice president, and Carl Troester from the United States the first secretary-general. Thus ICHPER was born in 1959.

Conferences on Physical Education. The custom of holding conferences on isolated subjects related to physical education apart from the annual conventions of the national, district, or state meetings, was slowly developing following World War II.

Foreign Service. Following World War II, worldwide opportunities for foreign service opened for physical educators, coaches, and athletes of the United States through Fulbright Professorships, Special Services assignments, the Job Corps, and the Peace Corps, all of which claimed the attention of hundreds of Americans.

LEADERS OF PHYSICAL EDUCATION AT MID-CENTURY

The American Association for Health, Physical Education and Recreation established three national awards in this era: in 1931, the Honor Award to be conferred upon several physical educators each year in recognition of notable leadership in the profession; in 1944, the Gulick Award as discussed earlier; and in 1949, the Anderson Award, to be conferred upon one or more persons each year in recognition of their work either in a specific branch of the Association's concerns (health education, sports, or recreation) or to a non–physical educator for his or her work in an allied field (medicine, physiology, sociology, etc.) that has specifically affected physical education.

The Gulick awards conferred from 1923 to 1929 by the New York City Physical Education Society went to six physical educators, members of the New York City group, who were among the most notable members of the profession of their day. This was the only award conferred in those years by any professional group in the country and therefore, the National Association has always looked upon those awards conferred before 1944 as its own. (The Gulick awardees have been so listed in the Appendix from 1923 on.)

The first set of outstanding leaders of the mid-century to be discussed consists of names of six leaders all of whom were born in the 1880s and 1890s and are named in order of their birth year.

Agnes Rebecca Wayman (1880–1968)

Agnes R. Wayman was born May 13, 1880, in Auburn Park, Illinois, a suburb of Chicago. She attended high school in Calumet, another suburb, and entered the University of Chicago in 1899, graduating in 1901 with an Associate Degree in 1901 and an A.B. in 1903. She proved to be such an excellent player at field hockey that Miss Dudley, head of physical education for women under Director Stagg, kept her for several years as women's hockey coach and finally appointed her an instructor on the physical education staff, which position she held until 1916. During that time, she served the year 1913–1914 as president of the University of Chicago Alumni Association.[11]

Although there is a lack of firm record of Agnes Wayman's commitments from 1916 to the early 1920s I know she was head of physical education at Barnard College by 1922.

Although Agnes Wayman no doubt found her greatest professional satisfactions in the area of sports for girls and women, she first came to national attention through her work in physical efficiency testing. She developed this work under the banner of the NAPECW, serving that college women's group as chairwoman of its test projects. In the November 1923 issue of APEA's *Review* she published her first article on physical efficiency tests for college women—a first such in the field for women by a woman. Earlier in that same year she accepted Mrs. Herbert Hoover's invitation to come to Washington, D.C., in April to consider the founding of the Women's Division of NAAF. Miss Wayman was elected a member of the Founding Executive Committee and was later appointed chairwoman of its first study which was on physical achievement tests for girls and women.

Figure 13. Agnes R. Wayman (1880–1968). (From a photograph presented to the author by Miss Wayman in 1942.)

In the Women's Division she found her real niche in national organization work, serving for many years on its Executive Committee from its founding in 1923, then as its chairwoman from 1931 to 1933. After that she moved on to the Board of Directors where she served until 1940 when the Women's Division was absorbed by NSWA of AAHPER.

During these years she also had "other irons in the fire," publishing her first book in 1934 and her second in 1938. After years of behind-the-scenes work on all sorts of important committees in her Eastern District Association of Physical Education, NAPECW, and APEA, she, from 1935 to 1936 became the third woman to be president of the American Physical Education Association. In the mid-1930s she was elected a Fellow in the American Academy of Physical Education, the second woman so honored after the four women charter members.

In 1942 Russell Sage College conferred upon her the honorary degree of

Doctor of Pedagogy and the University of Chicago gave her its Alumni Citation. Then in 1952 AAHPER conferred upon her its William G. Anderson award for distinguished service. In 1955 she retired from her position at Barnard College at age 75, and in 1968 after several years of volunteer community service to her new home, Brielle, New Jersey, she died, having organized a woman's club, a library, and other projects for the enrichment of the community.

Miss Wayman will go down in history as a staunch and effective promoter and defender of the Platform of the Women's Division of the National Amateur Athletic Federation which called for wholesome and sane athletics for all girls and women of America.

Mary Channing Coleman (1883–1947)[12]

Mary Channing Coleman was born July 11, 1883, in Halifax County, Virginia, and attended South Boston, Virginia, schools, finishing high school at age 15 in 1898. She then attended the State Female Normal School at Farmville, Virginia, for two years after which she taught for two years at Birch School, a one-room school near South Boston, Virginia. In 1903 she taught in evening schools of the New York Public School system. For the next four years she was an assistant in the office of Walter Truslow, M.D., a famous orthopedic surgeon of that day. By then she had learned of the Boston Normal School of Gymnastics and so attended that school for its last year in Boston (1908–1909) and its first year as the Department of Hygiene and Physical Education of Wellesley College (1909–1910).

Certified to teach physical education she entered upon her chosen career, teaching from 1910 to 1913 as head of physical education at Winthrop College in Rock Hill, South Carolina. The next four years (1913–1917) she taught in the public schools of Detroit under Ethel Perrin. The next three years (1917–1920) she was head of physical education at Margaret Morrison College, the Women's College of Carnegie Institute of Technology in Pittsburg. Then in 1920 she became head of physical education at North Carolina College for Women at Greensboro where she served until her death, October 1, 1947, from a heart attack just before her scheduled retirement at age 67. During these years she procured the bachelor's and master's degrees the hard way—during summers.

Born in Virginia and having taught physical education for three years in South Carolina and twenty-seven years in North Carolina, she was deeply conscious of the backwardness of many Southern schools, even in those several decades since the devastations of the Civil War. She threw all her energies into helping the South in its efforts to equal the educational standards of the nation as a whole and, when the Southern District Association of American Physical Education Association was founded in 1927, she was the prime force in swinging the few women workers into line and was the first woman to serve as president of the organization (1931–1932) following the first three men presidents. Two years later she stepped into the national association presidency (1933–1934), the second woman so honored. In

Figure 14. Mary Channing Coleman (1883–1947). (From a photograph presented to the author by Miss Coleman in 1938.)

that position she pushed for still more changes in APEA's constitution to advance the several moves of 1930 and 1931 to democratize the national organization.

In 1923 she was one of the group of women physical educators called to Washington, D.C., to help establish the Women's Division of NAAF, and she threw herself unstintingly into rallying Southern support in particular of the Women's Division Platform for Girls' and Women's Sports.

Charles Harold McCloy (1886–1959)[13]

Charles H. McCloy was born March 30, 1886, in Marietta, Ohio, but spent his early boyhood years on a cattle ranch near Dickinson, South Dakota. After grade school he returned to Marietta where he graduated first from the Academy and then from Marietta College, in 1907. Three years later he procured the master's degree at Marietta College, studying summers and teaching during the regular school years.

Then following the same pattern of teaching and study he procured the Ph.D. degree at Columbia University in 1932.

As a young boy, distressed over his poor physique, he came into possession at the age of 12 of a copy of Spalding's *The Athletes Guide* which recommended running to develop the legs. Thus started his self-planned, self-taught physical fitness program. At Marietta College he learned of the Harvard Summer School of Physical Education and attended it faithfully each summer of his college years 1905 on. He was so dedicated and enthusiastic about physical development work that for his last two years in college he was employed part time as a physical education instructor. He knew from then on that physical education was to be his career.

The first year out of college, 1907 to 1908, he was director of physical education at Yankton College, in Yankton, South Dakota, and the next year he moved on to directorship of physical education at the Danville, Virginia, YMCA

Figure 15. Charles H. McCloy (1886–1959). (Courtesy of University of Iowa.)

where he taught for three years. The next two years, 1911 to 1913, he was director of the Baltimore Public School Athletic League, and while there studied at the John Hopkins Medical College, not sure whether he should go on for the medical degree as most of the early leaders in the profession had done or go after the Ph.D. which the new day seemed to be calling for.

At this time the National Council of the YMCA offered him a position in China as secretary for the YMCA department of physical education for China, which he accepted in 1913. He spent the next thirteen years in that country, the first eight years in the original job, the next five as Director of the School of Physical Education at National Southeastern University at Nanking.

He returned to the United States in 1926 going to Detroit Teachers College for a year as a research specialist and then to New York City for three years as secretary of research in physical education for the National YMCA. During this time he also served for the year 1928–1929 as a lecturer at Teachers College, Columbia University, under Dr. Thomas D. Wood. In 1930 he went to the University of Iowa, at Iowa City, as research and anthropometry professor, in a dual position with both the Division of Physical Education and the Child Welfare Station, spending the rest of his career there.

During World War II he was frequently on leave of absence as well as on emergency calls to serve in the Surgeon General's Office as consultant in physical fitness and physical training of the armed forces. He also served on the Civilian Advisory Committee for the navy's Physical Fitness Program and on the Joint Army and Navy Welfare Committee. He was consultant to the Army and Navy Ground Forces, and also the Army and Air Force branch. It became a common occurence during those war years for an army or navy plane to land near Iowa City, pick up Dr. McCloy, and rush him to some army or navy conference where "higher-ups" needed his advice and/or suggestions on some sudden problems of the physical training work.

Dr. McCloy was the star linguist of the profession of his day. He could speak and write proficiently in English, Chinese, and Spanish, and could handle French in some measure for conversation. He wrote many books and a great number of articles for periodicals, in both English and Chinese, and some in Spanish for Central and South American readers. A few of his books and some articles were published in eight different languages. In addition to preparing eighty-four publications in Chinese, he served as editor of a professional Chinese journal, *New Education*, in China.

In the United States he received many honors and recognitions: charter member of the American Academy of Physical Education; recipient of both the Honor Award and the Gulick Award of AAHPER, the Hetherington Award of the American Academy of Physical Education, four honorary doctorates, honorary membership in the International Federation of Ling Gymnastics, and in the International Federation of Sports Medicine; president of the Central District of AAHPER

(1933–1934), of AAHPER (1937–1938), of the Academy of Physical Education (1947–1949), and of the Pan-American Institute of Physical Education. In 1958 he (with Seward Staley) received the first award conferred for distinguished service by the American College of Sports Medicine. In 1980 the C. H. McCloy Research Lecture Series was initiated within AAHPERD to be delivered in his memory annually at the national association convention. (The first lecture was delivered in Detroit in 1980 by William P. Morgan of the University of Wisconsin, Madison, and the second in Boston in 1981 by Walter Kroll of the University of Massachusetts, Amherst.)

As early as 1907, at age 21, he conceived the idea of rehabilitation exercises in hospitals for persons recovering from operations or from lengthy stays in bed—years ahead of the times. Almost forty years later he was working hard to convince the top echelon of officers of the U.S. Army of the value of reconditioning in all army hospitals.

As early as 1915 in China, at age 29, he was experimenting with the idea of building a natural gymnastics around activities of everyday life to replace the old German and Swedish forms still popular in America, unknowingly following Hitchcock's experiments of the last decades of the nineteenth century at Amherst College and unaware as yet of Thomas D. Wood's advocacy of such ideas of the 1890s at Stanford and later at Columbia University, where he was destined to work under Wood for a year in the late 1920s.

He was a great advocate of the values to the profession of intensive research work if its mission in education is to benefit humankind. And he practiced what he preached. In fact for many years the faculty and graduate students of physical education at the University of Iowa under his direction published more research reports than any other institution in the country.

Charles McCloy was a hard-working person. He gave unstintedly of his time and talents, not only to his students but to all workers in the profession who sought him out for information, opinions, or advice. His close friends warned him constantly against "burning the candle at both ends" and urged him to slow down upon retirement in 1954. Five years later he died, almost to the very end still giving of himself to help others. William P. Morgan sums up his career: "The McCloy story has a certain Horatio Alger dimension to it" and he was "a scholar of the first rank."[14]

Jay Bryan Nash (1886–1965)[15]

Jay Bryan Nash was born October 17, 1886, in New Baltimore, Ohio. In 1911 he received the A.B. degree at Oberlin College and in 1927 the A.M. degree and in 1929 the Ph.D. degree, both at New York University. In the summer of 1912 he studied under Clark Hetherington at the University of California and that fall be-

Figure 16. Jay B. Nash (1886–1965). (Courtesy of AAHPERD.)

came superintendent of playgrounds and director of physical education of the public schools of Oakland, California, a position he held for many years. From 1915 to 1918 he held a position as instructor in education at the University of California. From 1918 to 1919 he worked on Hetherington's staff at the State Department of Public Instruction as a field supervisor of physical education. From 1919 to 1926 there is a break in information in his *Who's Who in America* information, but it states that he was successively teacher and director of physical education and superintendent of playgrounds of Oakland for a period of fifteen years, which would have engaged him from 1911 to 1926 when he joined Hetherington's staff at NYU. Evidently from 1911 to 1926 when not otherwise engaged in work at the University of California or on Hetherington's staff in the California State Department of Education he was at work in Oakland. In 1930 he succeeded to Hetherington's position as head of physical education at NYU where he served out his active teaching career.

While at NYU he served for several years on a government appointment as director of Indian Emergency Conservation affairs. Also he gave outstanding leadership to many professional organizations: he was a charter member, and secretary of the American Academy of Physical Education (1926–1930); president of Eastern District Association of AAHPER (1933–1935), of AAHPER (1942–1943), and of the Academy (1945–1947); he served as president of the School Health and Physical Education Section of NEA, as vice president of the Camp Fire Girls of America, as a member for several years of the Advisory Committee of the Boy Scouts of America. For distinguished services, AAHPER conferred upon him both its Honor Award and the Gulick Award; the Academy gave him its Hetherington Award, and he was the recipient of the Medal of the Royal Hungarian College of Physical Education.

From 1930 to 1948 he authored or coauthored over a dozen books on physical education and recreation. He was a dynamic speaker and was in great demand at conferences, commencements, and conventions all across the country. A student of Delphine Hanna at Oberlin and a co-worker and protégé of Hetherington both in California and New York, he quickly rose to prominence in the profession, and there grew up around him a great following of enthusiastic and devoted admirers.

Elmer Dayton Mitchell (1889–)[16]

Elmer Dayton Mitchell was born in Negaunee, Michigan, September 6, 1889. He graduated from the University of Michigan in 1912 and, after graduate study at the University of Wisconsin in 1913, returned to the University of Michigan for his A.M. in 1919 and his Ph.D. in 1938. In college he was a member of the varsity baseball team for three years (captain his senior year) and a member of the varsity band.

From 1912 to 1915, he was a teacher and athletic director at Grand Rapids Union High School; from 1915 to 1917 he was athletic director and assistant professor of physical education at Michigan State Normal College at Ypsilanti. In 1917 he became a member of the varsity athletic coaching staff of the University of Michigan where he remained for the rest of his career, filling several different posts. In 1919 he became director of intramural sports, one of the very few persons of that day holding such a position. In 1921 he became assistant professor of physical education and rose to a full professorship in 1938, becoming chairman of the department of physical education for men in 1942 until he retired in 1958.

From 1923 to 1927 he served as a member of the Rockefeller Foundation Study of Motor Ability Tests. During the period 1931 to 1950 he taught at Utah State University (two summers), New York University, University of Iowa, University of Southern California, and Sul Rose Teachers College, Texas. Throughout his career

Figure 17. Elmer D. Mitchell (1889–   ). (Courtesy of his daughter, Mrs. Ann Dailey.)

he served many organizations as consultant and advisor, such as the National Congress of Parents and Teachers, the Educational Policy Committee of NEA, and the committee on training of recreation leaders of the United States Office of Education. Within the profession of physical education, he served the Middle West Society of Physical Education as secretary and editor (1928–1930); APEA (later AAHPER) as executive-secretary and editor (1930–1938) and as editor (1938–1943); president of the College Physical Education Association for the calendar year of 1953; charter member of the Academy of Physical Education and its president from 1954 to 1955. In 1949 AAHPER conferred both the Honor Award and the Gulick Award upon him for his distinguished service to it. The Academy conferred upon him its Hetherington Award in 1960. He also worked on the Intramural Directors Association and served as president of its Western Conference. He was honored by election into five professional fraternities.

He was a prolific writer within the profession, authoring and coauthoring at least a dozen books, most on sports or recreation, and contributing a long list of articles for educational journals. In 1921 he invented the game of speedball to be played in the fall by physical education classes and used in intramural programs.

During World War II he served from 1943 to 1945 as Lt. Commander U.S.N.R., Officer in Charge of Physical Training, Eighth Naval District, New Orleans. He retired in 1958.

The first intramural sports building in the country had been constructed at the University of Michigan under his direction and dedicated in 1928. Fifty years later Michigan's latest athletic field, providing play space for a great variety of games and to be used for the exclusive use of intramural sports, was dedicated in his honor. At age 92 Elmer D. Mitchell was present for the ceremony on September 25, 1981.

Dr. Mitchell gave the world *Intramural Sports,* the first book on the subject. After an earlier start by others, he served as the first director of intramural sports to put this activity on its feet and to nurse it along to success and national acclaim. No wonder he is hailed as the Father of Intramural Sports. Students and professional workers reading the *Journal of Health, Physical Education, Recreation and Dance* and the *Research Quarterly for Exercise and Sports,* should remember that Elmer Mitchell was also the founder of these periodicals.

Dorothy Sears Ainsworth (1894–1976)[17]

Dorothy S. Ainsworth was born March 8, 1894, in Moline, Illinois, and received her lower school education there. She attended Smith College from 1912–1916 and there she became interested in physical education. Returning home to Moline after graduation, she taught physical education until 1919 when she joined the Smith College Relief Unit of volunteers to go to France (March 1919–February 1920) to do rehabilitation work in towns and villages devastated during World War I. Upon her return she continued in volunteer work through the War Camp Community Service until Smith College offered her a position in the physical education department to teach dance and coach basketball. She had no professional training for this work but as a college student there she had been an enthusiastic pupil in both subjects. In the summer of 1922 she went to the University of Wisconsin to study dance under Margaret H'Doubler and there decided that physical education was to be her career. After two years of teaching at Smith, she resigned to attend Columbia University to enter upon professional preparation in physical education under Thomas D. Wood. In two years there (1923–1925) she earned her M.A. She then went to Skidmore College to teach for the years from 1925 to 1926, resigning to take over the directorship of the Department of Physical Education at Smith College, which position she held from 1926 to 1960, when she retired at 66 years of age.

For three years, beginning in 1927, she attended classes at Teachers College

Figure 18. Dorothy S. Ainsworth (1894–1976). (Courtesy of AAHPERD.)

Columbia University on Saturdays, commuting to New York City every weekend. She received her Ph.D. in November, 1930.

For her dissertation she did a history of physical education in the leading women's colleges of the United States. This has stood for more than fifty years as the definitive study of that topic up to 1930.

During her thirty-four years of teaching at Smith College, Miss Ainsworth made unusual contributions to the profession. From the late 1930s on for the next twenty-five years she played a strong leadership role. She served as president of three important professional groups: NAPECW (1937–1941), Eastern District Association of AAHPER (1948–1949), and AAHPER (1958–1959). But district and national work was not enough. In 1949 in a meeting in Copenhagen she with Agnete Betram of Denmark founded the International Association of Physical Education and Sport for Girls and Women and served that organization as founder from 1949 to 1953 and as president for the next twelve years after its formal birth in Paris in 1953.

In 1958 in Rome she initiated and chaired the founding of the International Council of Health, Physical Education and Recreation and served for six years (1959–1965) as its first president and from then on as honorary president for life.

Dr. Ainsworth's honors make a long list, chief among which are an honorary doctorate conferred by Smith College in 1956, the Gulick Award of AAHPER in 1960, the Hetherington Award of the American Academy of Physical Education in 1962, dedication of the Dorothy Ainsworth Gymnasium at Smith College in 1976, and prestigious foreign awards from Sweden, France, Finland, and Japan. In 1968, during the twentieth anniversary of the Universal Declaration of Human Rights, she received the Woman of Conscience Award conferred by U.S.A. National Council of Women at a ceremony in New York City, and in 1974 the U.S.A. Presidential Recognition Award in appreciation "for her outstanding contributions to International Friendship, Goodwill and Understanding through Sports." In the words of Catherine Allen, who paid her tribute at the Eighth Congress of IAPESGW in Capetown, South Africa, in 1977 following Dorothy Ainsworth's death:

> The profession's "First Lady of the World . . . kind and compassionate, without discrimination, gracious, wise, softspoken, cultured, affectionate, a prophet of the years-to-come with the conviction that we shall all be ONE WORLD."[18]

Other Leaders

There were many exceptional leaders in physical education in mid-twentieth century. Those already mentioned were but a fraction of the large numbers effectively at work all across the country establishing physical education in its various aspects within the wider world of education in general. Following are mentioned briefly seven other workers, three men and four women, they, also, born in the last two decades of the nineteenth century. The oldest of this group was born in 1880, the youngest in 1897. Of the seven, two women and one man were still living January 1, 1982, aged 83, 84, and 92 years. The six are as follows arranged according to the birth year.

They have been chosen as representative of this era for a variety of interests: the last woman with an M.D. within the profession to offer outstanding leadership, the profession's first black leader, foremost dance leader, popular woman lecturer and author, the profession's first executive-secretary of its national organization, a foremost leader in the battle for recognition of women's sports within the national professional organization, and the leading physiologist of the profession.

Gertrude Evelyn Moulton (1880–1964).[19] Born in Rio Grande, Ohio, June 5, 1880, Gertrude Moulton received the B.A. degree from Oberlin College in 1903 and the M.D. from the University of Illinois Medical School in 1919. Ever the student, she studied at Western Reserve University, Harvard Summer School of Physical Education, Columbia and New York universities, and in 1936 received the

A.M. degree at New York University. She taught physical education in the public schools of Cleveland, 1904 to 1907, and for the next eight years was a member of the staff of physical education for women at the University of Illinois (Champaign), serving first as an instructor and from 1909 to 1915 as director of the department. After a break of four years to study medicine, she returned to the University as medical adviser to women, 1919 to 1923. From then on until her retirement in 1946, she was director of physical education for women and medical adviser at Oberlin College, a period of twenty-three years. During her professional career, Dr. Moulton led the women of the profession in setting up proper standards and procedures for lower school and college physical examinations for girls and women. She took active part in the work of NAPECW, serving it as president from 1929 to 1932. She was president of the Mid West Association of Health, Physical Education and Recreation, 1946 to 1947, and was one of the few women elected into membership of the American Academy of Physical Education in its early years. She was among the still active group of younger leaders recognized by APEA's Honor Award at its first Award ceremony in Detroit in April 1931. She was active in the Camp Movement and into her late seventies was still enjoying canoe trips across the Canadian border into the Quetico Forest.

Edwin Bancroft Henderson (1883–1976).[20] Educated in the public schools and at Teachers College in Washington, D.C., and at Harvard Summer School of Physical Education, with graduate work at Columbia University, Edwin Henderson became a coach and teacher in Negro schools of the District of Columbia from 1904 until his retirement in 1954. He was head of the Physical Training Department of high schools, Washington, D.C., 1925–1951; Director of Physical Education and Safety and Athletics of schools of Washington, D.C., 1951–1954; founder of Negro Public School Athletic League, 1910; and co-founder and president of Affiliated Board of Officials for black schools of southeastern United States. He introduced intramurals into black high schools in 1904; was author of *The Negro in Sports* (1939); wrote many articles in *JOHPER* and *Journal of Negro Education* and newspapers and periodicals; served as consultant to the National Physical Fitness Committee of the Federal Security Agency, 1944 to 1945; was a member of the Board of Directors of United Service Organization (USO), 1945, Chairman of Civil Rights Commission of Washington, D.C., 1948, recipient of awards of several organizations, receiving a special tribute at the fiftieth anniversary banquet of the National Association for Advancement of Colored People (NAACP), 1965. He was inducted into the Black Sports Hall of Fame in 1974, along with Willie Mays, Jesse Owens, Henry Aaron, and several others. He held many firsts—as a black sports historian, black professional football player, black coach in the National Football League. In the realm of education, he was an innovator of physical education for blacks, and in the realm of Civil Rights, a leader in behalf of blacks—a quiet, calm force in many just causes. He was physical education's earliest black leader of the twentieth century.

Margaret H'Doubler (1889–1982).[21] Margaret H'Doubler, born of Swiss parentage in Kansas, received her lower school education in Warren, Illinois, and when her family moved to Madison, Wisconsin, she entered the University there and received the bachelor's degree in 1910 in biology. Because of her enthusiasm for and skills in sports, she was offered an assistantship in the department of physical education for women there where she spent all the years of her professional career, except the year 1916–1917 when she was on leave to study at Columbia University in search for some substitute for the stilted "esthetic dance" of earlier years. From this searching she developed her own dance forms which brought about a revolution in dance in the college field. She is proclaimed today as the founder of modern dance in the college programs.

She was the founder, at the University of Wisconsin, of the first collegiate dance major in the United States and in 1926 founder of Orchesis, an honorary college dance organization. One of the first authors of books on dance in education, she was the recipient of the AAHPER Gulick Award in 1971 and in the late 1970s was the Heritage Honoree of the National Association of Dance of AAHPER.

Rosalind Cassidy (1890–1980).[22] Rosalind Cassidy was born in Quincy, Illinois, in 1890. She graduated from Mills College in 1918, and from Columbia University she received the A.M. degree in 1924 and the Ed.D. in 1937. Her teaching career from 1918 to 1947 was spent at Mills College, and at UCLA from 1947 until her retirement. At Mills she spent the years 1918 to 1924 in the physical education department, moving into the chairmanship in 1925, after the year 1924–1925 she served as assistant to the president. After 1947 she served several years on the National Board of Girl Scouts.

Within the profession she served as president of NAPECW, 1934 to 1937, and as president of the American Academy of Physical Education, 1950 to 1951. She received an honorary doctorate, L.H.D. from Mills College in 1950, and the AAHPER Gulic Award in 1956. She was an advocate of Wood's natural gymnastics, and an advocate of the search for the democratic process in all facets of physical education. She was a popular lecturer and author.

Helen Hazelton (1894–). Helen Hazelton was born September 8, 1894, in Montague City, Massachusetts, and attended lower grade schools there to 1908 when she entered high school at Greenfield, Massachusetts. She attended Mount Holyoke College, 1912 to 1916, and from 1917 to 1919 Wellesley College where she received the Certificate of Physical Education under Miss Homans's directorship. Following that she held the position of instructor at Northwestern University for four years, 1919 to 1923, followed by five years as an assistant professor at the University of Minnesota, 1923 to 1928. For the year 1928–1929 she attended Columbia University where she procured the Master's Degree in Physical Education from Teachers College. Then from 1929 to 1963 she was professor and Head of Physical Education for Women at Purdue University, Lafayette, Indiana.

She has received many honors and held many important positions within the profession, such as: Chairman of Women's Athletic Section, APEA, 1930 to 1931; President of Middle West Society of Physical Education, 1939 to 1940; President of MWAPECW, 1945 to 1947 and of NAPECW, 1947 to 1949; first Secretary-Treasurer of International Association of Physical Education and Sport for Girls and Women, 1949 to 1953 and 1957 to 1961, and Vice President, 1961 to 1965; a leader of the struggle for the rights of women in sports to have voting membership in the APEA national council[23] in the APEA constitution reorganization years of 1930 to 1932; champion of correct sports for girls and women within the education field. She is a member of the Academy of Physical Education, an honorary Fellow of the Indiana AHPER, 1950, and of AAHPER, 1938, and recipient of the Presidential Citation Award of NASGW, 1975.

Neils Peter Neilson (1895–).[24] Neils Neilson was born November 20, 1895, in Milville, Utah. In 1919 he received the B.S. degree from Utah State Agricultural College, Logan; in 1923, the A.M.; and in 1936 the Ph.D. from the University of California. From 1921 to 1926 he was head of physical education for boys at a high school in San Francisco, during which time he worked toward his master's degree at Berkeley. From 1926 to 1934 he was California State Supervisor of Health and Physical Education, during which time he started work at Berkeley toward the Ph.D. degree. As associate professor of physical education at Stanford University from 1934 to 1938, he completed his doctoral work. At the same time he was given a special assignment at Stanford to assist Clark W. Hetherington in preparing his writings for publication.

In the spring of 1938 he was elected president of AAHPER and in the fall resigned that office since AAHPER had offered him the position of first executive-secretary of the national association—which then was setting up a permanent office in the NEA Building in Washington, D.C. He held this position for five years and then resigned to return to teaching, this time to the chairmanship of physical education at the University of Utah, which position he held from 1943 until his retirement in 1964. After that he taught at Utah full-time for another five years, and after that still stayed on, at age 86, part-time to work with graduate students.

He served the Society of State Directors of Health and Physical Education as the president, 1933 to 1934; president of AAHPER, April–September, 1938; and president of the American Academy of Physical Education, 1953 to 1954. He has authored and co-authored many books. His *Physical Education for Elementary Schools,* written with Winifred Van Hagen, was prepared as a state syllabus when both authors were in the State Department of Public Instruction. Later when it became popular nationally it was permitted to be published commercially for general use. For many years it was declared to be the profession's all-time best seller.

Chapters 5, 6, and 7 of Dr. Neilson's latest book, *Concepts and Objectives in the Movement Arts and Sciences,* of 1978, are built around Hetherington's original concepts as he talked them over with Dr. Neilson and which Hetherington, himself, never got into final form for publication. The current edition takes into account the changing times in the forty years since Hetherington's death. In 1961, AAAHPER honored Neils Neilson with its Gulick Award.

Arthur H. Steinhaus (1897–1970).[25] Arthur Steinhaus was born in Chicago in 1897. He was educated in Chicago schools and attended the University of Chicago, receiving the B.S. degree in 1920. In 1921 he obtained the B.P.E. degree at George Williams College; in 1925, the M.S. at University of Chicago; in 1926, the M.P.E. at George Williams College; and in 1928, the Ph.D. at the University of Chicago. From 1920 to 1928 he was an instructor in biology at George Williams College and in 1928, with his Ph.D. completed, became professor of physiology at George Williams College where he served out the rest of his teaching career, becoming Dean of the College before his retirement.

In 1935–1936 he was deeply involved in the work of the International Congress of Physical Education, and the International Student Sports Congress in connection with the eleventh Olympic Games in Berlin. From 1937 through 1946 he was deeply involved for seven summers as a visiting professor at the Universities of California, Colorado, and Wisconsin, except for the World War II years when he was on leave from George Williams College to work with the U.S. Office of Education under the Federal Security Agency and with the Robinson Foundation on health education work. Also during the war he served as a consultant to the Secretary of Navy on physical fitness problems.

In 1931–1932 he also had a leave to study in Europe on a Guggenheim Fellowship. In later years he made several trips to Europe on lecturing engagements. He was a charter member of the American Academy of Physical Education and served as its secretary for several years and its president from 1943 to 1945. He also served the Middle West District Association of Health, Physical Education and Recreation as its president in 1955–56. In 1940 he received the YMCA Roberts-Gulick Award and in 1969 the AAHPER Gulick Award. He was a prolific writer on physiology and its relation to exercise, also on physical fitness, and, with a great knack for expressing his view in an entertaining way, he was a greatly sought speaker in the profession.

PHYSICAL EDUCATION IN THE LATTER TWENTIETH CENTURY

14

Events and Movements of the Latter Twentieth Century That Affect Physical Education and Its Activities

Times have changed greatly since World War II. Further increase of mechanization has robbed ever larger segments of society of opportunities for physical exercise, which formerly existed both in the home and at work. Also leisure time has increased. Because of the advances of technology the way of life has changed markedly. Physical education and sports activities have also changed. This is discussed in the material that follows.

EVENTS AND MOVEMENTS AFFECTING PHYSICAL EDUCATION DIRECTLY

The old question of the early twentieth century, Why can't Johnny read? has by the latter century years turned into Why Johnny still can't read, and added to it are the questions, Why can't Johnny spell? (or do simple arithmetic or respond to discipline for the common good), and to claim physical education's special attention, Why isn't Johnny physically fit? Part of the answers may be found in a study of the Recreation and Camping Movements of today, in physical education's efforts to meet today's challenges in the schools, in Physical Fitness Movements, and in Civil Rights Movements, all of which are discussed in the material that follows.

The Camping Movement

The Camping Movement of this era has suffered serious setbacks. Contributing factors fo this were the ever-increasing numbers of automobiles owned by people in all walks of life, the sudden fad of the camping van, the mobile home and the like, and the greatly increased wages of the worker so that families could afford these heretofore luxuries. Also now came the gradual spread throughout the country of the great four-lane interstate highway, bypassing villages, towns, and even cities, contributing in a large way to the call to all citizens "to take to the roads" for their family vacation. More and still more national parks increased their camping facilities, as did more and still more private owners of lakes, mountain meadows, river resorts, ocean beaches, forests and ranches. The heyday of the Camping Movement seems to be over but it still serves fairly large numbers during summer vacations. As the all-summer children's camps have decreased, the municipal and local camps for shorter camp periods—one to two and three weeks—have increased.

Many camps still advertise annually for counselors. Physical activities are still the backbone of their programs in camps for boys and girls. And many camps still exist in all parts of the country with their program built largely around some single activity—such as field hockey camps, archery camps, volleyball camps, running many short sessions in a season. Such camps call for professionally trained physical educators and coaches.

The old-style family camp set in some specific location has just about been replaced by family camping in a new form. It is usually not held to one definite site but instead by camping van moves about around the country, briefly here, briefly there.

There are today many school camps near home where groups of children go for a week or two during vacations. Physical education staffs put on programs of physical activities, home economics staffs take charge of the nutrition program, and art and music staffs lead in the recreation of quiet and evening hours.

The Recreation Movement

Recreation in the United States today is still sponsored by many agencies. The activities of the National Recreation Association have multiplied so markedly since the last war that it has materially increased its headquarters staff. In 1965 it changed its name to the National Recreation and Park Association (NRPA) and the following year changed the name of its official magazine from *Recreation* to *Parks and Recreation*. The Association has come to stand for many things to different communities. Some of the services provided include: personnel service to private, voluntary, and governmental agencies; special consultant services for all phases of areas and facilities; service to industrial concerns engaged in recreation; consultant and correspondence services to agencies and individuals; special publications about problems concerning recreation; publication of their magazine; annual convention or congress for the professional leaders in the field; and research on various aspects of recreation.

The National Parks System offers unusual recreation for all citizens who visit the various parks, each patterned after the particular type of entertainment each park can offer, each according to its particular type of setting. Whereas in 1956, 30 million people visited the various National Parks, in 1966, 130 million had checked in.

The Physical Fitness Movement

In February 1961 the Department of Health, Education, and Welfare held a Conference on Youth Fitness, for which it called upon the profession of physical education for help from the early planning stage. Following this the Council on Youth Fitness produced a booklet, *Youth Fitness,* that was widely circulated throughout the nation. It carried a suggestion for a school-centered program of fitness, calling attention to the use of calisthenics as a way to develop fitness quickly, but stressing that the fitness program should not consist only of calisthenics. Shortly many states established state fitness programs, although a few, notably Oregon since 1945, and California were already at work on such projects.

Following President Eisenhower's lead, President Kennedy carried on his Council on Fitness for Youth and his Citizen's Advisory Committee, naming Charles B. "Bud" Wilkinson (1916–   ), nationally known football coach, as Special Consultant to the President on Physical Fitness. He also issued, in July 1961, a *President's Message to the Schools on Physical Fitness of Youth* that urged expansion of physical education programs and facilities, as he said, "to give a high priority to a crusade for excellence in health and fitness," and he set aside April 30–May 6, 1961, as National Youth Fitness Week. Following this many states held state fitness conferences, and others held clinics and workshops on fitness. The AAHPER set up fitness tests for the schools.

Following President Kennedy, President Johnson carried on this movement, naming Stan Musial (1920–   ), baseball star, as his Special Consultant to succeed Wilkinson, and for administrative purposes he placed the Council under the Department of Health, Education, and Welfare. In 1967 Lt. Commander James A. Lovell, Jr. (1928–   ), a NASA astronaut, was appointed Special Consultant on Physical Fitness to the President. In 1966 President Johnson established the President's Physical Fitness Award, which was sponsored by the AAHPER and the Council on Physical Fitness. In 1967, 50,000 boys and girls in the ten-to-seventeen-year range qualified for the award, with schools from all states, the District of Columbia, and Puerto Rico participating.

Succeeding presidents have each appointed his own Special Consultant to carry on this work. Today there is a great awakening in this movement and practically all states have their own state physical fitness organization with the state head of physical fitness serving as a governor's appointee. These groups are lending support to physical education in the schools through national awards which thousands of children have received to date. Pressure is made for physical fitness activities to be made available to all students, handicapped as well as the nonhandicapped, the poorly skilled as well as highly skilled. They are also pushing for physical fitness of adults, encouraging all to become physically active.

The Jogging Fad. In the late 1970s there developed a nationwide interest and participation in running which has engaged vast numbers of citizens, old and young, men and boys, women and girls. Nothing like it in the way of exercise has ever before caught the fancy of the entire nation in so firm a grip. True enough the pleasure of running itself is no doubt as old as humankind but at the turn of the twentieth century it was confined almost exclusively to a few college men who went out for cross-country running as they called it as an event in their competitive intercollegiate program. It was a rare young woman who took up such an activity at that time and then only on the running track in the gymnasium away from public gaze. Now "everyone is doing it," as the popular song of pre–World I years stated it in speaking of the then fad of ragtime dance.

The Marathon Races. As related in earlier chapters marathon races became popular in the late nineteenth century—at least as popular topics of conversation and popular for spectators—and in the 1960s and 1970s they were still growing stronger than ever. The Boston Marathon—the United States' first one—today engages hundreds of runners, mostly boys and men of all ages into the sixties but in 1981 also engaging women. Today marathons are organized and run off all over the country, and women are entering in increasing numbers. Most marathons attract runners from several states.

Rope Jumping[1]. Rope jumping, very popular in the Gay Nineties as a home physical activity for play periods, died out in the early twentieth century. But it is now enjoying a revival which far exceeds the rope-jumping dreams of any Victorian-age children. While they did single-rope jumping with a partner skipping in now and then for duet jumping, and long-rope jumping with two swingers and several jumpers dodging in and out at random, they knew nothing of the fantastic skills of today's jumpers, as singles, duets, trios or in groups with both single and long ropes.

Devised as a project of today's physical fitness movement, it was promoted as a fad to bring in money for the national heart fund, and it caught on so quickly and successfully that under the slogan "Jump Rope for Heart," it has raised millions of dollars for the fund. The report for 1981 was for $12,995,897 gross—$9,421,142 net—with 579,169 children participating in the project from 7759 schools in 49 states (Nevada not participating), 2 large cities counted apart from their states, and the District of Columbia.

A few of these school teams demonstrated their skills at group rope-jumping at the AAHPER conventions in Boston, April 1981, and Houston, April 1982. Their performances were breathtaking in the skills and dramatic patterns of activity. Today's rope jumpers have skilled teachers to lead them, schools that accept this activity as a part of the physical education program, and many books or pamphlets on the market to guide the novices.

In the World War II years, Alice Marble who kept herself fit for tennis tried to popularize rope jumping for the Physical Fitness Movement but there was no American Heart Association to back her then, as today.

The General Exercise Fads. Radio and TV programs offering exercise routines to do at home are popular all across the country and groups of women get together in homes, dance studios, or church or club gymnasiums to "do their exercise thing" together for the fun of it as well as for good health. Also, aerobic dancing claims the attention of many such groups.

Quackery in Fitness. All manner of people are taking advantage of the physical fitness fads of today and opening physical fitness salons, exercise rooms, and private gymnasiums, all across the country. Patrons are flocking to them, little knowing whether the people offering these services are properly prepared for such work. Some of these "teachers" are no doubt adequately prepared for this task, but it is quite probable that many are merely opportunists making the most possible financially out of this fad while it lasts and stating without benefit of any certificate or license they are qualified to handle such work. Perhaps such people should be licensed by the town or "city fathers" and the quacks put out of business. As early as 1975 one writer in the physical education field has suggested that AAHPER work for consumer protection bills in Congress to protect the lay public but such a move has not as yet developed.[2]

Research in Fitness. A tremendous amount of research in the field of physical fitness is being carried on in many colleges and universities across the country—all to the benefit of the movement and the entire profession of physical education. AAHPERD supports a *Research Quarterly* within its own framework, a Research Section, and a Research Consortium. The American College of Sports Medicine, discussed in a later chapter, carries on much research in this field.

The Civil Rights Movement

The Civil Rights Act of 1964. In 1964 Congress passed the Civil Rights Act, calling for an end to discrimination in all facets of life because of race, color, religion, sex, or national origins. Several facets of this act concerned education, and thus physical education directly. Specifically it concerned physical education and sports for girls and women.

Outlawing Sex Discrimination. Shortly after passage of the Civil Rights Act, a U.S. citizen, an Olympic equestrienne, was refused a jockey's license by the Maryland Racing Commission because of her sex. She took her case to court and won, and her license was issued at once. About that same time a woman who was a sports writer was refused admission in the Yale University press box. She, too, took her case to court and won. Such incidents began to multiply throughout the country. Women were becoming restless over the slow process of achieving equality and many took to militancy in making their demands heard. Feminists arose in protest, and a Feminist Movement was a natural outcome.

Sex Discrimination in Education. Over 2000 years ago, Plato in his *Republic* was advocating that education of women be equal to that of men but that their education could differ in detail according to differences in character not because of difference in sex.[3] Modern philosophers are still calling for equality of the sexes in education. It was still at mid-twentieth century in many ways but an unrealized dream. Although women and blacks were accepted into a college for the first time in America in 1833 (at Oberlin College), there were still more than 130 years later many barriers to be swept away before full equality in education would be achieved.

To women senior citizens of the 1980s who were following a career in the early twentieth century, the inequality in their schooling was not as memorable as the inequalities they experienced in employment, status, and pay. Today there is still a long way to go.

There was little discrimination against women in physical education from men in the field. Discrimination came from men who were heads of athletics and physical education in the early years of this century (and frequently had not one modicum of training as educators) and from men administrators in higher echelons of authority. These men approved of the women's lower paychecks and their slower rate of advancement to higher positions, or gave preference for employment to less qualified and/or less experienced men. The men of industry, business, or other professions held these same beliefs that women should not be paid as much as men. They were seemingly universal beliefs.

The one great argument they all held in support of paying women less than men was that men had spouses and children to support and working women did not. (In early years of women entering upon careers, it was almost exclusively the unmarried woman who posed a career threat to men. Almost invariably in the late 1890s and early 1900s a woman gave up her employed position when she married. In fact many schools and businesses had rules against employing married women. Even some colleges would not admit married women as students.

Today's women who are senior citizens must have vivid recollections of how girls and women were treated as second class citizens in their physical education classwork and sports, were permitted the use of gymnasium floors and play spaces only at hours when they were not desired for the boys and men.

The Educational Amendment Act of 1972 (Title IX, Section 901). The passage of the Educational Amendment Act of 1972 (Title IX) has decidedly upset the old ways in all schools and colleges that accept government aid in any form. This act mandates that no person in the United States shall, on the basis of sex, be excluded from participation in, be denied the benefits of, or be subjected to discrimination under any education program or activity receiving federal financial assistance. This has affected physical education and sports in a large way since discrimination in both has been rampant since the earliest years of their claim on education. How it has affected both is discussed later under these topics, both in this and in the following chapter.

Educational Mainstreaming of Disadvantaged Children[4]

In 1973 the Rehabilitation Act was passed by Congress, calling for all children disadvantaged in any way to be given public education to suit their needs and to approximate as nearly as possible the general public school education offered to all children. Unfortunately this law was not implemented until 1977. In the meantime two law suits arose that attracted much attention to disadvantaged children and their rights to an education at public expense. One was brought by the Pennsylvania Association for Retarded Citizens (PARC) in 1971 which was settled with a decision that all children including the mentally retarded have a right to quality education. The second, *Mills* v. *the Board of Education of District of Columbia,* in 1972, brought a favorable decision, demanding that all children of school age, mentally retarded, physically handicapped, or with any sensory impairment or emotionally disturbed, must be accepted into the public schools and given quality education.[5]

The Education for All Handicapped Children Act of 1975. These two court cases awakened Congress to pass the Education for All Handicapped Children Act (Public Law 94-142) which President Ford signed into law November 1975. This act specifically mandates special physical education, including athletics, for all handicapped children. Implementation was soon underway in schools all across the country and the year 1981 was designated as the International Year of Disabled Persons. Many athletic contests for disabled children and even Olympics for the handicapped were run off in various parts of the country.

As a result of these special acts in behalf of the disadvantaged there are now laws to the effect that all new buildings for public use, also all old public buildings being renovated, must include barrier-free access for the handicapped. Also laws require that access to such buildings from the streets be barrier-free at curbs and entrances.

PHYSICAL ACTIVITIES AFFECTED BY THE ABOVE LISTED EVENTS

The Physical Fitness and Civil Rights Movements have markedly affected dance, gymnastics, and sports of the latter twentieth century.

As girls and women are today going out for interschool and intercollegiate sports as never before, so boys and men are getting the coeducation idea and are taking to dance in its various forms as never before. No longer is a boy or man considered effeminate if he joins a contemporary dance class or group just as a girl or woman can go out for sports of a more varied nature than in earlier years and not be considered "mannish." There is an awakening to the idea that all physical activities are for both sexes. Of course the folk dance forms have always been considered coed forms although some sports (the body contact sports such as regulation football) even yet today are frowned upon as coed activities.

Dance

Folk Dance. Less is heard today about folk dance clubs than was heard in the 1930s and 1940s before World War II. Nor does folk dance appear as frequently in school programs. However there are still many communities in several states, mostly in small towns, where a certain national strain still prevails, such as Czech, German, Norweigan, Scotch, or Irish where through annual festivals the older generations have kept the Old-Country dances alive for the younger generations. Some of these towns maintain active folk dance clubs all the year around. However the great wealth of folk dance on the whole is sadly neglected in the schools of our country.

A 1970s fad has grown up around belly dancing of the Orient and there are thriving Belly-Dance Clubs in some of our large cities. This has escalated to embrace other Mid-East dances so that the 1980s have opened with much enthusiasm in some cities for this activity in club form, or in colleges.

Square Dance. A revival of square dance that started in the 1940s has carried over to today's world. It is going on in all sections of the country, and not only state but also regional and national festivals are held. But in the 1960s square dancers began creating their own dances, building on the fundamental forms and figures of the old but transforming them into new patterns that form altogether different dances. In some of these new dances they use the two-step or waltz instead of the shuffle or skipping steps of the older forms. A local club creates a new dance and passes it on to other clubs and demonstrates it at some festival, and it may become popular and well known. There are new calls and jingles and whereas in the old square dancing anyone gave the calls, there has today grown up a group of professional callers, in great demand at festivals, who travel about the country and are paid large fees for their services. In today's square-dance world, it is frequently the caller rather than the dancers who receive public acclaim.

International Folk Dance. At one of its sessions, the International Association of Physical Education and Sport for Girls and Women (IAPESGW) at its quadrennial congress in Capetown, South Africa, in the summer of 1977, staged a huge program of dances of the nations of the world. An estimated 500 delegates from thirty-two different nations performed in these dances. One news commentator reported:

I have watched these delegates join hands, literally spiritually, and emotionally, irresponsive of colour, creed, race or politics, and together learn and perform each other's National Folk Dance.[6]

At this congress, on another occasion, a dance group from the University of Utah presented an entire program of dance of various forms.

Contemporary or Modern Dance.[7] The name *modern dance* for the new forms of rhythmic activity that in the 1920s and 1930s replaced the older so-called nature and interpretive dance seemed to have worn out its welcome to many by the 1960s and the title *contemporary dance* was replacing it; but John Martin, noted dance critic, in an interview on a television program, "Dance of Today" (November 1967), spoke of the unfortunate new name as being as poor as the old one. He expressed the hope that some name for this form of dance might yet be devised which would not be tied to any period of time. But by the 1980s such a name still eludes the profession. Some schools now use *modern dance,* others use the *contemporary.* Which name is preferred seems to be decreed by the head of dance in each school.

The early forms of modern dance denied the classical ballet forms but today, ballet is considered a worthy partner of the world of dance in education.

Aerobic Dance. This exercise form recognized by the lay world as a dance form is disowned by bona fide dance teachers, and for the purposes of this book is discussed under the heading of gymnastics.

Gymnastics

Following World War II, physical educators were taking a new look at gymnastics, which had been crowded out of the physical education program largely to make way in the preceding period for sports and dance. Now physical educators were returning to their earlier acknowledged responsibility toward all children—a responsibility peculiarly their own—of developing in each child the aspects of physical fitness that depend upon participation in physical activity for its accomplishment. Accompanying this renewed acknowledgement was the recognition of gymnastics as having intrinsic values in the development of physical fitness and as such as having a place in the physical education program.

The New Gymnastics. Out of a critical investigation of the old forms of gymnastics came a very different and new form—so different that it seems that it should take on a new name. To older citizens, the word *gymnastics* calls forth images far different from the response to the word for today's young people.

Gymnastics used to mean free standing exercises of the German, Swedish, Danish, or other national variety plus work on pieces of apparatus such as the horse, buck, vaulting box, parallel bars, stall bars, overhead ladders, flying rings, traveling rings, Swedish boom, and climbing ropes and ladders. Today most of these pieces of apparatus are gone, as forgotten as the old formal exercises of German and Swedish styles. The flying rings are still in service but they are no longer allowed to fly. They are now called "still" rings and the person exercising on them must do so in such a way that they are still. The pommel and long horse, the parallel bars, and the vaulting box are still in use mostly for boys and men. For the girls and women there are now uneven parallel bars and the high balance beam.

The trampoline became a popular piece of gymnasium equipment in the 1940s and 1950s and for a while into the 1960s. In fact college men did not stage the first national championship (put on by NCAA at the University of Michigan) until April 19, 1969. Shortly after that, no doubt due to the safety hazards connected with it, the trampoline quickly disappeared from school gymnasiums.[8]

Until the Educational Amendment Act of 1972 physical education recognized two classes of gymnastics: gymnastics for boys and men, and gymnastics for girls and women. Now it recognizes just one gymnastics which the two sexes take together.[9] However within that grouping there is recognized two classes of work, one for apparatus work for male students and another for females. For the boys and men today, there are six parts to gymnastics: (1) floor routine of tumbling; (2) vaulting on the pommel horse; (3) vaulting on the long horse; (4) work on the "still" rings; (5) work on the parallel bars; (6) work on the horizontal bar. For the girls and women, there are four parts to class work: (1) a floor exercise routine done to music (a seeming combination of dance steps, tumbling, and warm-up exercises); (2) vaulting on the side horse; (3) work on the uneven parallel bars; (4) work on the high balance beam.

The general class work opens with group warming-up routines done in unison or sometimes individually, and then the class divides into squads for apparatus work.

Since these routines and various pieces of apparatus work follow the guidelines for Olympic competition, perhaps this is history repeating itself—teaching today as an Olympic Committee dictates rather than according to the dictates of educational objectives, thus possibly repeating the error of World War I when many teachers hoping to make a good record for their pupils in physical achievement tests to boost their school's rating were teaching to train their pupils specifically to pass these tests rather than teaching to meet general physical fitness standards. It was a great bone of contention in mid-1910s as today's teaching of gymnastics may in the 1980s become a similar bone of contention, once administrators ask just what are the aims of school gymnastics—to prepare pupils to try out for the Olympics or to prepare them to be fit for whatever life offers—relegating the Olympics to their proper niche in life, not as the end of all life's dreams. In the meantime it is an interesting bit of teaching to investigate, with a questioning of its aims.

Gymnastic Fads. Triggered by the great widespread interest in physical fitness, exercise fads have arisen and caught the fancy of a great many people. No doubt some good results come from "aerobic dances" and "jazzercises" for the individuals who engage in them if they are aware of what their hearts can tolerate in terms of strenuous, prolonged exercise mixed with the emotional stresses that usually accompany such activity when pushed to great public acclaim. Because this exercising is done to music, it is confused with dance. Long-playing records are on the market to accompany the class activities that may engage such huge numbers that sometimes it takes huge halls to accommodate the participants.

Adapted or Individual Gymnastics. Following the passage of the Educational Amendment Act of 1972, physical education school programs have gradually come to include specialized classwork to meet the needs of disadvantaged children. This holds true in the lower schools as well as in high schools and colleges.

Ever since the late 1880s, followers of the Swedish gymnastics system have tried to educate the general public about the need for specialized physical education. At the turn of the century such work was called corrective gymnastics, but since few schools or colleges offered such classwork it was little understood and there became attached to the title a seeming stigma belittling those pupils who were placed in these highly specialized classes. The name was gradually dropped and the titles *adaptive gymnastics* or *individual gymnastics* came into preference.

In the early years of this century teachers prepared to offer such specialized work were rare and schools hiring such teachers rarer yet. In colleges it was almost exclusively the women's physical education departments that offered this work, presumably because the women's staff was not as busy with intercollegiate sports as the men's. So female students profited from this specialized work. This work was usually offered not because the board of education or regents or trustees mandated it but merely because the female head of physical education insisted on it. Also not all teacher-training schools of physical education offered preparation in such work, thus lessening the chances that it would be offered in the schools.

But today it is a "new ball game." The government mandates that special classwork be offered to all pupils and students needing it. Because of Title IX the general public now hears about these children through the attention to their plight of newspapers, popular periodicals, radio, and TV. Professional periodicals inform us of the several books already coming off press to guide teachers in this specialized work with today's latest knowledge of kinesiology and physiology of exercise applied to the subject.

Today teacher-training schools and departments are putting such training into their curricula, and special schools for such training are springing up across the country. Soon there should be such a core of special teachers of adaptive gymnastics that every department of physical education anywhere will not be considered properly staffed until it has a special teacher on its roster.

Research will no doubt in the years ahead guide the program builders into a better knowledge of the exercises best suited for the varied types of physical disadvantages encountered by children. It is a new world of education opening up.

Sports

There has been in the latter twentieth century such an explosion of sports all over the country (in fact all over the world) that to present this topic calls for an entire book by itself. Therefore, the topic is treated in this book almost entirely as it relates to education in general, with mention of a single sport only if it presents some particular aspect out of the ordinary. Students of history of physical education can supplement this text from the wealth of information in newspapers, popular periodicals, special sports publications, and radio and television programs.

Bicycling. Bicycling aroused new interests in the 1960s and 1970s which give promise of increasing in the 1980s. Perhaps the most promising of all new twists to get youth out into the countryside is Iowa's Rag Brai put on annually since 1976. Rag Brai means The Register's Annual Great Bicycle Ride Across Iowa, which is sponsored by the Des Moines *Register* with the cooperation of the State Highway Patrol, and a large number of civic groups all along the route selected for each year.

This annual ride has developed into a great event with hundreds of bicyclers, old and young, boys and men, girls and women from all over the country entering the "ride." It is in no sense a race or contest. It is just what its name proclaims it to be—a ride across the state from the Missouri River to the Mississippi. The route from west to east is different each year, and they are planned to avoid main highways. An article about it in *Smithsonian* magazine[10] gives the full story of its origins and the first five rides.

Cricket. Although cricket has never become a popular game in the United States it has been played (as related in an earlier chapter) at the University of California, Los Angeles, (UCLA) since the 1930s and since 1960 has been recognized by the awarding of a varsity letter. By 1960 there were eight cricket clubs actively functioning in the Los Angeles area. The Westwood Cricket Club was made up of UCLA students and alumni, its first captain an American who had learned the game in Australia.

In the late 1960s there were twelve such clubs in the Los Angeles area alone, with seven playing fields at their disposal. Among them they carried on a six-months schedule of games, all played on Sundays, with three different trophy tournaments to end the season. On the East Coast the game was played as early as

1910 at Wellesley College but by the time the West Coast had taken up the game at Los Angeles, the game had long died out at Wellesley.

Bowling. Bowling is having a big revival not only as recreation for the citizenry in general but also as a feature in school and college intramural sports. And now it has even invaded the extramural field. In the mid-1970s, nine states—California, Hawaii, Iowa, Maine, New Hampshire, New Mexico, New York, South Carolina, and South Dakota—were reporting high school teams entered in interscholastic contests. New York State alone boasted 336 high school teams.[11] However, it has not as yet invaded the intercollegiate field.

English Field Hockey. This King of Sports for women has suffered because it requires eleven players to the team, and the equipment is expensive. These two counts against the sport have prevented its being offered by schools in small towns and by some small colleges. Perhaps if someone had done for field hockey what Stephen Epler in the 1920s did for football field hockey (with six women on a team) might have had a better chance. At any rate it has survived in some city high schools, in the women's colleges, in many universities, and in many small colleges, and above all as a sports club activity for women in large city areas.

In the mid-1970s a survey reported that field hockey was being played by girls in 1534 high schools in seventeen states (eight Eastern states, six Middle West states, two West Coast states, and one Southern state).[12]

Since men have not taken to this sport, varsity field hockey is not in general offered by intercollegiate athletic departments, hence there is no ignoring of the mandate of Title IX when women who want varsity field hockey are denied it from the standpoint of expense. The survival of this sport seems to depend upon the classwork offered in college and high school departments where activities that appeal only to girls and women may be offered with impunity. Otherwise the sport is relegated to intramural programs or to sports club organization.

Equitation. Although horseback riding has long been a part of physical education programs in many schools and colleges, especially in women's colleges, it has never received national organization attention until 1967 when a National Riding Committee under the NAGWS of AAHPER went into operation. Since then, this activity has been growing in intramural programs more as a club activity than as a competitive one.

Tennis. There was a great outburst of enthusiasm for tennis after 1970 not only in colleges but in the lay world where tennis clubs have multiplied materially, both private and public, so that many cities and larger towns support large tennis facilities through their municipal recreation departments or through privately owned courts used by tennis clubs. America's first tennis stadium, recently built at the University of Wisconsin, is discussed in Chapter 15 under Facilities.

Volleyball. Thirteen states reported 450 high school teams entered in interschool volleyball contests: Maine, Maryland, New Hampshire, New York, Pennsylvania, and Vermont in the East; Colorado, Missouri, and Wisconsin in the Middle West; California in the Far West; and Georgia, Oklahoma and Texas in the South.[13]

Other Sports. Several new indoor sports are being tried out in different parts of the country but since they are still in a first trial stage they are not yet of historical interest.

CHAPTER 15

Amateur Sports of the Latter Twentieth Century

AMATEUR SPORTS ORGANIZATIONS OF LATTER TWENTIETH CENTURY

Participation in amateur sports of a highly competitive nature has increased so markedly in these latter years of the twentieth century that organizations to promote and regulate all of them have also proliferated. In the following material only those organizations that have a great impact on education and national life will be discussed.

Amateur Sports Organizations of the World of Education

The government's Educational Amendment Act of 1972 focused on the integration of females and disadvantaged persons into all phases of education. The world of sports has been materially affected by this. No longer are the educational institutions to be looked upon as primarily a world for advantaged boys and men only. In the 1980s transition is still being made from the old to the new thinking.

In the minds of educators sports have developed in America in the past 150 years into two classes—highly competitive sports for highly skilled boys and men only, and sports for girls, women, and poorly skilled boys and men but only "within the walls" of the home school (intramurals). Now things have suddenly changed. All sports are for all pupils. And if sports are to be offered at all then they must be offered in sufficient variety to meet the needs of girls, women, and the disadvantaged, as well as those of boys and men.

Today many more women participate in highly competitive sports than in earlier years so they attract less attention than in earlier times. There has developed a large body of women trained in physical education who are capable of handling women's sports participation. The attitude of the profession in regard to the participation of women in highly competitive sports situations has changed with the times. The National Association of Girls' and Women's Sports is making every effort to hold the line for standards based on sound education principles and philosophy, and urges all groups that sponsor extramural competition for girls and women to hold to high standards such as these set forth in its own publications.

High School Amateur Sports Organizations. Not all states for their interscholastic sports function under the set title of State Association of High School Athletic Associations. Nebraska high schools, for example, belong in their sports participation under an organization named the Nebraska State High School Activities Association, which is an umbrella group to legislate about and for high school bands, high school debate clubs, and all manner of extracurricular activities with management and promotion of sports but one section of its total organization. However, its sport section is affiliated with the National Federation of High School Athletic Associations.

Boys Organizations. The Federation frowns upon the signing of school boys to professional sports contracts, and one state, Washington, has even passed a law against such activity on the part of professional sports groups. Also, the Federation has definite standards for interschool contests, to which all its member schools subscribe. By 1965 it was sponsoring thirty-three sports for boys, the activities ranging from archery to wrestling. By 1980, there was a still greater variety of sports offered.

Today the State High School Athletic Associations of all fifty states except Texas belong to this Federation including groups in four Canadian provinces. It checks adherence of all state groups to eligibility rules for all sports contests, holding all to local, district, and state level.[1]

By mandate of the State Legislature of some states this organization at the state level is under the State Department of Public Instruction.

Girls' Organizations. In most states, the Girls Division of the State High School Athletic Association takes over all girls' sports.[2]

Title IX has caused all state high school athletic associations to review their purposes and government policies to take in girls' interscholastic sports. By 1974, twenty-nine state associations were known to have added to their boards an advisory group on girls' athletics but this did not mean that women were added to their boards. A 1975 survey by National School Boards Associations showed that women represented only 5 percent of the membership of governing boards for athletics. Five years later that figure had increased to 7 percent.

By 1980 only ten states within NFSHSAA had a girls' advisory board in their athletic set-up and six states had a joint boys' and girls' advisory group; both men and women made up membership in all these groups. Each of ten states had a woman voting representative on the board, and Delaware had two women voting representatives. New York state now includes a woman representative of girls' athletics on its slate of officers of its state organization and the state presidency rotates from a superintendent to a principal to a representative of boys' athletics to a representative of girls' athletics.

Intramural Organizations. Although intramural sports have been engaged in through departments of physical education with little publicity in the schools and colleges from late nineteenth century to today, it has taken over eighty years to awaken the lay world to this type of sports competition. Within the late 1970s there has been born the National Intramural Sports Council (NISC), a joint project of NAGWS and the National Association of Sports and Physical Education of the AAHPERD. Born to promote intramural sports in all levels of education, it is open to membership of all persons involved in the administration of such sports programs whether at elementary, secondary, or college level. This Council functions through the national office of AAHPERD.

The President's Commission on Olympic Sports, in its Report of 1975 to 1977[3] revealed that, as of 1971 to 1972, 1,676,995 men and 276,167 women students in the NCAA colleges took part in the intramural sports programs they offered in over fifty sports, with basketball, softball, and touch football being the most popular with the men, in that order, and with volleyball, softball, and basketball being the most popular with the women, in that order. But such a count of participants (not different individuals) would not have included women's participation in the intramural programs put on for them by the departments of physical education for women in these NCAA schools.

For over thirty years, Girls Athletic Associations (GAAs) and Womens' Athletic Associations functioned at the local high school and college levels sponsored by departments of physical education for girls and women, and at state levels in a few states by State Leagues of High School Girls Athletic Associations, and at college level by ARFCW with their play days to take the place of interscholastic athletics. But the strange interpretation of the mandates of Title IX in many places has come to mean giving up all old single-sex organizations, offering nothing to take their place, with intramural sport being abandoned. In many schools the rich programs of intramurals offered to high school and college girls through the local GAAs and WAAs no longer exist. Gone also are the departments of physical education for girls and women that fostered them. This in the name of equality for women.

College Sports Organizations for Men. Within the college world of sports organizations, the men's full attention seems to turn exclusively to intercollegiate sports which are largely governed by the National Collegiate Athletic Association (NCAA). However, the National Association of Intercollegiate Athletics (NAIA), made up of the smaller colleges and universities and founded in 1945, boasted of 465 college members by the mid-1960s. It was offering a program of nine of the more popular sports. The junior colleges also have their own organization, the National Junior College Athletic Association (NJCAA), to promote their sports competition. It offers both intramural and intercollegiate sports programs within the twenty-two regions in the United States, and each region has its own board of directors.

NCAA. By 1980 this organization was made up of over 900 member institutions, with over 50 percent of them small schools that do not compete on the major college level.

NCAA has had a dramatic growth in membership in the latter years of this century. From 567 college members in the late 1950s it grew to 905 members by 1981. It supports 72 national championships in 21 sports with over 16,000 student-athletes competing under its jurisdiction[4] annually.

NCAA and Its Awakening to Women's Sports. From the NCAA's birth in 1906 until April 1964 not one mention is made of the sports for women in some twenty-three pages of chronology of the main events of its functioning of its first seventy-five years.[5] From the very start it declared itself to be concerned only with inter-collegiate competition but there is no mention that NCAA originated or carried on as an organization for college sports for men only. However, it was clearly so assumed.

The mandates of Title IX of 1972 changed NCAA's "men only" thinking of the past sixty-seven years. However the records show that even a few years before that there had been some push developing for recognition of women.

For April 18, 1964, the chronology carries the following, almost sixty years belated: "Acting upon the request of female college sports leaders, the NCAA Executive Committee amended the executive regulations to limit participation in NCAA championships to undergraduate male students." A day later, the record shows that the Council appointed a Special Committee on Women's Competition to serve as a liaison agency with all other interested groups.

A year later (May 1974) this entry appears in the chronology: "Interpretations by the Department of Health, Education, and Welfare of antidiscrimination provisions of Title IX of the Education Amendments of 1972 threatened the financial structure of intercollegiate athletics." Two months later the NCAA Council called "for the orderly development of women's intercollegiate athletics."

Organizations for Amateur Sports for College Women. Since their beginnings in the late 1890s all organizations for sports for college women have functioned through the AAHPER (under its various titles of 1885 on), thus keeping in close touch with the world of education. This is not true of men's sports organizations which have never been tied to the education world in such manner.

Association for Intercollegiate Athletics for Women (AIAW).[6] This organizaton was born as a substructure of the National Association for Girls' and Women's Sports (NAGWS) to promote women's intercollegiate sports. It was not until 1957 that there developed sufficient interest in intercollegiate sports for women that a need for some form of organization to promote and control it was felt. At that time under the NSGWS of AAHPER a joint committee with the NAPECW was set up to investigate the intercollegiate possibilities but it had no power. Then in 1966 the Division for Girls and Women's Sports (DGWS), a new name for NSGWS, took over the former joint committee work as its own project and developed a Commission for Intercollegiate Sports for Women (CISW) whose purpose was to promote such sports on the basis of DGWS standards. A year later it changed the name to CIAW, substituting the word *athletics* for *sports*. In 1972, the title was changed again to the Association of Intercollegiate Athletics for Women (AIAW), a substructure of DGWS.

The purpose of the AIAW was announced as "to foster broad programs of women's intercollegiate athletics which are consistent with the educational aims and objectives of the member schools."[7] It was hoped that it would be able to avoid the excesses and evils of the men's intercollegiate sports competition—this referring chiefly to the granting of athletic scholarships, recruitment of players, compulsory gate receipts, and a philosophy that winning contests is the all-important thing. It also hoped to avoid for women in sports contacts with sports promoters.

In 1969 it announced national competition in gymnastics and in track and field; in 1970, in badminton and volleyball; in 1972, in basketball. Only colleges that hold membership in AIAW could enter its tournaments and all must accept AIAW rules and regulations. Following the mandate of Title IX, there was a great expansion in women's intercollegiate sports, with the Men's Athletic Departments forced by government decree to finance women's intercollegiate competition as well as that for men.

During the 1970s the number of colleges that became members of the AIAW grew from 206 to 970, a larger figure than NCAA produced for men's sports: On July 1, 1979, AIAW separated from NAGWS/AAHPER to become a completely independent organization with every determination to continue its original focus on education and to keep close ties with NAGWS.

Because of controversy over control of women's intercollegiate sports with NCAA (as related later in this chapter), an antitrust suit against NCAA was filed by AIAW in October 1981, which was to come to trial in October 1982. As this book goes to press, AIAW has suspended operations temporarily as of June 30, 1982. If it wins the case it will renew operations for the school year 1983–1984; if it loses, it will dissolve the organization.[8]

College Women in Sport (CWS). This organization now functioning under NAGWS was originally an independent group known in 1917 as the Athletic Conference of American College Women, in 1933 as the Athletic and Recreation Federation of American College Women, and since 1957 as the CWS. From its very beginnings it was the governing body for intramural sports for college women. The rich programs of intramural sports put on in colleges all around the country for female students from the early 1890s through mid-twentieth century through the local Women's Athletic Associations (WAAs) were sponsored by the local departments of physical education for women.

In its heyday in the 1930s, 1940s, and 1950s, the ARFACW had triennial national conferences which were inspiring occasions when young college girls came together not to try to beat each other at some game but to play together and exchange points of view on intramural sports and to trade ideas about sports programs. From the twenty-three schools that were represented in the charter membership, the organization had grown as of 1967 to a membership of 198 colleges and universities, including junior colleges. Since then, this Federation has aligned itself with the AAHPER, and its organizational work is under the charge of a consultant in the AAHPER National office. Today the old WAAs have largely died out, killed by strange interpretations of what equality in sports means as mandated by Title IX. Gone are most of the strong WAAs of mid-twentieth century which supported rich intramural programs for women in hundreds of colleges. Gone, also, in the name of equality, are the departments of physical education for women.

The United States Collegiate Sport Council. In October 1967 the United States Collegiate Sport Council, made up of the NCAA, NAIA, NJCA, and the National Student Association, held its first meeting. It was established to represent all colleges and universities in the United States in the *Federation Internationale du Sport Universitaire*. World university games were held in Tokyo in 1967, and schools in the United States sent eighty-two athletes. In 1968 the U.S. Department of State allocated $15,000 to help defray expense to U. S. athletes to the World Winter Games in Innsbruck, Austria, and again helped out financially for the summer games in Spain and Portugal in 1969.

National Association for Girls' and Women's Sports (NAGWS). The NAGWS, today's outgrowth of the 1899 effort by Senda Berensen to get national recognition for a basketball rules-making body for girls and women, is a far cry from what it was during the Gay Nineties awakening of American women to the world of sports participation. (The various forms this organization has taken throughout the years are listed in the Appendix.) This group is not a sports-promoting group. Instead it is the rules-making body, the standards setter for sports for girls and women, whether in school or out of school. For the past sixty years it has been an organization backed by hundreds of volunteer workers from within the profession of physical education.

It is doubtful if there is any other group in the profession of physical education that turns out more work or engages more volunteer workers within the profession in its various projects than does the NAGWS. In 1967 over 10,000 women were at work on its many and varied committees and projects, not only putting out the rules of many sports for women but setting standards for sports participation—a task handed on to it by the Women's Division of the NAAF on its demise—publicizing its activities putting on clinics, holding sports officiating training projects, to name only the more important of its many areas of work. Its earlier work along this line has grown until it now maintains local officials rating boards in forty-seven states. Since World War II the NAGWS has also been represented on the National Gymnastic, Track and Field, and Swimming Committees, and in the U.S. Track and Field and Gymnastic Federations. It also worked with the Women's Board of the U.S. Olympic Development Committee.

Although there are other groups in the United States that make rules for various women's sports, the profession of physical education looks upon the NAGWS as the official rules-making body for sports for girls and women. In the year 1966 to 1967 alone it put out eighteen sports guides.

Amateur Sports Organizations of the Lay World

The Amateur Athletic Union. Through the many years of the AAU's functioning from the late nineteenth century on, it has been a bone of contention of all other sports organizations. It has, so it seems, tried not only to be all things to all people in the amateur sports world but also to control it all, and in these efforts it has caused much dispute. There have been years of dissension with college men physical educators of the early twentieth century who wished the AAU to keep its hands off men's intercollegiate sports and individual college men athletes, with lay women and women physical educators of the 1920s and 1930s who wished AAU to keep out of the promotion of girls' and women's sports, with the army and navy, with college men's athletic directors of the 1920s who wished AAU to stop trying to take over U.S. sports for the Olympics, with various mixed groups of both men and women of the World War II era, finally culminating in 1968 with the AAU giving up all attempts to promote and control track and field sports in America.

However, as of 1980, the AAU was still active in promoting a variety of sports for men, women, girls, and boys, outside the jurisdiction of the schools and colleges. This is discussed later under Controverses and Sports Competition.

As of 1980 the AAU was on the U.S. National Governing Board for the Olympics as holder of the franchises for water polo, bobsledding, boxing, lunge, weight lifting, and wrestling; and for the U.S. Governing Board for such non-Olympic sports as baton twirling, handball, horseshoe pitching, karate, synchronized swimming, and tumbling.[9] It reported as of 1975 to 1977, 7000 local sports clubs covering 115 regions and 300,000 volunteer coaches, referees, and sponsors of competition, and 332,000 athletes, 35 percent of whom are girls and women. For men their greatest enrollment is in karate; for women, in baton-twirling.

United States Track and Field Federation. History has a way of repeating itself, and as the National Amateur Athletic Federation was born in the 1920s out of the discontent of many groups with the dictatorial policies of the AAU, so the United States Track and Field Federation (USTFF) was born in 1962 out of continued discontent with those same policies. Founded by fourteen national amateur athletic groups and twenty-one amateur athletic conferences the following charter members were largely instrumental in its birth: National Collegiate Athletic Association, National Junior College Athletic Association, National Federation of State High School Athletic Associations, National Track and Field Association, and the American Association for Health, Physical Education and Recreation. Associate members include among other groups the Athletic Institute, United States Track Coaches Association, and the President's Council on Physical Fitness. It functions under five divisions: intercollegiate, interscholastic, club groups, unattached groups, and allied groups.

Quoting from its publication, *Record,* June 1966: "the members of the United States Track and Field Federation comprise nearly the complete sum total of the grass roots track and field programs of the nation and provide the United States its basic strength and resources in the sport of track and field." Through its member groups it actually covers over 90 percent of all track and field athletes in the country, over 90 percent of all track coaches and all track facilities, and over 90 percent of all money spent on the sport. Similar organizations exist for other sports, but they are too numerous to discuss individually in a brief history of physical education.

As of 1964 the USTFF was made up of the National Federation of State High School Athletic Associations, NCAA, National Junior College Athletic Associations, and National Track and Field Associations, covering over 20,000 high schools and 600,000 male student athletes out for track and field; 559 colleges and universities with 36,300 male students out for track and field; 300 junior colleges with 6240 male students out for track; and over 130 track clubs representing 11,300 athletes. The AAHPER was an allied member with one representative, Dr. Roswell Merrick, on its Governing Council. The Federation claimed a total of 670,901 athletes under its jurisdiction with 27,353 coaches and 13,075 indoor and outdoor tracks at its disposal.[10]

In 1978 the USTFF merged with another group, the USA Track and Field Association (TFA—USA) to become a member of the U.S. Athletic Congress, familiarly spoken of as TAC. It governs track and field sports in both indoor and outdoor meets all over the country.

The Athletic Congress (TAC). The Athletic Congress is the U.S. governing body within the International Amateur Athletic Federation (IAAF) which through merger in 1982 has taken over the functions of former USTFF.

The United States Gymnastics Federation. The United States Gymnastics Federation is made up of representatives from high schools, colleges, YMCA's, and the AAU, and turners, Sokols, and like groups. It was accepted in October 1970, as the official U.S. representative on the International Gymnastics Federation replacing AAU.[11]

Organizations for International Amateur Sports

The United State Olympic Committee[12]. The USOC is the organization within the United States that controls the U.S. entries into the Olympic Games. Above it and in certain authority over it and similar committees of all other nations wishing to take part in an Olympiad is the International Olympic Committee (IOC) which determines where the Games will be held and which sports will be included in the program. Under IOC is an International Sports Federation (ISF) which controls the events within the various approved sports and appoints the officials for these. The national committees of the various nations that wish to enter athletes select their own teams and are responsible for sending them to the games.

The U.S. Olympic Committee was born in 1906, the tenth anniversary of the first modern Olympiad in Athens, but it was 1911 before it took charge of the participation of U.S. athletes preparing for the 1912 games. In 1921 it developed into a permanent organization with its membership made up of a federation of independent organizations. Since then it has been at work for each succeeding Olympiad.

From the very beginnings of the USOC, AAHPERD has appointed a representative on this committee. For many years, Vaughn Blanchard (1889–1969), head of physical education and sports for the public schools of Detroit and president of AAHPER (1947–1948), served as that representative, followed for the past several years by Ross Merrick of the National Staff of AAHPERD.

The USOC, as of the late 1970s a committee of more than 200 members, is made up of nine groups of members. Most members were national organizations, each of which sent a representative to the national committee. Group A had twenty-seven members, each representing a national federation of a given sport (eight sports called Divisions were controlled by AAU and nineteen sports were each represented by its own association). Group B had ten members, each representing some national organization interested in Olympic competition such as: NCAA, NAIA, NJCIA, AAU, AAHPER, Catholic Youth Organization, National Jewish Welfare Board, YMCA, armed forces, and NFSHSA. Group C had thirteen members, each representing a national association of some lesser Olympic sport not covered by members in Group A. The other six groups were made up of an assortment of individuals, fifty of them each representing one of the fifty states.

Relation of National Olympic Committees (NOCs) to the International Olympic Committee (IOC). The IOC, with a membership of seventy-seven individuals all elected by its own members, is a self-perpetuating body. Its headquarters are in Lausanne, Switzerland, and its main function is to supervise the summer and winter Olympics (it also has control over the Pan-American Games). There are 134 NOCs under its jurisdiction although no NOC sends a representative to the IOC. Instead when an NOC is accepted into membership, the IOC chooses one of its seventy-seven members (preferably a citizen of the NOC country if one is a member) who serves as the representative of that nation and its NOC.

Although NOCs are not members of the IOC, each is subject to the rules of IOC, which dictate certain conditions to each NOC, such as (1) all members of an NOC must serve as volunteers, being reimbursed only for travel expenses and per diem to attend the National Olympics Committee meetings; (2) each NOC must have under its jurisdiction the national federation of at least five or more sports that are recognized in the Olympic program, and each of these must belong to its own International Sports Federation (ISF); (3) no professional athlete or coach may serve on an NOC; (4) each NOC controls itself completely as to its own administration, functions, and fund raising; (5) each NOC must have under its jurisdiction a National Governing Body (NGB) for each sport and for which it wishes to enter an athlete in Olympic competition.

The President's Commission on Olympic Sports. Beginning in 1962 such deep problems arose over men's sports between AAU and NSTFF on the one hand and between AAU and NCAA on the other that the President of the United States stepped in to try to get the problems resolved (as is related later in this chapter). As the problems dragged on unsettled into the 1970s, the U.S. Senate in 1974 took a hand in the disputes and passed bills 1018 and 3500 providing for a federal review of procedures for administration of amateur international competition. As a result, the President's Commission on Olympic Sports was established in 1975.

This Commission consisted of twenty-two members, four U.S. senators, four U.S. representatives (all men), and fourteen private individuals (twelve men and two women—Dr. Barbara Forker, head of physical education and athletics at Iowa State University, Ames, and president of AAHPER, 1972 to 1973, and Donna de Verona, a 1964 Olympic swimming medalist. After a two-year study, 1975 to 1976, the Commission reported to the President in a two-volume statement its major conclusions and recommendations. In 1978 Congress passed the Amateur Sports Act of 1978 and the President signed it in November, 1978. This act mandated among many things that the USOC be reorganized, that each National Governing Body (NGB) of each sport under the U.S. Olympic Committee be composed of at least 20 percent athletes at the administration level, that the rights of athletes be guaranteed, that the less influential sports group be involved in the funding of the committee, that disputes be dealt with firmly and settled quickly, and that no power blocs be recognized. It specifically called for attention to sports for the handicapped and for athletes of racial and ethnic minorities.

These federal interventions have not imposed restrictions on the USOC. Direct intervention of government in sports would be against the will of the American people, also against IOC rules and would jeopardize any nation's NOC that bowed to them as permitting nationalistic political influence to enter into their functioning.

The President's Commission recommended that there be established under the USOC a new national organization to be known as the Central Sports Organization (CSO) which would bind together for administration all the NOBs of all the sports considered for Olympic consideration. These transition years may bring about such an organization.

In 1980 the president of AAHPER appointed a committee of five members to represent it in the Delegate Assembly of USOC and to prepare a position paper defining to USOC, AAHPER's role in regard to amateur athletics. Dr. Barbara Forker was appointed chairwoman of this committee for a four-year term, 1980 to 1984, as AAHPERD's representative on the fifty Member Executive Board of USOC.

U.S. Olympic Education Council and the Olympic Academy. In 1934 Dr. Carl Diem of Germany, spiritual successor of Baron de Coubertin for Olympic affairs, visited Greece to plan the arrangements for a first torch-lighting ceremony in which the torch lighted in Greece at the site of the ancient games would be borne by a relay of runners to Berlin where the 1936 games would be held. There in conversations with John Ketsian, a business man and sports enthusiast of Athens, he developed the idea of an Olympic Academy to educate lay people about the possibilities of Olympics if properly administered and supported aiding materially in bringing about a real brotherhood of humankind. The second World War delayed things but by the time of the first games to follow in London in 1948, he had plans ready to submit to the IOC. IOC approved the plans. By 1961 a two-week Academy was held near the village of Ella, 200 miles west of Athens near the site of the ancient games. Two hundred young men and women in the age bracket of 18 to 35 years were to be brought together from several different countries. Lectures were to be given in Greek, French, and English.[13]

From this start plans developed for each contributing nation to develop its own Olympic Education Council within its own Olympic Committee to prepare young people to be chosen to attend the International Academy meetings held each summer in Greece. In the United States the first Olympic Academy was held in 1977 at the University of Illinois, Chicago Circle; in 1978 at the University of Southern Illinois, at Normal; in 1979 at Brigham Young University, in Provo, Utah; in 1980 at the University of Indiana, Bloomington; in 1981 at the Olympic Training Center, Colorado Springs; and in 1982 at Pepperdine University, Malibu, California.

These Academies are gatherings of several days and are open to anyone desiring to attend. From those who have attended, the USOA Committee selects the persons to represent the United States at the next International Academy in Greece.

As of 1980, forty-seven nations were supporting Olympic Academies. For each National Academy (NOA), its Education Council sets up the program and there is serious discussion of the philosophy of the Olympics, their objectives and high goals. Out of these gatherings of recent years has developed the word *Olympism* which connotes a highly idealistic philosophy of sports.

To be considered a candidate of a country to attend the International Academy in Greece, one must have attended the National Academy, (preferably) be of age 18 to 35 years, and be a citizen of the country to be represented. The USOA pays travel expenses from New York City to Greece and return, also room and board at the Academy, and Academy fees.

Olympic Training Centers. In 1976, the USOC set up a training center at Squaw Valley for the athletes who will try out for the games, and in 1977 moved it to Colorado Springs where it was still located in 1982.

The Women's Board of the U.S. Olympic Development Committee. The Board of Directors of the U.S. Olympic Development Committee created a Women's Advisory Board in 1961, which two years later dropped the word *Advisory;* the Women's Board became a functioning group with the following duties: (1) to increase opportunities for girls and women to participate in sports; (2) to help women physical educators to become competent in teaching and officiating in sports; (3) to provide opportunities for women physical educators to give leadership toward properly organized and administered sports experiences for girls and women; (4) to interpret for women the place of competition in our culture; (5) to encourage research in women's sports. In 1963 the Olympic Development Committee approved DGWS as the agent to put on promotional institutes in Olympic sports for women and between 1963 and 1969 it offered five such conferences.

Under the sponsorship of both DGWS and the AAHPER, the Board put on sports institutes in 1963, which were attended by hundreds of teachers from all states, who in turn put on workshops in their respective states, reaching hundreds of other teachers. The institutes in 1963 were on gymnastics and track and field; in 1965, on gymnastics, track and field, kayaking, fencing, and diving; and in 1966, on skiing and figure skating, and on coaching basketball and volleyball.

Other Amateur Sports Organizations

The YMCA's and YWCA's across the country offer a great variety of sports to citizens of all ages. Unlike so many sports groups, they own their gymnasiums and swimming pools and are equipped to carry on on their own. As of 1977, there were 1800 clubs with 6,169,537 members functioning under the YMCAs in the United States and a large majority of these were sports clubs. Through their World Alliance these clubs are readily in touch with similar clubs in eighty other countries. The YWCAs as of 1976 had over 500,000 girls and women participating in their aquatics programs alone. It was the one sport for women offered in competition within the YWCAs and that was conducted at local, state and national levels.

Little Leagues. All over the country are all sorts of youth sports clubs sponsored by local groups, using school and church and community recreation facilities. Perhaps none receive more publicity than the Little Leagues. These leagues have flourished locally for the past several decades but they have grown to such an extent that in latter twentieth century they are organized nationally. A National Pony League conducts national championship contests in Little League baseball, a National Biddy Basketball organization takes care of that sport, and a Pop Warner National League for Little League covers football. Thousands of young boys play in these leagues locally and since spring of 1973 girls also play with some of them.

Sports Organizations for the Handicapped. Following passage of P.L. 94-142, the Education for All Handicapped Children Act in 1975, there were established organizations to care for sports participation for handicapped children.[14]

Before legislative action forced the schools to accept handicapped children within their programs, various lay groups were already organized to help. As early as the 1930s the head of physical education at the School for the Blind in Nebraska City, Nebraska, was putting on an ambitious sports program there. Groups within veteran organizations were in action from late 1940s on.

By 1945 the American Athletic Association for the Deaf (AAAD) boasted 120 clubs with 15,000 members in seven regions, carrying on in softball, volleyball, and basketball. In 1946 the hospitals of the Veterans Administration founded the National Wheelchair Basketball Association (NWBA) which became popular. As of today it has 110 teams playing in twenty conferences. In 1958 the National Wheelchair Athletic Association (NWAA) was founded and that same year put on a national wheelchair games event. As of the late 1970s it claimed around 2500 members. It recognizes thirteen regions in the United States, and U.S. teams are selected to compete every two years in the Pan-American Games and every four years in an Olympiad for Physically Disabled.

In 1968, Special Olympics, Inc. (SOI) was founded for the mentally retarded. As of today it claims that 600,000 are taking part in programs in all fifty states, the District of Columbia, Puerto Rico, and sixteen other nations. But this involves only 15 to 25 percent of all U.S. mentally retarded. The Kennedy Foundation gives this organization $1.4 million annually.

Other sports organizations for the handicapped are the National Handicapped Sports and Recreation Association (NHSRA), the National Therapeutic Recreation

Society (NTRS), the National Wheelchair Athletic Association (NWAA), and the United States Association for Blind Athletes (USABA).

AMATEUR SPORTS COMPETITION OF LATTER TWENTIETH CENTURY

Although there was a tremendous increase in participation in sports in the 1960s and 1970s, there was still a tremendous interest throughout the country in spectator sports, both professional and amateur, so that sports coverage now takes up much of both radio and television time, as well as much space in the newspapers. Also, many new periodicals were established to cater exclusively to the sports scene. Through the promotional efforts of the many sports leagues and associations, both professional and amateur, there has been a great deal of competition going on all the year round in many different parts of the country and in many different sports, with men's baseball, basketball, and football, both professional and amateur, holding the limelight in public attention, with ice hockey, golf, and tennis increasing greatly in spectator sports appeal.

Whereas in years past the seasons of various sports were well defined and did not overrun each other's schedule on the calendar, today these seasons have become so prolonged to meet public interest that the closing dates of one sport's season overlap the opening dates of another sport's season. It has become commonplace to have baseball and football games claiming public attention at the same time in early fall, football and basketball in early winter, and basketball and baseball in early spring.

Since World War II, as in earlier periods, public interest in sports competition still lies mainly with men's sports. Only an infinitesimal number of girls and women go out for the sports that involve gate receipts and "spectatoritis" with their resultant objective of winning at all costs and the settling of important championships. Only a very few American girls and women are of interest to the sporting public. Also, not many women's sports teams achieve even statewide attention, let alone national. However, many small towns throughout the country still develop considerable interest and excitement, over girls' high school basketball teams in particular. But for the great majority of American girls, participation in sports competition is confined to the intramural scene and to the out-of-school world.

The mottoes of the first group of women who organized and promoted sports for girls and women, "A sport for every girl and every girl in a sport" and "Play for play's sake," are not heard so frequently today, although a check with many women leaders in physical education who are teachers first and coaches only second, shows that they still have them in mind.

Workers in NAPECW, DGWS, State Leagues of High School GAAs, and the Women's Division of NAAF who were at work in the 1920s and 1930s will recall the years of fighting AAU in its attempts to take over women's athletics. The real struggle was to protect the factory working girls and the business and office girls without school affiliations, and also to educate AAU to sanity in sports for girls and to the idea that winning at all costs and big gate receipts were not desirable goals in women's sports.

Interscholastic Competition

For Boys. Competition in the United States at high school level is largely controlled, as in earlier years, by the National Federation of State High School Athletic Associations. Highly organized by today, this Federation has splendid control of all interschool sports competitions for high school pupils. It opposes athletic competition on the national level but does sanction sectional events provided they are held in strict observance of Federation rules on distance to be traveled, type of sponsor, and extent to which the event might interfere with smaller events that will include greater participation. It permits no international competition without the sanction of the National Federation and permits no tournaments to determine a national or regional championship. It also prohibits postseason all-star games. It prohibits the transportation of high school pupils to colleges for try outs for future considerations and forbids all home interviews with high school athletes except in the school guidance office.

In the 1970s, 20,000 high schools belonged to the NFSHSA, with over 3 million boys and girls competing in sports in their programs. These 20,000 high schools have 20,000 gymnasiums, 17,000 tracks, 4000 pools. Since 1940, this Association has maintained a full-time staff with headquarters in Elgin, Illinois. Under the National Association are the fifty state organizations and each state group has a State Board of Control. In some states the sports competition is a part of an overall State High School Activities Association and that part of their state association functions according to National Federation Rules and Regulations plus the overall rules and regulations of its State Activities Association.

Throughout the National Federation, depending upon the male student enrollment football is played as six-man, eight-man, eleven-man or twelve-man football. In 1975 the NFSHSAA estimated that high school boys that year had competed in 500,000 basketball games, 250,000 football games, 250,000 baseball games, and 250,000 track meets.[15]

March is tournament month all over the United States for high school boys' basketball. In 1964 to 1965 the greatest number of schools participating in any one activity in state programs were 19,112 schools in basketball, with 639,755 boys entered in the state tournaments. There were 15,524 schools entered in the various state track and field meets, with 512,271 boys taking part; and 13,248 schools in the state baseball tournaments, with 357,145 boys participating. On the other hand, there were only two schools entered in a field hockey tournament engaging 40 boys. These were Canadian schools. Overall in 1964 to 1965 there were 2,891,930 high school boys engaged in various sports activities in the various state tournaments conducted by the state associations of the National Federation. Communities throughout the nation have become interested in having their high schools sponsor winning football, basketball, baseball, and track teams. This has made it possible to erect large gymnasiums, playing fields, and stadiums in which public school students participate. Support for such ventures has come from public taxation, school bonds, or donations from business organizations.[16]

For Girls. Since the Education Amendment Act of 1972 with its mandates of Title IX all schools receiving federal aid must offer sports opportunities for girls equal to those for boys. This has opened the use of physical education facilities to girls' departments of physical education such as they have never known before except in rare schools. The doors of state high school athletic associations which were open almost 100 percent for boys only are now opened to girls too, not only for intramural play but also for interscholastic games.

In most states the State Federation of High School Athletic Associations has taken over jurisdiction of interscholastic sports for girls by creqting a Girls Division within their already well-established state organization, which has from their very foundings of fifty and sixty years ago been aligned with the school administrations. This tie-up means bringing in women physical educators, women coaches, and women sponsors from the school's staff to administer the girls' programs, while binding the girls' programs to the same rules and regulations that control the boys' interscholastic sports, insofar as they are applicable to both sexes. This interpretation of the mandate of Title IX does not mean that girls to be treated equally with boys must be absorbed into the boys' programs but that, whereas the boys have their own program administered through a Boys Division by the SFHSAA, so now in most states the girls have their own program through a Girls Division, administered by women of the school's staff.

Intercollegiate Competition

Many physical educators believe that the emphasis on winning which pervades college athletic competition, if not curbed, will lead to the eventual deterioration of all athletic competition. There is also much concern in education circles over the present-day form of subsidization of college athletes and a growing desire that all colleges follow the example set by the ivy league schools, or, better still, follow the original example of AIAW in regard to women: ban the use of athletic scholarships in all amateur sports.

For Men. Each college member of NCAA is assigned to one of its divisions within which it carries on its competitive program in all its sports. Out of 905 school members as of 1981 there are about 470 schools that do not engage on the major competitive level.[17]

Under NCAA are the Big Ten (Michigan State, Ohio State, Purdue, and universities of Illinois, Indiana, Iowa, Michigan, Minnesota, Pittsburg, and Wisconsin), the Big Eight (Iowa State, Kansas State, Oklahoma State, and universities of Colorado, Kansas, Missouri, Nebraska, and Oklahoma), and Pacific Coast League of ten schools (Arizona State, Oregon State, Washington State, Stanford, and universities of Arizona, California Los Angeles, California at Berkeley, Oregon, Southern California, and Washington). And the East Coast Ivy League is listed below. the U.S. army and navy military academies, and schools like Pennsylvania State and Notre Dame, and many others of athletic fame carry on their competition under the banners of a variety of sports clubs. At the end of the football seasons, the great Bowl Games are played when schools cut across regional lines. There are also basketball interregional games at the end of the season.

In the 1970s collegiate television revenue in football and basketball alone brought in over $25 million per year for several years. NCAA's budget for 1981 to 1982 was $27,889,000 derived primarily from Division I's championships with men's basketball bringing in around 63 percent of the total revenue.

Today NCAA conducts tournaments in twenty-one sports and championships in thirteen sports, with over 16,000 student athletes competing annually.

Although NCAA is generally looked upon as the organization that controls competition within the larger colleges and universities, it does have many member schools within divisions II and III that are small private and church-related colleges. However, many such schools belong to NAIA rather than NCAA. As of the mid-1960s, NAIA had 465 college members and was sponsoring football, baseball, bowling, golf, soccer, cross country, swimming, wrestling, and track and field. Following this lead, the junior colleges under NJCIA joined forces and maintain their own league and foster their own competition.

Competition in the Ivy League. In the college Ivy League (Brown, Columbia, Cornell, Dartmouth, Harvard, Pennsylvania, Princeton, and Yale) the members of the football teams are students in every sense of the word—not men brought in to play in various sports. Strictly amateur, these teams nonetheless draw large crowds and hold student, as well as public, interest.

These ivy league colleges play round-robin schedules with each other, completely under the control of the academic authorities. There are no athletic scholarships. No student who was subsidized as a high school player is eligible to play on these college teams. Each player must be working in earnest toward a college degree, and there are no snap courses or special tutors for athletes. Players receive the same consideration for scholarships as do all other students. The amount of scholarship granted to an athlete is determined by educational authorities and not by coaches or athletic directors. All gate receipts from games go into the college treasury.[18]

Competition in the Sports Clubs. An interesting new development has arisen in the late 1960s in the college sports field that shows how history does at times repeat itself. In several colleges where intercollegiate sports competition has been dropped since 1965, club sports have arisen, all student originated, student managed, student financed as was the situation with intercollege sports during almost the entire nineteenth century. In the fall of 1967 there were thirty-six such college clubs playing games against other colleges. The members of these clubs hire the coaches, buy their own equipment, carry their own insurance, and arrange their own pep rallies. Most of the colleges where these sports clubs exist permit the use of the college facilities. As a rule coaches for these clubs are volunteers who enjoy the sport and thus keep in touch with it. At Marquette University, for example, the 1967 chief coaching staff for the club activities consisted of three high school coaches and a dental student.[19]

Postseason Regional Games. The postseason interregional games as well as the in-season regular games within the various regions have become enormous business today. In early 1968 talk arose within the NCAA about national championship games in college football but nothing came of it. Many college stadiums have been enlarged in recent years to accommodate the greatly increased crowds that turn out for games.

Since then the post-season Bowls have multiplied. As of 1982, there were fifteen postseason bowl games approved by NCAA. There are still others played by lesser leagues.

With most of these games played on New Year's Eve or New Year's Day, the football season in the United States "goes out with a roar." For the 1982 New Year's Day match at the Orange Bowl game, the University of Nebraska squad flew in a few days early in two chartered planes, carrying a squad of around 150: 120 football players, 15 coaches, and around 35 medical staff, trainers, and administrative staff.

Controversies over Men's Intercollegiate Sports. Since it is the NCAA that as of 1982 holds the strings of the largest sports purse in the educational world, it is around NCAA that much controversy over sports exists. Also since it is NCAA that controls most of the male athletes of the college world and has opened the door to get control of the college women athletes, too, it is around NCAA that much controversy has existed in the past and still exists over control of student athletes. The story of early controversies in the man's world has been told in Chapter 8. The ongoing story from the mid-1930s on is revealed in the following record.

During the depression matters drifted. In 1936 the NCAA urged the American Olympic Association to change its constitution to give better representation to athletes from the college world, who by then were beginning to dominate the track and field sports. But things still drifted, and World War II came and went. Throughout the late 1940s and 1950s, controversies multiplied. Finally in 1960 the AAU brought down the wrath of the International Basketball Federation on its head by trying to deny U.S. college basketball teams the privilege of playing a touring Swedish amateur team. Following this the NCAA canceled its Articles of Alliance, drawn up some time before with the AAU, and refused from then on to recognize the AAU's suspension of athletes. In early 1962 the NCAA attempted to bring about a reconciliation with the AAU, but after several meetings, when the AAU refused permission for any other group to attend meetings even as observers and insisted upon a union in which the AAU would have thirty-two out of fifty votes on the Foreign Relations Committee, the NCAA abandoned all hopes for reconciliation. Then the other groups decided to organize the U.S. Track and Field Federation. The AAU was invited to be one of the organizing groups, but it refused to attend the organization meeting. Later it was invited to join the new Federation, but it declined the offer. Following this, increased controversies arose, so that the federal government stepped in and requested that the AAU, the new Federation, the U.S. Olympic Committee, and other interested parties meet in Washington in October of 1962 for open discussion of their difficulties. At this meeting the Washington Alliance agreement was reached as to *closed* and *open* meets and other moot points of contention, and the agreement was referred to the boards of each group concerned for ratification. The USTFF approved the agreement at once but the AAU rejected it. Then the U.S. Attorney General, Robert Kennedy, was drawn into negotiations. This step resulted in the Olympic House Coalition, which was accepted by the representatives of both the AAU and the USTFF. This plan gave equal voting power to the two groups and established a coalition governing body for all U.S. track and field athletics, which was commissioned to petition the International Amateur Athletic Federation for recognition as the U.S. governing body for track athletics. But within a few weeks, the AAU rejected the plan. Then President Kennedy (1917–1963) stepped in and requested arbitration by General Douglas MacArthur, to which the USTFF agreed but the AAU objected. But the MacArthur meeting was held anyway in January of 1963, and a four-point program was drawn up, which among other things set up an Olympic Eligibility Board of three men each from the USTF and the AAU and recommended that following the 1964 Olympic Games the President of the United States would arrange a meeting of all amateur athletic groups to draw up a permanent plan for the control of amateur sports.

That fall, the USTFF issued a notice that its athletes could take part in all amateur meets without the necessity of joining the AAU and paying its membership and entrance fees and obtaining AAU travel permits. This notice was approved in advance by General MacArthur. In 1964, as a result of the MacArthur Agreement, the amateur athlete who was not a school or college athlete, known as an *open* athlete, was also freed from the necessity of joining the AAU in order to compete and was granted the privilege of affiliating with a club of the National Track and Field Association, which is a member of the USTFF. Thereby, *open* athletes can enjoy the advantages of the coaching, facilities, and competition of this national federation.

Then in 1966, as the U.S. efforts in track and field appeared to be jeopardized by continuing controversy, the Vice President of the United States, Hubert

Humphrey, was empowered to select an arbitration panel of five persons, which was made up of a distinguished labor arbiter and attorney of New York City, a former commandant of the U.S. Marines, a former famous U.S. Olympic champion sprinter, a nationally known newspaper editor, and a Harvard law professor who had served as United States Solicitor General under President Kennedy. This Board "directed the AAU to take no action (declaration of ineligibility) against the 300 athletes who participated in the U.S.TFF meets." Despite many meetings of this Arbitration Board, much was left unresolved.[20]

In 1970 the U.S. Gymnastics Federation which had been recognized by the International Gymnastics Federation in 1968 was selected as the U.S. representative for gymnastics, replacing AAU. Then in 1974 the U.S. Amateur Basketball Association was taken into membership in the International Basketball Federation recognizing it as the holder of the United States franchise for amateur basketball. Thus was brought to an end AAU's control over international basketball for the U.S. Gradually AAU's long dictatorial hold on U.S. sports was being broken.

Whereas in 1957 NCAA hired a full-time investigator to look into complaints of broken rules of that day, today it employs thirteen full-time investigators to see that rules are obeyed by schools, coaches, and athletes.[21]

For Women. Winds of change were already blowing before the Feminist Movement brought about the 1972 mandates of Title IX of the Educational Amendment Act. Immediately the question arose as to what was meant by "equality of opportunity for girls and women." High schools and colleges accepting financial aid from the government needed a quick answer to that question. Athletic departments in particular were pushed for the answer. Girls and young women looking forward to interscholastic and intercollegiate sports equal to boys' and men's programs were pushing for the answer.

In the late 1960s the little intercollegiate sports competition for women going on in the United States (compared to the enormous programs of intramural sports carried on in hundreds of schools all over the country) occurred mostly in the individual sports. With the establishment in 1966 of the Commission on Intercollegiate Sports for Women (CISW), under AAHPER-DGWS control, there was considerable growth in such sports. The Commission sanctioned only competition that would involve only full-time college students, was open to all such students, and involved five or more colleges. It was not to select all-star teams.[22]

In 1967 the CISW sanctioned two intercollegiate events, an archery meet in Arizona and a swimming meet at the University of New Mexico. In 1968 it sanctioned a college women's golf tournament and planned for 1969 an intercollegiate gymnastic meet and a track and field meet, and for 1970 a swimming meet and badminton and volleyball tournaments. This changed attitude came about through improved facilities and programs and a larger body of professionally trained women to promote and control these sports. There is still, however, a large group of women leaders who would have sports competition for women held to the intramural form only; others approve of extramural competition but in individual sports only; others approve of extramurals also in a few selected team sports if held to strict standards of participation and conduct; and a few would let down all bars, opening competition for girls and women into a world of sports comparable to that now engaged in by men and boys.

AIAW Takes Over. Immediately after Title IX became known in 1972, AIAW proceeded in the name of equal opportunity to demand recognition by all college educational groups dealing with sports or women. This meant invading the strongholds of NCAA, NAIA, and NJCIA. All AIAW member schools under the jurisdiction of these three organizations for men's intercollegiate sports were soon aware of AIAW's intentions to push women's sports under their own woman's organization, with expectations that each school with membership in both AIAW and one of the men's organizations would see to it that necessary funds and facilities would be made available for the women as well as for men.

NCAA has vast amounts of money for sports—the departments of athletics of their member schools bring in the huge gate receipts from games and income from TV and radio contracts. For the purposes of this book, the NCAA/AIAW encounter suffices as an example of what transpires.

Unlike NCAA, AIAW in its competition in sports does not function through regional groups or leagues. All the sports it sponsors are open to all member schools within any one grouping made up of NCAA, NAIA, and NJCIA member schools.

As early as March 1973, NCAA, apparently not sure of the meaning of the government's interpretation of equal opportunity, accepted a woman athlete of Wayne University to compete in their swimming and diving championship contest along with the men. But it soon developed that equal opportunity did not mean taking women into men's sports groups.[23] No doubt NCAA was relieved to awaken to the realization that AIAW existed to take over women's sports and offer opportunities to women.

The men's athletic department of some colleges that had been begrudgingly paying out from their large gate receipts a wee token in way of cash to finance women's intramural programs in years gone by were now forced by interpretation of Title IX to pay out hundreds of thousands of dollars for this phase of women's sports, alone. Naturally, directors of men's athletic departments of NCAA schools were alarmed. Also, whereas the college athletic departments had heretofore borne no expense for travel for women's teams, they now had such demands made upon their treasuries, and when they tried to hand out women's travel funds only for bus or railroad travel while the men's teams traveled by air, the feminists quickly stepped in and made demands for equal treatment. This plus many more seemingly reasonable demands have caused much controversy—it is a strange new world of sports for both the men and women.

After the 1973 threatened court action that forced AIAW to rescind its rule against athletic scholarships for women, as related below, NCAA athletic directors were claiming that this was threatening the very financial structure of intercollegiate sports. Also NCAA was showing signs of intending to take over women's intercollegiate sports. Opposition of women's athletic directors and coaches began to grow. AIAW, a substructure of DGWS or AAHPER, had no intention to give up its control of women's sports.

In 1974 DGWS as related earlier changed its name to the National Association for Girls' and Women's Sports (NAGWS) although it still maintained its relationship with AAHPER, as one of several national associations. Then in 1980, AIAW, a substructure of NAGWS, petitioned for and was granted separation from NAGWS/AAHPER to become an independent national organization in its own right but retaining close association with both groups.

For almost a full decade AIAW has offered college women a great variety of intercollegiate sports. College women in colleges whose men's intercollegiate sports are controlled by NCAA do not have to confine themselves to sports with these schools only. All women athletes of AIAW member colleges can play women of any other AIAW member college no matter under what organization the men of the same school play.

Many national championships have been run off by AIAW in several sports. Thousands of young women have played in these games. In 1977 it offered nineteen championships in twelve sports. Surprisingly, AIAW has built up a considerable body of women coaches. But in all this activity AIAW has "played it low key and cool" as women prefer their sports. Although the news media is awakening to this new field for public consumption, the women prefer to place the public emphasis on the sport rather than on the individual athletes. It has taken the lay world a long time to realize that equal opportunity does not necessarily mean, for example, that if football is offered to men it must also be offered to women, or that women should be accepted on men's football teams. But equal opportunity does mean that if an intercollegiate sports program is open to men in a college receiving federal aid, one must also be offered to women but not necessarily in the same sports. After 1972 there had to be some effort to allow men and women equality of facilities, equipment, programs, coaching, etc.

Since the AIAW has established its identity as an organization on its own, it has engaged in serious controversy with NCAA.

Controversies over Women's Intercollegiate Sports Competition. With the entrance of women into the intercollegiate sports program supposedly on an equal opportunity basis with men, both the NCAA and the AIAW found that they had many new problems on their hands. The first controversy over women's rights in intercollegiate competition came to AIAW when early in 1973 some women athletes at a private college in Florida were refused permission to play in an inter-collegiate tennis tournament on the grounds that they had accepted athletic scholar-ships. This was against the AIAW rules under which the physical education director and the tennis coach were functioning for intercollegiate competition for women. The student plaintiffs filed suit against a long list of defendents, among them the college, the physical director and tennis coach, AIAW, DGWS of AAHPER, NAPECW and other organizations behind AIAW, attacking AIAW's ruling ban-ning athletic scholarships for women. The ruling was idealistic, hoping to keep women's sports free as much as possible of the evils surrounding men's intercollegi-ate sports; this was AIAW's first serious challenge. Men had been dealing in athletic scholarships for many years. If women were to enjoy "rights" that men enjoyed, so, too, it now seemed they should accept "wrongs," as true educators look upon athletic scholarships. Under legal advice, also advice of DGWS/ AAHPER in the face of threatened law suit, AIAW deleted its rule against athletic scholarships, and the case was settled out of court. But in the wake of this sudden facing up to the realities of a man's world, the AIAW made new rules reluctantly accepting athletic scholarships for women and safeguarding as much as possible the granting of such scholarships with strict regulations for recruiting.

By the late 1970s a struggle had developed as to which—NCAA or AIAW would control women's sports in the colleges under NCAA's control as to men's sports. By 1975 the NCAA reported that 663 NCAA colleges were sponsoring two or more sports for women. In January 1980 NCAA approved within both Divisions II and III five women's championships that it would sponsor—basketball, field hockey, swimming, tennis and volleyball—effective for the 1981 to 1982 school year. At the same time it announced there would be women representatives on the governing bodies of all three Divisions.

Then when the school year 1981 to 1982 arrived the NCAA announced it would offer twenty-nine championships for women: nine each in Division I, eight in Division III, and three open to women in all three Divisions playing together. There upon in October, 1981 the AIAW filed an antitrust suit against the NCAA in the Federal District Court of the District of Columbia[24] and requested the issuance of a preliminary injunction to prevent the NCAA from sponsoring any women's champi-onships while the suit was in progress. The District Court denied the injunction as did the District of Columbia Circuit Court of Appeals. Upon this the AIAW sus-pended operations as of June 30, 1982 awaiting the court decision of October 1982 on the antitrust case.[25]

This seems to be a clear-cut case of history repeating itself. For over 70 years the NCAA fought the efforts of AAU to take over control of men's intercollegiate athletics. Now a women's national intercollegiate sports group is waging battle against the NCAA attempts to take over the control of women's intercollegiate sports from the AIAW.

Nonschool Sports Competition

Little Leagues. These leagues are growing in number. Today many of them are open to little girls as well as to little boys—the ages when the sexes are integrated naturally for play when left to their own devices within neighborhood settings. However, these little leagues are frowned upon by the profession of physical education, and by many physicians, as being far removed from the goals of education and as being a far cry from the normal natural play life of children.

With the advent of Title IX, disputes arose around the country over the one-sex rule and the use of public property. In 1973, the city of Ypsilanti, Michigan, challenged the National Little League over its "boys only" rule declaring that the local Little League could not use city facilities if girls were not allowed to play on Little League teams. In retaliation, the National Little League revoked the Ypsilanti charter. The dispute was finally settled in court with the local league winning the case. But that did not settle the dispute for everyone. In June 1973, U.S. Representative Martha W. Griffith presented Bill H.R. 8854 into the House of Representatives calling national attention to these disputes. In August 1973, the Little League World Series of Games were picketed by the National Organization of Women (NOW), demanding the rights of girls; in November 1973, the New Jersey Civil Rights Division ruled that girls must be admitted in Little League teams; in February 1974, the Appelate Division of Superior Court ruled in favor of girls' equal rights with boys in their sports.

Extramural Sports Competition for Girls and Women. Many girls and women outside the schools engage in sports competition today, no doubt a larger percentage than in any other period of our history. These activities are sponsored by YWCAs, YMCAs, church leagues, sports clubs, and recreation organizations. Archery, basketball, bowling, golf, field hockey, shooting, skiing, softball, swimming, tennis, and volleyball each claim a large following today. Never have American girls and women been so sports-participation minded, and never before have interests, both public and private, made facilities for women's sports so readily available.

Competition for the Handicapped.[26] There are an estimated 35 million handicapped persons in the United States, and since the passage of the Rehabilitation Act of 1973 prospects of hundred of thousands of them for a better life have changed materially. This act of Congress mandates that no person by reason of a handicap may be denied benefits or be subjected to discrimination under any program receiving federal financial assistance. In two of its sections it particularly singles out any organization of any sort receiving federal aid that offers physical education activities or sports in any form to any one. Today, thirty regional and national organizations are promoting physical education and athletics for around one million handicapped persons.

The public and news media are somewhat apathetic to these sports which for their major thrust are mostly concerned with the importance of participation rather than in producing superior performers. There are serious problems of funding and lack of coaches qualified to handle the various types of handicaps.

A brief discussion of the competition that is offered today by a few of the many organizations that exist for sports for the handicapped is offered in the material that follows. The oldest of these organizations is the National Wheelchair Basketball Association (NWBA). By 1948 there were teams in six of the Veterans Hospitals and in 1949 the Association was established and claimed as of the late 1970s that there were 110 teams in twenty conferences. The National Wheelchair Athletic Association (NWAA) started out with a track meet in 1958, with 60-, 100-, and 220-yard dashes and a 100-yard shuttle relay. Since then there have been added the discus throw and an obstacle course, also track and field events, swimming, archery, table tennis, and weight lifting. The Association in the late 1970s claimed a 2500 membership and was holding annual regional meets in thirteen regions.

The American Blind Bowling Association (ABBA) claims thirty leagues in the United States and Canada. It uses a 15-foot guide rail in its national competition. The American Association of Blind Athletes (AABA) started its competitive program in 1977.

For the deaf there is the American Athletic Association for the Deaf (AAAD) which has been a member of AAU for over twenty years. This organization holds Quadrennial International Games for the Deaf, the first being held in 1977 in Budapest.

For the mentally retarded there is the Special Olympics Inc. which, prospering since 1965, culminates in International Games involving basketball, bowling, swimming, diving, gymnastics, dance, soccer, softball, tennis, and touch football. As to the title (which seems to imply that these competitions are a part of the Olympic Games but are not), the U.S. Olympics Committee with its blessing granted these groups the official use of this title.

To prepare for these games there are first the local games in which thousands compete, followed by Area Games which in 1976 were offered in 700 areas. Next come the Chapter Games which in 1976 drew 80,000 competitors and were held in all fifty states and the District of Columbia. The next step is the National Games. In 1976 eight nations held these Games at the national level but it has not yet been determined whether national area games are desirable. Some people are in favor of the games culminating at the state level. However the climax of all these sports is the International Games, put on by Special Olympics Inc. In 1975 over 3000 athletes who had won in local, area, regional, and national meets took part in the International Games.

In regard to all these organizations promoting physical fitness of the millions of disabled persons of our country, who can contemplate the victories of persons who are Gold Medal Olympic winners despite hardships and not realize the value of the work of these organizations. To name but two such persons, Tenley Albright, disabled by polio as a child, won the Gold Medal in figure skating in the 1956 Olympics and is a successful surgeon today, and Bill Toomey won a Gold Medal in the 1968 Olympics in the decathlon despite three paralyzed fingers in his right hand limiting action in handling the equipment for the discus, javelin, and shot put.

International Sports Competition

Today there is much international competition in sports going on all over the world, promoted by a great variety of nonschool organizations and sponsored by a great variety of interests, but none holds the interest of the entire world as much as the Olympics.

Since World War II the U.S. State Department has used athletes as goodwill ambassadors to various foreign countries and has sent athletic coaches to less developed countries to help them set up athletic programs and to prepare teams for Olympic and other international competition.

The Olympics of Latter Twentieth Century. The 1960 Olympics in Rome were historically dramatic, with the marathon race starting at the foot of the steps leading up to the Capitol; passing the Colosseum, dating from A.D. 80, where gladiators fought; and going out into the country, by way of the Appian Way, dating from 312 B.C., where Caesar's Legions marched. The gymnastic events were held in the ancient Baths of Caracalla, the equestrian sports in the famous old Borghese Gardens. For the other sports, Rome built ten new stadiums, a large gymnasium, two sport palaces (including seven swimming pools), and an Olympic Village to house 8000 athletes.[27]

The 1964 Olympics were the first to be held in the Orient. Although ninety-four nations competed in these Olympics, the bickering and quarrels such as accompanied the Olympics of the early twentieth century seemed to have taken on less importance, and the friendships of the athletes to have taken on greater significance.[28]

In the summer games of the nineteenth Olympiad, held in Mexico City in 1968, the bright spot for the United States was Al Oerter in track events, winning his fifth Gold Medal in his fourth entrance into the Olympics, earning them previously in 1956, 1960, and 1964. In the winter games, Peggy Fleming also of the United States stole the show with her figure skating.

In the summer games of the twentieth Olympiad held in 1972 in Munich the Russians produced the fastest man in the world, the highest jumper, the best all-round athlete, the strongest man, and the most exciting female athlete, and to cap it all defeated the United States in its own game of basketball. However, Mark Spitz of the University of Indiana won seven gold medals in swimming.

The summer games of the twenty-first Olympiad were held in Montreal in 1976 where the United States won a few gold medals, mostly in swimming. However, in the winter Olympics at Innsbruck, Dorothy Hamil of the United States played a stellar part in figure skating. The twenty-second Olympics were held in Moscow in 1980. The United States boycotted them because of the Soviet invasion of Afghanistan, but as host to the winter games in Lake Placid, the United States won a surprise victory in ice hockey, stopping the USSR's four straight Olympiad wins in that sport.

International Sports Competition for Women. Since the Education Amendment Act of 1972 was passed many new doors have been opened in sports for women. Although U.S. women have taken part in Olympics since 1920 the way to achieve high goals has been made easier today for those who wish to try for top athletic honors. Since 1952 when U.S. women won their first gold medals in winter sports (introduced into the Olympics in 1924) the United States has developed wonderfully talented women skaters. But it was in swimming that U.S. women first entered the Olympics in 1920 began to "bring home" gold medals, and it is in swimming, thus far, that U.S. women have made the greatest all-round showings, with winter sports taking second place and track and field, third.

It is doubtful whether any women Olympic gold medal winners have created more interest in a sport, worldwide, than the two youthful girl gymnasts of the 1972 and 1976 Olympics, Russian Olga Korbut and Roumanian Nadia Comaneci. As they have traveled about the world with TV appearances displaying their unusual skills they have generated great enthusiasm for gymnastics for women.

CHAPTER 16

The Status of Physical Education in Latter Twentieth Century

During and following World War II, as related earlier, a great population movement began from the rural areas to the large cities, as the country, heretofore largely agricultural, changed to a society that was largely industrial. As a nation we had become enormously wealthy.

NEW DIRECTIONS FOR PHYSICAL EDUCATION

Despite the frustrations, harrassments, and turmoil of the times, the citizenry in general kept relatively calm in the 1960s and 1970s. Several movements and events contributed toward a sane and sound physical education for the latter twentieth century, a few of which are discussed below.

Reawakenings of Earlier Movements

Rediscovery of Dewey's Philosophy. As the passing years give perspective, it appears that the complaints that Dewey's philosophy caused the disappearance from the schools of disciplined work were misplaced, and that it was the radicals among his followers who misinterpreting the philosophy (as he in his book of 1938 insisted that they had) caused the disappearance. Dewey's philosophy, where correctly interpreted, brought about an awakened social consciousness that has strongly affected education in America. At the same time there has developed a swing back to an appreciation for discipline in all facets of life. This awakened social consciousness with a renewed interest in discipline is bringing about an educational philosophy acceptable to the majority of parents and educators. This philosophy is being strongly felt in latter 20th century.

State Legislation. As of 1968, forty-five states were maintaining within state departments of education some person to be responsible for the state program for physical education in the schools. Most people engaged in this special work full time are recognized as state directors of health, physical education, and recreation, but some attend to physical education only as an adjunct to other unrelated work; some look after both physical education and athletics; some, physical education and health education; and some, health education only. Some are designated as supervisors, some as consultants, some as bureau chiefs of HPER, some as coordinators of HPER, some as specialists in physical education, although the title *state director* seems to be the most commonly used.

In the late 1960s, Ohio was maintaining four state directors of physical education (one a woman), and Washington two (one a woman as supervisor of health education and the other a man as supervisor of physical education and recreation). Only two states, Connecticut and Hawaii, had a female director of all health and physical education.

Most states have a state law requiring that physical education be taught in the schools but they vary widely in regard to the number of times a week and number of years of the requirement. In 1967, a group in the California legislature attempted to drop a part of the state physical education requirement but their efforts were defeated. In some states, where the law is permissive, the department of education merely appoints a state director, procures budget support for the work, and goes forward without a time allotment set by law.

As of 1981, Puerto Rico and all states except South Dakota were maintaining state directors of physical education who in most cases were also state directors of health education. Colorado, as South Dakota, does not have a person assigned at the state level for physical education but unlike South Dakota does have a state health education director. Several states have more than one person assigned to physical education at the state level, on a geographical assignment within the state or on grade levels (some overseeing elementary schools, some secondary), so that there are today 124 state physical education directors on the job. Of these only a small percentage are women. As to state directorships in physical education, only five states as of 1981 supported women in this top position: Alabama, California, Indiana, Nebraska, and Oklahoma.

Three states are organized in unusual fashion: Alabama maintains five directors, divided between health education, physical education, health and physical education, physical education at elementary level, and physical education at secondary level; in Indiana, physical education functions at state level not under the State Department of Education but under the State Board of Health; and Mississippi has a state consultant in physical education and recreation but no health education specialist. Some states function on the city–county directorship level for their larger cities.

Rediscovery of Physical Education through the Physical Fitness Movement. The great popularity of the Physical Fitness Movement and its related crazes, such as jogging, marathon runs, aerobic dancing, "jazzercises," and the like have made physical education seem as if it is education's opening of a door to the good life. School children and college youth flock cheerfully to the physical education departments to learn to dance, swim, do gymnastics, or to learn fundamentals of some sport to use in the outside world. It is a great change from the years gone by when girls in particular maneuvered in every way imaginable not to have to "take gym," as a physical exercise class was called. Now it is the "in" thing to acquire skills in physical activities. The old foot-dragging over registering for "gym" is largely a thing of the past.

The Recreation Movement Contributes to the Good Life. An estimated 130 million people visited our National Parks in 1966. The upheavals following the Civil Rights Act of 1964, which opened public doors to all Americans, brought about a new look at many facets of education. It also brought out increased awareness in regard to the recreational needs of all students, including all ethnic groups, females as well as males. The exceptional male students who looked to intercollegiate or interscholastic sports for their recreational outlet had been well cared for in colleges and high schools from the very beginnings of the twentieth century, but not the great majority of boys and men and not girls and women except in those schools where there existed good physical education departments that offered intramural sports and strong Girls' and Women's Athletic Associations (GAAs and WAAs).

In the 1960s there developed an outspoken desire for coed recreation. Physical education departments of a few schools had been offering a few coed activities since the 1930s but they did not reach a large body of students. The 1960s brought a great ground swell from students for such activities and the administrative branches of colleges "got the message." Bypassing physical education departments that had not become aware of this student demand, they brought in recreation experts as nonacademic staff members, or permitted students to organize Student Recreation Associations on their own. They granted them use of college facilities as needed and some set up a student fee for their financing. In the larger schools and universities these recreational activities have grown rapidly with large staffs (still nonacademic personnel) offering a great variety of coed sports, some activities for men, some for women, some of them gradually taking over intramural sports that had been heretofore the sole responsibility of the physical education departments crowding the former GAAs and WAAs off the campus.

Physical education departments in many schools that had not been keeping in touch with the realities of the 1960s had only themselves to blame for this turn of events and lessening of their prestige. The variety of physical activities offered by many of these so-called student recreation groups is a great service to the college communities involved. Some of them today own or have at their disposal their own tennis courts, swimming pools, and three-hole and six-hole golf courses quite apart from any such facilities at the disposal of academic physical education departments. Hundreds, thousands of students (male and female, of all imaginable national origins and races, of all forms of religion—all students enrolled in a college) take part in these student organizations all over the country. All are largely staffed by student volunteers; only the top administrators are on salary and that is not a part of the school academic budget.

Federal Legislation and Physical Education

Justice for Blacks. The Civil Rights Act of 1964 paved the way for today's acceptance of blacks in all phases of public life. It did not disrupt physical education in general for never has physical education on its own discriminated against blacks. Wherever they have been accepted in a school, physical education has not injected discriminatory actions against them on their own as some other departments were now and then accused of doing. In fact, there are no departments of the world of education where blacks have been so welcomed as in interscholastic and inter-collegiate sports. The Federal Act of 1964 posed no problem to physical education other than that encountered by schools on the whole.

Justice for Girls and Women. The year 1972 was quite a year for women's rights. Congress in that year passed one amendment and one act in their favor: one the Equal Rights Amendment of 1972 (ERA), the other the Educational Amendment Act of 1972. The first failed to muster favorable votes from a number of states sufficient to make it a law.

The second was signed quickly into law by President Nixon. Title IX, a part of that act, directly dictated to physical education and sports equal opportunity of females with males in all institutions receiving federal aid. That meant equal pay, equal opportunity in scheduling and programs, and equal use of facilities and equipment, and the like. Many administrators interpreted this to mean, as far as students and their physical education were concerned, males and females treated exactly the same and to achieve that throwing all into classes together. There were no longer to be separate departments of physical education for boys or men and for girls or women. One department head or chairman would now take care of both sexes. This meant that either the male or female chairmanship was closed out and, fearful that they might be accused of discriminating against women, many administrative officers with the power to act at first assigned these united departmental headships to women. The dislocated men in the lower schools who all too frequently in the smaller schools were functioning as part-time coaches were easily absorbed full time back into the classroom. They were not physical educators in the first place. But as the women heads of the new sex-integrated departments retired or resigned, they were too frequently replaced by men so that today the women's former positions as heads of departments largely disappeared within the profession. This in itself has been a loss not only to career women in the profession, but also to the profession.

In some small schools where the limited facilities and equipment were no more than enough for the boys and men alone without making them equally available to girls and women, the administrators chose to meet the challenge by dropping all physical education and sports from their school programs—a grevious loss.

There are scattered about the country some lower schools, and some colleges and universities, where enlightened educators have refused to accept the early strange interpretation as to what *equal opportunity* really means for education. They have maintained departments of physical education for boys and men, and also departments for girls and women. They have also retained male heads for male students and female heads for female students but have coordinated the two departments with some activity classes for females only, some for males only, and some for both sexes together.

Apparently "equal opportunities" to many administrators means "the same," closing their minds to the facts of life—in relation to some branches of education boys and men are not the same as girls and women, and girls and women are not the same as boys and men. These are inescapable facts and should not be ignored in education, especially not when dealing in physical activities of a highly competitive nature. From the very nature of highly competitive sports they need to take into account the physiological, sociological, and psychological differences between the sexes. These differences do not affect the sexes taking academic courses together nor physical education courses together such as dance and some sports.

When it comes to sports, there is a great difference between the sexes from adolescence on in how they relate and react to sports in their own participation, enough difference that in educational settings girls' and women's sports as a rule should be headed by women educators just as men's as a rule should be headed by men educators.

It is going to take many years to undo the harm to physical education that has come about not because of Title IX of the Educational Amendment Act of 1972 itself, but because of the misinterpretations by some administrators of today.

Ask women interested in education what they hoped to win in their Feminist Movement in education for girls and women through physical education and sports and they will most surely say: "Not the same thing as boys and men have but an opportunity to have use of facilities and equipment and teaching staff on an equal basis with boys and men relative to enrollment figures for both sexes and to have the privilege to 'do their own thing,' not imitate the male pattern".

There is a marked difference between the great run of men and women over the philosophical concepts of sports. Women (also many men) concerned about the education of girls and women want above all else to keep girls' and women's sports free of what to them are excesses and misplaced emphasis of men's sports that have come about from commercialization. The typical male sports coach does not seem to understand this, just as does not the great run of male educators in administrative posts.

Justice for the Disadvantaged within Physical Education. From the earliest days of the profession of physical education there have always been a few teachers who have strived to aid disadvantaged children in their physical development, but these were not a specific concern of the schools. The physically crippled child in particular received some special attention as early as the 1890s in a few schools when the Swedish system of gymnastics came to this country; but this was mainly the concern of hospitals and private clinics, which undertook to train physical educators in the specialization of physical therapy work. Following this lead, a few schools did employ specialists in so-called corrective work and did what they could for the school children who needed such help.

Today, awakened by Dewey's philosophy of the early twentieth century and the recent laws of 1970s, physical education is taking a renewed interest in the handicapped. Special training in physical development for the various forms of abnormality is being devised in training schools.

The Rehabilitation Act of 1973 (discussed in Chapter 14) called for every disadvantaged child to be granted public school education equal as far as possible to that given all regular students. It specifically called for physical education and sports according to each child's needs insofar as a child could handle what the schools could offer. This brought about a growing appreciation that disadvantaged children can be trained in physical developmental needs and can handle physical education work of higher quality than heretofore considered possible. There was new interest in classes in adapted physical education. It had been offered in a few schools and in many colleges through their departments of physical education for women, if there was a teacher available trained in Swedish gymnastics as early as the turn of the century. School children and college youths considered unable to handle classwork in regular classes, who had heretofore usually been excused from physical education because there was no course offered to meet their special needs, are now given attention. Special courses for handling such work are increasing markedly in physical education's professional training departments as demands for such special teachers are increasing.

STATUS OF PHYSICAL EDUCATION OF THE LATTER TWENTIETH CENTURY

For the past few decades some physical educators have been questioning the early twentieth century terminology: *physical education* supplanted the nineteenth century *physical culture* and *physical training*. Many have proposed that the term *movement education* or *movement arts* replace the old terms, but by 1982 it has not been generally accepted. As Earle Ziegler, 1982 president of the Academy of Physical Education, points out, it is the experimentalist within the profession who objects to the old terminology and the realist who does not object to staying with the old term.[1] As in all other branches of education, physical education has its pragmatists, realists, idealists, reconstructionists, experimentalists, and essentialists. They counterbalance each other, and together are producing a physical education quite different in many respects from that of any preceding era—a kind of physical education that can be judged best only in the years that are ahead.

The Situation in the Schools

The Lower Schools. The 15,503,000 children reported by the U.S. Office of Education as enrolled in the public schools at the turn of the century had grown to 26,678,000 by 1930 and to 36,087,000 by 1960. The early 1970s brought an estimated figure of 50 million. As of 1980, 57,348,000 are enrolled in public schools; 47,873,000 are white, 8,251,000 are blacks, and 1,224,000 are members of other racial groups.[2]

A decade of adjustment to Title IX has brought about a general acceptance of the idea that if a school has a department of physical education for boys it must also have one for girls, and that if there are already both there, it is not necessary to merge (or submerge one) to achieve equality for both sexes. However, if there are already both established, equality requires both to be so organized that they have equal opportunities in the use of facilities and equipment and in the choice of hours for use and equal treatment in quality of teachers employed to handle the two departments. In pursuit of their physical activities, this plan permits girls to be treated as girls, and boys to be treated as boys. Of course, in some activities that are suited to integration, there should be coed participation.

Certainly even in the chaotic conditions physical education is in, in some schools today, girls have gained in that the boys no longer have, as formerly in many schools, the greater use of physical education facilities and at the choicest hours and with the greatest attention of the teachers and authorities to their needs. But no doubt they have lost considerably in their pursuit of sports, since for their sports they are largely under the supervision of men coaches rather than under physical educators, either men or women. (Generally speaking, there is a big difference between a coach and an educator.) There are few principals or superintendents or coaches (most of whom are usually men) who understand the female philosophy of sports participation. The gulf between male philosophy and female philosophy about amateur sports of intense competitive nature is indeed a deep chasm. However, there are all kinds of shadings to these generalities. Some coaches are also good educators. Some educators are also good coaches.

Equality of Education for the Disadvantaged. The mandate for equal rights to an education for the disadvantaged has also affected physical education deeply but it does not relate to the merging of departments as does the sex issue. In the case of the disadvantaged, integration with regular students is not required for those whose education would be better advanced by their being segregated. Also, if intramural sports are to be offered regular pupils in a school, such sports tailored to their needs must also be offered the disadvantaged pupils under the supervision of physical education teachers. Today some High School Athletic Associations have assimilated some disadvantaged pupils into their regular sports programs.

In the late 1960s, "Bud" Wilkinson, head of AAHPER's Lifetime Sports Education Project in the schools reported that 90 percent of all schools involved had accelerated their physical education programs.

Colleges and Universities. With the rapid growth of new colleges throughout the country in the 1960s and an equally rapid increase in enrollment in the established colleges and universities, physical education, as all other departments in colleges, was "straining at the seams." By 1967 it was estimated that one new college per week was added to the collegiate world, while the state universities were proliferating through the opening of new branches. New junior colleges were also being established in scores of communities. In 1967, there were estimated to be 6 million students enrolled in standard colleges and universities, with another 1.5 million in junior colleges.[3] (California alone supports eighty junior colleges.) Since World War II, there has developed a tendency to cut or drop the requirement in physical education. This has become an actuality in several colleges and universities.

Requirements. In a survey of 1960 to 1961 of college physical education programs, it was shown that 84 percent of those surveyed (and the survey included institutions of all sizes) have a requirement in physical education. Of these, 5 percent had a requirement for four years; 3 percent, for three years; 68 percent, two years; and 25 percent, one year. Of those institutions with a requirement, 76 percent give credit for the work, with the larger institutions predominating in this group. Fifty percent of the institutions of over 5000 enrollment have a swimming requirement for all students.[4]

Facilities. With inflation rampant these latter years of the twentieth century, the few new buildings for physical education that have been erected recently have cost a seeming fortune. Vassar College, one of the more prestigious of the women's colleges, has become coeducational and in 1981 completed a $5 million physical education project which has among its many wonders a solar-collector system to heat water for baths and its six-lane swimming pool. (The University of Nebraska—Lincoln was one of the earliest institutions to try out the solar-collector system to heat water for the gymnasium baths and pool—this in its 1968 new women's gymnasium.) The natatorium in Vassar's old gymnasium has been converted into a dance center.

In many colleges and universities, former men's or women's gymnasiums have been changed into coed gymnasiums, but many of these conversions have been makeshift. New structures intended from the first as coeducational buildings should prove more satisfactory.

The Nielsen Tennis Stadium, at the University of Wisconsin, dated 1968, was a $2.4 million gift and is claimed to be the world's largest such facility. It has eighteen courts and can serve 6000 players per week, all year round, in all weather, all seasons, day and night. Of its eighteen courts, six are squash racquets courts (one of them double), and twelve are tennis courts (two of them exhibition courts). The entire building is air-conditioned for all seasons of the year. The tennis courts are forty-two feet high for high lobs. There is provision for as many as 1500 spectators, and dressing room lockers for over 1000 participants. Besides the usual dressing and shower rooms, there is a players' lounge.

The building is 392 by 330 feet in size, with eight separate building sections, each with its own high roof. It is conveniently located near the University Intramural Sports Field. For a small fee, it is available for physical education classes, intramural and intercollegiate sports, and to all students, faculty, and staff.

Recently an alumnus of Coe College presented that Iowa school a gift of over $2 million for a similar facility to be erected on that campus.

The Elmer D. Mitchell Recreation Field at the University of Michigan, dedicated September 25, 1981, is most unusual in that it provides for a variety of recreational sports and for its six softball diamonds all lighted for night play. This new field at Michigan added to the older intramural field makes that institution unusually well equipped to care for the sports interests of the great majority of students who do not care to participate in intercollegiate sports.

A Question of Woman's Place. The Feminist Movement with its drive for women's rights seems to have backfired as far as women teachers in physical education are concerned. The great drive for "oneness" or "the same" which higher-up men administrators have interpreted Title IX to demand, has developed not in a union of men's and women's departments to work out together a new form of joint organization but in a submergence of women's departments under almost total male management.

When the mandate first came which was interpreted that men's and women's departments must give up their old identities and become a new joint group, out of fear of being accused of favoring men over women the headship of the new joint department was in many cases given to the former woman head rather than to the former man head. (A few higher administrators took their chance at the criticism and cries of "foul" from radical feminists and gave the headship of the new joint group to the former man head.) In the very nature of the changeover, one of the two former heads was out of a position—at least out of a chairmanship of a department. Many found employment elsewhere, some left the profession for other careers. The ones who stayed on were absorbed into heavier teaching roles—no one was actually dismissed as the records seem to reveal the story.[5]

In a few years, as the women who stayed on in the headship retired or resigned, a man was frequently appointed to fill the vacancy until today the majority of these positions are filled by men. In 1980, eight out of the nine merged departments of physical education of the Big Ten universities were headed by men. As of the school year 1981–1982 only a few of the merged departments were headed by women of the physical education profession. However, in a few colleges and universities (probably four or five), the directorships of all athletics and all physical education for both men and women students were held by women physical educators (for example, Mary Jean Mulvaney at the University of Chicago). A survey of 1977 shows that men's salaries were still higher than women's in the field of physical education, men's teaching loads on the whole were lighter than women's, men were assigned to more graduate courses than were the women, and men attain higher professional rank more readily than do the women.[6]

Before these mergers young girls in the lower schools and young women in colleges had the woman head of the physical education department to turn to for many of their problems, as young boys and college youth had their man head to turn to for theirs. It has throughout this entire century been general knowledge among school children and college students of both sexes that their physical education teacher can usually be counted upon for help in times of emotional stress. Students come to feel at ease with their physical education teacher who has led them in sports, gymnastics or dance, and mingles with them in the relaxed, familiar atmosphere of the locker and dressing rooms.

Some schools, some colleges (a small percentage of the whole) have higher administrators who have refused to bow to these interpretations of what is meant by "equal opportunity" and have kept their two segregated departments of the years before Title IX intact, but coordinated the two where coordination had not existed before to see that girls and women are receiving their just share of facilities, equipment, funds, and teachers. In these schools and colleges, the philosophical, subtle, immeasureable relationships between women teachers and girl students and between men teachers and young men students have been maintained, and equality is achieved without the great harm to women's physical education encountered today by forced integration of the sexes in all physical education work.

Research for the Profession. The greatest amount of research in the field of physical education is carried on in colleges and universities. As of 1980, the Editor, the four members of the Advisory Committee, and all fourteen Section Editors of AAHPERD's *Research Quarterly* were persons located in universities stretching from the Atlantic to the Pacific and practically all the published articles came out of the research laboratories of colleges from all over the country.

The profession's research work had increased so markedly by the late 1960s that the national professional office added to its staff a Research Consultant. At the same time, AAHPER increased the size of its *Research Quarterly* in an attempt to keep abreast of the enlarged accumulation of reports of research. In 1980 the old

Quarterly of 1930 changed its name to *Research Quarterly for Exercise and Sport,* which more clearly defines its present scope of interest.

The national professional organization maintains a Research Consortium and a Measurement and Evaluation Council. It conducts research into the problems of the aged, the physiology of space flight, physical fitness, and a great array of investigative topics. A sampling of the great number of researches in progress can be seen in the kinds of offerings by the Research Consortium at the 1982 AAHPERD convention in Houston: 155 research papers, 158 research abstracts, 19 research symposiums, and the reports on the results of 36 research projects.[7] This research work covers health education and recreation as well as sports and physical education.

Professional Preparation. As of 1965 there were 539 colleges and universities offering professional preparation in physical education. Figures as recent as 1980 are as yet unavailable. But today some institutions offer professional preparation in health education only, a few in recreation only, and some in physical education only. Some offer preparation in both health education and physical education, some in both recreation and physical education, and some in all three fields. These institutions are located in every state of the Union and in the District of Columbia, some offering only an undergraduate major in the department of physical education; some offering also graduate work there; others functioning within a university as a school or college of physical education, combined with health and recreation training at both graduate and undergraduate levels; and some offering highly specialized training leading to work with people needing special education or in the field of dance. The world of professional education in physical education is a changed world since the turn of the century, even since World War II.

This era has produced many conferences on professional preparation, many sponsored by the AAHPER, some on undergraduate and some on graduate preparation. Out of these has developed self-evaluation checklists for the training program and for the institutions involved, and also a directory of institutions offering professional preparation. From these conferences has come an approach at standardization and an upgrading of specialization.

Today in some quarters there is renewed talk (as there had been in the 1920s following the lead of Wellesley College, which required five years for a major in physical education) of making the requirement five years for a bachelor's degree with specialization in this field. The talk claims justification in the curtailment of cultural subjects that occurs in a four-year program when the heavy science requirements added to the heavy physical activity requirements cut a student's time available for valuable liberal arts courses to a minimum. From others comes talk of requiring all physical education majors to complete a full academic major as well as the professional one, which also would tend to extend undergraduate work into a fifth year.

A study of the institutions offering graduate work in physical education raises some doubts as to the quality of the graduate work being done, when one contemplates the inadequacies of size of staff, the facilities, and the equipment available in some of these schools. Also, how much of the so-called graduate work is actually of graduate level rather than being merely more undergraduate work following the bachelor's degree, the profession needs to determine for the protection of its professional standing in the world of education.

Final Disposition of the Last of the Early Private Schools. Of the several private schools of physical education which had flourished in late nineteenth and early twentieth centuries, all had closed their doors or found final collegiate homes by 1960 except the Bouvé–Boston and the Sargent School of Physical Education. After eleven years of affiliation with Simmons College and twenty-two years with Tufts University, the Boston-Bouvé School of Physical Education withdrew in 1964 to become the Bouvé College of Northeastern University.

The early Sargent Normal School of Gymnastics which had since 1933 been Sargent College of Boston University was in 1967 renamed the Sargent College of Allied Health Professions to reflect its broadened scope which had embraced physical therapy in 1951, therapeutic recreation in 1960, occupational therapy in 1963, and a graduate program in physical therapy in 1966.

Specialization in Dance. The seventeen colleges and universities that were offering specialization in dance in 1947 had increased to fifty by 1967. Besides these, sixty-three other institutions were offering courses in dance concentration, and twenty, a dance minor. Of these many dance majors, some are in the field of dance education, others in the field of performing arts. Also as of 1967, twenty-nine schools were offering summer schools of dance. No doubt figures of early 1980s have increased even more. The National Association of Dance of AAHPERD releases the figures of the latest count. Dance seems to be one of the fastest growing specializations within the profession.

Accreditation. In 1960 the AAHPER voted to place itself under the accrediting jurisdiction of the NCATE. Now the AAHPER recognizes only those teacher-training programs approved by this organization, and urges state departments of education and the National School Board Association and local school boards to hire only physical education teachers who are graduates of departments, schools, or colleges of physical education approved by the NCATE.

Professional Literature

When an older member of the profession ponders the poverty of professional literature in the field of physical education at the turn of the century, even of the post–World War I era, it is difficult to realize the full extent of today's offerings of sixty to eighty years later. Today there are books on psychology of sports, philosophy of sports, sociology of sports, and the like. The inquiring reader and student need only to keep in touch with the *JOPERD* of AAHPERD to be continually alerted to the wealth of books coming off press from many different publishing companies.

The national association itself has developed a large publishing department, putting out several different magazines and a continual stream of books and booklets to serve its variety of members. A catalog of all its publishings is available. Its main on-going publications are the *Journal of Physical Education, Recreation and Dance* (nine issues per year) and *Research Quarterly of Exercise and Sport* (both free to members).

The profession also in the 1970s undertook a four-volume project—an *Encyclopedia of Physical Education and Sports*. Volume 1 under the editorship of Reuben Frost, Emeritus Professor of Springfield College, *Sports, Dance, and Related Subjects*, came off press in 1977; Volume 2, under the editorship of G. Allan Stull of the University of Minnesota, *Training, Environment, Nutrition and Fitness*, was off press in 1980. Starting in the late 1950s, NAPECW and CPEAM jointly published *Quest*, which is in 1982 running the thirty-fourth volume, and the new North American Society for Sport History puts out its *Journal of Sport History*, the 1982 volume being the eleventh.

As to history, the profession has been slow in awakening to its potentialities in that field. For over thirty years, Edward Hartwell and Fred Leonard, to whose memories this book is dedicated, served the field unchallenged. Then in the 1920s following Fred Leonard's death, Emmet Rice took up the challenge, unopposed except for brief historical articles in magazines on specific topics published by a variety of writers. It was then another thirty-five years before the Association's seventy-fifth Anniversary Celebration (1960) kindled a spark for an awakening.

Preceding that by a few years, Elmer Mitchell, Debold Van Dalen, and Bruce Bennett in 1953 published their *World History of Physical Education*, which was issued in 1971 in a second edition by Van Dalen and Bennett alone. In 1958, John L. Hutchinson and I took up the challenge to revive the earlier Rice book, *A Brief History of Physical Education*, bringing it out in a fifth edition in 1969. In 1966 Charles W. Hackensmith offered the profession his *History of Physical Education*.

Following the publication in 1960 of the seventy-five-year history of the national association,[8] which Bruce Bennett and I had been invited to do, there developed a body of physical educators who, awakened to the profession's historical heritage, wished to delve into the histories of the district groups of the national professional organization. The first to awaken to this void in historical research was the Midwest Association of Physical Education, which persuaded me to write its history from its founding in 1912 on. Today's Central Assocaition had been a full half of that history, 1912 to 1933, when the old Middle West Society of Physical Education divided into two districts, one east of the Mississippi, the other, west, to make today's two districts. I volunteered my services to the cause provided the historical production would be a joint venture of both groups since the years of 1912 to 1933 marked a period of common history for the two groups. Both groups favored the plan and shared the costs of production equally. This first district-history came off press in 1963, entitled *The History of the Middle West Society of Physical Education.*[9]

Four years later this venture was followed by Part 2—*History of the Central District of Physical Education, 1933–1963.*[10] The Midwest District also started to prepare its history, 1933 on, but the venture was never completed. Various writers have offered in isolated magazine articles bits of histories of other districts, but no book or booklet with a full history has as yet been published on other such regional histories. For the Centennial of AAHPERD in 1985 a hundred-year history is planned under the direction of AAHPERD historian, Harold Ray.

Of recent years there have been published several compilations of articles by several authors, each dealing with specific phases of the profession's history in America, all excellent supplementary reading materials in any course in the history of physical education.

Physical Education in Nonschool Groups

Physical education is very much alive in latter twentieth century in many organizations not connected with the schools—organizations knowledgeable about and sympathetic toward education's aims and objectives for physical education. The more far-reaching of these are discussed in the material that follows.

The YMCAs. As of today the World Alliance of YMCAs is made up of YMCAs in eighty countries. As of 1982, the YMCAs of the USA have increased over 50 percent and the number of its physical directors has doubled since mid-century.

The YMCA has materially increased its service to women and girls, particularly in communities where there are no YWCA programs. About 70 percent of all newly established associations make provisions for them in their sports and recreational offerings. As of 1977 there were 1800 YMCA clubs with 6,169,537 members, about 35 percent of whom were women. The physical activities alone account for 75 percent of their memberships. In the 1970s they were offering eleven Olympic sports with track and field being offered at both local and state tournaments. As a rule, they use AAU sports guides for boys' sports.[11]

In this era they have put on nationwide many sports conferences and tournaments. Aquatics play a big role in their programs.

The YWCAs.[12] The YWCA of today, with World headquarters in Geneva, Switzerland, claims to be the "oldest and largest women's membership organization in the world." Out of 183 countries it serves, it maintains 6000 locations in the United States alone, with 2.5 million members, as of August, 1979.

For the year 1978 to 1979, the National YWCA reported 1,038,597 members enrolled in the physical education and athletics classes, about one-fifth of them boys and men. In the camping program that year, 25,700 girls and women were registered, and 18,317 boys and men. Out of a total of 5182 locations it used for its physical activity classes located n all fifty states, it used in addition to its own facilities those of 1035 schools, 451 churches, 744 parks, pools, golf courses, tennis courts, and bowling alleys.

Many YWCAs have their own swimming pools, and many others rent them from local sources. Thousands of girls and women as well as boys and men enroll in their swim, dance, gymnastics, and sports classes, and thousands more enjoy their camping programs. Several hundred women are employed full time and head their physical education departments.

Other Related Groups. Girl Scouts, Boy Scouts, the Young Men's Hebrew Association, the Young Women's Hebrew Association, and many other like groups offer boys and girls, young men and women, many opportunitites to engage in physical, educational, and recreational activities in all-year-round programs. In response to the federal government's drive of the 1960s and 1970s for equal treatment of the sexes and integration of races, the Camp Fire Girls organization has responded in an unusual way by opening its doors to boys as well as girls and dropping the word *girls* from its 60-year-old name to reflect its new status. It is now known as Camp Fire, Inc. Wherever possible, it offers its members programs of camping, outdoor living, wilderness experiences, canoeing, and the like. For years it claimed to be "the first national non-sectarian, inter-racial program for girls," it has now gone "coeducational."

NATIONAL PROFESSIONAL ORGANIZATIONS

Several of the national professional organizations that are serving the profession today are discussed below in the order of their founding. The presidents of AAHPERD and presidents of other early national groups through their early years are listed in the Appendices following this chapter. The form of organization of the over-all mother professional group, AAHPERD, is discussed in the material that follows in the hope that the student in training or young teacher in reading this will become somewhat acquainted with this organization, will be aware of its subdivisions, and will take out early membership and become an interested working member. Entering into the work of some of its subdivisions gives meaning to a career and advances the profession.

The American Alliance for Health, Physical Education, Recreation and Dance

The oldest national organization has been in continuous service to the profession, the AAHPERD, was founded in 1885 as related in an earlier chapter. It has been known by the present title since 1974 when it changed its form of government to embrace a group of national associations, which had grown in importance to the profession from their earlier years of functioning as sections and/or divisions of interest within the Association. It then took on the title, Alliance, thus retaining its former alphabetical abbreviation of AAHPER. Then in 1981, it recognized the former Dance Section, born in 1932, as a National Association of Dance (NAD) and added the word *Dance* at the end of its already lengthy title.

Form of Government of AAHPERD. The original American Association for the Advancement of Physical Education (AAAPE) of 1885 was "going strong" as it approached its centennial year. Earlier chapters (7, 10, and 13) give the story of its growth through the years.

There was now a more logical form of government and an all-inclusive one covering the entire nation geographically and opening doors to all logical interests of all members—truly national in every way.

In 1960 the Association celebrated its seventy-fifth anniversary at its April convention in Miami Beach. That month's issue of the *Journal of HPER* was devoted to the story of its full history and to biographical sketches of its early leaders.

Beginning in 1965, the Association has sponsored a Life-Time Sports Education Project. The project was set up on a three-year trial basis, and through its many clinics it has brought about a marked increase of interest in lifetime sports in school programs.

As of 1968 the Association took on a Territorial organization, the Guam Association of HPER, and in the early 1970s added to that the Puerto Rico Association.

By 1967 the divisions had grown to eight and the sections under them, to thirty-two. In 1968, AAHPER established the McKenzie Award for outstanding contributions to the welfare of man through service to the profession and participation in wider education and community relationship. With the passage by Congress of various acts of the 1970s, AAHPER has been deeply involved in the problems of equality for girls, women, and the disadvantaged. In 1974, as related above, the association again changed its form of government becoming the American Alliance for Health, Physical Education and Recreation, and in 1980 added Dance to its title, although Dance had long been a concern of the physical education section.

Today's Organization. Fifty states support a state association of HPER, also professionals in the District of Columbia, Puerto Rico, the Virgin Islands, and Guam are organized, each with a representative on AAHPERD's Alliance Assembly. All of these grass-roots also belong to their respective District Associations, with the six Districts also represented on the Alliance Assembly.

Since 1980 it maintains national headquarters in its own new building in Reston, Virginia,[13] near Washington, D.C., where it maintained headquarters in the NEA Building from 1938 to 1980. As of 1981 it had a national headquarters staff of thirty-three paid workers, plus the necessary secretorial and office assistants. Aside from this staff there are continuously several hundred members of the Alliance who serve untold hours per week all the year around in its various subdivisions and on its various committees. All of these are volunteer workers, as is generally the case in all like educational and professional organizations.

The Board of Directors is made up of the President, Immediate Past-President, President-Elect, Executive Vice-President (ex-officio—a full-time employee, head of national headquarters), a representative from each of the six District Associations, and heads of the several national associations. The seven national associations under AAHPERD are as follows: American Association for Leisure and Recreation (AALR), American School and Community Safety Association (ASCSA), Association for Advancement of Health Education (AAHE), Association for Research, Professional Councils and Societies (ARPCS), National Association for Girls' and Women's Sports (NAGWS), National Association of Sport and Physical Education (NASPE), and National Association for Dance (NAD).

In the national office the Alliance maintains specialists on programs for elementary schools, handicapped persons, and student services. It also assists members through a job exchange and through its several publications. For the latter, it has a publications department and each year it puts out many pamphlets, booklets, and a few books to aid the profession (listed in its publications catalog). It puts out three monthly periodicals: the *Health Education Journal,* the *Journal of Physical Education, Recreation and Dance* (each nine issues per year), and *UPDATE* (a newspaper type of monthly of ten issues per year); and one quarterly, the *Research Quarterly of Exercise and Sport.* Besides these, it also puts out for various subdivisions, news bulletins, and like materials.

National College Physical Education Association for Men (NCPEAM)

The original Society of College Gymnasium Directors of 1897 became the Society of Directors of Physical Education in Colleges in 1908, the College Physical Education Association in 1935, and in the 1960s it took on the long title above. By 1960 it had a membership of 675, representing 45 states and 320 colleges and universities. For over seventy years it has been a strong influence in the promotion of the best interests of the profession. Gradually losing its effectiveness after World War II it joined forces with the women's group, to be discussed later. In 1977 it ended its career as a one-sex organization.

National Association of Physical Education for College Women (NAPECW)

From the small group of sixteen women physical directors (representing three district groups previously established) who were present when the NAPECW was officially declared established in 1924, it had grown to a membership of 1481 as of May 1967, representing over 200 colleges and universities from all sections of the country with membership open to all college women staff members. It developed into a working organization with over 10 percent of the members actively at work on committees promoting improved physical education for women in colleges. For the past several years the organization has sponsored workshops which have been held biennially.

In 1963, in conjunction with NCPEAM, it initiated the joint publication of *Quest,* a quarterly magazine, which beginning with the 1979 volume has been published by the new joint organization NAPEHE discussed below. In 1967 NAPECW established a lecture series to the memory of Amy Morris Homans.

This national group had a long and meaningful career as a one-sex organization until 1977 when it joined forces with the waning CPEAM to create a new cooperative endeavor. Unlike the men's group it had a splendid treasury, a large membership, and was still a strongly felt force in the profession on women's affairs and the professional preparation of women physical education teachers. But the Feminist Movement was crying out for integration of the sexes all along the line of education. The decision in 1977 to consolidate with the former college men's group was of course decided by majority vote but the losing minority was a large bloc. It was not a case of the younger women out-voting the older ones. There were many women both older and younger, who felt that girls' and women's physical education under varied circumstances still needed to be looked at from a woman's point of view, and a woman's philosophy of physical activities for girls and women. NAPECW had been doing this for over fifty years, and many felt that the need still exists. There is no other organization to fill this place. But the majority voted for union with the men's group, and NAPECW as a woman's organization ceased to exist as of 1977, except through its various district groups, which with the exception of the central group, have maintained their one-sex status.

Society of State Directors of Health and Physical Education

Although there were state directors of physical education or of health and physical education as early as 1916, it was not until 1926 that there were as many as twelve states so organized in their state departments of education. At that time these few came together and with Carl Schrader of Massachusetts as their first president founded the Society of State Directors of Physical Education. Five years later Jessie R. Garrison of Alabama was the first woman to hold such a position. (She had served two years previously as acting director.) This organization has been functioning over fifty years now and from its very nature is a small group which is a great source of support to its members.

The American Academy of Physical Education (AAPE)

From the group of twenty-nine charter members of 1930, this organization has grown until in 1981 it has a membership of 107 active members, 64 retired fellows,

26 associate members from related professions, and 63 corresponding fellows from 29 foreign countries. Through its many foreign contacts, it serves as a liaison group between physical educators of America and those of the rest of the world. Its "steadfast belief in the integrity of physical education as a significant attribute to the perpetuation of American culture" is the keystone of its functioning.

American College of Sports Medicine (ACSM)[14]

The American College of Sports Medicine was founded in 1954 through the initial efforts of three physicians and a physical educator: Joseph B. Wolffe, M.D., Director of Valley Forge Heart Institute, Albert S. Hyman, M.D., a cardiologist, Ernest Jokl, M.D., then working with Dr. Wolffe but for many years before on the physical education staff of the University of Kentucky, and Grover W. Mueller, Director of Physical and Health Education, Philadelphia Public Schools. The founding meeting was held in connection with the AAHPER convention in New York City, April 1954, when all delegates attending those meetings were invited to come to a meeting to consider the founding of such an organization as those four had contemplated. Out of the group that responded favorably to this invitation, eleven persons definitely expressed a desire to become charter members and thereupon the organization was born with Dr. Wolffe elected president, Peter V. Karpovich, M.D. of Department of Physical Education, Springfield College, and Neils Neilson of the University of Utah as vice-presidents, and Grover W. Mueller, secretary. Of the eleven charter members, five were M.D.s (two of whom, Karpovich and Jokl, were looked upon also as physical educators) and six were physical educators, so the ties of this organization with physical education have from the beginning been very close. The four physical educators who were not also M.D.s, besides Mueller and Neilson mentioned earlier, were all Ph.D.s—Clifford Brownell of Columbia University, Leonard Larson of Springfield College, Josephine Rathbone Karpovitch, the only woman in the group, of Columbia University, and Arthur H. Steinhaus of George Williams College. All charter members were physicians, physical educators, and physiologists organizing for the purpose of promoting scientific studies in relation to the effect of sports on health and fitness, to cooperate with other groups concerned with human fitness, and to initiate and encourage research on the subject. The organization holds workshops (frequently in conjunction with the annual convention of the AAHPER), makes postgraduate education in sports medicine available, and publishes a scientific journal dealing with human fitness. The permanent office has been located on the University of Wisconsin campus since 1965.

By 1982 it claims 9000 members and affiliation with several professional organizations, chief among them the American Medical Association and AAHPERD as well as its international contacts through the Federation Internationale de Medicine Sportive. It publishes a scientific journal five times a year and a quarterly *Sports Medicine Bulletin* and holds annual conventions covering all parts of the country.

North American Society for Sport History (NASSH)

Following World War II interest in historical research in sports gradually awakened. With this aspect of research neglected by both AAHPER and the Academy of Physical Education a group of interested parties founded NASSH in May 1973, with its founders meeting at Ohio State University, with Bruce L. Bennett serving as host. The first officers were Marvin Eyler, University of Maryland, president; Guy Lewis, University of Massachusetts, Amherst, president-elect; Ronald A. Smith, Penn State University, secretary–treasurer; and Bruce L. Bennett, Ohio State University, Betty McCue, University of Oregon, and Mary Lou Remley, University of Wisconsin, as members of the Executive Committee. Alan Metcalfe, University of Windsor, Canada, was chosen as Editor. Seward Staley, former head of the School of Health and Physical Education, University of Illinois, was the main influence behind the founding of its *Journal of Sport History,* and each year the Society presents a lecture in his honor. The wealth of historical research attested to in the variety of articles in the first eight volumes of its quarterly *Journal* bespeaks its hewing to the line to carry out its original purpose to help preserve the history of sports in North America.

National Association of Physical Education in Higher Education (NAPEHE)

The latest national organization grown from physical education is NAPEHE which was born in 1978 from a uniting of the earlier CPEAM and NAPECW, as discussed above. It is carrying on NAPECW's earlier Amy Morris Homans Lecture Series, which is given each year in connection with the AAHPER convention. In 1980 it initiated a commerative lecture series honoring Dudley Allen Sargent, given annually at NAPEHE convention.

American Association of Fitness Directors in Business and Industry

Business and industry have become sufficiently concerned about physical fitness of both their employers and employees that there has developed a group of directors of physical fitness in business and industry that has organized for mutual help and inspiration. The American Association of Fitness Directors in Business and Industry (AAFDBI) was established in 1975 by a group of thirty-nine persons representing large corporations and organized for mutual benefit as an affiliate of the President's Council of Physical Fitness and Sports. By 1982 this group had grown to a membership of 2200.

It holds an annual national conference and puts out a monthly bulletin, AAFDBI ACTION. It maintains close ties with the American College of Sports Medicine for advice on its fitness programs. Through the nation's business and industrial groups this organization conducts fitness programs reaching hundreds of thousands of the citizens all across the country.

INTERNATIONAL PROFESSIONAL ORGANIZATIONS

International Association of Physical Education and Sports for Girls and Women (IAPESGW)[15]

In the latter twentieth century the International Association of Physical Education and Sports for Girls and Women has held its quadrennial conferences in Washington, D.C. (1961); Cologne, Germany (1965); Sappora, Japan (1969); Teheran, Iran (1973); Capetown, South Africa (1977); and Buenos Aires, and Argentina (1981). In 1965, Liselott Diem (wife of Carl Diem, heir-apparent of Baron de Coubertin's role in the Olympics) was elected president, serving through 1981. In the thirty-two years of functioning since its organizing Congress in 1949, it has met in four European countries, one North American country, one Far East country, one Middle East country, one African country, and one South American country. It has made itself felt worldwide for great betterment of physical education to all girls and women.

International Council on Health, Physical Education and Recreation (ICHPER)[16]

Through the years, ICHPER has filled a great gap in the educational world's understanding of the importance of health education, physical education, and recreation in the education of all children in the world. In its first eight years of existence after the initial talks in Rome in 1958, it held annual international conferences in Washington, D.C., Amsterdam, New Delhi, Stockholm, Rio de Janeiro, Paris, Addas Ababa, and Seoul. Since then it has met in fifteen different countries in sites scattered all around the globe. It has reached thousands of educators worldwide.

As of 1960 it established contacts with the World Health Organization (WHO), Food and Agricultural Organization (FAO), and United Nations Educational, Scientific, and Cultural Organization (UNESCO) for mutual help. In 1961 it started publication of its *Bulletin,* a quarterly periodical published in English, French, and Spanish; in 1963 it started the quarterly *International Journal of Physical Education* and also its quarterly *Gymnasion,* both edited and published in Germany; beginning in 1965 it started serious observance of United Nations designation of various years as special international years, such as 1975 as International Year of Women, 1978 as International Year of the Child, and 1981 as International Year of the Handicapped. The year 1985 is scheduled as International Youth Year.

In 1966 it began support of plans for the international exchange of faculty and students working in the fields of health, physical education, and recreation. From

1966 to 1977 it published ten monographs on *Physical Education around the World;* beginning in 1969 it put out the *ICHPER Asian Journal,* two issues per year edited and published in Manilla; in 1972 it published in cooperation with AAHPER a book on *International Understanding.*

In support of this organization, the United States Office of Education assigns a staff member, Elsa Schneider, as a consultant. Continuing work includes securing sports equipment and advice for underdeveloped countries, and in recent years the cooperation with the Organization of American States (OAS) in providing physical education and sports for the handicapped of the countries of the Caribbean area.

As of 1981, ICHPER included members from 114 countries, covering all continents. For its July 1981 conference, it met in Manilla with 1200 delegates in attendance. Its present plan is to hold an international Congress in the odd years (1983 in Nigeria) and regional meetings in the even years.

Dorothy Sears Ainsworth who served as president until 1965 was elected Honorary President, a position she held until her death in 1976. Carl Troester, Jr., executive secretary of AAHPER, 1948 to 1974, served as secretary–general from the organization's founding with his office in the AAHPER building in Reston, Virginia.

CONFERENCES ON PHYSICAL EDUCATION

Conferences on a great variety of topics related to health education, physical education, recreation, sports, and dance, in various aspects of each discipline, are being held all the year round in all parts of the country. Announcements about them are carried in various issues of *JOPER, UPDATE,* and the several bulletins issued by subdivisions of AAHPER. Many of these meetings, aside from the usual annual conference put on by some professional organization, are offered by various colleges and universities in forms of symposiums or clinics.

LEADERS OF PHYSICAL EDUCATION OF LATTER TWENTIETH CENTURY

The number of leaders in the field of physical education has grown tremendously since World War II. All parts of the country are now covered by well-trained and effective men and women who are working in its service.

The American Alliance for Health, Physical Education, Recreation and Dance confers five types of awards in recognition of leadership in the profession listed in the order of their establishment:

1. The Gulick Award, established in 1923 in memory of Luther Halsey Gulick and conferred upon one physical educator a year for unusually significant leadership to the profession.[17]

2. The Honor Award, first conferred in 1931 honoring several persons each year in recognition of notable leadership.

3. The Anderson Award first conferred in 1949 in memory of William G. Anderson and conferred upon two or more persons a year who work in allied field and have rendered distinguished service to physical education.

4. The McKenzie Award first conferred in 1968 in memory of R. Tait McKenzie honoring one person each year "for outstanding contributions to the welfare of man through service to the profession and participation in the wider education and community relationship."

5. The Mabel Lee Award established in 1975 in recognition of that year as the International Year of Women and conferred annually upon one or two young teachers who have not yet reached the age of thirty-six and already give promise of unusual leadership in physical education.

Information about and photographs of each year's Award Fellows are published in some issue of the profession's monthly *Journal* or *UpDate* of the year of the award. Also biographical material on many of these leaders appears in *Who's Who in America* and other biographical publications in their various editions, particularly of the years of the heights of their careers. Biographies of many of these have been written, largely as doctoral dissertations in behalf of historical research within the profession. A perusal of the Appendix that follows this chapter will reveal the names of many outstanding leaders of the profession of physical education who have through the years served as presidents of the four leading national groups listed there and/or have been winners of some of the Alliance's top awards listed there. (There is no listing in the Appendix of Honor Awardees, since this award has been conferred for fifty-one years as of 1981 with usually five or more honored each year.) There are many fine leaders whose names are not in these lists but who were or still are exceptional and superior leaders. (Probably no one as yet had taken the time to nominate them for consideration by the Awards Committee. These committees consider for honors only those whose names are sent to them accompanied by professional biographical information.)

Also there was born at the turn of the century a large group of people whose careers in physical education were at their heights by 1960, with retirement just around the corner. They and their careers are too close to the present for final assessment. From a rough appraisal of this new group of leaders and the many promising young teachers coming after them, it seems quite in order to say that the profession is in excellent hands.

Appendix

NATIONAL ASSOCIATIONS OF PHYSICAL EDUCATION

American Alliance for Health, Physical Education, Recreation and Dance

Titles through the Years

1885–1886 American Association for Physical Education

1886–1903 American Association for the Advancement of Physical Education

1903–1937 American Physical Education Association

1937–1938 American Association for Health and Physical Education

1938–1974 American Association for Health, Physical Education and Recreation

1974–1980 American Alliance for Health, Physical Education and Recreation

1980–date American Alliance for Health, Physical Education, Recreation and Dance

Presidents through the Years[1]

1885–1887 Edward Hitchcock (1828–1911)

1887–1890 (2⅓ years) William Blaikie (1842–1904)

[1]Terms of office through the years. 1885–1889, Fall to fall: 1889–1900, Fall to spring (transition year): 1890–1906, Spring to spring: 1906, Spring to end of year (transition year): 1907 through 1931, Calendar years: 1932, January 1 through April (transition year): 1932 to date, Spring to spring.

1890–1891 Dudley A. Sargent (1849–1924)

1891–1892 Edward M. Hartwell (1850–1922)

1892–1894 Dudley A. Sargent

1894–1895 Jay W. Seaver (1859–1915)

1895–1899 Edward M. Hartwell

1899–1901 Dudley A. Sargent

1901–1903 Watson L. Savage (1859–1931)

1903–1907 (3⅔ years) Luther H. Gulick (1865–1918)

1907–1912 George L. Meylan (1873–1960)

1912–1916 R. Tait McKenzie (1867–1938)

1916 Earnest H. Arnold (1865–1929)

1917–1920 William H. Burdick (1871–1935)

1920–1923 Dudley B. Reed (1878–1955)

1923–1926 Carl L. Schrader (1872–1961)

1926–1929 Charles W. Savage (1869–1957)

1929–1931 Frederick W. Maroney (1884–1958)

1931–1932 (1⅓ years) Mabel Lee (1886–)

1932–1933 Jesse F. Williams (1886–1966)

1933–1934 Mary Channing Coleman (1882–1947)

1934–1935 Strong Hinman (1893–)

1935–1936 Agnes R. Wayman (1880–1968)

1936–1937 William G. Moorhead (1886–1954)

1937–1938 Charles H. McCloy (1886–1959)

1938 (6 months) Neils P. Neilson (1893–)

1938–1939 (6 months) Frederick W. Cozens (1890–1953)

1939–1940 Margaret Bell (1888–1969)

1940–1941 Hiram A. Jones (1899–1945)

1941–1942 Anne Schley Duggan (1905–1973)

1942–1943 Jay B. Nash (1886–1965)

1943–1944 August H. Pritzlaff (1894–1975)

1944–1946 William L. Hughes (1895–1957)

1946–1947 Helen Manley (1894–)

1947–1948 Vaughan S. Blanchard (1889–1969)

1948–1949 Ruth Evans (1908–)

1949–1950 Carl L. Nordly (1901–)

1950–1951 Dorothy S. Ainsworth (1894–1976)

1951 (April 20–22) Frank S. Stafford (1903–1951)

1951–1952 Bernice R. Moss (1906–1978)

1952–1954 Clifford L. Brownell (1895–)

1954–1956 Ruth Abernathy (1908–)

1956–1958 Ray O. Duncan (1906–1967)

1958–1959 Pattric R. O'Keefe
(1902–1959)

1959–1960 Arthur A. Esslinger
(1905–1973)

1960–1961 Minnie A. Lynn
(1902–   )

1961–1962 Arthur S. Daniels
(1906–1966)

1962–1963 Anita Aldrich
(1910–   )

1963–1964 Ben W. Miller
(1909–   )

1964–1965 Catherine L. Allen
(1909–   )

1965–1966 Rueben B. Frost
(1907–   )

1966–1967 Leona Holbrook
(1909–1980)

1967–1968 Joy W. Kistler
(1898–   )

1968–1969 Mabel Locke
(1907–   )

1969–1970 John M. Cooper
(1912–   )

1970–1971 Laura Mae Brown
(1918–   )

1971–1972 Louis E. Alley[2]

1972–1973 Barbara E. Forker

1973–1974 Willis J. Baughman

1974–1975 Katherine Ley

1975–1976 Roger C. Wiley

1976–1977 Celeste Ulrich

1977–1978 Leroy Walker

1978–1979 Margaret Coffee

1979–1980 Glen M. Smith

1980–1981 Fay Biles

1981–1982 Peter Everett

1982–1983 Mary Beyrer

1983–1984 Wayne H. Osness

Recipients of Gulick Awards

1923 Luther H. Gulick
(Posthumous award)

1924 Jessie H. Bancroft

1925 Thomas D. Wood

1926 Thomas A. Storey

1928 Clark W. Hetherington

1929 George J. Fisher

1939 Jesse F. Williams

1940 Jay B. Nash

1944 Charles H. McCloy

1945 William G. Anderson

1946 Ethel Perrin

1947 Blanche M. Trilling

1948 Mabel Lee

1949 Elmer D. Mitchell

1950 Elizabeth Burchenal

1951 William Ralph LaPorte

1952 Charles W. Savage

1953 Frederick W. Cozens

1954 William L. Hughes

1955 Carl L. Nordly

1956 Rosalind E. Cassidy

1957 Clair V. Langton

1958 Helen Manley

1959 Delbert Oberteuffer

1960 Dorothy Ainsworth

[2]Presidents from 1971 on are as of 1982 all actively engaged in their careers and their birth years are not listed.

1961 Neils P. Neilson

1962 Clifford Lee Brownell

1963 David Kingsley Brace

1964 Ruth Glassow

1965 Ruth Abernathy and Elwood Craig Davis

1967 Arthur A. Esslinger

1968 Minnie L. Lynn

1969 Arthur H. Steinhaus

1970 Catherine Allen

1971 Margaret H'Doubler

1972 Julian Smith

1974 Laura Huelster

1975 Thomas K. Cureton

1976 Ben W. Miller

1977 Eleanor Metheny

1978 H. Harrison Clarke

1979 Ruth Murray and Elena Slipvovich

1980 Aileene Lockhart

1981 Gladys Scott

1982 LeRoy T. Walker

Substructure for Women's Sports

Titles through the Years

1899–1905 Women's Basket Ball Rules Committee

1905–1917 National Women's Basket Ball Committee

1917–1927 National Committee on Women's Sports

1927–1931 Women's Athletic Section

1931–1952 National Section on Women's Athletics (NSWA)

1952–1958 National Section on Girls' and Women's Athletics (NSGWA)

1958–1974 Division for Girls' and Women's Sports (DGWS)

1974–Present National Association for Girls' and Women's Sports (NAGWS)

Chairman through the Years

1899–1905 Alice B. Foster

1905–1917 Senda Berenson

1917–1921 Elizabeth Burchenal

1921–1925 Blanche Trilling

1925–1927 Katherine Sibley

1927–1930 Florence Somers

1930–1931 Helen W. Hazelton

1931–1932 Grace Jones

1932–1934 Grace B. Davies

1934–1936 Eline Von Borries

1936–1938 Elinor Schroeder

1938–1940 Jane Shurmer

1940–1942 Ruth D. Atwell

1942–1943 Alice Shriver

1943–1946 Anna S. Espenschade

1946–1948 Alfreda Mosscrop

1948–1949 Martha A. Gable

1949–1952 Laurie Campbell

1952–1954 Josephine Fiske

1954 (June–December) Aileene Lockhart

1954 (December)–1956 Grace I. Fox

1956–1958 Mabel Locke

1958–1959 Jane A. Mott

1959–1960 Thelma Bishop
1960–1961 Anne Finlayson
1961–1962 Sara Staff Jernigan
1962–1963 Katherine Ley
1963–1964 Marguerite Clifton
1964–1965 Betty F. McCue
1965–1966 Phebe M. Scott
1966–1967 Frances McGill
1967–1968 Lucille Magnason
1968–1969 Alyce Cheska
1969–1970 E. Ann Stitt
1970–1971 Edith Betts

1971–1972 Jo Anne Thorpe
1972–1973 Betty Grant Hartman
1973–1974 Frances Koenig
1974–1975 Mildred Barnes
1975–1976 Lou Jean Moyer
1976–1977 Jo Anna Davenport
1977–1978 Carole Oglesby
1978–1979 L. Leotus Morrison
1979–1980 Phyllis A. Blatz
1980–1981 Doris Corbett
1981–1982 Helen Knierim
1982–1983 Bonnie Slatton

District Associations of AAHPERD and Dates of Establishment

1912 Middle West Society (in 1933 it divided into Mid West and Central Associations)

1919 Eastern Association of Physical Education

1927 Southern Association of Physical Education

1930 North West Association of Physical Education

1934 South West Association of Physical Education

College Physical Education Association for Men

Early Presidents (first twenty)

1897 Edward Hitchcock (organizing chairman)
1898 Jay W. Seaver
1899 Dudley A. Sargent
1900 William G. Anderson
1901 R. Tait McKenzie
1902 Paul C. Phillips
1903 Watson L. Savage
1904 R. Tait McKenzie
1905, 1906 George L. Meylan
1907, 1908 Thomas A. Storey
1909 R. Tait McKenzie

1910, 1911 Amos Alonzo Stagg
1912 Fred E. Leonard
1913 W. A. Lambeth
1914 James Naismith
1915 Charles W. Savage
1916 C. V. Young
1917 Joseph E. Roycroft
1918 Joseph E. Roycroft
1919 Edwin Fayer
1920 Edwin Fayer
1921 Frederick Luehring
1922 Edgar Fayer

National Association of Physical Education for College Women

Early Presidents (first sixteen)

1924–1925 Lydia Clark	1941–1943 Elizabeth Kelly
1925–1926 Alice Belding	1943–1945 Elizabeth Halsey
1926–1927 Mabel Lee	1945–1947 Gertrude Manchester
1927–1929 Mary E. Gross	1947–1949 Helen W. Hazelton
1929–1932 Gertrude E. Moulton	1949–1951 Irene A. Clayton
1932–1934 Ruth Elliott	1951–1953 Pauline Hodgson
1934–1937 Rosalind E. Cassidy	1953–1955 Laura J. Huelster
1937–1941 Dorothy S. Ainsworth	1955-1957 Ruth M. Wilson

Society of State Directors of Health and Physical Education

Early Presidents (first sixteen)

1926–1927 Carl L. Schrader	1935–1936 G. K. Hendricks
1927–1928 William H. Burdick	1936–1937 Jessie R. Garrison
1928–1929 Allen G. Ireland	1937–1938 W. H. Orion
1929–1930 E. W. Everts	1938–1939 Hiram A. Jones
1930–1931 Elliott V. Graves	1939–1940 Harry Edwards
1931–1933 William G. Moorehead	1940–1941 Jess W. Hair
1933–1934 Neils P. Neilson	1941–1942 Bernice R. Moss
1934–1935 C. J. Prohaska	1942–1943 Alice G. Aldrich

American Academy of Physical Education

Charter Members (according to numbers assigned to fellows)

1. Clark W. Hetherington	12. Amy Morris Homans
2. R. Tait McKenzie	13. William A. Stecher
3. William H. Burdick	14. Earnest H. Arnold
4. Thomas A. Storey	15. George L. Meylan
5. Jay B. Nash	16. (Cancelled)
6. Carl L. Schrader	17. William Ralph LaPorte
7. James H. McCurdy	18. Charles W. Savage
8. Jessie H. Bancroft	19. John F. Bovard
9. Wilbur P. Bowen	20. Paul C. Phillips
10. Dudley B. Reed	21. Arthur S. Lamb
11. Howard S. Braucher	22. (Cancelled)

23. John Brown, Jr.
24. J. Anna Norris
25. E. C. Schneider
26. Elmer D. Mitchell

27. Charles H. McCloy
28. Elizabeth Burchenal
29. Arthur H. Steinhaus

Presidents (first sixteen)

1926–1930 Clark W. Hetherington (organizing chairman)

1930–1938 R. Tait McKenzie

1938–1939 R. Tait McKenzie (two weeks) and Mabel Lee (acting)

1939–1940 John Brown, Jr.

1941–1943 Mabel Lee

1943–1945 Arthur H. Steinhaus

1945–1947 Jay B. Nash

1947–1949 Charles H. McCloy

1949–1950 Frederick W. Cozens

1950–1951 Rosalind E. Cassidy

1951–1952 Seward C. Staley

1952–1953 David K. Brace

1953–1954 Neils P. Neilson

1954–1955 Elmer D. Mitchell

1955–1956 Anna S. Espenschade

1956-1957 Harry A. Scott

EARLY STATE DIRECTORS OF HEALTH AND PHYSICAL EDUCATION

1916 New York, Thomas A. Storey

1918 California, Clark W. Hetherington

1918 New Jersey, Frederick W. Maroney

1918 Maryland, William Burdick

1919 Michigan, Floyd A. Rowe

1920 Alabama, O. C. Bird

1922 Massachusetts, Carl L. Schrader

1922 Missouri, Henry S. Curtis

1922 Pennsylvania, Charles H. Keene

1923 Minnesota, E. W. Everts

1925 Virginia, Elliott V. Graves

1926 Delaware, P. S. Prince

1926 Ohio, Clifford L. Brownell

1927 Florida, Caswell Miles

1929 Illinois, Louis Kulcinski

1930 Texas, R. N. Sandlin

(In 1919, Jessie R. Garrison was appointed Acting Physical Director for the State of Alabama succeeding Jackson R. Sharman, and two years later she became Director—the first woman to hold a state directorship of physical education.)

References

Chapter 1

1. Seton Lloyd, *Foundations in the Dust*. London: Oxford University Press, 1949, p. viii.
2. _____, *op cit.*, pp. 22–24. R. Campbell Thompson, *The Epic of Gilgamesh*. Translated into English blank verse. London: Oxford University Press, 1929.
3. James Henry Breasted, *History of Egypt*. New York: Charles Scribners, 1921.
4. For material on Greece, the author is indebted to the following sources: William Leonard Langer, Editor, *Encyclopedia of World History*. Boston: Houghton Mifflin Co., 1948, p. 46. Clarence A. Forbes, *Greek Physical Education*. New York: Century Co., 1929.
5. Jean E. Chrysosfis, "Plato on Physical Education," *The Pentathlon*, May 1, 1929, p. 10. (first issue of a shortlived periodical of the Middle West Society of Physical Education, Elmer D. Mitchell, Editor)
6. For source material on Rome and the Middle Ages, the author is indebted to: W. L. Langer, *op. cit.*; various encyclopedia; Paul Monroe, *Source Book in the History of Education for the Greek and Roman Period*. New York: Century Co., 1920. Fred Eugene Leonard and George B. Affleck, *A Guide to the History of Physical Education*. Philadelphia: Lea and Febiger, 1947.
7. Barbara Schradt, "Sports of the Byzantine Empire," *Journal of Sport History*, Vol. 8, No. 3, Winter 1981. Langer, *op. cit.*, pp. 70, 170.
8. Allan Cameron, *Porphyrius The Charioteer*. London: University of Oxford Press, 1973, pp. 63, 155, 276.
9. Phillip K. Hitti, *History of the Arabs*. London: MacMillan, 1937.
10. Recorded in the fifteenth century by Sir Thomas Malory in his *Morte d' Arthur*, and still later by the modern poet Sir Alfred Tennyson (1809–1892) in his *Idylls of the King*.
11. Sir Thomas Elyot, *The Boke Named the Govyernour*. (Everyman's Library) London, 1885. Book I, Section 16–20 on exercise and dancing.

12. As depicted in Michel Olmert, "Points of Origin," *Smithsonian*, Sept. 1981, p. 40.
13. *Ibid. Ibid*, pp. 142–44.
14. *National Encyclopedia*, New York: Collier & Sons, 1935, Vol. 3, pp. 396–397.
15. Langer, *op. cit.*, pp. 365–368.

Chapter 2

1. Paul Monroe, *Founding of American Public School System*. New York: The Macmillan Co. Vol. I, 1940, pp. 188, 446.
2. Benjamin Franklin, "Proposals Relating to the Education of Youth," *Report of U.S. Commissioner of Education*, Vol. 1, 1902, pp. 182–185.
3. For information on this topic the author is indebted to the following sources: Robert W. Henderson, *Early American Sport*. New York: A. S. Barnes & Co., 1953, pp. 25–34, 95–96, 116–125, 155–156, 224. Herbert Manchester, *Four Centuries of Sport in America*. New York: The Derrydale Press, 1931. Robert B. Weaver, *Amusements and Sports in American Life*. Chicago: The University of Chicago Press, 1939, p. 112.
4. T. D. Wood and C. L. Brownell, "Discipline of the Methodist Episcopal Church," *Source Book in Physical Education*. New York: The Macmillan Co., 1925, p. 352.
5. Copy preserved in New York City Public Library.
6. Foster Rhea Dulles, *America Learns to Play*. New York: Appleton–Century–Crofts, 1935.
7. According to p. 11 of a town law passed Sept., 1701 and p. 43 of a law passed in 1780 (Boston City Archives).
8. Benjamin Rush, *Sermons to Gentleman upon Temperance and Exercise, 1772*. Richmond, Va.: Franklin Office, 1820.
9. Henderson, *op. cit.*
10. As recorded in Princeton College Archives.
11. John Locke, *Some Thoughts Concerning Education*. London: Cambridge University Press, 1902.
12. Rousseau, *op. cit.*
13. R. H. Quick, *Essays on Educational Reformers*. New York: D. Appleton Co., 1912, Chaps. 14, 15.
14. Franklin, *op. cit.*
15. Copies of these books are preserved by the American Antiquary Society in Worcester, Massachusetts, the Boston Athenaenum, the Library of Congress, and the New York City Public Library.
16. R. Tait McKenzie, "Benjamin Franklin—Illustrious Pioneer in Physical Education," *Journal of Health and Physical Education*, Vol. 7, 1936.
17. R. F. Seybolt, *Source Studies in Colonial Education: The Private School* (Bulletin No. 28.). Urbana: Bureau of Educational Research, College of Education, University of Illinois, 1925.

Chapter 3

1. Thomas Woody, *A History of Women's Education in the United States*, Vol. 1. New York: Science Press, 1929, pp. 329–342.
2. Lawrence A. Cremin, *Transformation of the School*. New York: Alfred A. Knopf, 1961, pp. 128, 279.

3. Elmer Brown, *The Making of Our Middle Schools*. 3rd ed. New York: Longmans, Green & Co., 1907.
4. Alma Lutz, *Emma Willard, Daughter of Democracy*. Boston: Houghton Mifflin Co., 1929.
5. Catharine Beecher, *Educational Reminiscences and Suggestions*. New York: J. B. Ford & Co., 1874.
6. George Winship, "Autobiographical Sketches of a Strength-Seeker," *Atlantic Monthly*, Jan. 1862, pp. 102–115.
7. Dio Lewis, *The New Gymnastics for Men, Women, and Children*. Boston: Ticknor and Fields, 8th ed. 1864.
8. Leon Burr Richardson, *History of Dartmouth College*, Hanover, N.H.: Dartmouth Publications, 1932.
9. Robert W. Henderson, *Ball, Bat and Bishop*. New York: Rockport Press, 1947, pp. 163–165.
10. *Ibid.*
11. *Ibid.*
12. Henry L. Baker, *Football: Facts and Figures*. New York: Rinehart & Co., 1945, pp. 9–11. John Tunis, *Sports for the Fun of It*. New York: A. S. Barnes & Co., 1940, p. 34.
13. Robert Kelly, *American Rowing, Its Background and Tradition*. New York: Rinehart & Co., 1945, pp. 9–11.
14. Frederick Leuhring, *Swimming Pool Standards*. New York: A. S. Barnes & Co., 1939, p. 23.
15. John F. Watson, *Annals of Philadelphia and Pennsylvania in the Olden Times*, Vol. 3, Philadelphia: Leary, Stuart & Co., 1900.
16. R. Tait McKenzie, "Benjamin Franklin—Illustrious Pioneer in Physical Education," *Journal of Health and Physical Education*, Vol. 7, 1936.
17. *Ibid.*
18. ———, "Physical Education at Girard College," *Mind and Body* Sept., 1923, pp. 197–203.
19. Guy M. Lewis, "America's First International Sport—The Regattas of 1852 and 1875," *Research Quarterly* of AAHPER, Vol. 38, No. 4, Dec. 1967, p. 637.

Chapter 4

1. Bruce L. Bennett, "The Making of Round Hill School," *Quest*, Monograph 4, April 1965, p. 53.
2. Horst Ueberhorst, *Friedrich Ludwig Jahn—1778–1978*. Translated by Timothy Nevill. Bonn–Bad Godesberg: Inter Nationes, 1978, p. 107.
3. John C. Warren, *The Importance of Physical Education, Lecture No. 1*. Boston: American Institute of Instruction, 1831.
4. E. D. Neill, *History of Minnesota Schools*. St. Paul: State Office, 1858.
5. Robert Knight Barney, "The Allen School: Pioneer in Institutional Physical Education," *Proceedings: North American Society for Sports History*, 1974, p. 43.
6. John Swett, *Public Education in California*. New York: American Book Co., 1911.
7. Dudley S. DeGroot, *A History of Physical Education in California—1848–1939*. Doctoral dissertation, Stanford University, 1940.

8. Catharine Beecher, *Educational Reminiscences and Suggestions*. New York: J. B. Ford & Co., 1874.

9. William Bentley Fowle, "Medical Intelligences," *American Journal of Education*, 1820, pp. 698–699.

10. Dudley A. Sargent, "Beginnings of Physical Education in America," *American Physical Education Review*, Vol. 25, Nov. 1920.

11. Leon Burr Richardson. *History of Dartmouth College*. Hanover, N.H.: Dartmouth Publication, 1932.

12. Edward Mussey Hartwell, *Physical Training in American Colleges and Universities* (Circular No. 5). Washington, D.C.: U.S. Bureau of Education, 1885.

13. J. Edmund Welch, *Edward Hitchcock, M.D., Founder of Physical Education in the College Community*. Greenville, N.C.: Published privately, P.O. Box 2043, 1966.

14. Charles A. Bennett, *A History of Manual and Industrial Education to 1870*. Peoria: Peoria Press, 1926.

15. Kenneth D. Miller, "Stearns, Hitchcock, and Amherst College," *Journal of Health and Physical Education*, Vol. 25, May–June 1957, pp. 29–30.

16. Paul C. Phillips, "Historical Data Regarding Construction of College Gymnasia," *American Physical Education Review*, Vol. 30, Oct. 1916, pp. 434–435. Frederick Luehring, *Swimming Pool Standards*. New York: A. S. Barnes & Co., 1939, p. 23. Edward M. Hartwell, *The Rise of College Gymnasiums in the USA*. Washington, D.C.: Government Printing Office, 1886. Special report of U.S. Bureau of Education given at World's Industrial and Cotton Centennial Exposition in New Orleans, 1884 and 1885. Fred Eugene Leonard and George B. Affleck, *A Guide to the History of Physical Education*. Philadelphia: Lea & Febiger, 1947, pp. 273, 329.

17. Emil Rinsch, *History of the Normal College of American Gymnastic Union of Indiana University—1866–1966*. Bloomington: Indiana University Press, 1966.

18. Robert Knight Barney, "A Historical Reinterpretation of the Forces Underlying the First State Legislation for Physical Education in the Public Schools of the U.S.," *Research Quarterly* of AAHPER, Vol. 40, No. 3, Oct. 1973, p. 357.

19. Leonard and Affleck, *op. cit.*

20. Rinsch, *op. cit.*

21. Richard C. Morse, *The History of the North American Young Men's Christian Association*. New York: Association Press, 1918.

22. Ueberhorst, *op. cit.*, p. 107.

23. *Ibid.*, p. 93.

24. Fred Eugene Leonard, *Pioneers of Modern Physical Training*. New York: Association Press, 1915. E. L. Follen, *Life of Charles Follen*. Boston: Thomas H. Webb & Co., 1844.

25. Leonard, *op. cit.*, p. 235.

26. Thomas S. Perry, *Life and Letters of Francis Lieber*. Boston: James R. Osgood & Co., 1882.

27. Willystine Goodsell, *Pioneers of Women's Education in the United States*. New York: McGraw–Hill Book Co., 1931. Discusses educational theories of Emma Willard, Mary Lyon, and Catharine Beecher. Thomas Woody, *A History of Women's Education in the United States*, Vol. 2. New York: Science Press, 1929.

28. Mary F. Eastman and Ceilia Clark Lewis. *The Biography of Dio Lewis*. New York: Fowler & Wells Co., 1891.

29. *The Massachusetts Teacher*. Vol. 13, pp. 378–393.

30. Disagreeing with some of Lewis's theories, Miss Beecher shortly resigned. Many years later Delphine Hanna, M.D., of Oberlin College, in speaking of Dio Lewis to some of her pupils, told them that she had investigated his training school with the thought of probably adopting his system of exercises but when she questioned some of his theories and challenged them as being scientifically unsound, he replied: "Oh, well. People like to be humbugged." Gertrude Moulton, M.D., who was a pupil of Dr. Hanna at Oberlin heard this remark of Dr. Hanna and in the late 1950s repeated it to the author of this book.

Chapter 5

1. Claës Enebuske, *Progressive Gymnastics Day's Orders*. New York: Silver Burdette Co., 1890.

2. Emily Bishop, "Americanized Delsarte Culture," *AAAPE Proceedings, 1885–1895*, No. 9, 1892, pp. 80–96. Genevieve Stebbins, *Delsarte System of Expression*. New York: E. S. Werner, 6th ed., 1902.

3. John Richards Betts, *America's Sporting Heritage—1850–1950*. Reading, Mass.: Addison–Wesley Publishing Co., 1974, p. 84.

4. *Ibid.*, p. 69.

5. David Quentin Voigt, *American Baseball*. Norman: University of Oklahoma Press, 1966, p. 24.

6. Betts, *op. cit.*, pp. 69, 71.

7. Bernice Larson Webb, *The Basketball Man James Naismith*. Lawrence: University Press of Kansas, 1973. James Naismith, *Basketball. Its Origins and Development*. New York: Association Press, 1941. The author's own memories of conversations with Dr. Naismith during his last years at the University of Kansas.

8. Webb, *op. cit.*

9. Edith Naomi Hill, "Senda Berenson," *Supplement to Research Quarterly* of APEA, Vol. 7, Oct. 1941, pp. 658–665. Senda Berenson, "Basket Ball for Women," *Physical Education*, Sept. 1894, p. 106.

10. Webb, *op. cit.*, p. 70.

11. Albert G. Spalding, "Story of Women's Basket Ball Rules Committee," *Women's Basket Ball Guide*. New York: American Sports Publishing Co., 1911.

12. Frank W. Schwinn, *The Story of the Bicycle and Its Contribution to Our Way of Life*. Chicago: Arnold Schwinn & Co., 1945, pp. 31–51.

13. Betts, *op. cit.* Herbert Manchester, *Four Centuries of Sport in America*. New York: The Derrydale Press, 1931.

14. F. G. Menke, *Encyclopedia of Sports*. New York: A. S. Barnes & Co., 1947.

15. Parke H. Davis, *Football, the American Intercollegiate Game*. New York: Charles Scribner's Sons, 1911. Alexander M. Wayand, *The Saga of American Football*. New York: The Macmillan Co., 1955.

16. Betts, *op. cit.*

17. John Tunis, *Sports for the Fun of It*. New York: A. S. Barnes & Co., 1940.

18. ———, "Women and Sport Business," *Harpers Weekly*, Vol. 160, July 1929, pp. 211–221.

19. Betts, *op. cit.*

20. Robert Kelly, *American Rowing, Its Background and Tradition*. New York: G. P. Putnam's Sons, 1933, pp. viii, xvii, 25, 73, 101, 162.

21. F. M. Peterson, *The History of Olympic Skiing for Women—A Cultural Interpretation*. Doctoral dissertation, University of Southern California, 1967.

22. G. W. Hangar, *Public Baths in the United States*. U.S. Bureau of Labor Bulletin, No. 54, Sept. 1904.

23. Frederick Luehring, *Swimming Pool Standards*. New York: A. S. Barnes & Co., 1939, p. 23.

24. Betts, *op. cit.*, p. 156.

25. *Ibid.*

26. *National Encyclopedia*. New York: Collier & Sons, 1935, Vol. 10, pp. 77–78.

27. Menke, *op. cit.*

28. *Ibid.*

29. Betts, *op. cit.* James E. Sullivan, "First Athletic Clubs in the USA," *American Physical Education Review*, Vol. 8, March 1903, p. 268.

30. Betts, *op. cit.*, p. 109.

31. Source for this and following paragraphs on this topic: Betts, *op. cit.*, pp. 69–79.

32. *Ibid.*, p. 15.

33. Menke, *op. cit.*

34. Betts, *op. cit.*, p. 104.

35. *Ibid.*, p. 189.

36. John S. Watterson III, "The Football Crisis of 1909–1910, The Responsibility of the Eastern Big Three," NASSH *Journal of Sport History*, Vol. 8, No. 1, Spring 1981, p. 38.

37. Amos Alonzo Stagg, *Physical Culture and Athletics* (University of Chicago Decennial Publications, Vol. 1). Chicago: University of Chicago Press, 1904, pp. 336–372.

38. Guy M. Lewis, "America's First International Sport—The Regattas of 1852 and 1875," *Research Quarterly* of AAHPER, Vol. 38, No. 4, Dec. 1967, p. 637.

39. C. Ward Crampton, *The Public School Athletic League of New York City*. Sept. 1936. Unpublished paper, a copy of which is in the AAHPER Archives.

40. Fred Eugene Leonard and George B. Affleck, *A Guide to the History of Physical Education*. Philadelphia: Lea & Febiger, 1947, pp. 220–223.

41. Information discovered by the author, October 9, 1966, in the library of University of North Carolina at Greensboro, in a faded newspaper clipping from some unclearly marked *Herald* and dated March 3, 1931, attached to the flyleaf of a copy of one of Blaikie's books on file there in their Amy Morris Homans' Collection of Books.

42. Virginia C. Gildersleeve, *Many a Good Crusade*. New York: The Macmillan Co., 1954, p. 21.

43. Ellery H. Clark, "The Olympic Games," *American Physical Education Review*, Sept.–Dec. 1896, pp. 14–22.

44. John Kieran, *The Story of the Olympic Games—776 B.C.–1936 A.D.* New York: Frederick A. Stokes Co., 1936. *National Encyclopedia*, Vol. 7, pp. 401–402, New York: Collier & Sons, 1935.

45. Hill, *op. cit.*

46. Harold C. Evans, "Some Notes on College Basketball in Kansas," *Kansas Historical Quarterly*, Vol. 11, No. 2, May 1942, pp. 199–215.

Chapter 6

1. Robert Knight Barney, "A Historical Reinterpretation of the Forces Underlying the First State Legislation for Physical Education in the Public Schools of the USA," *Research Quarterly* of AAHPER, Vol. 44, No. 3, Oct. 1973, p. 346. _____, "Adele Parot: Beacon of the Dioclesian Lewis School of Gymnastic Expression in the American West," *Proceedings of North American Society for Sport History*, 1973, pp. 43–44. John Swett, *Public Education in California*. New York: American Book Co., 1911. Barbara J. Hoepner, "John Swett," *Research Quarterly*, Vol. 41, No. 3, Oct. 1970, p. 365.

2. Dudley A. Sargent, *Autobiography*. Philadelphia: Lea & Febiger, Publishers, 1927.

3. Catharine Beecher, *Educational Reminiscences and Suggestions*. New York: J. B. Ford & Co., 1874.

4. Grover Mueller, "A Hundred Years of Physical and Health Education in Philadelphia," *Report to Philadelphia Board of Education*, 1938.

5. Patricia Patterson, "The History of Physical Education in Minnesota Schools." Paper published in Newsletter of Minnesota AHPER, in 1960s. (Minnesota AHPER Archives, undated.)

6. E. H. Fellows, "The Founding of Physical Education in the Public Schools of Kansas, City, Missouri," *AAPE, Index-Proceedings 1885–1895*. No. 2, p. 9.

7. John Richards Betts, *America's Sporting Heritage—1850–1950*. Reading, Mass.: Addison–Wesley Publishing Co., 1974, p. 84.

8. James C. Boykin, "Physical Training," *Report of U.S. Commissioner of Education*, Washington, D.C.: Government Printing Office, 1891–1892.

9. Edward M. Hartwell, *Physical Training in American Colleges and Universities*. Washington, D.C.: U.S. Bureau of Education, Circular No. 5, 1885.

10. Sargent, *op. cit.*

11. Frederick Luehring, *Swimming Pool Standards*. New York: A. S. Barnes & Co., 1939.

12. Amos Alonzo Stagg, *Physical Culture and Athletics*. University of Chicago Decennial Publications, Vol. I. Chicago: University of Chicago Press, 1904.

13. Sargent, *op. cit.*

14. Ruth Elliott, *The Organization of Professional Training in State Universities*. New York: Teachers College, Bureau of Publications, Columbia University, 1927.

15. Nancy Truna and Mary L. Remley, "Physical Education for Women at the University of Wisconsin—1863–1918—A Half Century of Progress," *Canadian Journal of History of Sport and Physical Education*, Vol. 4, No. 1, May 1973, pp. 8–26.

16. Mabel Lee, *Seventy-five Years of Professional Preparation in Physical Education for Women at the University of Nebraska–Lincoln—1898–1973*. Lincoln: University Print Shop, 1973. Parts 1 and 2 of a four-part history.

17. Dorothy S. Ainsworth, *History of Physical Education in Women's Colleges*. New York: Columbia University Press, 1927, pp. ix, 24, 27.

18. Secretary of Department of Physical Education for Women, Oberlin College, "Delphine Hanna." Supplement to *Research Quarterly* of APEA, Oct. 1941, p. 647.

19. Monroe, *op. cit.*, p. 281.

20. Hartwell, *op. cit.*

21. Fred Eugene Leonard and George B. Affleck, *A Guide to the History of Physical Education*. Philadelphia: Lea & Febiger, 1947, p. 342.

22. *Ibid.*

23. *Pioneer Women in Physical Education:* Supplement to *Research Quarterly* of AAHPER, Oct. 1941, pp. 664, 680.

24. Emil Rinsch, *History of the Normal College of American Gymnastic Union of Indiana University—1866–1966*. Bloomington: Indiana University Press, 1966.

25. Horst Ueberhorst, *Friedrich Ludwig Jahn—1778–1978*. Bonn–Bad Godesberg: Inter Nationes, 1978, p. 96.

26. Sargent, *op. cit.*

27. Delphine Hanna, "The Present Status of Professional Training in Normal Schools," *American Physical Education Review*, Vol. 8, No. 1, March 1903, pp. 293–297.

28. Sargent, *op. cit.*

29. Leonard and Affleck, *op. cit.*, p. 376.

30. Robert A. Reilly, "Luther Gulick and the YMCA Training School Curriculum— 1887–1903," *NASSH Proceedings*, 1977, p. 30. Luther H. Gulick, "Physical Education in the YMCA," *Proceedings*, AAAPE, 1891.

31. Hanna, *op. cit.*

32. Boston Public School Teachers. *Memorial Services in Honor of Mary Hemenway*. Boston: George Ellis Press, 1899. Contains material on the founding of the Boston Normal School of Gymnastics.

33. Thomas Hines, *History of the Posse School of Gymnastics*. Paper read at the 75th Anniversary Convention of AAHPER, 1960.

34. Edward M. Hartwell, *Physical Training in American Colleges and Universities* (Circular No. 5). Washington, D.C.: U.S. Bureau of Education, 1885. Secretary, Department of Physical Education for Women, Oberlin College, "Brief Outline of Life and Work of Delphine Hanna," Supplement to *Research Quarterly* of APEA, Oct. 1941, pp. 646–652.

35. Walter Kroll and Guy Lewis, "The First Academic Degree in Physical Education," *Journal of Health, Physical Education and Recreation*, June 1969, pp. 73–74.

36. *Ibid.*

37. Information from correspondence of author with Archivist of Stanford University, in September 1972.

38. Hanna, *op. cit.*

39. Letter to author, December 13, 1976, from Mrs. Katherine Strobel, Middle Tennessee State University, Murfreesboro, Tennessee.

40. Emil Rinsch, *History of the Normal College of American Gymnastic Union of Indiana University—1866–1966*. Bloomington: Indiana University Press, 1966.

41. Laurence Doggett, *Man and a School*. New York: Association Press, 1943. Story of Springfield College.

42. Elizabeth Wilson, *Fifty Years of Association Work Among YWCAs*. New York: National Board of YWCA of U.S.A., 1916.

43. Elmer D. Mitchell and Bernard Mason, *Theory of Play*. New York: A. S. Barnes & Co., 1948.

44. Ida B. Crawford and Viola Mitchell, *Camp Counseling*. 3d ed. Philadelphia: W. B. Saunders Co., 1961.

45. Issues of some of these early magazines are available in microcard from the School of Physical Education, University of Oregon. They make interesting reading.

Chapter 7

1. Mabel Lee and Bruce L. Bennett, "This Is Our Heritage," *Journal of Health, Physical Education and Recreation*, Vol. 31, No. 4, April 1960, pp. 25–33, 38–48, 52–58, 62–73, 76–86. This is the seventy-five year history of AAHPER.

2. AAAPE, *Proceedings—1885–1895*. (AAHPERD Archives). William G. Anderson, "The American Association for the Advancement of Physical Education," *American Physical Education Review*, Vol. 25, Nov. 1920, p. 312. "Organization of Ohio State Physical Education Association," *Mind and Body*, Vol. 7, April 1895, p. 38.

3. Harry A. Scott, "The Society of Directors of Physical Education in Colleges," *Journal of Health and Physical Education*, Vol. 3, April 1923, p. 3.

4. Isabel Barrows, *Conference on Physical Training—1889*. Boston: George Ellis Press, 1899. For Sargent quotations, see pp. 66–68. The addresses reported in this book carry great significance for today's student.

5. The author is indebted to the following sources for information on the life of Edward Hitchcock: Fred Eugene Leonard, *Pioneers of Modern Physical Training*. New York: Association Press, 1915. Kenneth D. Miller, "Edward Hitchcock," *Journal of Health, Physical Education and Recreation*, Vol. 31, No. 4, April 1960, p. 35. ———, "Stearns, Hitchcock, and Amherst College," *Journal of Health, Physical Education and Recreation*, Vol. 25, May–June 1957, pp. 29–30. Paul C. Phillips, "Dr. Edward Hitchcock," *American Physical Education Review*, Vol. 16, March 1911, p. 217. J. Edmund Welch, *Pioneering in Health Education at Amherst College*. Paper presented at Research Section of MWAHPER in Charleston, West Virginia, April 25, 1969.

6. John Richards Betts, *America's Sporting Heritage—1850–1950*. Reading, Massachusetts: Addison–Wesley Publishing Co., 1974.

7. The author acknowledges indebtedness to the following sources: "Eliza Maria Mosher, M.D.," autobiographical sketch published under title "Hisory of American Medical Women" in *The Medical Woman's Journal*, Vol. 24, No. 10, Oct. 1922, p. 253. Reprinted in Supplement to *Research Quarterly* of APEA, Vol. 12, No. 3, Oct. 1941, pp. 628–632. Esther A. Coster, "Eliza M. Mosher—50 Years a Woman Doctor," *Independent Woman*, 1925, (Magazine of National Federation of Business and Professional Womens' Clubs). "Hundreds Gather to Commemorate Fifty Years of Service," *The Michigan Alumnus*, March 1925. "Dr. Eliza Mosher, First Dean of Women, Dies," *The Michigan Alumnus*, Nov. 1928.

8. Josephine Rathbone, "Amy Morris Homans," *Journal of Health, Physical Education and Recreation*, Vol. 31, No. 4, April 1960, p. 37. William Skarstrom, "Life and Work of Amy Morris Homans," Supplement to *Research Quarterly* of AAHPER, Vol. 2, No. 3, Oct. 1941, pp. 615–627. Mabel Lee, *Memories of a Bloomer Girl*. Washington, D.C.: AAHPER Publications Dept., 1977. There is much material about Miss Homans in this book, pp. 81–199. ———, *Memories beyond Bloomers*, Washington, D.C.: AAHPER Publication, 1978, sequel to *Memories of a Bloomer Girl*. Much material on Homans as indicated by index, pp. 11–421.

9. Author acknowledges indebtedness to the following sources: Bruce L. Bennett, *Dudley A. Sargent*. Doctoral dissertation, University of Michigan, 1948. George K. Makechnie, "Dudley Allen Sargent," *Journal of Health, Physical Education and Recreation*, Vol. 31, No. 4, April 1960, p. 51. Dudley A. Sargent, *Autobiography*. Philadelphia: Lea & Febiger, Publishers, 1927. "Tributes to Dudley A. Sargent," *American Physical Education Review*, Vol. 29, 1924, pp. 436 and 484. This issue of the magazine carries several tributes by many different people under the one title.

10. Isabel Barrows, Editor, *Conference on Physical Training—1889*. Boston: George Ellis Press, 1899.

11. "Edward Mussey Hartwell," *National Cyclopedia of American Biography*. New York: James J. White & Co., 1929, pp. xx, 132–33. Fred Eugene Leonard, *Pioneers of Modern Physical Training*. New York: Association Press, 1915. Dudley A. Sargent, "Tribute to Edward M. Hartwell," *American Physical Education Review*, Vol. 27, March 1923, p. 116. Fred Eugene Leonard and George B. Affleck, *A Guide to the History of Physical Education*. Philadelphia: Lea & Febiger, 1947, p. 384.

12. Vol. 16, 1887. March 31, pp. 271–302, and April 19, pp. 321–327, as reported in Leonard and Affleck, *op. cit.*, p. 384.

13. The following sources contributed to this biographical sketch: "Brief Outline of the Life and Work of Dr. Delphine Hanna," Supplement to *Research Quarterly* of AAHPER, Vol. 12, No. 3, Oct. 1941, pp. 646–652. Minnie J. Lynn, "Delphine Hanna," *Journal of Health, Physical Education and Recreation*, Vol. 31, No. 4, April 1960, p. 51. J. H. Nichols, *Oberlin College, Delphine Hanna and Fred E. Leonard*. Paper read at 75th Anniversary Convention of AAHPER, 1960.

14. George Brosius, *Fifty Years Devoted to Physical Culture*. Milwaukee: Germania Publishing Co., 1914. Emil Rinsch, *History of the Normal College of the American Gymnastic Union of Indiana University—1866–1966*. Bloomington: Indiana University Press, 1966. A. M. Kerr, "Dr. W. G. Anderson," *Journal of Health and Physical Education*, Vol. 6, April 1935, p. 31. R. Tait McKenzie, "William G. Anderson," *American Physical Education Review*, Vol. 34, (1920), p. 311, 363.

15. Luther H. Gulick, "Physical Education in the YMCA," *Proceedings*, AAAPE, 1891. B. Deane Brink, *The Body Builder, Robert J. Roberts*. New York: Association Press, 1916.

16. Aside from the author's several chats with William G. Anderson in the 1930s and early 1940s about his childhood and early career years, the author is indebted to sources as follows: Margaret Brown and Josephine Beiderhase, "William G. Anderson," *Journal of Health, Physical Education and Recreation*, Vol. 31, No. 4, April 1960, p. 34.

Chapter 8

1. Margaret M. H'Doubler, *Dance and Its Place in Education*. New York: Harcourt, Brace Co., 1925.

2. Agnes L. Marsh, *Dance in Education*. New York: A. S. Barnes & Co., 1926.

3. Irene and Vernon Castle, *Modern Dancing*. New York City: DaCapo Press, 1980. Reprint of 1914.

4. Luther H. Gulick, *Physical Education*. Philadelphia: Blakiston's Sons & Co., 1907.

5. G. Stanley Hall, *Adolescence*. New York: Appleton–Century Co., 1901, pp. 200–207.

6. Dudley A. Sargent, "Speech at APEA Convention," *American Physical Education Review*, Vol. 25, Nov. 1920, p. 365.

7. Thomas D. Wood and Rosalind E. Cassidy, *The New Physical Education*. New York: The Macmillan Co., 1927.
8. Emily Andrews, *Fundamental Gymnastics of Nils Bukh*. Translated, rearranged, and adapted for use in America. New York: E. P. Dutton & Co., 1928.
9. The author played the game there in the fall of 1909.
10. Sydney Albright, "Wickets Spout in WLA," *Independent Press*, Los Angeles, July 10, 1960.
11. *American Physical Education Review*, Vol. 15, 1910. Reports of efforts at athletic reforms throughout this volume.
12. Frederick Luehring, *Swimming Pool Standards*. New York: A. S. Barnes & Co., 1939.
13. John Richards Betts, *America's Sporting Heritage—1850–1950*. Reading, Mass.: Addison–Wesley Publishing Co., 1974, p. 157.
14. C. Ward Crampton, *The New York City Public School Athletic League*. Sept. 1, 1936. Unpublished paper, a copy of which is in the AAHPER Archives.
15. C. W. Whitten, "History of the National Federation of High School Athletic Associations," *Journal of Health and Physical Education*, Vol. 4, No. 5, May 1933, p. 6.
16. Alice G. Bronson, *Clark W. Hetherington—Scientist and Philosopher*. Salt Lake City: University of Utah Press, 1958. David Starr Jordan, "Letter from the President of Stanford University," *American Physical Education Review*, Vol. 15, April 1910, p. 282. Paul Stagg, *The Development of NCAA and Its Relation to Intercollegiate Athletics in the U.S.A.* Doctoral dissertation, New York University, 1946.
17. *National Collegiate Athletic Association: 75 Years of Service*. Bulletin issued for sixteenth Annual Honors Luncheon, Jan. 12, 1981, at Fontainebleau Hilton, Miami Beach.
18. Betts, *op. cit.*, p. 217.
19. Marguerite Schwartz, "The Athletic Conference of American College Women," *Journal of Health and Physical Education*, Vol. 7, May 1936, p. 297.
20. Athletic Research Society. "Report of the Committee on Intramural Sport," *American Physical Education Review*, Vol. 23, April 1918, p. 198.
21. John L. Griffith, "Annual Report of NAAF," *American Physical Education Review*, Vol. 34, March 1929, p. 156.
22. Alice Sefton, *The Women's Division of NAAF*. Stanford: Stanford University Press, 1941. Agnes R. Wayman, "The Women's Division of NAAF," *Journal of Health and Physical Education*, Vol. 3, March 1932, p. 3.
23. John Tunis, *$port$: Heroics and Hysterics*. New York: John Day Co., Inc., 1928.
24. Charles W. Kennedy, "Self-Control and Chivalry through Sport," *Sportsmanship*, June 1929, p. 5.
25. Betts, *op. cit.*, p. 135.
26. John S. Watterson III, "The Football Crisis of 1909–1910: The Response of the Eastern Big Three," *Journal of Sport History*, NASSH, Vol. 8, No. 1, Spring 1981, pp. 33–37, 46.
27. Ronald A. Smith, "Harvard and Columbia and a Reconsideration of the 1905 Football Crisis," *Journal* of NASSH, Vol. 8, No. 3, Winter 1981, footnote 41 to p. 18.
28. Bronson, *op. cit.*, pp. 30–35.
29. Dudley A. Sargent, "History of Intercollegiate Athletics in the United States," *American Physical Education Review*, Vol. 15, April 1910, p. 252.
30. Howard J. Savage *et al.*, *American College Athletics*. Carnegie Foundation for the Advancement of Teaching, Bulletin No. 23, 1929.

31. John Tunis, "The Great Sports Myth," *$port$: Heroics and Hysterics*. New York: John Day Co., Inc., 1928.

32. *Information Please Almanac—1982*. New York: Simon & Schuster, 36th ed., 1982. John Kieran and Arthur Daley, *The Story of the Olympic Games, 1896–1956*. New York: J. B. Lippincott Co., 1957.

33. These Games did not represent an official Olympiad.

34. Sefton, *op. cit.*

35. Mabel Lee, "The Case for and against Intercollegiate Athletics for Women and the Situation as It Stands Today," *Mind and Body*, Nov. 1923 and *American Physical Education Review*, Vol. 39, Jan. 1924. _____, "The Case for and against Intercollegiate Athletics for Women and the Situation Since 1923, *Research Quarterly* of APEA, Vol. 2, May 1931, pp. 93–127.

36. Lucille Eaton Hill, *Athletics and Outdoor Sports for Women*. New York: The Macmillan Co., 1903.

37. Agnes R. Wayman, *Education through Physical Education*. Philadelphia and New York: Lea & Febiger, 1925.

38. E. E. Jacobs, *A Study of the Physical Vigor of American Women*. Boston: Marshall Jones, 1926.

39. Harold C. Evans, "Some Notes on College Basketball in Kansas," *Kansas Historical Quarterly*, Vol. 2, No. 2, May 1942, pp. 199–215.

40. Kieran and Daley, *op. cit.*

41. Sefton, *op. cit.*, item numbers I, III, IV, and V of *Olympic Protest* out of nine listed, pp. 82–83.

42. *Ibid.*, item number IX.

Chapter 9

1. "Report of the Athletic Program of the AEF," *American Physical Education Review*, Vol. 25, March 1920, p. 116; and Vol. 22, June 1917, p. 382.

2. John Richards Betts. *America's Sporting Heritage—1850–1950*. Reading, Mass.: Addison–Wesley Publishing Co., 1974.

3. Boyd Henry Bode, *Progressive Education at the Cross Roads*. New York: Newson & Co., 1938. Lawrence A. Cremin, *The Transformation of the School*. New York: Alfred A. Knopf, 2nd ed. 1961, pp. 141, 197, 213, 221. John Dewey, *School and Society*. Chicago: University of Chicago Press, 1900, pp. 10, 19.

4. Published by the University of Chicago Press in 1910.

5. Jesse F. Williams, *Organization and Administration of Physical Education*. New York: Macmillan Co., 1924, p. 9.

6. Charles H. McCloy, *Philosophical Basis for Physical Education*. New York: F. S. Crofts & Co., 1940, p. 97.

7. _____, "A Half Century of Physical Education," *Physical Educator*, Oct. 1960, p. 91. Published posthumously.

8. *White House Conference of 1930 on Child Health and Protection*. New York: Century Co., 1931, Forward and Children's Charter.

9. Frank Irving Cooper, "Report of Committee," *School House Planning*. Washington, D.C.: NEA, 1925, p. 144.

10. Ralph William La Porte, *The Physical Education Curriculum*. A committee report to

College Physical Education Association, 1937. In AAHPERD Archives. Clark W. Hetherington, *School Program in Physical Education.* Yonkers, New York: World Book Co., 1922.

11. Betts, *op. cit.,* p. 136.
12. George Meylan, "The Status of Physical Education in American Colleges," *American Physical Education Review,* Vol. 21, March 1916, p. 155.
13. Ruth Elliott Houston, *Modern Trends in Physical Education Facilities for College Women.* New York: A. S. Barnes & Co., 1939.
14. Amos Alonzo Stagg, *Physical Culture and Athletics,* University of Chicago Decennial Publications, Vol. 1. Chicago: University of Chicago Press, 1904. R. J. Kiputh, "The Payne Whitney Gymnasium of Yale University," *Research Quarterly* of APEA, Vol. 4, March 1933, p. 131.
15. Dorothy S. Ainsworth, *History of Physical Education in Women's Colleges.* New York: Columbia University Press, 1927. Harriet I. Ballantine, *The History of Physical Training in Vassar College—1865-1915.* Poughkeepsie: Lansing & Boas, 1915.
16. Dr. Mosher also held the position of Dean of Women, a prestige college title in the 1890s and at the turn of the century, which probably accounted for the professorship but nevertheless it accrued to the Director of Physical Education for Women if merely by association. But Dr. Hanna's title was held on her physical education work alone and therefore can be claimed as the first professorship conferred upon a woman physical educator solely in recognition of this discipline.
17. Mabel Lee, "Survey of Athletic and Gymnastic Costumes Used by American Girls and Women," *Research Quarterly* of AAHPER, Vol. 3, No. 1, March 1932. Includes a survey of college women's programs.
18. John Bovard and Frederick Cozens, *Tests and Measurements.* Philadephia: W. B. Saunders Co., 1930. Frederick Rand Rogers, *Physical Capacity Tests.* New York: A. S. Barnes & Co., 1931. Dudley A. Sargent, "A Physical Test of a Man," *American Physical Education Review,* Vol. 26, April 1921, pp. 188–194.
19. Harold Rugg. *That Men May Understand.* New York: Doubleday Doran & Co., 1941, p. 182.
20. Emil Rinsch, *History of the Normal College of the American Gymnastic Union of Indiana University—1866-1966.* Bloomington: Indiana University Press, 1966.
21. Mabel Lee, *Memories of a Bloomer Girl.* Washington, D.C.: AAHPER Publications Dept., 1977, chapters 6, 7, 8.
22. J. Edmund Welch, *The YMCA Graduate School of Nashville.* Paper presented at Research Section of AAHPER, St. Louis, March 30, 1968.
23. Harold T. Friermood, *et al., Continuing the Centennial Observance through YMCA Programs.* New York: National Council of YMCAs, 1944.
24. Avis Dinsmore and Edith Gates, "The National Association of Employed Officers of the YWCA," *Journal of Health and Physical Education,* Vol. 4, Jan. 1933.
25. Weaver Pangburn, "Play and Recreation," *Annals of American Academy of Political and Social Sciences,* Nov. 1940, p. 126.

Chapter 10
1. Mabel Lee and Bruce L. Bennett, "This Is Our Heritage," *Journal of Health, Physical Education and Recreation,* Vol. 31, No. 4, April 1960, pp. 25–33, 36–47, 52–59, 62–73, 76–86.

2. Mabel Lee, *History of the Middle West Society of Physical Education*. Lincoln, Nebr.: University of Nebraska Print Shop, 1963.

3. Harry Scott, "The Society of Directors of Physical Education in Colleges," *Journal of Health and Physical Education*, Vol. 1, No. 4, April 1930, p. 3. Glenn W. Howard, "The College Physical Education Association," *Journal of Health and Physical Education*, Vol. 17, Sept. 1946, p. 19.

4. Ethel Dorgan, *Luther Halsey Gulick*. New York: Teachers College, Bureau of Publications, Columbia University, 1934.

5. Dorothy S. Ainsworth *et al.*, "Women College Directors Society," *Journal of Health and Physical Education*, Vol. 6, No. 5, May 1935, p. 3.

6. Luther H. Gulick, "The Academy of Physical Education," *American Physical Education Review*, Vol. 15, May 1910, p. 342. R. Tait McKenzie, "The American Academy of Physical Education," *Journal of Health and Physical Education*, Vol. 3, No. 6, June 1932, p. 14.

7. Carl Schrader, "History of the Society of State Directors of Physical Education," *Journal of Health and Physical Education*, Vol. 4, Oct. 1933.

8. *White House Conference of 1930 on Child Health and Protection*. New York: Century Co., 1931, Forward and Children's Charter.

9. Ethel Dorgan, *op. cit.* J. B. Nash, "Luther Halsey Gulick," *Journal of Health, Physical Education and Recreation*, Vol. 31, No. 4, April 1960, p. 60. "Tributes to Luther Halsey Gulick," *American Physical Education Review*, Vol. 23, Oct. 1918; and Vol. 28, Sept.–Oct. 1923. The latter volume contains tributes to many different persons.

10. Christopher R. Hussey, *R. Tait McKenzie—Sculptor of Youth*. London: Country Life, Ltd., 1929. Andrew Kozar, *R. Tait McKenzie—Sculptor of Athletes*. Knoxville: The University of Tennessee Press, 1975. J. F. Leys, "R. Tait McKenzie," *Journal of Health, Physical Education and Recreation*, Vol. 31, No. 4, April 1960, p. 48. "R. Tait McKenzie," *Journal of Health and Physical Education*, Vol. 15, Feb. 1944. The entire issue of the magazine is devoted to articles about Dr. McKenzie.

11. Edith Naomi Hill, "Senda Berenson," *Pioneer Women in Physical Education* (Supplement to *Research Quarterly* of AAHPER, Vol. 12, No. 13, Oct. 1941, pp. 658–665.

12. Albert G. Spalding, "Story of Women's Basket Ball Rules Committee," *Women's Basket Ball Guide*. New York: American Sports Publishing Co., 1901.

13. Alice Bronson, *Clark W. Hetherington—Scientist and Philosopher*. Salt Lake City, University of Utah Press, 1958.

14. "Ethel Perrin—an Autobiography," *Pioneer Women in Physical Education*. (Supplement to *Research Quarterly* of AAHPER, Vol. 12, No. 3, Oct. 1941, pp. 682–685. Janice Carkin, *Biographies of Five Women Gulick Award Recipients*. Doctoral dissertation, Stanford University, 1952. (Ethel Perrin was included.)

15. Carkin, *op. cit.* (Elizabeth Burchenal was included.) Lucile Czarnowski, "Destined from the Start for Her Life Work," *Journal of Health, Physical Education and Recreation*, Feb. 1970, pp. 23–25. "Elizabeth Burchenal," *Notable Women of America—The Modern Era*, Vol. 4. Cambridge: Harvard University Press, 1980.

16. "Report of the Athletic Program of the AEF," *American Physical Education Review*, Vol. 25, March 1920, p. 116; and Vol. 22, June 1917, p. 382.

17. Bernice Larson Webb, *The Basketball Man—James Naismith*. Lawrence: The University of Kansas Press, 1973.

18. Mary Roberts Coolidge, "Clelia Duel Mosher—the Scientific Feminist." *Pioneer Women in Physical Education*. (Supplement to *Research Quarterly* of AAHPER, Vol. 12, No. 3, Oct. 1941, pp. 633–645.
19. Dorothy LaSalle, "Thomas D. Wood, M.D.—A Great Leader," *Journal of Health, Physical Education and Recreation*, Vol. 22, Nov. 1951, pp. 28–30. _____, "Thomas D. Wood," *Journal of Health, Physical Education and Recreation*, Vol. 31, No. 4, April 1960, p. 61.
20. "James Huff McCurdy," *Journal of Health and Physical Education*, Vol. 11, Oct. and Dec., 1940, pp. 476, 619.
21. Frederick Davis Shultz, *Fred Eugene Leonard, M.D.* Thesis for Master of Science Degree, Ohio State University, 1959.
22. Carkin, *op. cit.* (Bancroft was included.) Jessie H. Bancroft, "Pioneering in Physical Education—An Autobiography," *Pioneer Women in Physical Education*. (Supplement to *Research Quarterly* of AAHPER, Vol. 12, No. 3, Oct. 1941, pp. 666–678.
23. Published by McMillan Company.
24. Mabel Lee, *Biography of J. Anna Norris*. Paper presented at Conference of Mid West Association of Physical Education for College Women, Oct. 20, 1979. Copies on file with MWAPECW and University of Minnesota Archives.

Chapter 11

1. Theodore P. Bank, "Physical Fitness from the Standpoint of the Army," *Proceedings, National War Fitness Conference, 1943*. AAHPER Publication, 1944, p. 29.
2. War Department. *WAC Field Manual of Physical Training*, FM 35-20, July 1943, p. 15.
3. Louise Stitt, "Problems of Women in Industry," *Proceedings of Victory through Fitness Workshop*, NAPECW, June 1943, p. 21.
4. Major General Lewis B. Hersey, "Inside Story of the Rejection Rates," *Journal of Health and Physical Education*, Vol. 24, Jan. 1953, p. 9. Leonard Rowntree, "Education, Health, and Physical Fitness," *Journal of Health and Physical Education*, Vol. 14, Sept. 1943, p. 370.
5. Mabel Lee, *Memories beyond Bloomers*. Washington, D.C.: AAHPER Publications Dept., 1978, chapters 16, 17, 18. An account of the government's efforts at promoting physical fitness during a war emergency. The author served as Regional Director of Ninth Army Service Command under the O.C.D.
6. *Physical Fitness through Physical Education for the Victory Corps*. Washington, D.C.: U.S. Government Printing Office, 1943.
7. Hersey, *op. cit.*
8. Hans Kraus and Ruth P. Herschland, "Muscular Fitness and Health," *Journal of Health, Physical Education and Recreation*, Dec. 1953. This article reports the difference between American and European Children. Hans Kraus and Bonnie Prudden, "Minimum Muscular Fitness Tests in School Children," *Research Quarterly*, Vol. 25, No. 2, May 1954, pp. 178–188.
9. For several years from 1956 on, AAHPER devoted its September issue to the subject of physical fitness and reports of these conferences.
10. Phyllis Pier Valente, "The Dance in American Colleges," *Journal of Health, Physical Education, and Recreation*, Vol. 20, May 1949, p. 312.

11. Josephine Rathbone and Valerie V. Hunt, *Corrective Physical Education*. Philadelphia: W. B. Saunders Co., 1965.
12. John Tunis, *Sport for the Fun of It*, rev. ed. New York: The Ronald Press Co., 1958.
13. John Richard Betts, *America's Sporting Heritage: 1850–1950*. Reading, Mass.: Addison Wesley Publishing Co., 1974, p. 250.
14. Tunis, *op. cit.*
15. Sydney Albright, "Wickets Sprout in WLA," *Independent Press*, Los Angeles, July 19, 1960.
16. "Stephen E. Epler Fathered Six-Man Football," *Lincoln State Journal and Star*, Lincoln, Nebr., Sept. 2, 1959.
17. Tunis, *op. cit.*
18. Frederick Luehring, *Swimming Pool Standards*. New York: A. S. Barnes & Co., 1939, pp. 23, 34.
19. Beulah Gundling, *Exploring Aquatic Art*, 1963: Cedar Rapids, Ia.: Print Shop, 1963. *in the Water*, Marion, Ia.: Lynn–Litho Co., 1976.
2. pp. 245–246.

Chapter 12

1. John Betts, *America's Sporting Heritage: 1850–1950*. Reading, Mass.: Addison Wesley Publishing Co., 1974, p. 276.
2. Howard J. Savage *et al.*, *Current Developments in American College Sports* (Bulletin No. 26). Carnegie Foundation for the Advancement of Teaching, 1951.
3. NCAA, *Seventy-five Years of Service*. Pamphlet distributed at 16th Annual Honors Luncheon, January 12, 1981.
4. Joan Hult, "The Philosophical Conflicts in Men's and Women's Collegiate Athletics," *Quest*, Vol. 32, No. 1, p. 78.
5. Arranged from E. Jokl *et al.*, "Research on Olympic Athletes," *Journal of Health, Physical Education and Recreation*, Sept. 1956, p. 41.
6. NCAA, *op. cit.*

Chapter 13

1. P. Roy Brammel, *Health Work and Physical Education* (U.S. Office of Education Bulletin No. 19, Monograph No. 28), Washington, D.C.: Government Print Shop. 1932, pp. 79–80.
2. Elsa Schneider, *Physical Education in Urban Elementary Schools*. Washington, D.C.: U.S. Government Printing Office, 1943.
3. Jack Hewitt, "Status of Graduate Faculty," *Research Quarterly*, Vol. 37, Oct. 1965, p. 236. "Directory of Institutions Offering Professional Preparation Programs in Health, Physical Education and Recreation," *Journal of Health, Physical Education and Recreation*, Oct. 1965, p. 21.
4. Ida B. Crawford and Viola Mitchell, *Camp Counseling*. Philadelphia: W. B. Saunders Co., 1950.
5. *Hosteling—New Roads for Youth*. AYH Annual Report, 1950. Thomas Lewis Conrad, *Life and Professional Contributions of Dr. Ben W. Miller*, Vol. 1, 1909–1951. Thesis for Master of Science degree, U.C.L.A., 1971. Mabel Lee, "Gypsing by the Way of American Youth Hostels," *Journal of Health and Physical Education*, Vol. 7, April 1936, pp. 218–223.

6. Harold T. Friermood, *Highlights and Issues in YMCA Physical Education—Past and Present*. Paper presented to YMCA Curriculum Consultation at Lake Geneva Conference, April 24, 1967.
7. George Fisher and Jay B. Nash, "The Luther Gulick Award," *Journal of Health and Physical Education*, Vol. 17, June 1946, p. 302.
8. *Sports Medicine Bulletin*, April 1981. Madison: University of Wisconsin.
9. Hazel C. Peterson, *Dorothy S. Ainsworth—Her Life, Professional Career and Contributions to Physical Education*. Moscow, Idaho: University of Idaho Press, 2nd ed., 1975, chapter 10.
10. *Ibid.*, chapter 11. *A Decade of Progress—ICHPER, 1958–1967*. Washington, D.C.: ICHPER Pamphlet. (Carl Troester, Jr., Secretary General)
11. Courtesy of Archives of University of Chicago. Madge Phillips, "Agnes R. Wayman." One of *Eight Biographical sketches of leaders in physical education. Doctoral dissertation, University of Iowa, 1960.*
12. Data on Miss Coleman's early years in particular, courtesy of Department of Physical Education, University of North Carolina—Greensboro. The remainder is from the author's personal knowledge of Miss Coleman's career.
13. "Charles Harold McCloy," *Who's Who in America*. Chicago: Marquis Publications, Vol. 26, 1951–1952. "C. H. McCloy—Autobiographical Sketch," *Omnibus*. Washington, D.C.: AAHPER Publications, 1978, p. 203. C. H. McCloy, "Fifty Years of Physical Education," *Omnibus*. Washington, D.C.: AAHPER Publications, 1978, pp. 33–51.
14. William P. Morgan, "Charles Harold McCloy—A Biosketch," *Research Quarterly for Exercise and Sport*, Vol. 52, No. 3, Oct. 1981, pp. 386, 388.
15. Author is indebted to the following sources for information on Jay B. Nash: *Who's Who in America*, Vol. 26, Chicago: Marquis Publishing Co., 1952. Biographical sketches of early members in AAPE Archives, biographies of Gulick Awardees published in JOPER the year following the award; and biographical sketch in AAHPER, *Omnibus*, 1978, p. 202.
16. Author is indebted for biographical material on Elmer D. Mitchell to the following sources: *Who's Who in America*, Vol. 26, *op. cit.*; biographical sketches of early members in AAPE Archives; biographies of Gulick Awardees of 1949 in JOHPER, 1950; biographical information as of May, 1967, in the files of his daughter, Mrs. Ann Dailey of Ann Arbor, Michigan; and biographical information in *Ann Arbor News*, September 23, 1981, in reporting dedication of the Elmer D. Mitchell Recreation Field at University of Michigan.
17. Hazel C. Peterson, *Dorothy S. Ainsworth—Her Life and Professional Career*. Moscow, Idaho: University of Idaho Press, 1968.
18. Catherine Allen, "Dorothy Sears Ainsworth—Physical Education's First Lady of the World," NAPECW, *Spectrum*, Vol. 17, January 1978.
19. Madge Phillips. Section on Gertrude Moulton, *op. cit. Who's Who in America*, *op. cit.*, biography of Gertrude Moulton.
20. "Edwin Bancroft Henderson," biographical information on file with Awards Committee materials in AAHPER Archives; also newspaper articles about him in *Ledger-Enquirer*, East Alabama, Dec. 17, 1973, *The Montgomery Advertiser*, Dec. 1, 1975, and *New York Times*, March 15, 1974.

21. Madge Phillips, Section on Margaret H'Doubler, *op. cit.* Barbara Baxter Pillinger, "Margaret H'Doubler—Pioneer of Dance," *Quest,* Vol. 32, No. 1, 1980, pp. 103–109. "Margaret H'Doubler," *Omnibus,* AAHPER, 1976, p. 201.
22. *Who's Who in America, op. cit.* Biography of Rosalind Cassidy. "Rosalind Cassidy," *Omnibus,* AAHPER, 1976, p. 206.
23. Mabel Lee, *Memories beyond Bloomers.* Washington, D.C.: AAHPER Publication, 1978, pp. 184–201. A detailed story of women's struggle to have their National Section on Women's Athletics recognized as an official, voting power on AAHPER's National Council, and Miss Hazelton's leadership role in this battle for women's rights.
24. *Who's Who in America, op. cit.* Biography of Neils P. Neilson. "Neils Neilson," *Omnibus, op. cit.,* p. 209.
25. *Who's Who in America, op. cit.* Biography of Arthur S. Steinhaus. "Arthur Steinhaus," *Omnibus, op. cit.,* p. 214.

Chapter 14

1. "Jump Rope for Heart," AAHPERD, *Update,* Jan. 1982, p. 3.
2. Bob L. Beasley, "Physical Fitness Quackery," *JOPER,* June 5, 1975, p. 358.
3. Clarence A. Forbes, *Greek Physical Education.* New York: The Century Co., 1929.
4. T. M. Stephens, A. E. Blackhurst, and L. A. Magliocca, *Teaching Mainstreamed Students.* New York: John Wiley & Sons, Inc., 1982.
5. Peter M. Aufsessor, "Adapted Physical Education," *JOPER,* June 1981, p. 28.
6. Eve Borland, "Freedom in Dance," *The Cape News,* Aug. 18, 1977.
7. Ina Hahn, "Modern Dance for Modern Times," *Wellesley College Alumnae Magazine,* Jan. 1968, p. 22.
8. President's Commission on Olympic Sports, *Report 1975–1977,* Vol. 2. Washington, D.C.: Government Printing Office, Jan. 1977.
9. Blanche Jessen Drury, *Place of Gymnastics in a Physical Education Program.* Paper read at the National Institute on Girls' Sports, University of Oklahoma, Nov. 3–9, 1963.
10. Dora Jane Hamblin, "Rag Brai," *Smithsonian,* July 1981.
11. President's Commission on Olympic Sports, Vol. 2, *op. cit.*
12. *Ibid.*
13. President's Commission, Vol. 2, *op. cit.*

Chapter 15

1. NFHSAA, *Handbook,* 1964–1965 and 1965–1967.
2. Sandra E. Scott, "Women in State Athletic Associations," *Journal of Physical Education, Recreation and Dance,* Vol. 52, No. 9, Nov.–Dec., 1981, p. 59.
3. President's Commission on Olympic Sports, *Report, 1975–1977,* Vol. 1. Washington, D.C.: Government Printing Office.
4. NCAA, *75th Anniversary of the National Collegiate Athletic Association.* Pamphlet issued January 12, 1981. Contains twenty-three pages of chronology of its history, 1905–1980.
5. *Ibid.*
6. Joan S. Hult, "The Philosophical Conflicts in Men's and Women's Collegiate Athletics," *Quest,* Vol. 32, No. 1, Spring 1980, p. 82. This article should be required reading for all students of present-day history of physical education. (*Quest* is a quarterly maga-

zine born in the late 1940s of the National Association of Physical Education for College Women and now put out by the National Association of Physical Education in Higher Education.)

7. AIAW, *Handbook*, 1979, article III.
8. As reported to the author by Dr. Virginia Hunt, President-Elect of AIAW, in a telephone conversation, September 4, 1982.
9. President's Commission, *op. cit.*
10. USTFF, *For the Record.* Pamphlet of 1964.
11. NCAA, *op. cit.*
12. For much information on this topic the author acknowledges indebtedness to Vol. 2 of the President's Commission, *op. cit.*
13. *Ibid.*
14. Arranged from Peter M. Aufsesser, "Adapted Physical Education," *JOPER*, Vol. 52, No. 6, June 1981, pp. 28–31. President's Commission, Vol. II, *op. cit., pp. 467–473.*
15. NFHSAA, *Handbook*, 1964–1965, 1966–1967, and 1968.
16. *Ibid.*
17. NCAA, *General Information Folder*, Sept., 1981.
18. Howard J. Savage *et al. Current Developments in American College Sports* (Bulletin No. 26). Carnegie Foundation for the Advancement of Teaching, 1951.
19. "Rah! Club! Rah!" *Newsweek*, Nov. 6, 1967, p. 82.
20. NCAA, *75th Anniversary*, pamphlet, *op. cit.*
21. R. A. Swanson, *The Achievement of NCAA's—NAIA's Self-Imposed Educational Goals." Paper* given at AAHPERD convention in New Orleans, March 16, 1979.
22. Phebe Scott and Celeste Ulrich, "Commission on Intercollegiate Sports for Women," *Journal of Health, Physical Education and Recreation*, Vol. 37, No. 10, Oct. 1966, p. 10.
23. NCAA, *75th Anniversary, op. cit.*
24. *Report* of *President's Commission on Olympic Sports—1975–1977*, Vol. II, p. 378.
25. From information received from Virginia Hunt, President-Elect, AIAW.
26. President's Commission, Vol. 2, *op. cit.*
27. *Information Please—World Almanac.* New York: Simon & Schuster, 1982.
28. Donald Connery, "Tokyo Changes Face for Asia's First Olympics," *Sports Illustrated*, May 8, 1961, p. 38. Jhan and June Robbins, "Biggest and Most Beautiful Olympics," *Winnipeg Free Press*, July 2, 1960. As reported in *Reader's Digest*, Aug. 1960, p. 106.

Chapter 16

1. Earle Frederick Ziegler, *Philosophical Foundations for Physical, Health and Recreation Education.* New York: Prentice–Hall, 1964.
2. Figures from Department of Commerce, Bureau of Census.
3. Harold Howe (U.S. Commissioner of Education). Report of speech given before the National Student Association at College Park, Md., Aug. 22, 1967, as reported in *United States News and World Report*, Sept. 4, 1967, p. 14.
4. Joseph Oxendine, "Service Program in 1960–61," *Journal of Health, Physical Education and Recreation*, Sept. 1961, p. 37.
5. Mary J. Hoferek, "At the Crossroad: Merger or _____?" *Quest*, Vol. 32, No. 1, Spring 1980, p. 95. M. G. Fox, *Title IX—Equality, Reality or Myth?* Paper given at Conference

of Big Ten Physical Education Directors, Dec. 1977. C. J. Ansorge *et al.*, *The Merger Process as Perceived by Male and Female Physical Educators.* Paper at AAHPER Convention, Milwaukee, 1976.

6. *Ibid.*

7. *UPDATE,* Feb. 1982, p. 10. Monthly newspaper published by AAHPERD.

8. Published in *Journal of Health, Physical Education and Recreation,* April 1960.

9. Published by University of Nebraska print shop. A few copies should still be available from the Archivists of the two district groups.

10. When Miss Lee again volunteered her services to write it.

11. *President's Commission on Olympic Sports—1975–1977,* Vol. 2, Washington, D.C.: Government Printing Office.

12. *The Print Out, Program Year 1978–1979.* New York: National Board, YWCA, fall, 1980.

13. AAHPERD's address is 1900 Association Drive, Reston, Va.,22091.

14. J. Grove Wolf, "American College of Sports Medicine, History," *Sports Medicine Bulletin,* April 1981, pp. 11–12.

15. Hazel C. Peterson, *Dorothy S. Ainsworth, Her Life, Professional Career and Contributions to Physical Education.* Moscow, Idaho: University of Idaho Press, 1975, chap. 10. Report of Opening Session, July 18, 1949, of International Congress of Physical Education for Girls and Women, at University of Copenhagen.

16. *A Decade of Progress: ICHPER 1958–1967.* Washington, D.C.: International Council, 1969. Author's correspondence with Carl Troester, Jr., Secretary-General during years 1980 and 1981. Peterson, *op. cit.,* chap. 11.

17. This award was established by the New York City Physical Education Society and was confined to leaders who work in the New York area until 1944 when it passed into the possession of AAHPER. From then on it could be awarded to any outstanding leader from any part of the United States.

Index